SOCIAL PROBLEMS
AND
SOCIAL POLICY:
The American Experience

This is a volume in the Arno Press Series

SOCIAL PROBLEMS
AND
SOCIAL POLICY:
The American Experience

Advisory Editor
Gerald N. Grob

Editorial Board
Clarke A. Chambers
Blanche D. Coll
Walter I. Trattner

*See last pages of this volume
for a complete list of titles.*

PROSTITUTION IN AMERICA

Three Investigations, 1902-1914

ARNO PRESS

A New York Times Company

New York — 1976

Editorial Supervision: SHEILA MEHLMAN

———◆———

Reprint Edition 1976 by Arno Press Inc.

Copyright © 1976 by Arno Press Inc.

Reprinted from copies in the University of Illinois Library

SOCIAL PROBLEMS AND SOCIAL POLICY: The American Experience
ISBN for complete set: 0-405-07474-3
See last pages of this volume for titles.

Manufactured in the United States of America

———◆———

Library of Congress Cataloging in Publication Data
Main entry under title:

Prostitution in America.

   (Social problems and social policy—the American
experience.
   Reprint of the 2d rev. ed. of The social evil, with
special reference to conditions existing in the city of
New York, by the Committee of Fifteen, published in
1912 by Putnam, New York; of The Social evil in
Syracuse, published in 1913 in Syracuse, N. Y.; of
Report of the Commission for the Investigation of the
White Slave Traffic, so called, published in 1914 by
Wright and Potter Printing Co., state printers, Boston.
   1. Prostitution—United States. I. New York.
Committee of Fifteen, 1900. The social evil, with
special reference to conditions existing in the city
of New York. 1975. II. The Social evil in Syracuse.
1975. III. Massachusetts. Commission for
Investigation of White Slave Traffic. Report of the
Commission for the Investigation of the White Slave
Traffic, so called. 1975. IV. Series.
HQ144.P76 1976   301.41'54'0973   75-17240
ISBN 0-405-07511-1

CONTENTS

THE SOCIAL EVIL

WITH SPECIAL REFERENCE TO CONDITIONS
EXISTING IN THE CITY OF NEW YORK

A REPORT PREPARED [IN 1902] UNDER THE DIRECTION OF
THE COMMITTEE OF FIFTEEN

SECOND EDITION, REVISED, WITH NEW MATERIAL

EDITED BY
EDWIN R. A. SELIGMAN, LL.D.

MCVICKAR PROFESSOR OF POLITICAL ECONOMY, COLUMBIA UNIVERSITY

G. P. PUTNAM'S SONS
NEW YORK AND LONDON
The Knickerbocker Press
1912

The Knickerbocker Press, New York

MEMBERS OF THE COMMITTEE OF FIFTEEN
1900–1902

*WILLIAM H. BALDWIN, JR., *Chairman*,

FELIX ADLER,

*JOEL B. ERHARDT,

AUSTEN G. FOX,

*JOHN S. KENNEDY,

WILLIAM J. O'BRIEN,

ALEXANDER E. ORR,

GEORGE FOSTER PEABODY,

GEORGE HAVEN PUTNAM,

*J. HARSEN RHOADES,

JACOB H. SCHIFF,

ANDREW J. SMITH,

*CHARLES SPRAGUE SMITH,

*CHARLES STEWART SMITH,

EDWIN R. A. SELIGMAN, *Secretary*.

*Deceased since the publication of the first edition of the Report.

PREFACE TO THE REVISED EDITION

IN 1877, in the first attempt to grapple with the difficulties of the problem, Professor Sheldon Amos wrote in the preface to his great work[1]:

"The subject of this treatise encounters peculiar obstacles in the way of public and thorough discussion. It receives only scanty notice at the hands of public journalists. It can never form a topic of common conversation. It carries with it a reminder of shame, miseries, and wrongs which must be always distressing, and therefore instinctively shunned. One side of the subject, again, is appropriated, for the most part, by special members of a very special profession. On all these grounds it might be expected that laws and police regulations on the subject would resemble those plants which prosper best, or only, in the shade."

Since these words were written the conditions have changed materially. The discussion is no longer limited to the medical profession. It is being more and more recognised, and especially

---

[1] *A Comparative Survey of Laws in Force for the Prohibition, Regulation, and Licensing of Vice in England and Other Countries.* London, 1877.

by the broad-minded physicians themselves, that the problem is fundamentally a social and ethical problem. Slowly but surely there is emerging a recognition of the fact that while there are indeed grave dangers in indiscriminate discussion, no progress can be made without a frank and full treatment of the subject and a dissemination not alone of recent medical knowledge, but also of the teachings of modern ethics, economics, and social science, so far as they affect this entire topic. The battle has been half won when, as in America to-day, we find not only special associations devoted to this matter, but also its more frequent appearance on the programmes of many of our great scientific associations dealing with social and economic questions.

In the decade that has elapsed since the first edition of this book was published, there are several developments that call for notice: first, a growing feeling throughout the leading European countries that regulation is becoming more and more unsatisfactory; second, the portentous growth of the white slave traffic and the initiation of international legislation designed to cope with it; third, the continuance of the work of the Committee of Fifteen in New York City by the Committee of Fourteen and the attempts to deal in detail with the administration of the present laws; and finally, the awakening of interest throughout the United States as evidenced especially by the reports of the Chicago and Minneapolis commissions, and by the formation of the new national society.

When the publishers of this work approached me with the statement that the original edition had long been out of print, and asked me to undertake a new edition bringing the matter down to date, I felt that, however difficult it might be for me to turn aside from my other occupations, I owed it as a duty to my former colleagues to undertake the task. In these ten years eight out of the original fifteen members of the Committee of Fifteen, including its distinguished chairman, have passed away. It being, therefore, impracticable to issue this new edition under the auspices of the committee as a whole, I have, after consultation with the remaining members, decided to publish the additional matter on my own responsibility.

The report proper is re-issued without any changes. The new matter will be found in Part III. It has also been deemed wise to include a rather comprehensive bibliography on the subject.

In preparing this new matter I have been much helped by generous gifts of material from the leaders of the reform movement in Europe, notably from Mme. Avril de St. Croix of Paris, M. Henri Minod of Geneva, Frau Katharina Scheven of Dresden, and Dr. H. M. Wilson and Mr. W. A. Coote of London. My warm thanks are also extended to Miss Marion Dodd of the New York Vigilance Society for assistance in compiling the bibliography, to Mr. Frederick H. Whitin of the Committee of Fourteen for gifts of material, and to Dr. Prince A. Morrow for many suggestions and for assistance in reading the proof.

EDWIN R. A. SELIGMAN.

COLUMBIA UNIVERSITY,
January, 1912.

PREFACE TO THE ORIGINAL EDITION

In the fall of 1900, the city of New York was startled by discoveries in regard to the spread of the Social Evil in certain districts, and as to the extent of flagrant offences against public morality and common decency. A meeting of citizens was held at the Chamber of Commerce in November, as a result of which the Committee of Fifteen was called into existence. The objects which the Committee of Fifteen undertook to accomplish were thereupon stated as follows:

(1) To institute a searching inquiry, uninfluenced by partisan considerations, into the causes of the present alarming increase of gambling and the Social Evil in this city, and to collect such evidence as shall establish the connection between existing conditions and those who, in the last analysis, are responsible for these conditions.

(2) To publish the results of such investigations in order to put our fellow-citizens in possession of facts, and to enable them to adopt such corrective measures as may be needed.

(3) To promote such legislation as shall render it less difficult to reach offenders, and as shall put an end to the shifting and division of respon-

sibility in the local administration of the laws relating to vice and crime, to the end that public officers and their subordinates may be held to a strict accountability for their acts.

(4) To suggest and promote the provision of more wholesome conditions and surroundings, in order to lessen the allurements and incentives to vice and crime.

During the winter and spring of 1901 the Committee devoted its attention chiefly to the first object. Its corps of investigators collected a mass of information and evidence, a part of which was utilised in bringing some of the offenders to justice, and in exposing the notorious "cadet" system. The Committee also co-operated with the framers of the new Tenement House Bill in securing its enactment into law. As a result of this law and of the facts collected by the Committee, it became possible to take measures for the eradication of prostitution from the tenement houses.

The overthrow of the control of the municipal administration by Tammany Hall and the success of the Reform movement in the municipal campaign of 1901 (a campaign in which the information supplied by the Committee of Fifteen constituted a very important factor) rendered it possible for the Committee to abandon any further work of a police nature or having to do with the supervision of public morals.

The third object of the Committee, however, was to promote satisfactory legislation on the subject of the Social Evil. In order to make intelligent preparation for its recommendations, a sub-committee was appointed to make a study of the history of regulation and its application to present conditions in New York. The sub-committee was fortunate in securing for this work the services of Mr. Alvin S. Johnson, at the time University Fellow in Economics at Columbia University, and now Instructor in Economics at Bryn Mawr College. The investigation contained in Part I. is almost entirely the work of Mr. Johnson, to whom the thanks of the Committee are due. It is believed not only that the report constitutes a valuable scientific contribution to the subject, but that in no other publication can there be found so comprehensive or so clear a statement of the problems involved. Certain features of the Raines Law are so intimately connected with the existence of prostitution in New York that it has been deemed wise to include in the appendix an account of that law.

The conclusions and recommendations of the Committee itself are found in Part II. The appendix to this part contains a summary of the operations of the Committee with special relation to the "cadet" system and to the existence of the Social Evil in tenement houses.

New York, January 2, 1902.

CONTENTS

PART I

THE SOCIAL EVIL

CHAPTER I

CHAPTER II

CHAPTER III

Contents

CHAPTER IV

Regulation in Berlin and in Other Cities of Europe 32

CHAPTER V

The Sanitary Aspect of Modern Regulation   50

CHAPTER VI

The Moral Aspect of Regulation . .   59

Contents

PART I.

THE SOCIAL EVIL

CHAPTER I

THE PROBLEM OF PROSTITUTION

PROSTITUTION is a phenomenon coextensive with civilised society. Barbarous and semi-barbarous peoples have at times been free from it. The ancient Germans, we are told, tolerated no prostitution in their midst; and there are said to be Siberian and African tribes to-day of which the same thing is true. But no sooner has a people attained a moderate degree of civilisation than this social curse has fallen upon it; nor has any race reached a point of moral elevation where this form of vice has disappeared.

The most venerable traditions, the most ancient records, all bear testimony to the antiquity of prostitution. Even a careless reader of Scripture knows how constantly it beset the ancient Hebrews, and how vain were the efforts of sages and lawgivers to stamp it out. Nurtured by a vicious religion, it flourished throughout Asia Minor; and when civilisation moved westward to Greece and Rome, prostitution followed as its shadow. The rise of the mediæval cities in Western Europe was marked by the introduction of the brothel. The great development of trade and commerce that ushered in modern times was also responsible for the universalising of "the social evil."

Glancing at present conditions, we find that no important nation is free from the taint. The great cities of the world vie with each other in the vast numbers of those who gain their living by immorality. Nor is there reason to think that this condition is transitory. He would be an optimist indeed who could believe that a time will come when the problem of prostitution shall cease to be important. Like the pauper, the prostitute is a creature of civilisation, and, like the pauper, will continue to thrust her undesirable presence upon society.

The fact that prostitution is practically universal has impressed itself strongly upon the numerous writers who have dealt with the subject. The inference has frequently been drawn that all efforts to suppress or restrict vice must be vain, and that the only rational course to pursue is to recognise its existence and to minimise its attendant dangers. There have been authorities who held the view that vice is an essential element in society hence ineradicable. Others have gone so far as to affirm that what is best and purest in civilisation could not have existed but for the sacrifice of a portion of womankind to immorality.[1] The saner authorities, however, content themselves with stating that vice is the inevitable result of causes which society has never yet been able to control.

It is frequently said that vice is a constant and invariable element in social life. This is, however, obviously untrue. So far as one can judge from the fragmentary history of morality, periods of gross licentiousness have alternated with periods of comparative decency. The degrading influence that intercourse with a lascivious nation has exercised upon a people of comparatively pure morals is well known to every student of history. The Romans were disciples of the Greeks in immorality as well as in arts and sciences. The renewal of intercourse with the East that followed the Crusades was attended by a serious deterioration of European morals. On the other hand, the spread of Christianity, the Reformation, and the rise of chivalry, it is generally admitted, brought about a decided improvement in the moral tone of Europe.

Social and economic changes have frequently been marked by an increase or a diminution in

[1] Lecky, *History of European Morals*, ii., 299; Hügel, *Zur Geschichte, Statistik und Regelung der Prostitution*, 76.

vice. A prolonged war, more especially if it be a civil war, has generally resulted in an exaggeration of this evil. The Thirty Years' War and the French Revolution are notorious in this respect. Even minor phenomena, such as commercial disturbances, are not without a demonstrable effect upon the volume of vice.

That vice is a varying phenomenon, bearing no constant relation to population, is evident to any one who has studied the conditions of modern cities. It has been affirmed that the greater the city, the larger will be the proportion of the vicious. While this is probably true, yet certain cities have attained a pre-eminence in evil reputation that is not to be accounted for merely by their size and wealth.

This fact, that vice varies from age to age and from place to place, is a sufficient indication that the causes of which it is the result do not operate with uniform force. It suggests the idea that while it may be impossible to control all of the causes of prostitution, and so to eradicate it, certain of them may be brought under control, with the result of limiting the evil.

Not less striking than the variations in the volume of vice are the variations in its general character. In Rome the masculine factor in vice consisted in the soldiers and freedmen, the gladiators and ruffians, the throngs of the idle and turbulent that congregated in the great capital of the world. The feminine factor was made up chiefly of the vast numbers of slave women, captured in the unceasing wars of conquest. Roman vice reached its climax when these elements grew to such proportions as to overshadow orderly society. In the Middle Ages the masculine factor consisted in the soldiers of fortune, travellers and outlaws, apprentices and pseudo-clergy, that made up the floating population. The feminine factor was largely composed of women abducted by robber bands, captured in petty wars and abused by the soldiery, and of the neglected offspring of these unfortunates. As the floating population increased with the breaking up of the old order, as wars became more prolonged and their demoralising effect more general, mediæval prostitution attained extraordinary proportions. All society seemed to be demoralised. Modern prostitution bears the peculiar stamp of modern social and industrial conditions. The hosts of unmarried workers of the great trading or industrial city represent the masculine factor; the feminine factor consists of women and girls from the midst of the social organism who have been impelled by circumstances to make a quasi-voluntary choice of prostitution as a means of livelihood. Speaking generally, we may say that the ancient prostitute was a slave, the mediæval prostitute an alien, the modern prostitute is a citizen.

The fact is not to be overlooked that there is

an element in prostitution which remains fairly constant. In every society there have been women whom circumstances have destined for honourable life, but who from innate perversity chose the life of shame. Modern criminal anthropologists have shown that in physical, mental, and moral characteristics these women form a type which varies little with time and place. Some scientists have gone so far as to declare that these are the only real prostitutes.[1]

The truth seems to be, however, that the importance of this element is greatly overestimated. The victim of force or fraud, or of adverse social and economic conditions, soon reaches a point where she is indistinguishable from the congenital pervert.

It is a trite saying that the real cause, the *causa causans*, of prostitution is to be sought in the male factor. A community, it is said, will have as much vice as it is willing to pay for. "Demand will create a supply." In this bald and cynical form the statement is obviously untrue. There is not in any community an indefinite number of women who are ready to sell their honour for a sufficient price. The number who do so varies chiefly for reasons that are independent of the "demand." Nevertheless, the idea is not without a fraction of truth. Under existing conditions, many women are attracted, rather than

[1] Lombroso, B. Tarnowsky, Pauline Tarnowsky, Ströhmberg.

forced, into prostitution.   The greater the earnings of the prostitute, the richer her attire, and the more luxurious her mode of life, the stronger is the attraction for those who are upon the borderland of vice and virtue.   Accordingly, any account of the causes of prostitution may properly begin with a consideration of the general reasons that are responsible for an extensive "demand."

This problem is intimately connected with that of the movement of population toward the city. A great part of the population of a modern city consists of young men who have drifted thither from the country and small towns, attracted by the greater opportunities of rising in social life and by the greater degree of personal comfort that the city offers.   As a rule, the income that a young man earns, while sufficient to secure a fair degree of comfort for himself, does not suffice for founding a family.   As his income increases, his standard of personal comfort rises; accordingly, he postpones marriage until a date in the indefinite future, or abandons expectation of it altogether. His interests centre almost wholly in himself. He is responsible to no one but himself.   The pleasures that he may obtain from day to day become the chief end of his life.   A popular philosophy of hedonism furnishes him with a theoretical justification for the inclinations that are developed by the circumstances in which he is placed. It is not unnatural, then, that the strongest native impulse of man should find expression in the only way open to it—indulgence in vice.

At the same time that personal scruples with regard to continency dissolve in the crucible of city life, the main external check upon a man's conduct, the opinion of his neighbours, which has such a powerful influence in the country or small town, tends to disappear. In a great city one has no neighbours. No man knows the doings of even his close friends; few men care what the secret life of their friends may be. Thus, with his moral sensibilities blunted, the young man is left free to follow his own inclinations. The greater the city, as a rule, the more pronounced in this respect is its demoralising influence; and our cities are growing steadily greater and are in an ever greater degree setting the moral tone for the country as a whole. The problem of masculine vice, it will be seen, is an integral part of that infinitely complex problem, the "Social Question."

It would be impossible in a brief sketch to analyse the complicated phenomena of feminine vice. It is possible, however, to select a few of the most important and most characteristically modern elements. In the first place, there is a large class of women who may be said to have been trained for prostitution from earliest childhood. Foundlings and orphans and the offspring of the

miserably poor, they grow up in wretched tenements, contaminated by constant familiarity with
vice in its lowest forms.   Without training, mental
or moral, they remain ignorant and disagreeable,
slovenly and uncouth, good for nothing in the
social and economic organism.   When half matured they fall the willing victims of their male
associates, and inevitably drift into prostitution.
This element is to be found in almost every
large city; but it is in London where it is to be
found in the greatest extent and the greatest
hideousness.

Another form is closely connected with the
appearance of women in industry.   In many
cities there are great classes of women without
any resources excepting their earnings as needle-
women, day-workers, domestics, or factory hands.
These earnings are often so small as barely to
suffice for the urgent needs of the day.   A season
of non-employment presents them with the alternatives of starvation or prostitution.   These form
the "occasional prostitutes," who, according to
Blaschko, far outnumber all others in the city of
Berlin.   When employment is again to be had they
withdraw from the life of shame, if its irregulari-
ties have not incapacitated them for honourable
labour.

A third class, one which is more or less typical
of American prostitution, is made up of those who
cannot be said to be driven into prostitution either

by absolute want or by exceptionally pernicious
surroundings. They may be employed at living
wages, but the prospect of continuing from year
to year with no change from tedious and irksome
labour creates discontent and eventually rebellion.
They, too, are impregnated with the view that
individual happiness is the end of life, and their
lives bring them no happiness, and promise them
none. The circumstances of city life make it
possible for them to experiment with immorality
without losing such social standing as they may
have, and thus many of them drift gradually into
professional prostitution.

Any social problem, it must be remembered,
appears impossible of solution when whole classes
are viewed as units. The influences that are
chiefly responsible for the great mass of vice are
not within the control of government. Yet it
is evident that there are infinite gradations from
those who would remain pure under any circumstances to those who are almost destined by nature
or surroundings to succumb to vice, and that
those who are upon the margin of a life of shame
may be rescued or degraded by social action. By
private and public means something can be done
to improve the surroundings of poor children, to
relieve the distress of industrial workers in times of
non-employment, to improve the outlook of those
women whose lives are to be spent in the abnormal
environment of factory and shop. Experience

has shown the futility of measures that aim to abolish the evil. There is, however, every *à priori* reason to believe that its extent may be limited by a judicious policy of prevention.

CHAPTER II

REGULATION—ANCIENT, MEDIÆVAL, AND MODERN

Ancient Regulations.—Of the ancient nations with the life of which we are best acquainted, the Hebrews alone understood that prostitution is itself a serious evil. The Greeks and the Romans saw clearly that certain evils resulted from it, and it was their constant endeavour to divest it of those attendant evils. The trend of Jewish legislation may accordingly be described as repressive; that of Greece and Rome as regulative.

In Greece and Rome the evils that were the subject of legislation were religious, social, and political—never hygienic. Religion required that the family should be preserved in its integrity from generation to generation; hence anything that would make legitimacy of offspring doubtful was execrated. Politics required the greatest possible number of citizens of pure blood; hence anything that would incapacitate the daughters of citizens for marriage and motherhood was considered a public calamity. As a result, we find a body of drastic legislation which made the woman whose honour was tainted a total outcast from society.   It was the aim of the legislator to prevent, so far as possible, the fall of free women, and to make impossible the return to decent society of such as had fallen.

The social consequences of masculine vice practically escaped the notice of the Greek and Roman. Although there is evidence enough that venereal disease existed, its effect upon the welfare of the community was not understood.   The existence of a numerous class of slaves obviated the necessity of sacrificing free women to immorality. Accordingly, it is not surprising that the utmost latitude of conduct was granted to the freeman, while regularity of life on the part of free women was enforced with the utmost severity.   The preservation of city, clan, and family depended upon the chastity of the women; it did not depend in anything like the same degree upon the chastity of the men.

It was impossible, to be sure, to confine vice absolutely to slave women.   But if free women fell, they were assimilated to the class of slaves. In Rome they had no right to enjoy their property, they had no control over their children, they could not give oath or make accusation.   Their status differed from that of slaves in that they had no particular master.   They were, in a sense, public property, and were required to live in quarters set apart for them, and were subjected to regulations as to dress and conduct which might distinguish them as such wherever they might be. In Rome, as early as 180 B.C., they were registered in the books of the ædiles, in order that their peculiar status might be the more perfectly defined.[1]

After Rome had grown into a world empire, the line between slave and serf, freedman and free-born, tended to become obscure. At the same time, a thorough degradation of morals permeated all society, so that it was no longer possible to separate the immoral from the honourable. Prostitutes still formed a special class, but such regulation as continued to exist had for its chief purpose the collection of revenue from the earnings of the public prostitute. This end also was abandoned when a higher type of imperial authority realised the dishonour of public sharing in infamous gains. Under the Christian Emperors repressive laws were enacted, thus concluding definitely classical regulation of vice.[2]

Modern writers have sometimes claimed that prostitution was "tolerated" in Rome and Greece as a means of combating the unnatural vice which

[1] The origin of the special quarter and the special garb is probably to be found in the fact that the public women were originally "priestesses" of Venus, and lived in the precincts of the shrines and wore a garb indicating their religious office. The transition to the status of public slaves with the fading out of the religious idea can be easily understood.

[2] Parent-Duchâtelet, *De la Prostitution dans la ville de Paris*, 3d ed., vol. ii., 268.

was so common in ancient civilisation. It is a
sufficient refutation of this position that not until
a comparatively late date was unnatural vice
considered an evil, while prostitution was permitted
from the earliest times.   Moreover, so numerous
were the slave women devoted to infamy that it
is difficult to conceive how any one can believe that
it was dearth of "natural" vice that was responsible for the hideous development of unnatural
vice that disfigured the history of decadent Greece
and Rome.

Mediæval Regulation of Vice.—At the beginning of the Middle Ages the states of Western
Europe pursued a strictly repressive policy with
regard to prostitution.   The capitularies of Charle-
magne imposed upon the prostitute and those
who sheltered her imprisonment, whipping, and
exposure.   For this severity, the legislation of
the late Roman and Byzantine Emperors was no
doubt partially responsible.   A more potent influence was, however, exercised by the early
Teutonic customs and laws.   Tacitus states that
in some German tribes women of unchaste life
were punished by death.   The Salic law prescribed
banishment for them, and the laws of the Visi-
goths (600 A.D.) inflicted the penalty of beating
with rods.

But as population increased and became more
settled the treatment of the vicious underwent
a gradual change.   By the tenth century, the

persecution of the prostitute had practically ceased. Prostitution came to be tolerated, but under regulations that were aimed to divest it of the consequences that to the mediæval mind seemed evil. In 1180 Henry II. gave a royal patent for the legalisation of public houses of prostitution in London. They were established in Hamburg in the year 1272; Regensburg, 1306; Zürich, 1314; Basel, 1356; Avignon, 1347; Vienna, 1384. The ordinance of St. Louis, 1254, and the laws of Naples of the eleventh and twelfth centuries reflect the severity of early Teutonic legislation. These laws were, however, merely the outcome of the religious zeal of the rulers; they did not represent the public sentiment of the time. They do not appear ever to have been systematically enforced.

Mediæval regulation is best understood by reference to the ends it was designed to meet. Preservation of the existing order of things was regarded as of cardinal importance. The integrity of the family was looked upon as vital; accordingly, the severest penalties were inflicted upon unchaste wives and daughters of burghers. It was believed that if provision were made for the satisfaction of the vicious impulses of the floating population, the family would be secured from invasion. Therefore the brothel was not only tolerated; it was considered a necessary and a useful adjunct to city life. This will account for the fact that the house of ill fame was often built at public expense and managed on public account, and for the voting of funds for securing from abroad inmates for the public house. It also explains the condition sometimes imposed upon the citizen who leased such an establishment, that he should provide a sufficient number of suitable inmates.

It was also essential that public women should form a class absolutely distinct. They were normally secured from foreign countries, or, at any rate, from beyond the city's domain. They remained aliens; and if any woman from within the ranks of decent society fell from virtue, she became an alien in status and was for ever debarred from returning to her kin. They were required to live in a special quarter and wear a distinguishing mark upon their clothing, usually a yellow or red ribbon upon the sleeve, so that no mistake might be made as to their character.

There was no trace of the modern feeling that vice should be quite hidden from respectability, ignored by decent society. The prostitute played no mean rôle in the social life of the Middle Ages. As such, she took part in public processions, and even in sacred festivals. The brothel was bound to entertain notables who visited the city. In

---

[1] The student of the origin of social customs will at once suspect a relation between the functions of public women at festivals and the orgies in celebration of certain pagan deities. As a fact, the connection would not be difficult to trace.

2

short, the Middle Ages believed vice to be nothing evil, so long as it showed its true colours.

The second aim of the mediæval legislator was to prevent the brothel from becoming a centre of disorder. At all times the prostitute and the outlaw have been natural allies. Wherever houses of ill fame were grouped in special quarters, thieves and cutthroats congregated, menacing the persons and property of the citizens.[1]

It was the mediæval policy to fix responsibility upon groups, rather than upon individuals. This idea appears in the regulation of prostitution. Sometimes the public women were organised in guilds, which chose a head who was responsible for everything that might occur in the brothel. This was the case in Nuremberg; and, after the fashion of other guilds, the licensed prostitutes took it upon themselves to prosecute persons who infringed upon their monopoly. Sometimes they were placed under the charge of a special official who decided all cases of injury committed by them or against them; in still other places a special court was created for their control. Where a brothel was let to a responsible citizen, he was

---

[1] In 1367 two quarters were set apart by the Parisian authorities for prostitution, the *Glatigny* and the *Hueleu*. Great numbers of thieves, robbers, and vagabonds flocked together in these quarters, making of them veritable strongholds, whence vice and crime could raid the city with impunity. The police were defied and even royal edicts for demolishing the places were for decades set at nought.— Carlier, *Les Deux Prostitutions*, 11–13.

compelled to undertake all responsibility for the conduct of its inmates.

One further object held in view by the mediæval legislator was the organisation of prostitution for fiscal purposes. As possessors of a lucrative occupation, they were compelled to contribute to the public treasury. There seems to have been no hesitancy about accepting for public purposes a part of the earnings of shame. Even the Church did not stick at such revenues.[1]

Mediæval regulations, then, possessed generally these three aims: prevention of vicious conduct on the part of citizen women, collection of revenues from prostitution, and preservation of public order.

As in the case of classical regulation, aims that were possible of realisation while the cities were of moderate size and while social relations were fixed, were not capable of realisation when the old order broke up under the social and economic changes at the end of the Middle Ages. Society as a whole became corrupt; the alien character of prostitution disappeared. Sumptuary laws were enacted, because it was thought that it was the jewelry and fine clothing of the prostitute that attracted decent girls and women into the life of shame. At about the same time an epidemic of syphilis spread over Europe, assuming, as a result

[1] Clement VIII. compelled public women to give a part of their earnings to the Convent of St. Mary of Penitence.—Tammeo, *La Prostituzione*, 30.

of the general immorality, the proportions of a world plague.   Under the influence of this evil the licensed houses of prostitution were pretty generally closed during a considerable part of the fifteenth and sixteenth centuries.   Re-opened again, they lived by the strength of traditional usage until replaced by modern regulation of prostitution, or, as it is generally known, reglementation.

Modern Regulation.—Modern regulation is almost wholly distinct from that of mediæval and classical times, both in its ends and in the means it employs to secure them.   The mediæval city strove to insure the welfare of its own citizens; it cared nothing for the moral welfare of the aliens who were the victims of its policy.   The extension of the unit of society from the single city to the nation, from the nation to the civilised world, has awakened the public conscience to the fact that even the prostitute is a member of society.   Under modern conditions, it is inconceivable that a political body should aid in the securing of victims for vice, even if it were still believed that the existence of a vicious class is a safeguard for the virtuous; for the victims must necessarily be recruited from orderly society,—in the last instance, from the ranks of the virtuous.[1]

---

[1] Certain authors have caught at the idea of a supposed natural class of degenerate women, reversions to a non-moral type, as fitting victims for social vice.   It is no hardship, they claim, that such creatures should be permitted to follow their own natures.   This is evidently an attempt to restore the alien status of the prostitute.   It is not worth while to point out the weakness of the position.—See Ströhmberg, *op. cit., passim.*

Accordingly, the moral point of view has changed completely. Every modern system of regulation avows the purpose of preventing, as far as possible, the degradation of those who are not yet depraved, and the rescue and restoration to honourable life of fallen women who are still susceptible to moral influences.

But the chief distinguishing feature of modern regulation is its endeavour to stamp out the diseases that everywhere attend vice. Nothing analogous to this aim is to be found in ancient and mediæval regulation.[1]

So prominent has the sanitary aspect of the problem of vice become that the term "regulation" is used generally to denote sanitary regulation alone.

One end that modern regulation has in common with mediæval regulation is the dissociation of vice from crime. In the Middle Ages, this end was partially attained by fixing responsibility not upon the individual prostitute, but upon individuals or groups of individuals who could not so easily evade the law. A study of modern regulations will reveal the fact that not dissimilar means are employed for the same end.

---

[1] Parent-Duchâtelet cites regulations of Avignon of the 14th century, which required that public women should be visited weekly by a "barber." The regulations in question are, however, undoubtedly spurious.

CHAPTER III

REGULATION OF PROSTITUTION IN PARIS

DURING the Middle Ages, prostitution was tolerated in Paris as in all other important cities of Central Europe. But with the appearance of the epidemic of syphilis toleration ceased. The victim of that frightful malady fell heir to all the cruel maltreatment that had been the especial heritage of the leper. The prostitute, as the natural medium of the disease, came to be regarded with horror and hatred such as her mere moral delinquencies have hardly ever inspired. The ancient laws making prostitution a crime were restored, and not until the end of the eighteenth century did they cease to be enforced.

For a long time after the policy of expelling the male syphilitic from society had given way to the more rational policy of treating him, no provision was made for the relief of unfortunate prostitutes who were suffering from disease. It was only accidentally that certain features were inserted in repressive laws which pointed toward a system of sanitary control. As late as 1657 it was the practice to exclude infected prostitutes from the Salpêtrière, where the women charged with prostitution were confined. As the system of inspection was imperfect, many who were diseased were found among the prisoners. These were treated by order of the authorities of the prison, although this was strictly contrary to law. An edict of 1684 recognised the necessity of treating the diseased. This provision is regarded as the germ of the French sanitary control.[1]

By the same law, the lieutenant of police was given practically unlimited control over prostitutes. He passed sentence, nor was there any appeal from his decision. The length of time during which the prostitutes were imprisoned lay in his sole discretion. The determination of the criteria whereby a woman was judged guilty of debauch lay also in his province, as appears from the preamble of the law of July 26, 1713. It is easy to see in this the germ of the discretionary power that the police assume in dealing with prostitutes.[2]

For the rest, an effort was to be made to reform these women. They were to attend mass and hear prayers read, etc. They were treated, of course, as ordinary criminals: they were dressed in prison uniform and fed on prison fare and were

[1] Parent-Duchâtelet, *op. cit.*, ii., 5 *et seq.*
[2] Lecour, *La Prostitution à Paris et à Londres*, 407.

compelled to perform the hardest work of which they were capable.

By the law of 1713, above mentioned, the determination of the facts of prostitution was left to the royal commissaries or judges in the several quarters of the city. These were to receive as proof the declarations of the neighbours. The pronouncing of sentence and the discretionary power as to its severity still remained with the lieutenant of police.[1]

Such were the general regulations on the subject of prostitution down to 1768. In that year a royal ordinance decreed that prostitutes found with the army should be arrested and imprisoned by the military authorities unless they were domiciled in the vicinity. In that case they should be turned over to the civil authorities for imprisonment. Before being imprisoned, however, they were to be treated for disease if found ill.[2]

It is easy to see how the regulations of 1684, supplemented by the ordinance of 1768, should become in effect a system of sanitary control. The treatment previous to imprisonment was compulsory; the punishment lay in the discretion of the lieutenant of police. All that was necessary was to make periodical arrests with compulsory treatment and to discharge those who were cured without imprisonment. It appears

---

[1] Lecour, *op. cit.*, 409, 410.　　　　[2] *Ib.*, 411.

that a system something like this developed toward the end of the *ancien régime*.[1]

It was natural that the need for a system of permanent registration should arise. The first appearance of the idea of registration was in 1765. A police officer suggested in a report to the lieutenant of police that the existing disorder would be greatly diminished if all public women were registered by the police. It was rather with the hope of securing better order than with a view to sanitary control that the idea was then put forward. Some years later another memoir emphasised the sanitary bearing of registration. A commission was appointed to examine into the matter, but it pronounced the scheme impracticable.[2]

At the close of the reign of Louis XVI. the plan was again taken up, and two agents were ordered to proceed with the registration of prostitutes. The Revolution, however, prevented the order from being carried into effect. The principles of the Revolution were too uncompromising to permit of a policy so likely to infringe upon individual liberty.

Not until 1798 were any preventive sanitary measures taken. In that year a private physician undertook, under administrative patronage, the work of examining the prostitutes actively

[1] Carlier, *Les Deux Prostitutions*, 17.
[2] Reuss, *La Prostitution*, 231 *et seq.*

engaged in their occupation. Apparently, it was the understanding that he should communicate to the police the state of health of those whom he examined.[1]

In 1802 the prefecture of police proceeded to register public prostitutes and to impose upon them the obligation of submitting to fortnightly examination. Hitherto the courts had decided whether or not a woman was guilty of professional debauch; now the police proceeded to establish the facts in a purely administrative way. The ardour for personal liberty had cooled by this time so that no difficulties were thrown in the way of the carrying out of the plan of regulation. In 1805 a dispensary was established for the treatment of the diseased prostitutes. All expenses were to be met by fees collected by the physicians themselves. This system, it can easily be understood, led to great abuses. The examining physicians took care to make their fees as large as possible. Accordingly, in 1810, it was found necessary to make a change in this respect. The physicians were to report to the cashier of the administration the names, addresses, and the state of health of the women examined. That official paid the physicians and became responsible for the recovery of the sums from the prostitutes.[2]

By the second decade of the century the Parisian

[1] Lecour, *op. cit.*, 69.　　　　[2] *Ibid.*, 73.

police had developed a plan which they have cherished ever since—that of confining prostitution to houses specially licensed for that purpose. The difficulties that lay in the way of controlling the conduct of the prostitute by dealing with her directly were found to be almost insuperable. The keeper of a brothel or a house of accommodation, however low he may be morally, has nevertheless a property stake that will keep him within the bounds of the law. Prostitutes who were living in isolated quarters were ordered to betake themselves directly to the houses of accommodation. Soliciting upon the streets was forbidden again and again, but the prohibition was not capable of enforcement.

In 1828 the tax levied upon prostitutes for meeting the expenses of sanitary control was abolished. It had proven burdensome and injurious. Half the time of the special agents of the Morals Bureau was spent in hunting up prostitutes who were delinquent in their payments. Moreover, it acted as a deterrent to voluntary registration.[1]

Up to 1828 the police registered as a licensed prostitute any woman who desired it. No inquiries were made as to age, civil state, or antecedents. Young girls arrested for debauch were registered forthwith. According to Parent-Duchâtelet, the register of public women contained the names of

[1] Parent-Duchâtelet, *op. cit.*, ii., 224.

girls of ten, who had, of course, never been engaged in vice. In 1828 this outrageous policy ceased.[1]

In 1843 the service of morals was reorganised. The system then established is practically the one now in force. It has also served as a model for most of the systems of Europe. Prostitution is tolerated either in licensed brothels or in houses of accommodation where prostitutes at large are compelled to resort. Weekly examinations are imposed upon the inmates of brothels; these take place in the licensed houses. The prostitutes at large are obliged to appear once in two weeks at the office provided by the police for that purpose. Those found to be diseased are sent to the hospital of the prison of St. Lazare, and are not liberated until cured.

To insure a certain control over the conduct of these women, the keeper of a licensed house (always a woman) is responsible for good order in her establishment. A prostitute who lives alone in a rented apartment must own the furniture of the apartment, so that it will not be easy for her to disappear in case she has violated any of the regulations.

Women may be registered as prostitutes either by order of the chief of the Morals Bureau or at their own request. As a rule, inscription is voluntary. Clandestine prostitution is punished severely enough to make it worth while for the

[1] Carlier, *op. cit.*, 41.

notoriously debauched to avail themselves of the toleration offered by the police.

Originally, little attention seems to have been paid to the checking of the growth of vice. But there has been an increasing tendency to refuse the registration of minors. While this cannot be done in every case, minors are registered much less frequently now than formerly. The tenants of licensed houses are forbidden to admit boys under eighteen, or students of the various higher schools. Great care is also exercised in making it easy for a woman who desires to reform to do so.

The control of prostitution is given over almost entirely to a body of special agents who form a part of the general secret service. The ordinary police have nothing to do with prostitution, except in case of gross violation of public decency or public order. Between forty and fifty agents are required for this service. They must, of course, be men of great tact, they must be men upon whom reliance may be placed, since any mistake they may make entails the most serious consequences.

The medical service consisted in 1890 of a chief and assistant-chief surgeon, fourteen surgeons in ordinary, and ten adjunct surgeons. They are assigned to various quarters of the city, changing at intervals by regular rotation.

The first thing that strikes the student of the Parisian system is the weakness of its legal basis. Since the Revolution, no general laws on the subject of prostitution have been made. The Penal Code does not touch upon it. The police are therefore compelled to go back to the ordinances of 1684, 1713, 1768, and 1778 for their authority to regulate vice. According to these ordinances, prostitution was a crime, which the lieutenant of police could punish at his discretion. Clandestine prostitution is still punished according to those ordinances.[1]

The modern police are not, however, the successors to the powers of the lieutenant of police under the *ancien régime*. The lieutenant of police could pass sentence if his royal master authorised him to do so. The modern police commissary has no power to sentence a criminal; yet he appears to assume such an authority with regard to the so-called crime of debauch.

Another legal prop for the service of morals is the law of 1789 constituting the municipalities. By this law, the municipalities are assured the advantages of a good police system. The exact powers of the police are not enumerated, but by a law of 1790 it is specified that the police are to maintain public order and decency and to protect public health. It is assumed that this implies a system of police regulation of prostitution.[2]

There have been numerous attempts to pass general laws with regard to prostitution. In

[1] *Cf. Réglement du 13 Novembre, 1843*, Sec. 7.
[2] Lecour, *op. cit.*, 29.

1811 and in 1816, in 1819 and in 1823, eminent administrators, lawyers, and statesmen attempted to formulate special laws that would be appropriate to so delicate a subject. The task had to be abandoned, however. It was impossible to devise a law at once efficient and just. And so the police have continued to take matters into their own hands, changing their regulations from time to time to suit the exigencies of the occasion.

Doubtless the service of morals has gained rather than lost by the flexibility thus attained. But the lack of any other than a fictitious legal basis has always been a point of attack for the opponents of the system. While some of the supporters of the system of regulation acquiesce in the absence of general laws, believing it beneath the dignity of the State to notice a subject which is the cause of so many cares for the police, the majority would look with favour upon any measure which would free the police from the serious charge of illegal usurpation of powers.

CHAPTER IV

REGULATION IN BERLIN AND IN OTHER CITIES OF EUROPE

Berlin.—The Reformation and the great social and economic movements that were connected with it wrought a complete change in the character of the city of Berlin. From a conservative mediæval town, in which every person had his fixed place, it had become a large and wealthy city. The old regulations concerning vice had been quite outgrown. Although the old regulations, abolished at the time of the Reformation, were restored when the religious ardour had cooled, prostitution was no longer easily controlled by them. It had increased greatly in volume and in complexity. The inference of contemporaries was that the Reformation had thoroughly ruined the morals of society—an inference accepted by not a few modern writers.

In 1700 a system of regulation was adopted which contained the essential features of modern regulation. As one would expect, much was borrowed from the Middle Ages. The principle of dealing with groups of individuals under a responsible head appears in the provision which makes the keeper of the brothel responsible for the conduct of the inmates of his house. If any outrage were perpetrated, such as assault or robbery, the keeper had to make good the damage done. If a woman, known to be diseased, transmitted the malady, the keeper had to stand the costs of treatment. In this way it was thought possible to restrain effectively all tendency toward disorder.

For the sake of preserving the health not only of the prostitutes, but also of their visitors, an official surgeon was to examine them fortnightly. Those who were found to be diseased were to be confined to their rooms, if the malady were slight; if it were grave, they were to be sent to the Charity Hospital. This feature of the regulation is of course distinctly a modern innovation.

Another thing that strikes one as distinctly modern is the declaration that prostitution is not permitted, but tolerated—a bit of sophistry which marks a distinct advance over the naïve view of the Middle Ages. Instead of the mediæval tax upon prostitutes as the possessors of a lucrative trade, we find a fee of two groschen for medical examination. This, too, is modern. It shows that even then there was a feeling that it was dishonourable for the State to accept the earnings of so foul a trade, excepting for the expenditure of regulating the trade. One thing more that marks the regulation as modern is the provision that, if a prostitute wished to reform, the keeper of a brothel could not detain her, even though she owed him a debt.[1]

This regulation remained in force until 1792. With the growth of wealth and population, vice had increased enormously. In 1780 there were a hundred houses of ill fame, with seven to nine inmates in each.[2] There was, besides, a class of prostitutes who lived in rented lodgings and carried on their profession on their own account. These also were tolerated by the police, although the regulation of 1700 had made no provision for them. Moreover, clandestine prostitution throve, although the police dealt with unlicensed prostitutes in summary fashion, arresting them and registering them without formalities, and compelling them, under severe penalties, to appear for sanitary examinations. No special regard was had for the age or condition of those thus inscribed upon the register of infamy. Many of them were mere children.

In 1792 a new regulation was made. This was in many respects a mere amplification of the regulation of 1700. Licensed houses of prostitution were tolerated, as were also prostitutes at large. This was strictly contrary to the General

[1] Behrend, *Die Prostitution in Berlin*, 20.
[2] *Ibid.*, 26.

Code (*Allgemeines Landrecht*), which prohibited prostitution excepting in licensed houses. No attention was paid to this fact at the time.

The principle of placing the prostitutes under the control of persons who could be responsible for their conduct was still further developed. No one could open a brothel without first receiving permission from the police; no one could rent a room to a prostitute without permission. As in the older regulations, the tenant of the licensed house was responsible for any outrage or robbery committed upon his premises. Moreover, he was held to be an accomplice until he proved his innocence. Even if it could be proven that he was no partner to the outrage, he was subject to fine and imprisonment if he had not done everything in his power to prevent it. Prostitutes at large were compelled to live in certain streets. The person who let lodgings to them (always an elderly woman, single, widowed, or divorced) had to undertake responsibilities similar to those of the tenant of a licensed house.

Much greater emphasis was laid upon the sanitary feature of regulation. Any person who should transmit a venereal disease was to stand the cost of treatment and was subject to imprisonment for three months. While this provision applied to men as well as to women, it is easy to see that in practice it would hardly reach any one except the prostitute. The mistress of a brothel was held jointly responsible with the inmate for any disease transmitted, whether she knew that the disease existed or not. She was also under obligation to report at once any case of disease in her house. If she failed to do so, she was subject to fine and imprisonment.

The main sanitary measure was, however, the periodic examinations by the official surgeons. These took place weekly, at the domicile of the prostitute. Those who were diseased were disposed of as in the older regulation. To meet the expenses of treatment, a contribution was laid upon all prostitutes. As this proved insufficient, a tax was imposed three years later upon the tenants of licensed houses.

Much more attention than formerly was paid to the moral welfare of the fallen woman. If she wished to reform, she could not be detained for any reason. Minors could be registered only in case they were already utterly depraved.[1] Of this the police were the judges, since no girl could be admitted to a brothel without permission. Severe penalties were enacted against enticing young women into brothels.

For the preservation of public decency, soliciting in public places was prohibited, as well as indecent proposals from windows or doors of brothels. The brothel tenant or the woman who had let a room to a prostitute was responsible for

[1] The age of majority was twenty-four.

the enforcement of this regulation. Moreover, the sale of intoxicating liquors in brothels was prohibited, and, later, dancing and games, in order to prevent vicious resorts from becoming places of entertainment.[1]

No provision was made for compulsory registration. But the clandestine prostitute was punished by three months' imprisonment, followed by confinement in the workhouse until she should manifest a desire to enter some honourable employment, and should find an opportunity to do so.

This regulation remained practically unchanged until 1828. It was not, however, enforced with uniformity from year to year. The ideas of the French Revolution permeated German society to a certain extent, creating a feeling that it was an outrage upon justice to place a special class of human beings under the arbitrary control of the police. Moreover, it was felt that the intimate relations of the State with vice, which a system of regulation naturally creates, were degrading. Not only did this feeling exist in the general community, but it influenced not a little the ministry of the realm. Accordingly, the police of Berlin were subjected to hostility from above and below. In 1810 the ministry absolutely prohibited the registration of minors, a practice in which the police had hitherto persisted. The police were forbidden to grant permits for new brothels. They were to

[1] Behrend, *op. cit.*, 29 *et seq.*

examine closely into the antecedents of a woman who proposed to enter a house of ill fame, and to deter her from her purpose, if possible. Against this tendency was the sentiment of the army, which has generally been decidedly in favour of a system of tolerated vice. The military authorities at Berlin pleaded for the removal of the age limitation imposed upon those who wished to enter the ranks of registered prostitutes.[1]

After the "glorious victory" the sentiment against regulation diminished In 1814 permission was granted to register minors, although an attempt was first to be made to induce them to reform, and the consent of their parents was to be secured. Permission was also given to erect a new brothel in place of one that had failed, and to transfer the ownership of brothels. The consent of the police was of course to be secured.

In 1829 a new regulation was made, with the approval of the ministry. The only important change was the increased frequency of sanitary inspections. According to the new regulation, they were to be made twice a week instead of once.

At this time there were thirty-three licensed houses in Berlin. These were pretty well scattered throughout the city. There was no formal restriction as to their location, excepting that they were not permitted in the vicinity of churches and schools, or on crowded thoroughfares. A con-

[1] Behrend, *op. cit.*, 90.

siderable number of them, however, were grouped together in a small street, *an der Königsmauer.* This street had from a very early date been noted as a haunt of vice.

During the thirties, citizens who possessed property in the vicinity of brothels began to complain to the police and the ministry of the losses they suffered in consequence of the presence of vice, and to petition for the removal of the licensed houses. The police authorities paid no attention to the petitions, but in 1839 the ministry, again hostile to police regulation, ordered the removal of all such houses to the street *an der Königsmauer.* Accordingly, all were removed thither except two. Five failed, leaving twenty-six licensed houses in a street containing only fifty-two small houses. The street may fairly be said to have been abandoned utterly to vice, since its remaining inhabitants were largely panders and procurers, together with the workers and small traders who depended for support upon the custom of the brothels.

This measure was, however, very far from being satisfactory. It is a question whether the existence of isolated brothels in various parts of the city was as demoralising as the existence of a limited quarter in which vice ran riot. Whatever may be said of the demoralising effect upon respectable society of a number of prostitutes mingling with it, there can be no doubt that respectable surroundings have far more power than police regulations to keep the wanton woman from displaying the actual degradation of her character. In a limited community consisting wholly of immoral characters, in which respectable persons normally appear only in moments of immorality, this restraining influence is absent. An *esprit de corps* is created which is highly injurious to public morals and public order.[1] Furthermore, the existence of licensed houses side by side almost inevitably leads to an odious competition in indecency for the sake of attracting customers.

From the point of view of sanitary regulation, the plan was not successful. While the notoriety of the quarter naturally attracted the youthful and the reckless, the bands of students and apprentices, the strangers bent upon novelty, the publicity of it deterred those who had acquired caution without acquiring continence,—the greatest resource of prostitution. Hence clandestine prostitution increased throughout the city.[2]

A further result of the grouping of licensed houses was increased opposition toward any system of regulation whatever. The agglomeration upon one spot of so much vice opened the eyes

---

[1] Behrend, *op. cit.*, 114 *et seq.*

[2] This does not mean that prostitution in general increased. It merely means that the relative proportion of those who would submit to regulation declined.

of the better classes to the extent of the evil. Accounts, exaggerated beyond all semblance of truth, recalled the orgies of declining Rome. The abolition sentiment again gained credit with the higher authorities, and in 1843 the ministry issued an order that one half of the brothels *an der Königsmauer* should be removed beyond the *Stadtmauer*. All were to be subjected to close surveillance, and for three violations of the regulations, whether great or small, they were to be closed, nor were others to be opened in their place. The first part of the order was not carried out, as the police declared that it was impossible to find a locality which would receive the removed houses. Opportunity was not given for carrying the second part of the order into effect, as an order of the Minister of the Interior, issued in 1844, fixed January 1, 1846, as the date for the closing of all the brothels in Berlin. This order was duly executed.

It is not to be supposed that a let-alone policy was adopted. The police were ordered to take all needful measures for public safety and public health. Prostitutes were still compelled to submit to weekly medical inspections. A register was kept showing the state of health of the women, but no control-book was given them, and it was to be impressed upon them that they were not licensed, but merely tolerated. Clandestine prostitution was still subject to severe punishment.

Doubtless the police enforced the changed regulations with no very great enthusiasm; but, so far as the formal regulations were concerned, the only change was the abolition of the brothel and its replacement by tolerated prostitution at large. There is no ground whatever for the notion that all sanitary control was abandoned in 1846.

At the instigation of the military authorities, the licensed houses were opened again in 1851. The Penal Code of 1850 imposed the penalty fixed for procuring upon any one who should act as a mediator for professional vice or lend his aid to vicious practices.[1]

Another section, however, implied the right on the part of the police to make needful regulations for the preservation of public health and public order.[2]

It was upon the latter section that the police based the right of reopening the brothels. In 1856, however, a decision of the *Obertribunal* of Prussia pronounced the brothel an illegal institution, whereupon the licensed houses of Berlin were definitely closed.[3]

The "service of morals" as reorganised in 1850 and again in 1876 did not differ essentially from the system now in force. We may accordingly pass at once to the existing regulations. The

[1] Sec. 146.   [2] Sec. 147.
[3] Blaschko, *Conférence internationale, Brussels,* 1899; *Enquêtes,* i., 662.

sanitary feature is paramount. The registration of prostitutes is merely auxiliary to sanitary control, since it is absolutely necessary to register the women of loose life if they are to be subjected to periodical examination. A woman may be registered either at her own request or by the order of the chief of the police bureau. The police arrest any woman whom they have reason to suspect of clandestine prostitution. The grounds of such arrest may be direct observation by the special police agents of the service of morals, the denunciation of private persons, of registered prostitutes, or of men who believe themselves to be contaminated by the woman in question. When arrested, she is subjected to a physical examination, and if found to be diseased the police assume the power to place her upon the register. If she is not diseased, she receives a "kindly warning." In the warning-formula, especial emphasis is laid upon the fact that a second arrest would mean compulsory registration. It is assumed that if a mistake has been made in the first arrest, the woman arrested will take such pains to avoid further suspicion that a second mistake would be practically impossible.

Once registered, prostitutes are required to report every week at the public dispensary for sanitary examination. Failure to do so is punishable by imprisonment, the maximum sentence being six weeks. Examinations and treatment are gratuitous.

Every registered prostitute must give satisfactory information as to age and antecedents. Minors are not, as a rule, permitted to register.

There are, of course, numerous detailed regulations with regard to the localities where prostitutes may not appear, and with regard to the manner in which they must deport themselves. These it is unnecessary to discuss here.

Comparison of Reglementation Systems of Paris and Berlin.—If we compare the systems of Paris and of Berlin, we find that they do not differ greatly in essence. In both of them prostitutes are treated as a special class, bearing a relation to the common law essentially different from that of other members of society. A renowned French lawyer has clearly defined this point of view by declaring that prostitution is a status in the same sense that the army is a status, and, just as is the case with the army, prostitutes may be subjected to regulations that would be tyrannical if applied to the ordinary citizen.[1]

In Berlin this manner of regarding prostitution has been handed down from the Middle Ages, and may be considered a survival of a social system in which any body of individuals could be treated as a special status. In Paris it has

[1] M. Dupin, cited by Lecour, *op. cit.*, 41.

rather grown up as a result of the exigencies of police administration.

In both cities the need is recognised of a special body of police, acting with large discretionary powers. In both cities the sanitary features of control are paramount; nevertheless, public order, decency, and morals receive a certain attention. The Berlin authorities act, perhaps, with greater freedom in imposing registration upon prostitutes who will not submit to it voluntarily. This is probably owing to the greater legal authority which the Berlin police possess.

Much regard has usually been paid to the fact that in Paris it is the policy of the police to confine prostitution to licensed houses, while in Berlin the brothel is absolutely prohibited. How unimportant this feature is may be understood from the fact that not one tenth of the registered prostitutes of Paris live in licensed houses.[1] In practice, the administrations of the two cities have exactly the same problem to deal with.

There are, of course, innumerable minor regulations that show certain differences in policy. These, however, are of small interest to any one except the officials who have to administer the systems.

Finally, the sanitary service does not differ

[1] In 1897, out of about 6000 registered prostitutes only 490 lived in licensed houses.—Dr. Ozenne, *Conférence internationale, Brussels,* 1899; *Enquêtes,* i., 146.

in essence. It is true that all examinations in Berlin are held in public offices designed for that purpose, while in Paris those who live in licensed houses are examined at their domicile. This difference is of small significance, since the proportion of brothel inmates is so insignificant. In Berlin examinations are weekly, in Paris fortnightly. Examination and treatment are gratuitous in both cities.

Regulation in Other European Cities.—A study of the evolution of regulation in other European cities would reveal but few new features. Regulation has in general grown out of repressive legislation. Inability to enforce stringent measures against vice has generally given the policy of the police an arbitrary character that was easily changed into discretionary power. Sanitary features have been grafted upon systems of tacit toleration. As a rule, Paris and Berlin have served as models in this respect. Later systems, as the regulations of Italy, were modelled after that of Brussels, which in turn is in essence a copy of the Parisian system.

It may, perhaps, be worth while to touch upon a few of the peculiar features to be found in some of the other cities of Europe. Thus we find in Bremen the plan of confining prostitution to a single small street, which is so situated as to be easily controlled by the police. Prostitutes found elsewhere are arrested and punished by imprisonment. This plan has been partially adopted by several other of the smaller German cities. A similar policy is pursued in some of the smaller French cities.

No very large city has adopted such a policy. It seems probable that the enormous proportions such a quarter would assume in a city like Paris or Berlin would be a menace to good order and a centre of demoralisation. Where special quarters exist, it would seem that the interest of property owners in the vicinity of licensed houses, rather than a consideration of the moral interests of the community as a whole, was responsible for their creation.

In a large number of the cities of France, the police persist in attempting to confine prostitution to licensed houses. In some cities their efforts are not wholly unsuccessful. Thus in Marseilles the licensed houses hold their own. In other cities these houses are constantly declining. These differences are to be explained by the character of the clientage of prostitution. Where strangers are numerous, where sailors are accustomed to land, the licensed house thrives. It is the "law of supply and demand" that decides whether the efforts of the police can be fruitful or not.

Vienna presents several peculiarities in the system of regulation of vice. The Morals police and the Sanitary police are under different authorities. The supervision of public morals falls in the province of the Imperial police, while for the sanitary control the municipal authorities are responsible. As a consequence, there is a lack of harmony, the Sanitary police attempting to increase as far as possible the number of public prostitutes, the Morals police attempting to limit it. Examinations of licensed women are made by ordinary physicians, designated by the police. They are made either at the domicile of the physician or at that of the woman. They are thus designed to give as little publicity to the activities of police control as circumstances allow.

Extent of Regulation.—Regulation of vice is still properly in the experimental stage. Many believe, it is true, that its salutary effects are not to be challenged; others affirm that no such effects are to be found. It is accordingly necessary, as preliminary to examining the evidence as to the efficacy of regulation, to consider the extent of existing regulations.

In the first place, practically all the cities and large towns of France have systems of regulation much like that of Paris. So also have the cities of Belgium. German cities, as a rule, regulate vice. Hungary has what is considered an efficient system; Austrian cities regulate vice, but in no very efficient way. For the last half-century, Russian cities have persistently striven to keep prostitution under sanitary control. From the time of the union of Italy down to 1888, the larger Italian cities had a system of regulation modelled after that of Brussels. The Scandinavian states, with the exception of Norway, regulate vice in their largest cities; so also do Spain and Portugal. From 1866 until 1883, England tried the experiment of regulation in twelve districts in England and two in Ireland. In these stations prostitutes were registered and subjected to periodic sanitary inspection, and if diseased were detained in lock-hospitals until cured.

Outside of Europe similar regulations have been put in force. The most notorious were the regulations in India during the time of the Contagious Diseases Acts. Hong Kong also presented a system of regulation. In Japan prostitutes are confined to special quarters and are subjected to periodic examinations. Finally, mention may be made of the one experiment in our own country, in St. Louis, 1870–1873.

4

CHAPTER V

THE effect of vice upon the physical health of the community is receiving at present more attention than any other feature of the problem. Reglementists and abolitionists alike test their systems by the effect upon venereal disease. Nothing could be more natural, since it has at last become clear to almost every one that venereal diseases are frightfully common in every civilised country. Moreover, recent progress in medical science has demonstrated the fact that the diseases that have long been known to be the immediate effects of vice by no means make up the sum of the cost in health that results from it. Many constitutional maladies that were formerly ascribed to entirely different causes have recently been shown to be of venereal origin.

Unfortunately, it is impossible to form even an approximately correct idea of the actual extent of the ravages of venereal disease. One medical congress after another has urged the necessity of adequate statistics of venereal disease; but up to the present very little has been accomplished in this direction. In Norway alone are private physicians required by law to furnish reports of the cases treated by them. Everywhere else it is necessary to deduce the facts in question from the statistics of limited classes, such as the army and the navy, to piece together hospital records, or to depend upon the estimates of individual physicians.[1]

We may take as a starting-point the Norwegian statistics, since, with all their imperfections, they are the most complete in existence.

In Christiania, a city of over two hundred thousand inhabitants, during the period from 1879 to 1898, the yearly number of cases of venereal diseases of all kinds reported have ranged generally between ten and fifteen per thousand of population. The minimum was 5.7 in 1888; the maximum was 20.7 in 1882. Of these, about two fifths are cases of gonorrhœa; rather more than three tenths are cases of syphilis.

For the whole of Norway during the same period, the number of cases of venereal disease has varied from 2.14 per thousand in 1889 to 3.55 in 1882.[2]

---

[1] The Medical Department of Prussia has within the last year undertaken to secure statistics of venereal disease in the State of Prussia. A circular was issued by the Minister, April 30, 1901, requesting all physicians to report all cases treated by them during the current year.— *Bulletin de la Société Internationale de Prophylaxie Sanitaire et Morale,* Tome i., No. 3.

[2] Holst, *Conférence Internationale, Brussels,* 1899; *Enquêtes,* i., 126.

These figures are unquestionably too low. Many cases of disease are naturally treated by quacks, or by the patients themselves according to recipes borrowed from comrades. Again, although there is a law compelling every physician to report all cases, it is impossible to enforce such a law. The only motive that would induce a physician to comply with the law is scientific interest.

While cases of hereditary syphilis are reported, it is obvious that many will escape through insufficient scientific knowledge on the part of practising physicians. Finally, there is no place for the legacy of criminality, idiocy, and other forms of degeneracy that venereal disease entails upon society.

On the other hand, many of the persons diseased may be treated for several maladies during the same year, or for different phases of the same disease. Especially would this be true of prostitutes, who are, of course, included in the population at large. This would tend to make the number of venereally diseased seem greater than it actually is. Sufferers from such diseases are very apt to change their physicians; and this also would tend to make the figures too large.

Accordingly, these statistics can be considered as an indication only of the actual extent of disease. Nevertheless, it seems true that by far the greater proportion of the ills resulting from vice are recognisable by competent physicians. Christiania is a city in which, for half a century, much attention has been given to combating venereal disease. It may be assumed, then, that its physicians will generally have interest enough to report cases of disease according to law.

Where military service is compulsory, the state of health of the army will show something as to the extent of disease in population, since every able-bodied adult male must serve. The following table will show the extent of venereal diseases in various European armies[1]:

	German per 1000	French per 1000	Austrian per 1000	Italian per 1000
1881–86	35.1	58.2	73.6	102.9
1886–91	27.1	51.1	65.3	94.3
1891–96	29.1	56.7	61.0	84.9

As data for estimating the general prevalence of disease, these figures are, of course, to be used with a good deal of caution. The pay of the soldiers, the character of the discipline, the location of the barracks, and a number of other considerations must be allowed for before one can venture to affirm that venereal diseases are more common in Italy than in Germany. It is to be expected that disease will be much more frequent among soldiers than among citizens, owing to the fact that the soldiers are young and unmarried, free from arduous exertion, and exposed to the demoralising influences that always pervade military bodies.

[1] Blaschko, *Conférence Internationale, Brussels*, 1899; *Enquêtes*, i., 681.

When an army consists of volunteers, as the British army, statistics of venereal disease cease to have any value as an indication of the general state of health. It is not the typical British citizen who enlists in time of peace.

Where large standing armies do not exist, it is necessary to rely upon the records of hospitals and the estimates of physicians. The records of hospitals are worth little, as but a fraction of the diseased ever apply for admission. The estimates of physicians are of course mere guesses, most often evolved in the heat of argument, and hence worth practically nothing.

But however imperfect the data for estimating the true extent of the evil may be, they are sufficient to justify the opinion that venereal disease is one of the most serious that menace public health, and that no less energetic measures should be taken to stamp it out than are employed to check the ravages of other serious contagious diseases. Even if the shame and suffering which these maladies cause the individual are left out of account, there is no question that the burden which they impose upon society at large is a heavy one. Even if they do not utterly wreck the health of the individual, they impair his industrial efficiency and increase the chance of his becoming a burden upon society. In the long contest for survival among different nations, a high percentage of venereal diseases is a most serious handicap for any country.   It is the duty of a community to do everything in its power to disembarrass itself of them.

But the question whether society owes it to the individual to protect him from venereal infection has long been a subject of bitter controversy.   It is a common idea that, since such maladies are generally the result of immoral acts, the persons infected receive merely their due. They have knowingly exposed themselves to the danger; they have violated social laws in order to do so; let them take the consequences.

Another view, one which bears the stamp of modern evolutionary science, recognises the fact that there are individuals so constituted as to be unable to control their animal instincts.   These are, as it were, fatally devoted to expose themselves to contagion.   There can be no talk of free moral agency on the part of such persons; one cannot regard the misfortune that befalls them as a punishment for their acts.   Such persons are, however, unfit members of civilised society, and venereal disease merely acts to free society from their presence.

The latter view is the more easily disposed of. It is not merely the incompetent, the degenerate, the brutal, that fall victims to the scourge of syphilis.   The upper classes and the lower suffer alike.   In Russian cities, it is said to be the very flower of the youth, the young men in the universities, who are most frequently diseased. Similar observations have been made with regard to other European countries. Doubtless there is some exaggeration in such statements as these. But any practising physician will bear witness to the fact that among his patients the "unfit" form no inconsiderable fraction.

The other view deserves more extended consideration. It is an undeniable fact that, in the great majority of cases, venereal disease is contracted as the result of a voluntary act,—an act known by every one to be immoral. It is only natural to regard disease as a penalty for vicious conduct. In this respect there is certainly a valid distinction between venereal diseases on the one hand and all other contagious or infectious diseases on the other. An individual has a right to demand all possible protection from evils which he cannot avoid; his right to protection from dangers which he voluntarily encounters is not so clear.

Yet it is easy to carry the principle of personal responsibility for voluntary acts to an unwarranted extreme. The boy who yields to immoral impulses does not deserve the same penalty that falls upon the man of matured intelligence who lapses from virtue. The influence of the environment must be taken into account in judging the degree of personal responsibility. Now, it is well known that venereal disease is frequently contracted at a very early age. A considerable portion of the syphilitics treated in hospitals are boys still in their teens. Probably a majority of all sufferers from syphilis are infected before the twenty-sixth year.[1]

The penalty of disease, then, falls most heavily upon those who are least responsible for their acts. Accordingly, it is easy to see why many thinkers who are not in the least inclined to condone immorality look upon sanitary control of vice as of paramount importance. So long as society permits men to grow up in an environment inimical to virtue, they argue, it is idle to hold them strictly accountable for their conduct, and inhuman to permit them to suffer from diseases which might be prevented by systematic sanitary regulation.

There is one further fact which would seem to condemn the public policy of ignoring venereal diseases. Great numbers of people suffer from them by no moral fault of their own. It is, perhaps, not as well known as it should be, that men frequently transmit to their wives diseases contracted in their youth and folly, of which they believed themselves to be quite cured. It requires much moral cold-bloodedness to take the stand

---

[1] Of 10,000 syphilitics who came under the observation of Professor Fournier, 817 had been infected before the twentieth year, and 5130 between twenty-one and twenty-six.—*Conférence Internationale, Brussels*, 1899; *Rapports Préliminaires*, 41.

that this is merely a matter between husband and wife, with which society has nothing to do.[1]

Account must also be taken of the children brought into the world with the curse of hideous disease upon them; of the nurse contaminated by the child she nurtures; of the child diseased through its nurse; and of the numbers of persons who are infected by accidental contact.[2]

[1] Professor Fournier found that of one hundred women infected with syphilis, twenty had been contaminated by their husbands.— *Conférence Internationale, Brussels,* 1899; *Rapports Préliminaires,* i., 13. See also Flesch, *Prostitution und Frauenkrankheiten.*

[2] In some places, syphilitic disease is regularly contracted in such ways. According to the data at hand, as much as 80 per cent. of the syphilis among the Russian rural population is contracted thus. Even in the city population, extra-genital infection is responsible for from 1.5 to 3 per cent. This does not include hereditary syphilis.—O. V. Petersen, *Conférence Internationale, Brussels,* 1899; *Enquêtes,* i., 264.

CHAPTER VI

THE MORAL ASPECT OF REGULATION

THE prominence given in recent discussion to the sanitary evils that result from unchecked and unregulated prostitution has obscured, to a certain extent, the fact that there are greater evils than physical disease connected with vice. One who subscribes to the dictum, "Disease is a great evil, but vice is a greater," is almost certain to be subjected to the scorn of many practical men. Yet, when the controversial spirit subsides, all rational men will admit the gravity of vice, quite apart from its hygienic consequences. The history of decadent Greece and Rome will show to what depths of imbecility and shame it may cause a nation to fall. There can be no greater mistake than to believe that the impulses that lead to vice are constant and invariable, capable of complete satiation. They grow with feeding; if they are wearied with one kind of satisfaction, they seek not rest, but variety. This fact, rather than any other, will account for the hideous forms of vice that disfigured ancient society. One does not need a revealed religion or a subtle moral philosophy to teach him that unrestrained vice results in mental and moral disease and degeneracy far more hideous and far more dangerous to society than any form of physical disease.

Accordingly, if it is a dangerous policy for government to ignore the existence of venereal diseases and to neglect any possible means for preventing them, it is a still more dangerous policy to ignore vice and to permit it to grow unchecked. To limit the number of those who seek vicious pleasures, and to prevent the furnishing of such pleasures to those who are inclined to seek them, is one of the first duties of good government.

There is a widely-prevalent opinion that the moral task is too great for government to undertake, while sanitary improvements may be easily brought about; accordingly, it is expedient to limit governmental activity to the comparatively narrow field of sanitary regulation. Those who hold this view lose sight of the fact that humanity is not divided into two classes, the virtuous and the vicious, but that in it is represented every degree of virtue and vice, from the purest to the most utterly depraved. There will probably always be men who are swayed solely by animal passions, and it would be vain to hope to make them virtuous by legislative enactment. There will always be women who fall willing victims to vice, whom no governmental vigilance could save. A great part of vice withdraws itself as completely from social control as do a man's secret thoughts. The fact remains that the greater part of humanity stands midway between the two extremes and may be improved or degraded in morals by circumstances which lie within the control of society.

Indeed, it is almost inexplicable that any one should doubt that a more rational system of education, better housing conditions, the suppression of flagrant incitement to vice, and the dissociating of vice from legitimate amusement would diminish the number of patrons of prostitution, and would limit the extent to which the remainder indulge in illicit pleasures. The improvement in morals could not, of course, be very pronounced in its effects. A large part of the gain could appear only in a succeeding generation. It would certainly be worth none the less for that. It may be remarked that there is hardly a reputable defender of sanitary regulation who does not at the same time advocate measures of moral reform. The influence of pernicious surroundings in promoting immorality is everywhere recognised. Some writers expect much good from measures that tend to promote morality among men, but believe that nothing can be done to diminish the number of women who lead immoral lives. This is the view of Tarnowsky. It rests upon the theory of the innate perversity of all prostitutes, a theory which is not borne out by the facts. Without doubt, congenital perverts do exist among women. But there is no reason for believing that they form more than a negligible fraction of the entire number of prostitutes.

A very large number of prostitutes begin their career of shame when mere children. They may be the victims of procurers, or they may drift into vice without the deliberate incitement of any person who expects to profit from their shame. In any case, they can hardly be held responsible for their vicious conduct.

It is a disgrace to civilisation that panders are still permitted to betray neglected children and to take part of their earnings. In every large city those who have been attracted into prostitution before they were old enough to be responsible for their acts make up a very large proportion of the total number of vicious women.

It is undoubtedly true that a chronic state of poverty has à powerful influence in impelling women to accept a vicious life. Society has up to the present time proven unable to solve the problem of poverty; and until that problem is solved, there is little reason to believe that there will cease to be a class of women, not necessarily congenitally defective, who will choose a life of vice. But there are in every large city classes of working women whose normal income is sufficient to permit them to live honourable lives, but who are left at times of temporary depression with no means of escaping from starvation except prostitution.[1]

It is easily conceivable that society could furnish temporary relief to such unfortunates and thus diminish, to an appreciable extent, the volume of feminine vice.

Again, there still remains a class of women who are abducted and forced into prostitution by physical violence. The fact that they sooner or later accept their fate is the only thing that can account for the indifference of society toward such a shameful condition. This is certainly a factor within the control of government.

The possibilities of moral regulation are by no means exhausted when society has done all in its power to prevent women from entering upon a life of shame. It is a long-exploded fallacy that a woman who has once fallen must always remain in the lowest degradation of vice. Of the great numbers who have fallen through need or thoughtlessness, probably the majority are striving to rise out of the mire. It is a commonplace that modern prostitution, viewed as a whole, is a temporary, not a permanent state. After a few years of shame

---

[1] According to Blaschko, *Conférence Internationale, Brussels,* 1899; *Enquêtes,* i., 676, occasional prostitution far surpasses in extent professional prostitution in the great industrial centres of Germany. In such cities prostitution increases or diminishes inversely as employment in industry. In St. Petersburg it is common for domestics to practise prostitution when out of employment and to cease from it when work is offered.—Stürmer, *Die Prostitution in Russland,* 76.

the greater number of these women return to honourable employment, marry, or become kept mistresses,[1] a station degraded enough, to be sure, but infinitely less degraded than that of the public prostitute.

Even among the registered prostitutes of large European cities, there are many who are each year liberated from the control of the police, on the ground that they have ceased to prostitute themselves. Thus, in Copenhagen, from 1871 to 1896, twenty per cent. of the registered prostitutes were cancelled from the register because of marriage, thirteen per cent. returned to their relatives, and ten per cent. were taken in charge by private persons (institutions, etc.).[2] Of course, this would be much more frequently the case with occasional prostitutes, who have not formed the habits of a vicious life.

When the fact that prostitutes can and do reform is taken into account, it becomes evident that government has not performed all its duty as a moralising force until it has done everything in its power to make reform possible for those who desire it. The very least that common morality can demand is that no obstacle should be placed in the way of the unfortunates who are struggling to reform.

[1] Ehlers, *Conférence Internationale, Brussels,* 1899; *Enquêtes,* i., 98 *et seq.;* Schmölder, *Conférence Internationale, Brussels,* 1899; *Rapports Préliminaires;* Jeannel, *La Prostitution dans les grandes Villes du dixneuvième Siècle,* 263.

[2] Ehlers, *Conférence Internationale, Brussels,* 1899; *Enquêtes,* i., 121.

CHAPTER VII

FUNDAMENTAL OPPOSITION BETWEEN MORAL AND SANITARY CONTROL

IT is not difficult to understand that the sanitary and moral interests in the control of prostitution cannot be wholly in harmony with each other. Some features of sanitary control may be equally salutary morally, and *vice versâ*. Others may at least be indifferent morally, and so create no real opposition between the two groups of interests. But unquestionably many regulations which may be very good from a sanitary point of view are evil from the point of view of morals. And the reverse is likewise true.

It is not an accident that in Paris, where the sanitary branch of the service has been grafted upon the Morals Police proper, and is still subordinate to it, there should be constant friction between the medical men and the police. The police, as guardians of public morals, do not find it possible to put into force measures that the physicians consider absolutely essential. This is still more the case in Austria, where the two branches are independent of each other. The complaint is frequently made by the sanitary branch that the morals branch pursues its own ends, quite regardless of sanitary considerations. A learned Austrian writer has laid down the axiom that the less the attention that is paid to public morality, the better will be the state of public health, and *vice versâ*.[1]

The reason for this opposition lies upon the surface. Since venereal diseases are always the result of contagion, it is evident that if all those who are diseased could be isolated, and kept under treatment until entirely cured, venereal disease would disappear. But it is manifestly impossible to discover all cases of disease in the general population and to treat the patients discovered in isolation. Since, however, venereal disease is usually directly or indirectly traceable to prostitution, if prostitutes could be kept free from it, it would eventually disappear from society. To attain this end it would be necessary to discover every case of disease as soon as it appears, and to confine the patient until the disease is wholly cured. And this implies, of course, a rigid police control over every woman who sells the use of her person, whether publicly or not,—a control sufficient to compel her to submit to very frequent sanitary inspection, and to a long and tedious imprisonment whenever she is infected with disease. Naturally,

[1] Schrank, *Die Prostitution in Wien*, ii., 126.

the most violent opposition on the part of the prostitute must be expected. For several reasons, the periodic examinations are irksome to her; still more irksome is compulsory treatment, since the diseases with which she is infected may not be painful to her, and she cares not a whit whether she transmits them to her clients or not,—no more than do her clients care whether they transmit disease to her. According to this system of regulation, the police would treat her much as a chattel, and would keep her in good health for her clients' sake.

It is the habit of many who advocate such a system of regulation to paint all prostitutes as hideous, blear-eyed, degenerate creatures, recognisable at a glance, detestable to all, even to their "consumers," stained through and through with every form of vice. If such a characterisation corresponded with the reality, it would be comparatively easy to carry out such a system of regulation, and any moral opposition which might arise could be met by pointing out incidental effects that would make for morality and public order. The lodgings of the prostitute would be under police supervision and would be prevented from becoming dens of filth and contagion. The police would become acquainted with the general habits of such women, would know the individuals who prey upon them, and thus could prevent them from becoming the tools of low criminals, as they so often do under conditions of *laissez faire*. Moreover, the police would naturally inquire into their antecedents and would thus collect valuable data as to the causes, biological and social, which are responsible for such depraved forms of humanity.

Even if the premise of such a class of prostitutes is accepted, the objection might be raised that the semi-official position of the prostitute would seem to indicate a public sanction of debauch. The official guarantee of good health would remove any hesitancy to indulge in forbidden pleasures that fear of disease might create. Writers of the reglementation school claim, however, that as a practical fact the patrons of women of this class are not likely to be influenced much by sanction or lack of sanction on the part of the police, nor are they of self-control sufficient to restrain their passions for fear of disease.[1]

But it would be a grievous error to suppose that all prostitutes, or even a very large proportion of them, are thus easily distinguished from the decent classes of society. Modern prostitution is an infinitely complex phenomenon. It is intangible, indefinable. From its complexity arise not only the most serious practical difficulties, but moral difficulties as well.

With perhaps the majority of prostitutes, the

[1] As an example of this naïve type of reasoning, see *Report of Parliamentary Committee on the Contagious Diseases Acts*, 1882.

life of shame is only a temporary state.[1] In a time of distress, they resort to it as their readiest means of support.   Or, during certain years in which their native passions are strong, they accept such a life from choice, but, tiring of it, they seek to return into the society which they have left.   At first but a comparatively small number of them admit to themselves that they have taken an irrevocable step.   They conceal their life from their friends, they account in some fictitious way for their earnings.   It may be that they do not have the strength to abandon the life after once becoming accustomed to it.   But the majority, in all probability, do abandon it.

To the average individual, it is true, there is something exceedingly repulsive in the idea of the restoration to decent society of women who have lived a vicious life.   In the small city, the girl who has been the victim of the selfishness and treachery of the man whom she has trusted becomes a social outcast; how much more would society thrust from itself those who, even under the stress of starvation, have sold their honour.   Yet these women are members of society and can hardly be refused by government the right to reform.   And reform would be all but impossible if they were prevented from returning to some kind of society above the plane of the common prostitute.

Now, it is clear that to the woman who, in spite

[1] *Supra*, 74.

of her secret sin, still considers herself a member of decent society, any policy that would lay bare her doings, search out her antecedents, classify her with those whom she, at any rate, considers infinitely beneath her, would be a positive deterrent to reform. Hitherto, only those knew of her shame who shared in it; after she is placed under police control, a whole police system is privy to it. It does not matter that the Morals Service is bound not to disclose what it knows; the woman is certain that at any time in her life the knowledge of her previous conduct may in some mysterious way leak out; and the official record of her shame exists, to be consulted by favourites of the bureau, in spite of general regulations.

As would be expected, it is the opponents of a system of regulation who lay most stress upon the fact that subjection to any police control that would be sufficient for sanitary purposes is a serious check to reform,—an act calculated to transform the temporary state of prostitution into a permanent one.[1] But the more moderate and more rational supporters of reglementation admit that inscription upon the register of shame is a most serious step, and one to be taken only when the chances of reform are small.[2]

[1] See Yves-Guyot, *La Prostitution*, 218 *et seq.*, and Sheldon Amos, *Regulation of Vice*, 87 *et seq.*

[2] "Inscription upon the register of the bureau of morals is the final stage of vice, the final term of degradation. It is the official formality which, like the *licentia stupri* of the Romans, regulates and legitimates

Such are some of the moral considerations against forcing women to submit to police control against their own will. In many cases, however, the utmost willingness on the part of the prostitute will not morally justify her registration. This is especially the case with minors. In every large city there are numbers of very young girls engaged in professional vice. According to the theory of sanitary regulation, these ought to be subjected to periodical examinations as well as any others. But moral considerations forbid the public recognition of a right of children of thirteen, fourteen, and fifteen to prostitute themselves. It is a matter of sufficient gravity to register minors of more years than these. On the Continent, the consent of parents and guardians is usually required for their registration. It is difficult to see how the securing of the consent of a probably vicious and worthless parent can relieve the administration of any moral responsibility.

It would, accordingly, seem that while there is a class of prostitutes who would hardly be injured

the sad trade of prostitution. It is, in a word, that sinister act which severs a woman from society and which makes her a chattel of the Administration."—Mireur, *La Prostitution à Marseilles.*

"The system of supervision and regulation of vice which exists almost everywhere to-day is more designed to force into the depths the girls who are upon the downward path, and to retain in the profession of prostitution those who are already under police control, than to lighten their return to the right."—Neisser, *Conférence Internationale, Brussels,* 1899; *Rapports Préliminaires,* 5me Question, 14; also Jeannel, *op. cit.,* 315.

by sanitary regulation, whom it might be for the public welfare to subject to such regulation, there is also a class the subjection of which to regulation is inadmissible from the moral point of view. In practice, every system of regulation is compelled to take a middle course, sacrificing moral ends to sanitary and sanitary to moral. As a result, it is impossible to realise either end completely.

There are other moral difficulties in the way of a system of regulation. No amount of sophistical discrimination between the words "toleration" and "recognition" can conceal the fact that a system of regulation makes of prostitution a legitimate industry subject to regulations in the behalf of its patrons identical in nature with the early regulations as to the weight of the loaf of bread, or the size and quality of the yard of woollens. Almost every one is familiar enough with human nature to know that the notion that any indulgence is a general need, inherent in the state of manhood, creates in the growing boy an almost irresistible impulse to experience it. State recognition and regulation of prostitution would unquestionably tend to confirm the already common opinion that secret indulgence is an imperative need.

Again the creation of the impression that prostitution is safe is pretty sure to increase the patronage of the prostitute, and in so far to increase the material basis without which prostitution would perish. While there are large numbers of men who cannot be deterred from incontinence by fear of disease, yet even of these there are doubtless some who indulge less freely in vicious pleasures for that reason.   It is a notorious fact that travellers are less self-restrained in this respect in cities that have the reputation of possessing a good system of regulation than they are elsewhere.[1]

In the practical working of regulation systems, there are many features that are not in keeping with moral requirements.   The French system of encouraging the establishment of brothels is a case in point.   Any one knows that the assembling under one roof of a group of depraved women means a still further increase in their depravity. The creation of a propertied class which legitimately shares the profits of vice is in itself demoralising.   It means the recognition of pecuniary interests in the fall of women.[2]   In no country have

[1] It is sometimes argued that the fact that the "control-book" is very rarely shown by the prostitute to her patrons proves that little thought is given to the possibility of disease, and that hence the guarantee of good health does not add to the sum-total of immorality.   Of course it proves nothing of the kind.   In a city where sanitary regulation exists, the patron generally takes it for granted that such women are subjected to it and that the fact that they are at large proves their freedom from disease.   (For authority as to the popular belief in the safety of regulated prostitution, see Ströhmberg, *Die Prostitution*, 120.)

[2] France has long possessed a regular publication (*Annuaire Reïrum*) which gives the addresses of all houses of prostitution in the cities and towns of France, together with information of interest to the "trade," such as the towns suited by population and number of men in the garrison for the establishment of new brothels, etc.   The procuring of new recruits for the brothels is often undertaken by men representing groups of licensed houses.—Reuss, *op. cit.,* 151 *et seq.*

brothels existed without the rise of individuals who make seduction a profession. Of course, flagrant crimes against morality are sometimes punished. Nevertheless, if the brothel is to exist, it cannot be held too strictly to account for the measures it takes in securing the necessary number of occupants.

It has long been recognised that it is evil, from the moral point of view, to permit the sale of alcoholic liquors in brothels. The existence of places of amusement in connection with brothels is another serious evil; men who are simply in search of amusement that is harmless in itself are likely to be attracted there, only to become subject to temptations which they do not have the strength to resist. Accordingly, it was at first the policy in Paris to prohibit music and dancing, and the sale of intoxicants in public brothels. But it was found that the brothel could not exist under such conditions. And so the Parisian brothels have been permitted to transform themselves into luxurious cafés and the like, where every form of harmless entertainment is enlisted in the service of vice.

Again, public morals demand that solicitation upon the street and in public places[1] should cease.

---

[1] "From the moment that by inscription a semi-official seal is placed upon prostitution, one is morally bound to grant the women upon whom obligations are imposed the right to exercise their trade. For the great majority of public women, solicitation upon the street is the only kind that can be employed. The street, where they elbow the passers-by, furnishes them the means of their existence; forbid it them, and they die of hunger."—Reuss, *op. cit.*, 265.

But the prostitute at large would find it practically impossible to live if the prohibition were enforced. The enforcement of such a regulation is not in harmony with a system of toleration.

The licensed prostitute is perfectly aware of this fact, and her conduct is apt to be marked by a flagrancy which the clandestine prostitute would not dare to assume.

Of course it is perfectly apparent that a system of regulation which includes sanitary supervision may, from a moral point of view, be far better than a system of absolute *laissez faire*. Where prostitution is absolutely unrestrained, as it was in London some years ago, crimes against morality are without doubt more frequent than in a city like Paris. The debauching of minors was infinitely more frequent; the forcible detention in brothels, a thing not unknown in Paris, was fairly common. Organised societies for the debauching of little girls have existed, and probably still exist.[1] Solicitation is nowhere more open, more cynical.

But comparison cannot be made between a city in which there is practically no police control of vice, and one in which a most efficient police system has struggled with the evil for a century. Moreover, the conditions of the two cities are not such as to permit of a comparison of any value at all. One must rather compare the moral condition

[1] See *Revelations of the Pall Mall Gazette*, 1886; also *Select Report on Law relating to the Protection of Young Girls*, 1881, 579.

of a city in which sanitary control exists with the conditions that would prevail were sanitary control replaced by an equally efficient moral control.

There is one important consideration which may be noticed here, although it concerns itself immediately with public policy rather than with morality proper. Every student of political science knows that it is a serious matter to create laws or regulations which do not express the moral feelings of the more law-abiding class of society. The legal institution of *mala prohibita* which are not generally felt to be *mala in se* necessarily tends to diminish the feeling for the sanctity of the law,— a feeling without which laws can be effectively administered only by the strong hand of despotic government.

Infinitely more grave is the institution of laws which are, rightly or wrongly, felt by the moral classes of a state to be of execrable immorality. If, for example, it were agreed by sociological and political theorists that social welfare would be furthered by the literal enslavement of the idle and vicious, a law to that effect would be a menace to good government so long as the general public looks upon human liberty as sacred. It is conceivable that abstract thinkers might conclude that society would be better off if the congenitally defective, those of criminal instincts, and those who suffer from incurable, loathsome, and dangerous diseases could be put out of the way. But no sane legislator would be willing to violate the feeling of the sanctity of human life.

In every civilised country there is a large class of persons who look upon reglementation as a state iniquity exactly analogous to the above hypothetical policies. They consider that by legitimising vice the state identifies itself with immorality. By creating a class of administrative chattels for the use and enjoyment of the vicious, the state outrages the deepest sentiments of humanity. By discriminating between vicious women and vicious men, it insults womankind. By rendering vice innocuous, either in fact or in seeming, it incites the youth of both sexes to debauch. The defender of sanitary regulation will argue in vain against reasoning of this kind. He may try to prove that the countervailing good of reglementation would be so great that the sum of human happiness would be greatly increased by its introduction. But moral sentiments do not demand that society should be happy; they do demand that it should be moral.

Accordingly, even if it could be shown that sanitary regulation is actually as effective in checking disease as its supporters claim, and even if it were impossible to demonstrate a serious moral cost, the legislator would be compelled to take into account the existence of such general antagonism to the policy of reglementation. There is every reason for believing that, in an American city, the more moral element in the population would be practically a unit against it.

One further objection, also political rather than moral, may be added. It is the general belief of political thinkers, at least in Anglo-Saxon states, that every encroachment upon the liberty of the individual is an evil in itself, only to be justified by a very great good resulting from it. A system which makes it possible for the police to seize on suspicion any citizen and impose upon him an insulting examination for the purpose of discovering disease, and to imprison him on suspicion that he would immorally communicate it if left at large, cannot be said to be in harmony with the principles of personal liberty. Any person might be subject to such indignity, since the natural grounds upon which the administrators of such a system would act are the accusations of persons who have confessedly shared in immorality.[1]

It need not be supposed that the liberty of the average citizen is secured because the police in this specific case act only with regard to friendless women. One inroad into the domain of individual liberty is a precedent for another.

[1] In Paris and Berlin the registered prostitutes are recognised auxiliaries of the police in hunting down clandestine prostitutes. It can readily be seen that the personal liberty of any woman who is not of unquestioned standing in society may be jeopardised by the spite of a common harlot.

CHAPTER VIII

PRACTICAL DIFFICULTIES IN THE REGULATION OF PROSTITUTION

WE have seen that the ideal of sanitary regulation can, for moral reasons, admit of only an approximate realisation. It is of great importance to examine regulation as it exists to-day, with a view to ascertaining how far the approximation falls short of the ideal.

That part of prostitution which cannot be subjected to sanitary control is necessarily very large. Probably by far the greater number of prostitutes begin their career of shame before they have attained their majority.[1]

This fact is so well known that authority need hardly be cited to prove it. It stands to reason that the waif or neglected child of fifteen, sixteen, or seventeen should fall the easiest prey, first of the seducer and later of the procurer.

[1] Of 1000 prostitutes concerning whom Dr. Le Pileur was able to secure detailed information, 758 began to prostitute themselves before the twenty-first year; 109 were prostitutes before the sixteenth year.— Le Pileur, *Conférence Internationale, Brussels,* 1899; *Rapports Préliminaires,* 3me Question, 47.

Since the average length of time in which a prostitute exercises her trade is not more than half a dozen years, it is evident that the minors make up a considerable proportion of the total numbers of those who are at any time engaged in prostitution.

But minors, as a rule, cannot be subjected to sanitary control. In every country there is a strong public sentiment against the official recognition of minor prostitutes. Whether it is a sound moral sentiment or mere sentimentality, it must be counted with as a fact; and no administration dares to violate it to any great extent.[1]

With the minors may be grouped the very large numbers of prostitutes who will not voluntarily subject themselves to sanitary control, and whose conduct is not sufficiently notorious to justify compulsory registration. Naturally, most prostitutes begin in this class. They are not at first sufficiently hardened to be willing to be classed with notorious prostitutes; they still cherish the purpose of returning to honourable life. And although the police may suspect them, in probably nine cases out of ten it would be impossible

---

[1] In Berlin, 229 minors were registered in 1898. Any one can see that the number is wholly insignificant as compared with the number actually living in the state of prostitution. In Paris, from 1816 to 1832, 59% of those newly registered were minors. From 1851 to 1866 minors made up 33%. From 1880 to 1886 the minors were 20%. The percentage has declined since, but the exact figures are not at hand.

to obtain proof that would by any regular course of judicial procedure convict them of debauch. It is true that such proof is not absolutely necessary. Every police administration that undertakes to control prostitution pursues a more or less arbitrary policy. But experience has proved that such a policy must be pursued with great care. Otherwise the charge is sure to arise that honourable women have been seized and branded with the deepest infamy known to civilisation. It may be that the women in question are really what the police consider them to be. But if positive proof is wanting, as must generally be the case, the women stand innocent before the general public. And many such charges would annihilate any police organisation.

Continental defenders of sanitary regulation frequently deplore the violent opposition to the sanitary police that is aroused whenever the charge of arbitrary procedure is made. The system of sanitary control, they claim, is shorn of all effectiveness if the police are not empowered to act upon reasonable suspicion. Whether the popular feeling is sound or not, it is not necessary to inquire. The fact remains that it exists in every country, and that administrative systems find themselves compelled to respect it. Even in Russia, where, we are accustomed to believe, the police do much as they please, the high-class prostitute is seldom forced upon the register, for the simple reason that she can make her cause heard. It is the low-class woman[1] who is the subject of arbitrary disposal. In Germany, imbued as it is with military ideals, the police proceed with a good deal of freedom in registering women against their will. Lack of visible means of support, and the existence of venereal disease are taken as proof of prostitution. Of course, reflection will show that such proof is not absolute. But the public is generally willing enough to believe that a woman without support, especially if diseased, is of bad character; and doubtless mistakes would not be so very frequent. The experience of Berlin proves, however, that the great majority of those who are actually prostitutes cannot be discovered even in this way.

In Paris, the police are more circumspect in proceeding to register unwilling women as prostitutes. The movement for the abolition of control during the 'seventies and 'eighties brought to light some exceedingly unfortunate mistakes that had been made in the arrest of suspected women.[2] Doubtless the Bureau of Morals proceeded with as great caution as possible. But if compulsory registration is employed freely, some mistakes are inevitable.

It would be interesting to know how far such a policy could be pursued in a great city of England or America, with Anglo-Saxon notions of personal liberty and of inviolability of domicile, and with

[1] Stürmer, *Die Prostitution in Russland*, 107.
[2] Mrs. Butler, *Personal Reminiscences of a Great Crusade*, 285; Yves-Guyot, *op. cit.*, 126.

Anglo-Saxon dislike for police inquisition into private affairs. Of course a great number of low-class prostitutes could be picked up in notorious resorts, and public opinion might find little to object to. But as soon as the more notorious had been disposed of, it is difficult to see how the police could proceed farther.

Accordingly, it may be taken for granted that voluntary registration must chiefly be relied upon. Such is the case in the two cities we have selected as typical.[1] It may, further, be taken for granted that the very great majority of prostitutes will never submit voluntarily.[2]

[1] Of course, "voluntary" inscription must be understood to imply something quite different from free consent. By frequent arrests, by threats of long imprisonment, and the like, these women are compelled to submit. But of course no such persecution would compel a really innocent woman to consent to inscription.

[2] Every authority on prostitution will state that the unsubjected or "clandestine" prostitutes far outnumber those who are subject to control. Naturally, the number of the clandestine can be arrived at only by conjecture. Some of these conjectures may, however, be worth mentioning.

Barthélemy estimates that the clandestine prostitutes are from ten to fifteen times as numerous as the subjected. Reuss contents himself with saying that the clandestine are greatly in the majority. Lecour, writing in the 'seventies, estimated the number of prostitutes in Paris at 30,000, of whom about 4000 were subjected. At present, something over 6000 are subjected; and from the incessant complaints of the increase of clandestine prostitution, we may infer that the proportion has not changed for the better (from the reglementist point of view). Müller, writing in 1867, estimated the prostitutes of Vienna at 20,000. In all probability the number has since doubled. Those under sanitary control numbered 2400 in 1896. Nieman, in 1890, estimated that there were 50,000 prostitutes in Berlin; in 1887, 3063 were under sanitary control.

Without laying too great weight upon conjectural estimates (although the authors cited are entitled to the highest respect), one may consider it a very conservative opinion that in none of the great cities of Europe do the registered prostitutes make up more than from ten to twenty-five per cent. of the total number of those who gain their living by prostitution.

Without reflection, one would be inclined to suppose that the part controlled is the more dangerous from the sanitary point of view, since the more notoriously debauched. So far as syphilis is concerned, this is a mistake. It must be remembered that the syphilitic, after two or three years, does not normally transmit contagion, and that she is immune against fresh infection.

Syphilitic disease is so common among the patrons of prostitution that a prostitute rarely escapes the disease for more than two or three years after entering upon her life of shame.[1] It is, however, these years in which the prostitute is most averse to submission to control, and in which it is the most difficult for the police to force her to accept control.

Accordingly, it lies in the nature of the case that a very large percentage of those who submit to

---

[1] Out of the 718 syphilitic prostitutes observed by Le Pileur, 489, or 68%, were contaminated in the same year in which they began to be prostitutes; 101, or 15%, in the year following.—Le Pileur, *Conférence Internationale, Brussels,* 1899; *Rapports Préliminaires,* 3me Question, 49.

registration have gone through with their contagious period either partially or wholly.[1] This
would be especially true in the case of those infected while minors, since even just ground for
suspicion is not sufficient to permit of their registration. It will surprise no one to know that a
very large proportion of all prostitutes are infected
before their majority.[2]

When we take these facts into account, it seems
probable that of those who become registered
prostitutes, the dangerous period does not, on the
average, bear as great a proportion to the post-
contagious period of their career as registered
prostitutes as did the contagious period before
registration to the period before infection. Moreover, those who are never registered at all do not
continue in their life of dishonor as long after

---

[1] Of 431 registered prostitutes observed by the same authority, 318,
or 74%, were already syphilitic when registered; 147, or 34%, had been
infected a year or more before they were registered.—Le Pileur, Conférence Internationale, Brussels, 1899; Rapports Préliminaires, 3me
Question, 60.

[2] Dr. Le Pileur describes the early career of the typical prostitute
in the following "aphorism":

"Deflowered at 16,
Prostitute at 17,
Syphilitic at 18."

Out of the 718 syphilitic prostitutes, 498, or 69%, were infected
before the twenty-first year.—Le Pileur, ibid.

According to Fournier fils, 63% of syphilitic prostitutes under his
observation had been infected before the twenty-first year.—Conférence Internationale, Brussels, 1899; Compte Rendu, ii., 1re Question, 82.

Jullien finds that 65% are contaminated before twenty-one.—Conférence Internationale; Compte Rendu, ii., 1re Question, 58.

becoming immune as do those who are eventually registered.

One further fact to be taken into account is that the patron, or rather the consumer, of the child-prostitute, does not exercise the same caution that he would under other circumstances. He flatters himself that it is the first debauch or pretty nearly the first. In like manner, the man who has illicit relations with women who outwardly seem entirely respectable is unlikely to suspect disease.

Accordingly, there would seem to be a good *a priori* reason for believing that the clandestine prostitutes are far more dangerous than the registered; and this quite without regard for the greater or less degree of perfection of sanitary surveillance.

The comparative morbidity of the clandestine and the registered prostitutes has been very much discussed. As a rule, all supporters of regulation are agreed that the clandestine prostitute is far more likely to be diseased than the registered prostitute. The opponents of regulation hold the opposite view. The former party seem to have the better facts to support their contention.

One way of proving the dangerous character of clandestine prostitution is to make inquiries as to the source of contagion of men afflicted with venereal disease. But little information of value can be obtained in this way, since the patient is often uncertain as to which one of a number of prostitutes may have infected him. Again, if he knows it, he may refuse to designate the person, since that would render her liable to arrest. Moreover, since the clandestine are held to be not quite so low as the registered prostitutes, many men will give false information out of a species of pride.

But even if it could be certainly known how great the number infected by each class, no really valid comparison could be made, because no one knows the exact number of clandestine prostitutes.

A second way is to compare the state of health of the clandestine prostitutes who are arrested and examined with that of the registered prostitutes. This, too, can give no certain information, since those who are arrested are but a fraction of the total number, and may not be fairly representative of it at all. Such as it is, however, it is the only empirical evidence of any value that is attainable. This seems to be decidedly against the clandestine. From 1872 to 1888, the sanitary service of Paris examined 45,577 registered prostitutes and 47,340 clandestine. The average morbidity of the clandestine was 31.65%; that of the registered 13.47%.[1]

No separation of the various diseases is here made. It is generally claimed that the comparative proportion of syphilis alone is much more favourable to the registered. This is what one would expect, since gonorrhœa does not carry immunity with it, as does syphilis, and hence may be as

[1] Augagneur, *Conférence Internationale, Brussels,* 1899; *Rapports Préliminaires,* i., 65 *et seq.*

common among the older prostitutes as among the younger.

Older authoritites on prostitution try to establish the comparative morbidity from the number of examinations in which disease is discovered. This is, of course, a wholly absurd procedure. The registered prostitute who is diseased is removed to the hospital and ceases to figure in the statistics of examinations until she is cured, when she again helps to swell the number of examinations in which no disease is found. Whenever figures are cited showing that the clandestine are ten or twenty or fifty times as dangerous as the registered, one may be certain that this astonishing fallacy is chiefly responsible for them.

From such facts as we have, we may, however, conclude that the more dangerous prostitutes, from the sanitary point of view, are those who cannot be subjected to sanitary control.

It remains to consider how far that fraction of prostitution which can actually be brought under sanitary control is really rendered innocuous. This is, of course, a question for medical specialists to discuss rather than for laymen. Nevertheless, it is of the utmost importance for the layman to know what conclusions the specialists have reached.

It may be remarked, in passing, that the discussion of this question has taken an altogether new turn in late years. Twenty years ago it was only the moralist, who knew nothing of medicine, who dared to connect venereal disease with registered prostitution. It is difficult to find a single competent writer of the present day who does not deplore the imperfections of the system as it exists, and who does not admit that registered prostitutes are responsible for a vast amount of venereal infection.

In the first place, it is universally agreed that the manner of inspection is imperfect. In many places the inspection has to take place under circumstances that preclude the possibility of scientific accuracy. The apparatus needed is often wanting; the physicians appointed for the work are far too much overworked, and they are not men who have been specially trained for it. Consequently, many of the prostitutes who are dismissed with the official stamp of good health are capable of transmitting contagion. Cases are frequent where men who have accompanied them from the dispensary have been infected with venereal disease.[1]

These deficiencies, it would seem, are almost entirely due to lack of necessary funds. This is clearly the case with the imperfection of apparatus. The same reason explains the needless haste with which examinations are made. By methods known

[1] According to Carlier, there are frequently groups of cautious individuals prowling about the doors of the dispensary, waiting to accompany those who have been found by the physician to be in good health. It is hard to characterise the immorality of a system that wantonly deludes men of such exemplary prudence! What wonder that the doctors are sometimes threatened with assassination.

to modern science, gonorrhœa is practically always capable of being established.[1] The diagnosis of syphilis has never been especially difficult.

But the expense that the needed changes would involve would be considerable. Ströhmberg thinks that one physician could manage four hundred prostitutes. Finger would place fifty only under each physician. Other authorities are inclined to require fewer physicians than Finger, but more than Ströhmberg.

If we suppose that each physician could adequately examine and treat one hundred prostitutes, it is plain that the cost would not be light. In Paris, with six thousand registered prostitutes, sixty physicians would be needed instead of twenty-four. It is true that at Paris the salaries of professional men are ridiculously low, so that the charge would not weigh very heavily upon the budget. But if New York were to adopt a system of reglementation, controlling four or five thousand prostitutes (and few would advocate a system which should control less), the expense would be a matter of no small importance. The services of forty or fifty specialists could not be secured at a trifling cost.

To be sure, this point would not have much importance in the case of some other branch of sanitary service. But it must always be borne in mind that the great body of taxpayers would bear

[1] Kromayer and a number of other authorities deny this.—*Conférence Internationale, Brussels,* 1899; *Communications,* i.; Appendix, 26.

with very ill grace an expense created by other men's profligacy.

It is frequently suggested that by a system of charges for examination, a sanitary bureau may be made self-supporting.[1] Against the plan is the unanswerable argument of one hundred years of experience. Every city which has adopted sanitary control at first attempted to meet expenses in this way; and every large city has found that the plan works execrably. The most difficult part of a system of control is to induce prostitutes to submit to it voluntarily; and every burden imposed upon them will deter them from doing so. Accordingly, it has been suggested that those who do submit should receive a pension; nor is the suggestion unworthy of consideration, if sanitary control is to be adopted. It is time for every one to disillusion himself of the idea that the expenses of a system of regulation can be met from any other source than general taxation.

The second charge is that examinations do not take place at sufficiently frequent intervals. In Paris, excepting for the relatively small number of inmates of licensed houses, examinations are theoretically made every two weeks. As a fact, many delay their visit to the dispensary, so that the average time is longer. In Berlin, according to regulations, examinations are made weekly. In

---

[1] This view is advanced by Dr. F. R. Sturgis, in *Medicine*, June, 1901.

practice, the average number of examinations per annum is twenty-six.[1] In St. Petersburg, in 1893, the average number for prostitutes at large was twenty-seven; in Moscow, in the same year, it was only four.[2]

Of course, whatever good regulation may do must be greatly diminished when examinations are so infrequent. Disease may reach the contagious form soon after inspection and may be freely transmitted for two weeks or longer. The reasons why such a state of affairs exists are chiefly administrative. The examination is exceedingly irksome to the prostitute; and if it be made very frequent, she will do her best to evade control altogether. Were not this difficulty real, we may be certain that semi-weekly examinations would long ago have been instituted in all Continental cities.

The difficulty is much less in the case of the inmates of licensed houses. They cannot escape the examiner. This is one of the main reasons why the licensed house is so much favoured by the police, in spite of its moral defects. But the spirit of the times makes it impossible to confine any large part of the prostitutes in licensed houses.

Here, then, we have a difficulty which seems to be insurmountable. After a hundred years of experience, and with practically unlimited power to deal with prostitution as it will, the most perfect

[1] Blaschko, *Conférence Internationale, Brussels*, 1899; *Enquêtes*, i., 671.
[2] Stürmer, *op. cit.*, 121.

of police administrations, that of Paris, is manifestly unable to cope with it.

Under this head there is one further subtraction to be made from the efficacy of regulation. The prostitute who discovers herself infected is naturally in no haste to go to the dispensary, knowing, as she does, that weeks, perhaps months, of confinement will follow. Instead, she lingers as long as possible, or even disappears from her accustomed haunts and plies her vocation as a clandestine prostitute. She may be retaken by the police, and is subject to imprisonment after her recovery. But the future penalty does not outweigh the present prospect of being sent to the hospital.[1]

[1] Of 391 licensed prostitutes at large who were infected with syphilis, 74 per cent. were sent to the hospital in consequence of arrests made by the police. Of course, they would not have gone at once had they not been arrested.—Le Pileur, *Conférence Internationale, Brussels,* 1899; *Rapports Préliminaires,* 3me Question, 71.

It may be of interest here to note the number of prostitutes who attempt to escape from control, and the number retaken by the police.

	Total number registered.	Disappeared.	Restored to control.
1888	4591	1779	1491
1889	4951	2125	1309
1890	4770	1555	1234
1891	5015	1450	821
1892	5004	1436	869
1893	4793	1121	739
1894	5154	794	616
1895	5790	1456	494
1896	5900	1190	615
1897	5233	1599	454
1898	6018	344	498

—Louis Fiaux, *Conférence Internationale, Brussels,* 1899; *Rapports Préliminaires,* 2me Question, 121.

In the second place, it is generally admitted that the treatment is not sufficiently prolonged to cure the maladies discovered; that *as a rule*, in case of syphilis, the prostitute is dismissed from the hospital while quite capable of transmitting the disease. The external appearance of the disease is made to vanish; the disease remains. As a French writer has put it, the prostitutes are *whitewashed*, not cured. This is pretty largely the case with gonorrhœa also. For the first two or three years, the syphilitic may at any time transmit disease; gonorrhœa, if not completely cured, may be transmitted for an indefinite period. To cure the latter malady completely, several months of treatment may be required; it is still a disputed point whether or not there is not a large proportion of women infected with it who can never be cured at all.[1]

The question arises whether this can be remedied. From a practical point of view, it is hard to see how it can. It is out of the question to detain all the prostitutes with latent syphilis in the hospital

---

5609 prostitutes thus "disappeared" definitely in the eleven years. Of course many reasons besides desire to escape the hospital must have operated; but no one can doubt that many disappeared in order to prostitute themselves clandestinely either in Paris or in other cities, carrying disease with them.

[1] Kromayer makes this contention. Jadassohn, on the other hand, claims that in most cases it may be cured if time enough be given. But he frankly states that it is merely an opinion, and admits that it is not as yet proven. *Conférence Internationale, Brussels*, 1899; Rapports Préliminaires, 2me Question, 41.

until the two- or three-year period of contagion is over. Tarnowsky, Jadassohn, Finger, and a host of other medical men suggest the erection of asylums where they may be confined, and where the women afflicted with exceptionally stubborn cases of gonorrhœa may be kept.

According to Finger, about 25% of all licensed prostitutes are in the highly contagious stage of latent syphilis. From this we may form an estimate as to the practicability of the asylum scheme. In our hypothetical system of regulation in New York, we should constantly have from 1000 to 1500 persons serving two- and three-year terms in a species of health reformatory. We should also have a considerable number under indeterminate sentence for gonorrhœa,—a sentence which would in some cases expire only when old age should render the woman innocuous. The question of the costs at once looms up. But, quite apart from that, the plan is absurd, for no prostitute would submit to an examination that might lead to such consequences, if she could by any possible means escape it. Voluntary inscription would be unthinkable, and the difficulties of official inscription would be immeasurably increased.

There is a minor factor that may be taken into account before we leave the question of the safety of regulated prostitution. The question has often been raised,—generally by laymen, it is true,— whether contagion is not frequently *mediate*. When it is remembered how frequently a low-class prostitute performs the same office, it would seem reasonable that some of her patrons may receive the virus of disease indirectly from others. This has been adduced to explain the alleged fact that cases of disease traceable to inmates of licensed houses are likely to be more frequent, proportionately, than those originating with the isolated but registered prostitutes, in spite of the fact that the former may show a smaller percentage of disease.

It may be seen, then, that many subtractions from the ideal of sanitary control must be made before we reach the actual efficiency of existing and practicable regulation. If, as seems reasonable, a system of regulation encourages indulgence to a certain extent, it will be necessary to make a further subtraction.

If, however, the small sanitary good that is due to reglementation were a permanent acquisition of society, much might be said for the system. If venereal disease might in this manner be diminished, little by little, through the generations, it might be seriously considered whether the grave present costs ought not to be assumed. As a fact, so long as diseased patrons of prostitution are permitted to transmit their maladies without restraint, practically no permanent improvement is to be expected. A brief relaxation of sanitary control would restore exactly the conditions prevailing before its institution, provided the moral habits of the community remained unchanged. In undertaking one-sided regulation, society takes upon itself a burden which it can never lay down without losing every advantage gained by its assumption.

This fact has led to the demand that all visitors of prostitutes should be subjected to sanitary inspection. The scheme is obviously impracticable, since such inspection could take place only in the brothel. If physical examination were required of visitors of licensed brothels, the licensed brothel would disappear for want of patronage, and isolated and clandestine prostitution would take its place.

CHAPTER IX

THE ACTUAL EFFECTIVENESS OF SANITARY CONTROL

Since the system of sanitary control of prostitution has been tried in many parts of Europe, and since it has in some cities been consistently applied for over a century, one would naturally expect to find statistical proof of its effectiveness in preventing venereal disease.

In attempting to establish the usefulness of sanitary control, comparisons of morbidity have been made between cities subject to regulation and cities in which regulation does not exist; secondly, comparisons of morbidity before and after the introduction or abolition of regulation have been made; and thirdly, a study has been made of the comparative frequency of disease in cities and countries where severity of control has varied.[1]

The third method is, of course, the most doubtful of all. The degree of severity of control is a mere matter of opinion; the frequency of venereal

[1] Blaschko, *Conférence Internationale, Brussels,* 1899; *Rapports Préliminaires,* 1re Question, 76.

disease in the general population is also pretty much a matter of opinion. If we could rely implicitly upon the fairness of the men who furnish these opinions, we could still attach little importance to them. Under present circumstances, there are very few who are not prejudiced either against regulation or in favour of it. Still, we may cite the eminent Russian physician, Stürmer, as authority for the statement that in Russian cities, when the control is relaxed, disease increases, and the reverse.[1]

Of little value, if any, is the comparison of morbidity in different cities. The amount of disease may vary for reasons quite independent of the system of control, since the extent to which men indulge in vicious pleasures depends largely upon their resources, upon the moral tone of the community, and upon the number and character of those who offer such pleasures for sale. Moreover, the possibility of knowing the exact amount of venereal disease varies from city to city. Accordingly, unless there is an exceedingly marked difference in respect to disease, unless it may be shown to be exceedingly prevalent in one place and almost absent in another, it is impossible to demonstrate the influence of regulation in this way. As a fact, no reputable author would venture to affirm that venereal disease is more frequent in London or

[1] *Conférence Internationale, Brussels,* 1899; *Compte Rendu,* ire Question, 40.

New York than in Paris or Berlin. Assertions based upon *a priori* reasons are frequent enough, but they stand or fall with the reasoning upon which they are based.

Accordingly, it is upon statistics of morbidity for a period before and after the introduction or the abolition of regulation that we must rely, if we are to get statistical proof at all. Even here it is necessary to note many sources of error. Excepting in Norway, only a fraction of the actual number of cases of disease fall under official observation. From the reports of public hospitals and from statistics of disease in the army and navy, it is necessary to infer the extent of venereal maladies in the general population. But many causes influence the number of those who apply for admission to the public hospital. An economic crisis, for example, might compel some to seek admission who, under ordinary circumstances, would be treated by private physicians. If military service is compulsory, statistics for the entire army will show with some fidelity the curve of disease in the whole country. But if service is voluntary, disease will vary with the class of men who enlist, and that will in turn be affected by economic and social causes too numerous to mention. Changes may take place in the quality of medical skill, so that cases of disease not counted at one period will figure in the statistics of another. Moreover, it is a well-known fact that venereal disease is subject to great fluctuations, the causes of which are not sufficiently known. These fluctuations, while often extending over a great part of Europe, vary in degree from place to place. The effect of such fluctuations upon the statistical problem is obvious. A "spontaneous" oscillation, coinciding in time with the introduction or abolition of regulation, may greatly accentuate or may altogether neutralise the effect of the change.[1]

Such is the gravity of this source of error that so conservative a writer as Blaschko declares that in consequence of it the results of regulation, whatever they may be, either do not appear at all, or appear very indistinctly.

Nevertheless, it may be worth while to devote a brief space to such statistics as are most often cited in proof of various theses. The English venereal statistics may be taken first, as they are the best known, and have frequently been compared with the results of a laboratory experiment.

By the Contagious Diseases Acts, put into effect in 1866, twelve districts in England and two in Ireland, chosen on account of the number of soldiers and sailors stationed there and on account of the prevalence of venereal disease, were subjected to a system of regulation, modelled, so far as its sanitary features were concerned, after the

[1] *Report on Contagious Diseases Acts*, 1882, x.   *Conférence Internationale, Brussels*, 1899; *Rapports Préliminaires*, 1re Question, Augagneur, 61; *Enquêtes*, i., Ehlers, 106; *Enquêtes*, ii., *Annexe*, Tommasoli, 39.

Continental systems. In 1883 the Acts were suspended. Accordingly, it is possible to study the effect upon the army both of the introduction and of the abrogation of the Acts. In order to eliminate, as far as possible, the influence of the periodic oscillations of disease, the parliamentary reporters compared with the venereal statistics of the fourteen subjected stations those of all unsubjected stations.

	Primary Sores. Stations not Subjected. Per 1000 Men.	Stations Subjected.	Secondary Syphilis. Not Subjected.	Subjected.	Gonorrhœa. Not Subjected.	Subjected.
1861–1866	103	109.7	30.7	37.4	108.2	125.1
1867–1872	93.6	65.4	29.2	24.6	105.4	114.6
Decline	9%	40%	5%	34%	3%	8%
1860–1863	116.3	129.8	30.5	40	116.1	134.6
1870–1873	86	52.5	27.5	20.3	95	106.6
Decline	26%	60%	10%	49%	18%	24%[1]

The first impression created by these figures is that a very considerable reduction in disease is due to the Acts. But even a superficial examination is sufficient to show that the figures are deceptive.

Under primary sores are included both primary syphilis and *ulcus molle*. The latter disease, being easily discovered and easily cured when found, would naturally be the first to yield to sanitary control.[2]

[1] *Report, Contagious Diseases Acts*, 1882, xi.–xiv.

[2] "Prostitutes may conceal gonorrhœa, and physicians are not always able to determine whether or not a person is infected with syphi-

It would be of the highest practical importance to know how far the improvement in the subjected stations was due to the diminution in this form of disease. Few would advocate a system of regulation if its chief result were merely to eliminate that comparatively harmless malady.

The figures for secondary syphilis are no longer considered of any particular importance, since it is impossible to say where the primary syphilis, of which the secondary is a result, was contracted. The parliamentary reporters argue that in the shifting about of troops, fewer cases of latent syphilis left the subjected districts than were brought to them, assuming that there is a constant ratio between the number of cases of secondary syphilis and that of primary, and assuming that primary syphilis was less common in the subjected stations. The first of these assumptions is not exactly true, and the second is not proven, owing to the grouping of cases of the two kinds of disease. In default of actual proof as to the decline of primary syphilis, the statistics for secondary syphilis are devoid of all significance.

The decline in gonorrhœa is too slight to be of much importance. Even if such a decline were demonstrably due to regulation, one would hardly

lis; but *ulcus molle* will always be discovered if regulation is efficient. Consequently, regulation will always have an influence upon *ulcus molle*. With a good system it may become rare, and may even disappear."—Reimers, *Conférence Internationale, Brussels,* 1899; *Compte Rendu,* ii., 1re Question, 96.

find in it much of an argument for the introduction of a system of regulation.[1] Accordingly, all that is proved by the statistics of disease during the existence of the Acts is that a reduction in primary lesions was effected. This is shown conclusively, it would appear, by a comparison of the curve of primary sores in the fourteen subjected stations and the curve for fourteen unsubjected stations chosen for the sake of comparison.

But even if we grant that a decline in primary syphilis took place, it still remains a question whether any light is thrown upon the problem of reglementation in large cities. Most of the stations selected for the English experiment were towns and small cities. A moment's reflection will show that in such places the possibility of compelling all prostitutes to comply with the regulations is infinitely greater than in the great city. Clandestine prostitution can thrive only in great centres of population.

In a civil population, it seems reasonable that a general belief in the safety of prostitution will increase the patronage of vice, and thus neutralise to a certain extent whatever sanitary benefit may be due to control. In an army, the effect would probably be less marked, since soldiers are generally men whose habits are already formed, and who do not usually look upon venereal diseases

[1] Kromayer, after a detailed study of the English statistics, concludes that gonorrhœa was not really affected at all by the Acts.

with as much fear as does the civilian. Accordingly, there is reason to look for a much greater improvement in the health of an army, as a result of regulation, than in the health of the general population.

Norwegian statistics would seem to give more useful information than do those of England. In 1888 regulation was abolished for all of Norway excepting Bergen and Trondhjem. From the figures of Holst, it appears that immediately after the abolition of regulation a rise in the number of cases of venereal disease took place for all Norway.[1]

The statistics for Norway present, however, the same flaw that impairs the value of the English statistics. They do not enable us to know how far syphilis alone increased after the abolition of regulation. Moreover, we cannot be certain that cases of disease were as carefully reported before 1888 as after that year. In these respects the statistics for the city of Christiania are far more satisfactory. The curve of disease indicates that after the abolition of regulation, all three forms of venereal disease increased. The increase is particularly marked in the case of gonorrhœa.[2] This is somewhat surprising, since both *a priori* reasons and the facts of experience would lead one to expect a more radical change in the curve of *ulcus molle*, at least, than in that of gonorrhœa.

[1] Holst, *Conférence Internationale, Brussels*, 1899; *Enquêtes*, i., 128.
[2] *Ibid.*, 126.

The rise, however, is by no means such an extraordinary one as would be expected by those who look upon reglementation as the solution of the sanitary problem. Moreover, it is a question whether there were not other forces at work which tended to increase the volume of disease. From 1879 to 1888 the population of Christiania increased from 116,801 to 138,319. By 1898 the population had increased to about 220,000. The average annual increase for the former period was less than 2200; for the latter, about 8200. When it is remembered that the more rapid the growth of a city is, the greater the proportion of young and unmarried men and the greater the relative volume of vice will be, it does not seem unreasonable that an increase in disease would have taken place even if reglementation had not been abolished.

It is also a question whether 1888 did not introduce a period of spontaneous increase in venereal disease. The general oscillations of disease are not confined to any single country. Now, the nearest culminating point of syphilis in Copenhagen was in 1886, corresponding with a similar point in Christiania in 1882. In Copenhagen there was an abrupt descent of the curve of syphilis, reaching the lowest point in 1892, then rising again.[1]

At Lyons, a decline from 1883 to 1888 was followed by an increase from 1889 to 1893. At

[1] *Conférence Internationale, Brussels,* 1899; *Enquêtes,* i., 106.

Paris, a decrease from 1883 to 1888 was followed by an increase. In Colmar, the decline continued from 1882 to 1887, followed by an increase in 1888 and 1889.[1] In the Italian army, a decline from 1881 to 1888 was followed by an increase. Augagneur states that, for about the same period, the same thing is true of the French and English armies. Accordingly, it is an open question whether the increase that followed the abolition of regulation in Norway was due to it.

In Italy, a system of regulation which had been in force for about thirty years was abolished, nominally, in 1888. As a fact, the ministry did everything possible to discredit abolition. Statistics were collected and abused especially to that end. Moreover, the sanitary regulations were still enforced in many cities, in spite of the law. Accordingly, the statistics of Italy are worthless, so far as showing the effect of regulation is concerned.[2] The statistics of the Italian army show that after 1888 an increase in venereal disease did actually take place. But it cannot be demonstrated that the increase was due to the "abolition" of regulation. It was just as probably in part or wholly due to "spontaneous" oscillation.

The statistics of isolated cities or towns which have adopted or discontinued sanitary control are

[1] Augagneur, *Conférence Internationale, Brussels*, 1899; *Rapports Préliminaires*, 1re Question, 61.

[2] Tommasoli, *Conférence Internationale, Brussels*, 1899; *Enquêtes*, ii., Annexe.

sometimes cited as proof of the efficacy of regulation. It is obvious that such statistics can be of little value, unless the city is a great one, and unless the system is enforced for a number of years. Upon the introduction of a system of control, it is the most natural thing for prostitutes who know they are diseased to move to another town. It is only by degrees that they learn that it is possible to evade regulations that are inconvenient for them. Undoubtedly, such emigration would have an immediate salutary effect upon the city from which they go. The effect upon the country as a whole is, however, practically *nil*. The experience of Colmar, a small city in Upper Alsace, and of Glasgow, would seem to indicate that a policy of absolute repression would have the same effect. It is unfortunate that we have no reliable statistics for a great city which has introduced a really scientific system of regulation. For a small city, the town of Dorpat in Livonia has probably been more successful in making a good showing than any other. That city had always been noted for the severity of venereal disease, and was considered especially dangerous as a station for troops. In 1898, after three years of really efficient regulation, the commandant of the garrison reported that not one of the thousand men stationed there had contracted primary syphilis during the year.[1]

[1] Ströhmberg, *op. cit.*, 206.

The most absurdly imperfect experiment upon which arguments were ever based was that of St. Louis, from 1870–1874. According to this regulation, the city was divided into six districts. One physician in each district was to visit the houses of prostitution and the apartments where isolated prostitutes lived, and might make physical examinations *if he thought it necessary*. It is easy to imagine how much chance there was of detecting disease under such a system of regulation. The claim has been made that the number of prostitutes diminished, as well it may have done, since many prostitutes would prefer other cities, where they were free, to one in which they were taxed and controlled. It has been claimed by some that venereal disease diminished; by others, that it increased; neither claim being supported by facts worth anything. For all any one knows, disease may have decreased or it may have increased. Whatever the change in morbidity, such regulations can hardly be credited with it.

In view of the above considerations, it is no wonder that the enlightened supporters as well as the enlightened opponents of reglementation are practically agreed upon rejecting such statistics as we have at present, preferring to rely upon *a priori* reasoning and common-sense.[1]

[1] "It is a long time that I have studied statistics. Well, I do not believe that there are any that are of value."—Fournier, *Conférence Internationale, Brussels,* 1899; *Compte Rendu,* 1re Question, 29.

If it were true that the enormous sanitary improvements that the supporters of regulation expect from it could be realised, or if regulation brought about the thoroughgoing demoralisation that its opponents dread, statistics, imperfect as they are, would show it. But since the influence, whatever it may be, is comparatively slight, statistics cannot possibly establish it beyond cavil.

It is, then, upon common-sense that one is compelled to rely in deciding whether, with all its imperfections, existing regulation does much good. However imperfect the system may be, it nevertheless remains that many prostitutes who are capable of transmitting disease are discovered and sent to the hospital. The gist of the matter, according to Tarnowsky, is that a syphilitic prostitute when locked up in a hospital is less dangerous to society than when she is at large.[1]

Burlereaux, according to Barthélemy, observed thirty-five soldiers of a battalion infected with syphilis by the same woman. Would it not have been an advantage to have locked her up before so much damage had been done?

"It is my conviction, based upon studies continued, I am almost sorry to say, through years, that one cannot prove, by statistics, the effect of regulation of prostitution upon the spread of venereal disease."—Neisser, *ibid.*, 35.

"In general, one believes no statistics but his own. One may support a thesis by statistical data, but he will never convince an adversary by arguments of that kind."—Lassar, *ibid.*, 33.

[1] *Op. cit.*, 318.

Dr. Commenge has estimated the probable good due to Parisian regulation.[1]   From 1887 to 1897, 15,095 prostitutes have been sent to the hospital of the prison of St. Lazare to be treated for syphilis. Assuming that the average period of confinement was thirty days and that each one would have contaminated ten men, 150,950 men have been saved from a horrible disease.

There is something childish about such reasoning as this.   If venereal disease is as frightfully prevalent among the clandestine prostitutes as all supporters of regulation claim, and if the clandestine so far outnumber the registered prostitutes as they also claim, then the man who is saved from the great probability of being infected by the diseased registered prostitute runs almost as great a risk of infection from other prostitutes. Common-sense would admit that the risk is less, but how much less it is puerile to attempt to discover. One may be pretty sure that some of Burlereaux's thirty-five soldiers would have contracted syphilis elsewhere; but omniscience alone would make it possible to know how many.

It is obvious that if the number of prostitutes controlled is a small fraction of the total number, the value of control is zero, since the number of diseased actually removed from active commerce is but an infinitesimal part of the volume of disease

[1] *Conférence   Internationale,   Brussels,*   1899;   *Communications,* i., Appendix, 125.

to which the patrons of prostitution habitually expose themselves.[1] Regulation may be worth less than zero, if an impression of safety is produced without adequate reason.[2]

How near the efficiency of existing systems is to the zero point it is impossible to say. Some reliance may, however, be placed upon the opinions of those who have spent much of their life in studying the subject. It is worth noting that Parent-Duchâtelet, Behrend, Hügel, and almost all other writers of the first half of the nineteenth century, also many present-day writers in America,[3] never doubted that immense sanitary advantages from

[1] Ströhmberg, *op. cit.*, 144.

[2] "The public believes that this service" (sanitary control) "is very easy; that since the women have a direct professional interest in being well, there are practically no refractory ones at all, and that it is possible to have commerce with them without fear as though free from danger. It is here that the danger lies; it is this security that is perilous, since a man exposes himself without the habitual precautions."—Barthélemy, *Conférence Internationale, Brussels,* 1899; *Rapports Préliminaires,* 1re Question, 5.

[3] "One thing is certain, every one agrees,—the partisans of regulation not excepted,—that the methods actually in use for diminishing the evils of prostitution cannot be considered effective. The organisation and administration of the surveillance, medical and police, are so defective, in our opinion, that but little is to be expected from it."—Neisser, *Bulletin de la Société Internationale de Prophylaxie Sanitaire et Morale,* I., i.

"I am asked, 'Are you satisfied with the existing regulations?'—'No.'—'But you speak well of them.'—'Yes, for they do a *little good.*'"—Fournier, *Conférence Internationale, Brussels,* 1899; *Compte Rendu,* 1re Question, 100.

"A system of regulation in which arbitrary methods of registration are employed, which does not realise the purposes of sanitary inspection, which cripples the utility of compulsory treatment through premature

control were easily demonstrated. Modern authorities, on the other hand, are content to claim for regulation merely a modicum of good, or look upon it as a stock upon which really useful control may be grafted.

---

dismissal from the hospital,—such a system of regulation is certainly of little value."—Tarnowsky, *op. cit.*, 205.

Augagneur and Blaschko are inclined to deny that existing systems of regulation do any good at all. Kromayer is certain that one of the most serious diseases, gonorrhœa, is not influenced in the least by regulation as it exists.

8

CHAPTER X

PROBABLE EFFECTIVENESS OF REGLEMENTATION IN NEW YORK

THE problems which reglementation has to solve differ from city to city. Accordingly, it is not sufficient for the present purpose to show how far it has succeeded in other cities; but each problem relating to reglementation must be considered with respect to the legal institutions, the racial and local characteristics, the social and economic conditions of the city of immediate interest—New York.

The legal question is obviously one which can be decided only by legal specialists. It is in a way preliminary to all further discussion, since constitutional obstacles to reglementation, if such exist, are practically insurmountable. The regulation of prostitution can be a burning question only in the large city; and even if it were agreed by the inhabitants of the city that reglementation is expedient, the hostility or indifference of the country at large would make it impossible to carry a constitutional amendment for the sake of its realisation.

All that can be attempted here is to state the problem, and to indicate the main theories that have been advanced for its solution.

The essential features of a system of reglementation are the periodical examination and treatment in the lock-hospital for venereal diseases. No legal difficulty would arise if the prostitute could be induced to submit to the rules voluntarily. But a very large class will never submit; hence compulsion is absolutely necessary if the system is to be effective. Manifestly, it would be impossible to impose compulsory physical examinations and imprisonment for extended treatment without depriving the persons subjected to them of a large share of their personal liberty.

The most familiar line of defence for such a restriction upon individual liberty is the declaration that prostitution is a status, analogous to the military status, which limits the civil rights of the individual and subjects him to special regulations and, possibly, to special tribunals. This is practically the view of European reglementists. It is doubtful, however, whether American constitutional law would admit the right of a legislature to create a special status of this kind.

A second manner of defending reglementation is to classify prostitution with occupations that are subject to police regulation, such as cab-driving, the keeping of a hotel, and the like. Regulations may decide under what conditions such a trade may be carried on and under what conditions it is not permissible. Infractions of the rules may be subject to special penalties. The periodical examination could, perhaps, be·defended in such a manner.[1] Physical examination would be a condition precedent to the exercise of the trade. But imprisonment for treatment would seem to be more difficult to defend. Would it be possible to imprison a cabman whose license has been revoked and who is *suspected* of intending to carry on his occupation unauthorised? Such a procedure seems to be perfectly analogous to the forcible detention of the diseased prostitute. Accordingly, reglementation must discover some other basis than that of special regulation of a special trade.

But whether prostitution is viewed as a special status or a special occupation, some clear definition of prostitution and some workable method of establishing the fact of prostitution are essential. It is absurd to believe that the mere suspicion of police agents or the mere fact of venereal disease would be sufficient in America, as it is in France and Germany, to prove that a woman belongs to the status of professional prostitution, or exercises prostitution as a regular trade, so long as she denies the fact. Legal proof would be absolutely

---

[1] It may be remarked that in Russia, workers in factories are theoretically subject to periodical physical examinations, and that in Posen all barmaids are subjected to such examination before entering upon a position.

necessary for placing a woman in such a status or class, and such proof must necessarily in the majority of cases be difficult, if not impossible, to obtain.

Another common method of providing a legal basis for reglementation is to bring it under the class of police regulations for preventing the spread of contagious diseases. The analogy between the compulsory treatment of venereal disease and the isolation of those who suffer from other contagious maladies, would, perhaps, be perfect if all venereal patients were subjected to the same treatment. This would, however, be impossible under present conditions; and to make the regulation apply to a special class only, would, of course, require the creation of such a special class and thus would raise the difficulties which have been pointed out above.

A fourth plan is that of restoring ancient laws making prostitution a crime or a misdemeanour and of leaving to the police courts discretionary power as to the penalties imposed. It is conceivable that by a series of legal fictions the diseased prostitutes might be subjected to imprisonment in hospitals, while those not found to be diseased might be permitted to go unpunished. If such a procedure is not unconstitutional, it would probably provide a sufficient basis for a system of sanitary regulation of vice. The difficulty would still remain that sufficient proof of prostitution would be required,—a difficulty which is practically insurmountable.

It remains to be considered whether it would be possible to overcome the natural objections of women of this class to police regulations, so that submission to its rules might be voluntary. This could only be done by granting special privileges to those who submit. A relentless persecution of those who do not submit to the regulations, and immunity from arrest to those who do submit, would undoubtedly drive many to accept registration and periodical examination as the lesser of two evils. Accordingly, the question of regulation based upon quasi-voluntary inscription resolves itself into the question of the possibility of coping with "clandestine" or unsubjected prostitution.

The first question to be considered has to do with the efficiency of the police organisation itself. Experience has shown conclusively that for the morals service, special agents, endowed with rare qualities of tact, shrewdness, and integrity, are necessary. Doubtless the materials for a special force of agents can be found in an American city. But it stands to reason that it would take time to organise as efficient a force as that of Paris or Berlin. For this reason, it must be expected that for a time excess of caution, varied by unfortunate excess of zeal, would mar the working of the system. This defect would cure itself with time, however, and so may be dismissed.

But, granted a force of the highest degree of efficiency, it is evident that the problem of coping with clandestine prostitution in New York would be exceptionally difficult. The freedom with which women and girls of good character frequent public places unattended, or pass through the streets alone in the evening, is not paralleled in any European city. In Paris, Lecour could arrest a young woman who waited for her husband at the door of a shop, "because no decent woman lingered upon the sidewalk." Imagine a New York agent of police acting upon such inferences! It is needless to dwell upon this fact, since any one can understand that American habits of life make it possible for a discreet prostitute to exercise her vocation much longer without rousing the suspicion of a limited force of police agents than she could possibly do in Paris or Berlin.

A second consideration is the greater difficulty that an American morals police would find in acting upon its suspicions. On the Continent of Europe a person generally lives more or less under the eyes of the police. Birth certificates, passports, employment cards, and the like are in fairly general use, so that it is not difficult for the police to have an insight into the antecedents and means of livelihood of the resident population. It is easy to see how such data would be of the utmost importance in segregating that part of the population which will bear watching. The antecedents of any person who may immigrate into a city are likewise easily determined. But in New York the police would have no help from such data. A secret service, however ubiquitous, could acquaint itself with the life of only a fraction of the population of New York.

Again, it makes much difference whether the vicious element in the population is very migratory in its habits or not. It takes time before the conduct of a new arrival draws suspicion. Still more time elapses before the suspicion is sufficiently strong to justify police action. The person observed may be ready to remove to another city, or to another part of the same city, before anything can be done to fix her status.

The prostitute is notorious everywhere for her migratory habits. Self-interest may, however, compel her to remain in the same city when her whims would lead her to migrate. A city which is preëminently the centre of the life of a whole country will naturally be the place to which prostitutes will flock, and whence they may usually depart only with loss in earning power. Paris and Berlin occupy such positions. New York, on the other hand, is only one, although the greatest one, of a number of great American cities. As a centre of professional vice, it would be scarcely more attractive than Philadelphia or Chicago, or even a number of lesser cities. What is more, the far greater incomes of American prostitutes make it easier for them to move from place to place than it is for European prostitutes.

In view of these considerations, it is evident that the problem of combating clandestine prostitution in New York is far more difficult than in European cities. One fact is, however, to be set against these, and that is that the occasional prostitute, who merely ekes out an insufficient wage by vicious earnings, is probably less common in New York than in Berlin, and perhaps than in Paris. And this is the most difficult to cope with of all forms of clandestine prostitution.

It remains to consider whether it would be possible to retain as efficient a control over prostitutes once registered as it is in European cities. This also seems doubtful. It is well known that prostitutes are more or less refractory, according to the characteristics of the people from whom they spring. The American impatience of authority would certainly make itself manifest in the spirit with which these women would obey regulations. The Parisian authorities find great difficulty in following up the prostitutes who withdraw themselves from control by changing their habitations. In view of American notions of inviolability of domicile, it is hard to see why it would not be very easy for a prostitute to drop out of sight altogether by merely moving from one part of the city to another. Moreover, if diseased, she would be exceedingly likely to prefer a few months' sojourn in another city to a period of confinement in a lock-hospital. And while the amount of disease originating in New York might be diminished, the amount of disease in the country as a whole would remain practically the same. Under such conditions, it is evident that no permanent advance in the combating of venereal disease could be made, since a momentary relaxation of reglementation would mean a restoration of the conditions prevailing before its introduction.

In almost every respect, then, New York presents a more difficult problem with respect to reglementation than Paris or Berlin. If reglementation does only a "little good" in the latter cities, it would necessarily do less good in New York.

CHAPTER XI

MORAL REGULATION OF VICE

IT is customary to speak as though there were but three possible ways of dealing with prostitution, absolute *laissez faire*, absolute prohibition of vice, and reglementation.

It is very cogently argued that *laissez faire* is an inadmissible policy. Not only does venereal disease extend its ravages unchecked, but every sort of moral iniquity thrives wherever vice is a law unto itself. With equal cogency it is argued that no human legislator can make vicious men or women virtuous, or preserve so close a surveillance over them as to prevent the exercise of their evil propensities. Thus, by a process of exclusion, reglementation is arrived at as the only rational policy for government to pursue.

It is difficult to understand how such naïve reasoning can still be entertained by thinking men. Regulative and repressive systems differ in emphasis, rather than in essence. The first aim of the reglementist is to check disease; he recognises, however, the gravity of vice in itself, and admits that no measures that may limit its volume are to be disregarded. The opponent of reglementation, while believing that vice itself is an evil that completely overshadows any hygienic effects that result from it, will generally admit that all means for combating venereal disease should be adopted, provided that they are not directly antagonistic to moral ends. Accordingly, we find many elements, both moral and sanitary, upon which both parties agree. A system of control based upon such common elements and supplemented somewhat as common-sense suggests, would escape the serious charge, now brought against reglementation, of making itself ancillary to prostitution, and would at the same time be free from the moral and hygienic futility of violent repression. Such a system would abandon the task of effecting the impossible, in either morals or hygiene, and would reserve the powers at its command for the bringing about of such ameliorations as experience and reason have shown to be possible. Such a system we may term the Moral Regulation of Vice, since it would never lose sight of the fact that moral considerations are of paramount importance.

Repressive Features in Moral Control.—The first point upon which all are agreed is the necessity of suppressing, so far as possible, flagrant incitement to debauch. Solicitation upon the street and in public places should be restrained; haunts of vice should be compelled to assume the appearance of decency; in short, every method of conspicuous advertising of vice should be done away with. It is admitted that this can be only approximately accomplished. The prostitute will always contrive to make her presence known. But much would be gained if vice could be made relatively inconspicuous except to its votaries. The constant presence of women known to be immoral serves to recruit each year the patronage of prostitution by inciting to vice many who would not of themselves have sought illicit pleasures. From this point of view, it is far better that prostitutes should be clandestine in fact as well as in name than that they should appear in their true colours. A system which places moral ends before sanitary would be just as capable of dealing with this part of the problem as one which regards sanitary ends as paramount. As a practical fact, the former system would encounter less difficulty than the latter, since the exigencies of sanitary control require that a certain latitude of flagrancy should be given to the licensed prostitute.[1]

The pernicious effect of a league between vice and legitimate pleasures has been mentioned above.[2] Especially dangerous is vice in public drinking-places. Women are engaged to persuade men to drink alcoholic liquors to excess; the effects of alcohol, in turn, lend service to vice. To

[1] *Supra*, 74, note.   [2] *Supra*, 74.

what proportions this evil may grow, the Parisian *brasseries à femmes* (drinking-places with female service) will show. It will doubtless be impossible to keep the saloon absolutely free from the presence of prostitution, and to prohibit absolutely the sale of intoxicants in brothels. But a policy which should revoke the license of a saloonkeeper who permits unattended women to frequent his premises in the evening and night would assist in driving vice from the saloon proper. A supplemental policy of discouraging the sale of liquors in so-called hotels would be needed to make the plan effective.

In like manner, the dancing-hall or music-hall which lends itself to the purposes of vice is a public nuisance and could be reached by the police whenever immorality becomes flagrantly conspicuous.

Vice will naturally take refuge in private houses if denied the use of public places. It would still require regulation to keep it within the bounds of decency. It is in vain that it is driven into privacy if by conspicuous lights or signs or by noisy music it is permitted to make its presence notorious. An English law of the present day makes it possible to close a house if it is shown by the testimony of two responsible citizens to be used for immoral purposes.[1] While it is doubtful whether such a law would have any other effect than that of breaking

---

[1] The mere fact that men and women resort to a house in such a way as to give good ground for suspicion is accepted as presumptive proof.

up the house of ill fame and compelling prostitutes to resort to solicitation upon the street, an analogous measure which should permit aggrieved neighbours to close a house which is *obtrusively* devoted to immorality would be a most efficient force in compelling such establishments to conceal their true character.

We may here consider whether moral ends are best subserved by relegating vice to a single quarter of the city. It is a serious question whether the house of ill fame, situated in a respectable locality and compelled to preserve an outward air of decency is as dangerous to the community at large as a similar establishment surrounded by others of a like character and hence not under compulsion to refrain from flagrant devices for increasing its patronage [1]

Preventive Features.—A second point upon which all parties will agree, is the desirability of keeping growing children free from contact with professional vice. The child who knows all evil is almost destined to share in it. No child over three years of age should be permitted in a house where prostitution is carried on.[2] In tenement and flat-houses, parents of children should be able to bring complaint against tenants of tenements or flats in the same building when suspicion is created that

---

[1] *Supra,* 39 *et seq.*
[2] In Continental cities, the inmates of brothels are not permitted to keep even their own children with them after the third or fourth year.

prostitution is carried on in such tenements; and if the suspicion is found to be based upon reasonable grounds, the courts should require the landlord to evict the suspected parties. The evil is one of such gravity that it would seem to justify a measure which interferes, to a certain extent, with the principle of inviolability of domicile.

Even where the children of the poor are not in immediate contact with professional vice, their surroundings are frequently highly inimical to virtue. Where a whole family, adults and children of both sexes, is crowded together in a single room, moral degradation is almost inevitable. What the effects of such conditions may be, can be judged from the fact that in European cities an appreciable proportion of the prostitutes who are brought up in such circumstances trace their fall to incestuous relations. The problem is one of the most intricate with which society has to deal, since the incomes of the poor and the rents which they have to pay are almost entirely fixed by laws over which government has little control. Nevertheless, the question may be raised whether it is not possible, by means of restrictions upon the building and letting of houses, to discourage the formation of quarters that inevitably entail upon the community a most serious burden of vice and disease.

It has often been suggested that the present system of public education does not exhaust its possibilities as a moralising force. Frequently,

the child who leaves the public school loses the
only influence that makes for morality, and at the
time when the need for such influence is greatest.
There seems to be little doubt that an extension of
the years of public education for children whose
parents or guardians cannot show that they are
engaged in satisfactory employment or properly
cared for in their homes, would diminish the evil
of prostitution of young girls.   The child who is
left free to pursue her own inclinations, or who
is employed by unscrupulous parties, has always
been the easiest prey of the professional seducer.
Such additional education should naturally be of a
kind that would train the pupils for industrial or
household duties.   It must be remembered that
many girls become prostitutes simply because they
are so deficient in training as to be incapable of
earning their living in any other way.

All students of the social evil understand how
serious the problem of the prostitution of minors
has become.   Whether sanitary or moral ends are
considered to be of paramount importance, the
prostitution of children cannot be tolerated.   The
supporters of reglementation have for decades
pleaded for the establishment of reformatories or
asylums for the rescue of young girls who have
fallen into evil ways, or who are in danger of
falling.   The Morals Service constantly has to deal
with children who are much too young to be registered as public prostitutes, but who nevertheless

9

gain their living by professional vice. All that the judges can do is to give a useless warning, and to send them back to conditions in which moral improvement is impossible. In cities where no attempt is made to regulate vice, the general public is ignorant of the extent of this evil.

A Prussian law of July, 1900,[1] presents the first systematic attempt to grapple with this problem. By the provisions of this law, girls under eighteen who are found to be living a vicious life, or who fall into evil company so that they are in danger of being led into immorality, may be placed in institutions or under the charge of parties who will be responsible for their conduct. If necessary, they may be kept under guardianship until their twenty-first year. These provisions are applicable both to those whose parents or guardians connive at their downfall, and to those who cannot be controlled by their natural guardians. This law represents the consensus of opinion of the most profound students of the social evil.

Sanitary Features.—A system of moral control would not abandon all of the sanitary features that are embodied in reglementation. Both systems alike demand that general practitioners should be required to possess a high degree of knowledge in the treatment of venereal maladies. Both systems agree that the quack physician who practically fosters disease for his own ends should

[1] *Das Fürsorge-Erziehungs-Gesetz*, July 2, 1900.

be eliminated.[1] Treatment for venereal disease should be within the reach of all. The cost of adequate treatment for the more serious forms of venereal maladies is so great that the vast majority of patients cannot be treated at all except at public hospitals and dispensaries. These should, accordingly, be numerous enough to furnish gratuitous treatment to all who desire it. Patients should be encouraged to appear for treatment; every care should be taken to insure them against exposure, since many would rather endure their maladies in secret than permit it to be known that they suffer from a "shameful disease." If publicity cannot be avoided at public dispensaries, it would be for the general welfare to designate officially private physicians in each quarter of the city who should treat such patients free of charge, receiving their compensation from the public treasury.[2]

Objection will doubtless be raised that such

---

[1] This has already been accomplished in England.

[2] According to Dr. Prince A. Morrow (*The Prophylaxis of Venereal Disease*), the vast majority of syphilitic patients do not receive adequate treatment. "Not one in twenty, certainly not one in ten, receives a treatment sufficiently prolonged." The city of New York provides twenty-six beds for the treatment of female venereal patients. For male patients there are fifty-six beds in the City Hospital and a small number in the Metropolitan Hospital. It seems almost incredible that, at the dispensaries, women patients are received in the same room with men, so that the fact that they suffer from secret maladies becomes known. Such a policy reminds one of that pursued by Parisian hospitals toward venereal patients during the sixteenth and seventeenth centuries: They were well cudgelled upon their admission and upon their discharge, in order that the fact might be impressed upon them that they suffered from a shameful disease.

measures would minimise the deterrent effect that is exercised by venereal disease upon those who wish to indulge in vice. It is a sufficient answer that the chronic results of disease are frequently even more disastrous to innocent parties than to the sufferer himself. Moreover, the immediate consequences of disease are sufficiently grave to act as a deterrent for those who can be deterred from vice by fear of disease. It is doubtful whether the distantly remote consequences are weighed at all.

Finally, a system of moral control cannot overlook the fact that venereal disease is frequently transmitted to innocent persons. Most frequently, this results from the fact that men who believe that they are completely cured of such diseases still retain chronic accidents by which they transmit disease to their innocent wives. It is difficult to see how this evil can be remedied except by the requirement, as a preliminary condition to the issuing of a marriage license, of a certificate from an official physician showing the present state of health of each of the contracting parties. Such a requirement would work no real hardship to any one, since few persons who suspected the existence of a disease of this kind would apply for an official examination before health had been restored. It will be admitted that many difficulties would arise in the administration of such a law, and that it could only diminish somewhat the evil which it is designed to meet.   The evil in question is, however, one of so revolting a nature that any amelioration would be worth a heavy cost.

For the administration of any system of control of vice, experience has demonstrated that a special body of police agents is required.   If the ordinary police are permitted to arrest suspected prostitutes, or to raid houses of prostitution, the responsibility for the care of public morals is dissipated and unlimited opportunities for blackmail are created. The system which leaves the initiative to the private citizen is inadequate.   The citizen may be trusted to do whatever lies in his power to prevent resorts in his immediate vicinity from becoming especially offensive to decency.   This part of the system of control may wisely be left to him.   But for the discovery of prostitution of minors, for the control of prostitution in public places and upon the street, a limited body of agents selected for exceptional qualities of tact and integrity is absolutely essential.   Under a system of reglementation, the agents are handicapped by the fact that much of their time must be spent in hunting down prostitutes who fail to appear for periodic examination.   Divested of this responsibility, their efficiency in preventing the worst forms of vice would be vastly increased.

For the introduction of a system of control embodying the above features several State laws would be needed.   But whereas reglementation would with difficulty find a place under the Constitution, a system of moral control would be open to no objections on the score of constitutional law. What is of greater importance, any good that might result from reglementation is fatally tainted with evil; whatever good might result from moral control is good unmixed. Reglementation would arouse the uncompromising hostility of a great part of the community; intelligent moral control would meet with the approval of all, excepting of those who are not satisfied with a plan which would only gradually bring about moral and sanitary improvement, and who dream that there is some royal road to the instant abolition of either moral or sanitary evil.

APPENDIX

THE "RAINES LAW HOTEL" AND THE SOCIAL EVIL

No one who has lived in New York City can have failed to realise that there is a close connection between what is popularly known as the "Raines Law hotel" and professional vice. The term is rapidly coming to be synonymous with house of assignation. This does not mean that there are not many so-called hotels, organised for the sole purpose of evading the Raines Law, which have remained completely free from prostitution. Yet it can hardly be denied that there are forces at work which tend to make the decent Raines Law hotel the exception rather than the rule.

From time out of mind there have been inns and hotels in which no attempt has been made to conform to the rules of morality of the general community. The transient has always been of notoriously loose habits, and it is only natural that vicious women should congregate wherever he is entertained. Inn-keepers of unscrupulous character have winked at disreputable practices where they have not positively encouraged them and shared the resulting profits. It is easy to understand the transition from such inns to the house of accommodation, which does not derive any appreciable part of its returns from legitimate service, but depends upon the patronage brought to it by the professional street-walker. Wherever solicitation upon the street is permitted, such establishments will inevitably exist; and they will prosper or decay with the form of vice which supports them. Depending entirely upon vice, their location is necessarily limited to the quarters where the volume of vice is considerable. Solicitation upon the street is in turn limited to the vicinity of such houses, since the street-walker, in order to ply her vocation with profit, must have a place in the near vicinity to which she may bring her customers or victims. There is, accordingly, a natural tendency for vice to segregate itself, to a certain extent, from the general community, to form notorious districts in the various quarters of the large city.

New York, however, presents the unique feature of providing virtual houses of accommodation throughout the city, quite without regard for the actual demand for them. As a consequence, all difficulties that normally lie in the way of soliciting in other than notorious parts of the city are removed. The street-walker may make any place she chooses the scene of her operations. As a result, solicitation is probably more general in New York than in any other American city.

This abnormal and pernicious state of affairs is easily explained by reference to the local excise laws. By section 31 of the Raines Law the hotel is given a highly favoured position in the sale of alcoholic liquors, since it alone is permitted to sell such liquors on Sunday. It is a trite statement that the profits of a New York saloon are made on Sunday, the week-day trade merely sufficing to pay expenses. While this may be an exaggeration, the Sunday trade is certainly important, since the retention of regular custom frequently depends upon it. It was therefore inevitable that a great number of saloons should attempt to annex a sufficient number of rooms to pass under the definition of hotels.

For respectable purposes, however, the demand for rooms connected with saloons is necessarily very limited. And so the tenant of a "hotel" of this class has had the choice between paying rent for vacant space or permitting the use of his rooms for dishonourable purposes. ·Of course there are many men in the liquor business who have preferred a pecuniary loss to a shameful gain. But it is easy to see why, in a class of men who are held more or less in disrepute and who are repeatedly charged with making a gain out of other men's degradation, many will be found who will not stick at profits, however stained. It may be truthfully said that, under the most favourable circumstances, the more scrupulous among the dealers in alcoholic beverages are at a disadvantage. Under the Raines Law, as it has been applied, there is an active influence which favours those who do not hesitate to make themselves the abettors of vice.

Any one who is familiar with conditions in New York must admit that the effect of the Raines Law has been to provide unexampled accommodations for prostitution. The only questions that are open to discussion are whether the volume of vice is greater than it would be if the Raines Law hotel did not exist, and whether vice as it manifests itself in such institutions is more dangerous to public order and public health than it would be under normal conditions.

The patronage of vice may be divided into two parts: that which is given without the employment of any allurements on the part of those who provide vicious pleasures, and that which is procured by such allurements. It is manifest that nothing can be done to limit the patronage of the first class. It is by the influence upon the second class that the evil imputable to any institution must be estimated.

Nothing can be clearer than the fact that the possibility, due to the Raines Law hotels, of soliciting now in one part of the city, now in another, increases immensely the number of persons whom the prostitute can subject to her allurements. Moreover, so long as solicitation is confined to comparatively limited areas, it is possible for police agents to restrain, to a certain extent, the conduct of vicious women. When solicitation may occur in any part of the city, the task is made immeasurably greater. Accordingly, the power for evil of the prostitute is increased not only by the possibility given her of meeting greater numbers of men, but also by the greater freedom with which indecent proposals may be made.

More serious still, many of the Raines Law hotels are themselves the scene of most insidious and therefore most effective solicitation. The average citizen goes there to drink his glass of beer and to listen to the bad music and worse jokes that play so important a part in summer entertainment. When there, he becomes subject to solicitation which has the appearance of a mere flirtation; if he yields, it is with the least possible shock to his moral sensibilities; he may feel that he did not seek vice, but was overcome by circumstances. The convenient arrangement of rooms makes exposure unlikely. Persons who would hesitate to enter a brothel or notorious rendezvous are easily "victimised" in the Raines Law hotel with summer garden or roof garden or other facilities for public entertainment. The uncompromising moralist will probably say that it is a matter of small importance what befalls such moral imbeciles. He might, however, change his opinion if he knew how many of them there are.

Most serious of all, however, is the fact that the Raines Law hotel which stands on the line between vice and harmlessness is very frequently the place where the growing boy is introduced to the mysteries of immorality. Where popular entertainment is given, it is inevitable that a certain number of immoral persons will be found; and if accommodations for vice are present, the work of recruiting the patronage of vice among boys will certainly be active.

The effect of such institutions as the Raines Law hotel

in increasing the number of those who earn their living by immorality is no less obvious. Without them, the clandestine prostitute would necessarily take her patrons to brothels, houses of assignation, or to her own apartments. In any case the risk of discovery would be greater than at present. Many who are just starting upon the downward path would shrink from entering notorious haunts of vice. For such, the Raines Law hotel is naturally convenient. Just as the establishments which furnish free entertainment assist in the downfall of the young man, so they familiarise the young girl with the presence of disreputable characters and permit her to admire their stylish dress and flashy jewelry.

The most damning charge of all, however, is that the Raines Law hotel provides the greatest known facilities for seduction. Young girls, brought by unscrupulous escorts to enjoy the entertainment given, are regaled on beverages of the influence of which they are ignorant, and, by the aid and assistance of the hotel provision, fall easy victims. That this is no imaginary evil, nor one which is rare, is known to any one in New York who has eyes to see and ears to hear.

From the point of view of public order, the Raines Law hotel is unquestionably pernicious. It is impossible to form any idea of the number of thefts and robberies committed by prostitutes and their male retainers, since the victims do not usually make complaint. It is known, however, that such crimes are constantly taking place. They are naturally comparatively infrequent in the brothel and in the apartments of the isolated prostitute: in the former, because the proprietor of the establishment does not care to have the reputation for violence; in the latter, because the isolated prostitute does not wish her real character to be known to her neighbours. Even the house of accommodation is generally anxious to have a reputation for safety. But the criminal prostitute can take one client after another to a Raines Law hotel and plunder him with the aid of her male retainer; and if one were to make a complaint, it is a simple matter for the woman to choose another quarter for her crimes.

In like manner the brothel and the isolated prostitute with fixed station are anxious to avoid the reputation for disease. To the one who uses a score of Raines Law hotels indifferently, it makes no difference how many persons she contaminates. Accordingly, there seems to be good reason for the opinion, prevalent among New York physicians, that the Raines Law hotels are the chief factor in the spread of venereal disease.

It has been said that the evils above enumerated are due not to the Raines Law, but to the manner in which it is enforced. Probably not ten per cent. of the "fake" hotels comply with the regulations of the fire, health, and building departments. Accordingly, ninety per cent. could be wiped out of existence by simply enforcing the law. But would that end the matter? Hardly. Instead of going out of existence, the owners of such establishments would be slightly more careful as to the fulfilment of the requirements of those departments. At a somewhat greater expense, they would still be "hotels," and would still furnish accommodations for vice.

It is true that among the provisions of the law, the proprietor or tenant is required to prevent the premises from becoming "disorderly." If this provision were rigidly enforced, some of the evils could no doubt be reached. But when a hundred provisions of a law may be violated with impunity, there is little chance of enforcing any one.

Moreover, those who are best acquainted with New York City are agreed that there is no chance that the law will ever be enforced. The popular detestation of it precludes all possibility of enforcement.

So far as the problem of prostitution is concerned, the essential thing is to put an end to the abnormal tendency to make hotels out of saloons. And this can be done only by relieving the saloon proper of the disadvantages under which it now labours, or by imposing an additional burden upon the hotel. The latter policy would fall under the same popular detestation with the Raines Law itself, and so would seem to be out of the question. Accordingly, the only alternative which appears to be open is the removal of the restriction upon the selling of alcoholic beverages on Sunday. It is not claimed that even such a measure would remove all the evils that the Raines Law, as it has been applied, has created. It would, however, prevent the further growth of the evil and would assist in making possible an effective moral control of vice.

NOTE.—*Provisions of Raines Law discriminating between the hotel and other establishments for retailing liquor to be drunk on the premises. Definition of " Hotel" and "Guest."* *Raines Law,* §31:

"It shall not be lawful for any corporation, association, copartnership, or person, whether having paid such tax or not, to sell, offer or expose for sale, or give away, any liquor:

"a. On Sunday; or before five o'clock in the morning on Monday; or

"b. On any other day between one o'clock and five o'clock in the morning; or

"c. On the day of a general or special election, or city election or town meeting, or village election, within one quarter of a mile of any voting place, while the polls for such election or town meeting shall be open; or

"d. Within two hundred yards of the grounds or premises upon which any State, county, town, or other agricultural or horticultural fair is being held, unless such grounds or premises are within the limits of a city containing one hundred and fifty thousand inhabitants or more; . . .

.   .   .   .

"Clauses 'a,' 'c,' and 'd' of this section are subject to the following exception:

"The holder of a liquor tax certificate under subdivision one of section eleven of this act, who is the keeper of a hotel, may sell liquor to the guests of such hotel, . . . with their meals, or in their rooms therein, except between the hours of one o'clock and five o'clock in the morning, but not in the barroom or other similar room of such hotel; and the term 'hotel' as used in this act shall mean a building regularly used and kept open as such for the feeding and lodging of guests, where all who conduct themselves properly and who are able and ready to pay for their entertainment are received if there be accommodations for them, and who, without any stipulated engagement as to the duration of their stay, or as to the rate of compensation, are, while there, supplied, at a reasonable charge, with their meals, lodgings, refreshment, and such service and attention as are necessarily incident to the use of the place as a temporary home, and in which the only other dwellers shall be the family and servants of the hotel-keeper; and which shall conform to the following requirements, if situate in a city, incorporated village of twelve hundred or more inhabitants, or within two miles of the corporate limits of either:

"1.   The laws, ordinances, rules, and regulations relating to hotels and hotel-keepers, including all laws, ordinances, rules, and regulations of the state or locality pertaining to the building, fire, and health department in relation to hotels and hotel-keepers, shall be fully complied with.

"2.   Such buildings shall contain at least ten bedrooms above the basement, exclusive of those occupied by the family and servants, each room properly furnished to accommodate lodgers, and separated by partitions at least three inches thick, extending from floor to ceiling, with independent access to each room by a door opening into a hallway, each room having a window or windows with not less than eight square feet of surface opening upon a street or open court, light-shaft or open air, and each having at least eighty square feet of floor area, and at least six hundred cubic feet of space therein; a dining-room with at least three hundred square feet of floor area, which shall not be a part of the barroom, with tables, and having suitable table furniture and accommodations for at least twenty guests therein at one and the same time, and a kitchen and conveniences for cooking therein sufficient to provide *bona fide* meals at one and the same time for twenty guests. . . .

.   .   .   .

"A guest of a hotel, within the meaning of this exception to section thirty-one of this act, is:

"1.   A person who in good faith occupies a room in a hotel as a temporary home, and pays the regular customary charges for such occupancy, but who does not occupy such room for the purpose of having liquor served therein; or

"2.   A person who, during the hours when meals are regularly served therein, resorts to the hotel for the purpose of obtaining and actually orders and obtains at such time, in good faith, a meal therein "

PART II

RECOMMENDATIONS OF THE COMMITTEE

RECOMMENDATIONS OF THE COMMITTEE

A CAREFUL consideration of the foregoing report points unmistakably to the conclusion that the so-called system of regulation is not a radical or adequate remedy for the evils connected with prostitution, even in their merely physical aspect. For the members of this Committee, indeed, the moral grounds alone would have sufficed to stamp as intolerable the proposition that the public authorities should undertake the inspection of houses of ill-fame with a view to rendering the practice of vice innocuous to those who engage in it. We recommend to those persons who are wont to extol this system as a kind of panacea and to deplore, with something of impatience if not of contempt, the Puritanical sentiment which prevails in this country, and which renders any attempt to introduce such a system impracticable, an attentive study of the passages in the above report relating to regulation and its results. They will find, on a closer study of the results, as these appear where the system has been tried, that their vaunted panacea is no panacea at all, and that their confidence in its merits is far from being supported by the facts.

But, if not regulation, what then? The city of New York is rapidly expanding into metropolitan proportions. Within another ten years its aspect will, in many ways, be transformed. It is certain to become a more commodious and beautiful city than it has ever been before. But what will this material splendour avail if the forces that tend to debase the moral life of its people —and especially of its youth—are permitted to operate unchecked? The Social Evil is assuming alarming dimensions. What is needed at this time is a definite policy with regard to it; a policy that shall not attempt the impossible, that shall not be based on the delusive hope of radically altering in a single generation the evil propensities of the human heart, or of repressing vice by mere restrictive legislation, but which, none the less, shall ever recognise as an ultimate end the moral redemption of the human race from this degrading evil, and which shall initiate no measure and advise no step not conducive to that end; a policy that shall be practical with respect to the immediate future, and shall at the same time be in harmony with the ideals which are cherished by the best men and women in this community.

As an outline of such a policy we submit the following:

First, strenuous efforts to prevent in the tene-

ment houses the overcrowding which is the prolific source of sexual immorality. The attempts
to provide better housing for the poor, praise-
worthy and deserving of recognition as they are,
have as yet produced but a feeble impression upon
existing conditions, and are but the bare beginnings of a work which should be enlarged and
continued with unflagging vigour and devotion.
If we wish to abate the Social Evil, we must
attack it at its sources.

Secondly, the furnishing, by public provision
or private munificence, of purer and more elevating
forms of amusement to supplant the attractions
of the low dance-halls, theatres, and other similar
places of entertainment that only serve to stim-
ulate sensuality and to debase the taste. The
pleasures of the people need to be looked after
far more earnestly than has been the case hitherto.
If we would banish the kind of amusements that
degrade, we must offer to the public in this large
cosmopolitan city, where the appetite for pleasure
is keen, some sort of suitable alternatives.

Thirdly, whatever can be done to improve the
material conditions of the wage-earning class,
and especially of young wage-earning women,
will be directly in line with the purpose which is
here kept in view. It is a sad and humiliating
admission to make, at the opening of the twentieth
century, in one of the greatest centres of civilisation
in the world, that, in numerous instances, it is

not passion or corrupt inclination, but the force of actual physical want, that impels young women along the road to ruin.

The three suggestions mentioned above indicate permanent causes to which the increase of the Social Evil may be traced. A better system of moral education may also be mentioned as an imperative necessity in this connection. As Dr. Prince A. Morrow, in a paper on "The Prophylaxis of Venereal Diseases," says:

"This campaign of education should be extended to the high schools and colleges for young men. Unfortunately, this has always been a forbidden topic. There is no reason why young men should not be forewarned of the pitfalls and dangers which beset their pathway. Whatever may be thought of the innocuity of 'sowing wild oats,' its consequences are most often disastrous to the health of the individual. They should also be taught that self-restraint, personal purity, and respect for women are among the surest foundations of character."

But to come to the points that more directly bear upon the problem as it presents itself in the city of New York.

From a recent report of a committee of the County Medical Association, it appears that the great city of New York provides for the reception and treatment of women suffering from venereal diseases only twenty-six beds in the City Hospital on Blackwell's Island. We recommend the adequate increase of hospital accommodations for this class of patients. This recommendation is based on grounds of public health as well as of humanity to the sufferers. The public health is endangered, in so far as contagion is allowed to spread uncontrolled, and surely the sufferers themselves are entitled to the mercy of their fellow-beings. To justify the exclusion of such patients from the hospitals, and in answer to the question, What then shall become of them? it has been said: "Let them rot in their own vices." But this is a hard saying, all the more when it is remembered that not a few of the sufferers are but the victims of the sins of others, bearing in their shattered constitutions and in the loathsome disease inflicted upon them the penalty of suffering and humiliation which they themselves have done nothing to deserve.

The Committee further recommend that minors who are notoriously debauched shall be coercively confined in asylums or reformatories. The minors who are engaged in prostitution constitute at once the most dangerous and the most pitiable element in the problem of the Social Evil. They are the most active sources of contagion in every sense. In their case the prospect is, at the same time, most hopeful of waging effective warfare on the Social Evil, since they are young enough, if brought under the right influence, to be rescued from the army of the vicious and restored to honest callings.

But above all the Committee recommend a change in the attitude of the law. As it stands at present, the law regards prostitution as a crime. If we are ever to escape from the present impossible conditions, it seems imperative to draw the distinction sharply between sin and crime. The proposition is to exclude prostitution from the category of crime. We hasten to add that this proposition should by no means be understood as a plea in favour of laxer moral judgments. A sin is not less odious because it is not treated as a crime. Sins may even be incomparably more heinous than offences which the law visits with punishment. Nevertheless, some of the most grievous sins are not subjected to legal penalties, simply because it is recognised that such penalties cannot be enforced, and a law on the statute book that cannot be enforced is a whip in the hands of the blackmailer. Corruption in the police force can never be extirpated until this prolific source of it is stopped.

But it may be asked: What, then, is to be the status of prostitution in the city of New York? In the first place, it must be driven out of tenement and apartment houses; the evil must be rigidly excluded from the homes of the poor. Secondly, it must not be segregated in separate quarters of the city, for the reason that such quarters tend to become nests of crime and veritable plague spots, and for the further reason that segregation does not segregate, just as it has been shown that regulation does not regulate. Thirdly, all public, obtrusive manifestations of prostitution shall be sternly repressed. Not prostitution itself, when withdrawn from the public eye so as to be noticeable only to those who deliberately go in search of it, shall be punishable; but all such manifestations of it as belong under the head of public nuisance. The result of the adoption of this policy will be, indeed, the continued existence of houses of ill-fame, partly in streets formerly residential and deserted by the better class of occupants, partly scattered in the neighbourhood of the great thoroughfares and elsewhere, and these will remain undisturbed under the condition that they remain unobtrusive. The serious and weighty objections that lie against the existence of such houses are well known. But they are in every case objections which really apply to the existence of prostitution itself. They could only be removed if prostitution itself could summarily be extirpated. But this, in the present state of the moral evolution of the race, is as yet impossible. Recognising, then, that prostitution, although it ought not to exist, does and will for an indefinable time continue to exist among us, we are bound, as men advising for the moral welfare of our great city in the immediate future, to point out that form of the evil which, all things considered, will work the least harm.

The better housing for the poor, purer forms of amusement, the raising of the condition of labour, especially of female labour, better moral education, minors more and more withdrawn from the clutches of vice by means of reformatories, the spread of contagion checked by more adequate hospital accommodations, the evil itself unceasingly condemned by public opinion as a sin against morality, and punished as a crime with stringent penalties whenever it takes the form of a public nuisance: —these are the methods of dealing with it upon which the members of the Committee have united and from which they hope for the abatement of some of the worst of its consequences at present, and for the slow and gradual restriction of its scope in the future.

In addition, we would recommend the creation of a special body of morals police, analogous to the sanitary police already existing, selected on grounds of exceptional judgment and fitness, to whom and to whom alone should be entrusted the duties of surveillance and repression contemplated in the above recommendations.

APPENDIX

PRESENT CONDITIONS IN NEW YORK

TRADING in vice has had a rapid development in New York City within the last few years. A combination of circumstances has made this possible. Through the Raines Law, the entrance upon a life of prostitution became attractive and easy. The appearance of the "cadet" formed the connecting link between the Raines Law hotel and the house of prostitution. The partnership between some of the officials of the Police Department and the traffickers of prostitution resulted in a system of reciprocity. Immunity from arrest was exchanged for profits from the trade in vice. When a house containing not more than ten inmates, exclusive of the proprietress, and known as a "fifty-cent house," could afford to pay an initiation fee of $500 to the wardman, and $50 a month for the privilege of continuing in this illegal occupation unmolested, an estimate can be formed as to the amount of trade which must be carried on within.

In one police precinct, not more than a mile square, there were known to be in 1900 about forty such houses. In the same precinct there were some sixty well-known centres of prostitution in tenement houses. The employees of these houses openly cried their wares upon the streets, and children of the neighbourhood were given pennies and candy to distribute the cards of the prostitutes. A system of "watch-boys" or "light-houses" was also adopted, by which the news of any impending danger could be carried throughout a precinct in a very few minutes. Honest police officers who attempted to perform their duties were defied by the "cadets" and "light-houses." For a police officer to incur the enmity of a powerful "madame" meant the transfer of that officer "for the good of the service," if not to another precinct, at least to an undesirable post in the same precinct. A virtual reign of terror existed among the honest patrolmen and the ignorant citizens of these districts. Many times, citizens from such quarters have said that they would gladly tell what they could not help but see, were it not that they feared bodily harm and the destruction of their means of livelihood if they spoke. Little by little the facts were placed on record in the trials of police officers and "cadets."

The Cadet and his Victim.—The "cadet" is a young man averaging from eighteen to twenty-five years of age, who, after having served a short apprenticeship as a "light-house," secures a staff of girls and lives upon their earnings. He dresses better than the ordinary neighbourhood boy, wears an abundance of cheap jewelry, and has ususally cultivated a limited amount of gentlemanly demeanour. His occupation is professional seduction. By occasional visits he succeeds in securing the friendship of some attractive shop-girl. By apparently kind and generous treatment, and by giving the young girl glimpses of a standard of living which she had never dared hope to attain, this friendship rapidly ripens into infatuation. The Raines Law hotel or the "furnished-room house," with its café on the ground floor, is soon visited for refreshments. After a drugged drink, the girl wakens and finds herself at the mercy of her supposed friend. Through fear and promises of marriage she casts her fortunes with her companion and goes to live with him. The companion disappears; and the shop-girl finds herself an inmate of a

house of prostitution.   She is forced to receive visitors
of the house.   For each visitor the girl receives a brass
or pasteboard check from the cashier of the house entitling
her to twenty-five cents.   The "cadet" returns to the
house at frequent intervals, takes the checks from his
victim, and cashes them at the cashier's desk.

Within the last year, six "cadets" have been sent to
State prison for abducting girls under the age of eighteen
years.   The facts were substantially similar in all the
cases, and in a majority of them the victims were physical
wrecks when rescued.

The victim of the "cadet" is usually a young girl of
foreign birth who knows little or nothing of the conditions
of American life.   She has just reached womanhood, and
is taught by her parents that the time has come for her
to look forward to marriage.   Very often, the parents
themselves are highly flattered by the attentions which are
being paid to their daughter by such a prosperous-appearing
young man.   The conditions are all favourable for the
accomplishment of the purpose for which the "cadet"
began his attentions.   The early teachings of the young
girl are propitious for the consummation of her destruction.
She is taught that obedience should be unquestioned, and
that the word of the husband in the household is law.   The
"cadet" relentlessly uses these weapons which have been
placed in his hands, and he soon finds himself in possession
of this money-maker whose receipts will yield him ordinarily forty or fifty dollars a week.   If the young girl succeeds
in escaping from the house of prostitution, she prefers, in
a majority of cases, to become a street-walker rather
than to return home and to face the disgrace which awaits
her there.

Conditions in Tenement Houses.—The revenue-producing
power of the sale of immunity by the police seemed to make
the appetite of the police insatiable.   The infamy of the

private house, with all the horrors arising from the
"cadet" system, did not satisfy official greed. The tenement houses were levied upon, and the prostitutes began to
ply their trade therein openly. In many of these tenement
houses as many as fifty children resided. An acquaintance
by the children with adult vices was inevitable. Almost
any child on the East Side in New York will tell you what
a "nafke bias" is. The children of the tenements eagerly
watch the new sights in their midst. The statistics of
venereal diseases among children and the many revolting
stories from the Red Light district tell how completely
they learned the lessons taught them.

In the argument before the Cities Committee at Albany
in April, 1901, the Chairman of the Committee of Fifteen
presented certain statistics founded upon an inspection
of 125 tenement houses in which prostitutes were known
to reside and to ply their trade. This statement gave rise
to violent attempts at refutation by prominent officials
both at Albany and in New York City. An attempt was
made to becloud the issue by statements of these officials
that the virtue of the poor had been assailed by the Committee of Fifteen. Our then Police Commissioner, whose
ignorance of conditions would have been humorous rather
than pathetic were not the facts so serious, stated that
there was not a disorderly tenement-house below Fourteenth
Street; that he had lived in that neighbourhood for many
years and knew what he was talking about. In spite of
his vigorous denial, complaints were received by the
Committee of Fifteen and evidence was easily collected
against prostitutes in the street in which he himself resided.

In the work of the Committee of Fifteen, evidence was
secured in over three hundred[1] separate disorderly apart-

[1] It is impossible with such a limited staff of workers as were employed
by the Committee of Fifteen to approximate the number of prostitutes
or houses of prostitution in New York City. The figures given represent

ments in tenement houses in the city of New York. Over
two hundred of these tenants were removed under the
new Tenement House Law which went into effect July 1,
1901. Authentic reports reached the Committee that many
of the tenement-house prostitutes were retiring into private
houses of prostitution.

It is certain that the houses of prostitution are not
flaunting their wares upon the streets in the manner of a
year ago. Street-walking is also far less frequent. A
number of the more notorious dives have either changed
hands or have closed their doors. The most widely known
proprietor of houses of prostitution in New York City is
now serving a term in prison upon evidence secured by the
Committee of Fifteen. The proprietor of several of the
lowest dives is at the present time a fugitive from justice,
having forfeited his bail. Three police officers who were
shown to have been in partnership with vice have already
been convicted, and a half dozen are now awaiting trial.
As a result of the whole movement the prospect for a
reasonable control of the Social Evil in New York City is
more favourable at the present time than it has been for
many years.

---

cases where corroborated evidence was secured by the Committee.
There are no trustworthy statistics in existence covering the general
question of the Social Evil in New York.

PART III

THE PROGRESS OF THE MOVEMENT
1902–1912

CHAPTER I

IN the body of this book frequent references are made to the international conference held at Brussels, and many of the illustrations are taken from the discussions in that conference. Shortly after the first edition of this book appeared, a second conference was held, of still greater significance. It seems, therefore, eminently desirable to give some more information about these important conferences.

In order, however, to explain their origin, it is necessary to revert to the great struggle in England which was indirectly responsible for them. In the body of this work [1] several references are made to the English episode. As this has now been to a large extent forgotten, we shall attempt herewith a brief recital of the facts. [2]

[1] Pp. 101–105. See also pp. 68, 82.
[2] A good account of the movement is found in Benjamin Scott, *A State Iniquity: Its Rise, Extension, and Overthrow*. London, 1890. For the full title, see the Bibliography. A briefer work is *A Short Summary of the History of State Regulated Vice in the United Kingdom*. Compiled by the Friends' Association for abolishing State Regulated Vice. London, 1900. *Cf.* also in especial *Personal Reminiscences of a Great Crusade*. By Josephine E. Butler. London, 1876.

1. *The Repeal of the English Laws*

In 1862 a committee was appointed by the admiralty in London to inquire into the state of venereal disease in the army and navy, and to report upon the working of the regulation of prostitution in foreign ports. The committee reported against the introduction of the foreign system, but the contents of the report were not published. On June 20, 1864, Lord Clarence Paget, the secretary to the admiralty, introduced a "Bill for the Prevention of Contagious Diseases at certain Naval and Military Stations." It so happened that the public was at the time considerably exercised over the ravages of disease among cattle, and that parliament had passed various stringent acts under the title of "Contagious Diseases (Animal) Acts." When the new bill was introduced with the short title of "Contagious Diseases Prevention Act," 1864, the greater part of the public thought that it was another animals act. The bill received scarcely any discussion in parliament, and became a law on July 29, 1864. It provided, among other things, for the compulsory examination of these unfortunate women. The act was limited to three years, and applied to eleven military stations in Great Britain and Ireland. On June 11, 1866, it was continued, with two new features, namely, a register and a periodical examination, and it was now extended to Windsor. In 1869, a select committee was appointed to consider the advisability of extending the operation of the act to London, and on a favourable report from this committee the law of August 11, 1869, was enacted, increasing the number of localities subject to the law to eighteen. During the same year the system was extended to most of the military settlements abroad, as well as to Canada, the Australian colonies, and British India.

At the very outset a note of opposition was sounded by Harriet Martineau in a series of leading articles in the *Daily News*. But it was not until the extension of the system to London that organised opposition made itself felt. In 1869, Miss Martineau wrote four more letters to the *Daily News* over the signature "An Englishwoman," and on New Year's day, 1870, a formal protest was drawn up and signed by a number of prominent women, including Harriet Martineau, Florence Nightingale, Mary Carpenter, and Josephine E. Butler. The protest, to which thousands of names were subsequently added, was as follows:

We, the undersigned enter our solemn PROTEST against these Acts:

1st. Because, involving as they do such a momentous change in the legal safeguards hitherto enjoyed by women in common with men, they have been passed not only without the knowledge of the country, but unknown to Parliament itself; and we hold that neither the representatives of the People, nor the Press, fulfil the duties which are expected of them, when they allow such legislation to take place without the fullest discussion.

2d. Because, so far as women are concerned, they remove every guarantee of personal security which the law has established and held sacred, and put their reputation, their freedom, and their persons absolutely in the power of the police.

3d. Because the law is bound, in any country professing to give civil liberty to its subjects, to define clearly an offence which it punishes.

4th. Because it is unjust to punish the sex who are the victims of a vice, and leave unpunished the sex who are the main cause, both of the vice and its dreaded consequences; and we consider that liability to arrest, forced surgical examination, and (where this is resisted) imprisonment with hard labour, to which these Acts subject women, are punishment of the most degrading kind.

5th. Because, by such a system, the path of evil is made more easy to our sons, and to the whole of the youth of England; inasmuch as a moral restraint is withdrawn the moment the State recognises, and provides convenience for, the practice of a vice which it thereby declares to be necessary and venial.

6th. Because these measures are cruel to the women who come under their action—violating the feelings of those whose sense of shame is not wholly lost, and further brutalising even the most abandoned.

7th. Because the disease which these Acts seek to remove has never been removed by any such legislation. The advocates of the system have utterly failed to show, by statistics or otherwise that these regulations have, in any case, after several years' trial, and when applied to one sex only, diminished disease, reclaimed the fallen, or improved the general morality of the country. We have,

on the contrary, the strongest evidence to show that in
Paris and other continental cities where women have long
been outraged by this forced inspection, the public health
and morals are worse than at home.

8th. Because the conditions of this disease, in the first
instance, are moral not physical. The moral evil through
which the disease makes its way separates the case entirely
from that of the plague, or other scourges, which have been
placed under police control or sanitary care. We hold
that we are bound, before rushing into the experiment
of legalising a revolting vice, to try to deal with the *causes*
of the evil, and we dare to believe that with wiser teaching
and more capable legislation, those causes would not be
beyond control.

A ladies' national association was thereupon
formed, with Mrs. Butler as the leading force. It
was followed by a similar movement among the men,
known in London as "The Metropolitan United
Contagious Diseases Acts Association." The executive committee included John Stuart Mill,
Professor Sheldon Amos, Jacob Bright, M. P., A. J.
Mundella, M. P., Rev. Frederick D. Maurice, and
many other eminent men. Similar associations
were formed in other cities. Among the leading members were Professor Stuart, Professor F.
W. Newman, Herbert Spencer, and John Morley.
So vehement did the opposition now become
that a Royal Commission was appointed at the
close of 1870. This commission, however, brought
in a rather non-committal report. The protest-
ants now set to work vigorously to inaugurate a

national campaign. Owing to the difficulties of public discussion at the time the progress was at first slow. Various non-conformist religious organisations, like the Wesleyan, the Friends, etc., formed separate committees designed to secure the repeal of the Acts.

The Italian patriot Mazzini, the eminent Belgian economist de Laveleye, and the French poet Victor Hugo expressed their sympathy for the movement. Above all, the remarkable testimony of John Stuart Mill before the commission of 1870 was reprinted and spread broadcast.[1]

In 1875, an international association was formed in order to help the movement. By slow degrees and by dint of hard work, lavish expenditure, and numerous publications, most of which are noted in the bibliography at the end of this volume, public opinion was gradually influenced and won around. From year to year increasing minorities were obtained for the bills introduced to secure repeal. Finally, when Mr. Stansfeld moved on April 20, 1885, "that this House disapproves of the compulsory examination of women under the Contagious Diseases Acts," the motion was carried by a vote of 182 to 110. In the following year, the "Contagious Diseases Acts Repeal Bill" was passed without any opposition, becom-

---

[1] *The Evidence of John Stuart Mill taken before the Royal Commission of 1870 on the Administration and Operation of the Contagious Diseases Acts of 1866 and 1869.* 24 pp.

ing a law on April 16, 1886. Thus came to an end, probably for all time, the attempt to introduce into England the continental system of reglementation.

2. *The International Abolitionist Federation*

Reference has been made above to the international association. This was formed on March 19, 1875, under the title of "The International Federation for the Abolition of State Regulation of Vice." The founding of the international federation was due, in great measure, to the medical congress of Vienna in 1873. At that time the almost universal opinion of physicians was favourable to the system of regulation or reglementation, which always meant at least two things: the compulsory examination of prostitutes, and the registration or licensing of houses of ill-fame. For a long time the Belgian system was recognised as a model; and at the international medical congresses held in Brussels in 1852, in Paris in 1867, and in Florence in 1869, various propositions were advanced to extend this system throughout Europe and to make it uniform. Finally, the medical congress of Vienna, in 1873, passed a resolution demanding the prompt elaboration of an international law based on the Brussels system.

It was as an answer to this demand that the International Federation for the Abolition of

State Regulation of Vice was formed.   The impulse came largely from the English combatants, and especially Mrs. Butler.   Its headquarters were to be at Geneva, under the name of *Fédération Abolitionniste Internationale*, with national committees in the leading countries.   Its object was declared to be the abolition of prostitution, especially regarded as a legal or tolerated institution.   "Holding that the organisation of prostitution by public authority is a hygienic mistake, a social injustice, a moral monstrosity, and a judicial crime, the Federation endeavours to arouse opposition to the system and to secure its condemnation everywhere."   The Federation condemns in its platform the attempt to make women bear the sole burden of the system.   It maintains that the autonomy of the human being has its corollary in individual responsibility, and it declares that through the system of reglementation in vogue the state upsets the very conception of responsibility.   It declares that the state should limit itself in the domain of prostitution to the protection of minors, to the punishment of violence or fraud, and to the repression of public nuisances, and it contends that whatever laws are enacted be applied to men as well as to women.   Finally, it emphasises the need of a study of constructive measures to diminish the moral and economic causes of this social plague.[1]

[1] *Statuts, Fédération Abolitionniste Internationale*, Geneva March,

The International Abolitionist Federation holds annual conferences, the last having taken place in September, 1911, at Colmar in Alsace, where the regulation system was abolished twenty years ago. At intervals of every few years, moreover, the federation holds a more formal congress, in which it seeks to prepare the way for effective action. The first congress took place in Geneva, in 1877, and the tenth congress in the same city in 1908, the

---

1875: "Art. 4—La Fédération révendique, dans le domaine spécial de la législation en matière de mœurs, l'autonomie de la personne humaine, qui a son corollaire dans la responsabilité individuelle.

" D'une part, elle condamne toute mesure d'exception appliquée sous prétexte de mœurs;

" D'autre part, elle affirme qu'en instituant une réglementation qui veut procurer à l'homme sécurité et irresponsabilité dans le vice, l'État bouleverse la notion de responsabilité, base de toute morale.

" En faisant peser sur la femme seule les conséquences légales d'un acte commun, l'État propage cette idée funeste qu'il y aurait une morale différente pour chaque sexe.

"Art. 5—Considérant que le simple fait de prostitution personnelle et privée ne relève que de la conscience et ne constitue pas un délit, la Fédération déclare que l'intervention de l'État en matière de mœurs doit se limiter aux points suivants:

" Punition de tout attentat à la pudeur, commis ou tenté contre des mineurs ou des personnes de l'un ou de l'autre sexe assimilées aux mineurs. Chaque législation particulière doit déterminer exactement la limite et les conditions de cette minorité spéciale.

" Punition de tout attentat à la pudeur accompli ou tenté par des moyens violents ou frauduleux contre des personnes de tout âge et de tout sexe.

" Punition de la provocation publique à la débauche et du proxénétisme, dans celles de leurs manifestations délictueuses qui peuvent être constatées sans prêter à l'arbitraire et sans ramener, sous une autre forme, le régime spécial de la police des mœurs.

" Les mesures prises à cet égard doivent s'appliquer aux hommes comme aux femmes.

intervening congresses being held in the various capitals of Europe.[1]   At these congresses important papers were read, many of which have been published separately,[2] and were followed by interesting discussions.   The federation also publishes a monthly bulletin which has a wide influence.[3]

National committees were soon formed in the different countries, and are to be found to-day in England, France, Germany, Switzerland, Austria, Netherlands, Sweden, Spain, and Norway.   The most important of these committees are those of France, England and Germany.   In France, among the most distinguished and active members have been M. Yves Guyot, at one time minister of commerce, Mme. G. Avril de Sainte-Croix, the most indefatigable supporter of the movement,

---

"Toutes les fois que le proxénétisme tombe sous le coup de la loi, ceux qui paient les proxénètes et profitent de leur industrie doivent être considerés comme complices.

"La Fédération déclare donc que l'État ne doit ni imposer à une femme quelconque la visite obligatoire sous prétexte de mœurs, ni soumettre la personne des prostituées à un régime d'exception quelconque.

"Art. 6—Outre les questions qui sont en rapport direct avec le but spécial que poursuit la Fédération, celle-ci étudie scientifiquement la prostitution.   Elle poursuit une enquête permanente sur les causes morales, économiques ou autres de cette plaie sociale, sur ses effêts, sur les moyens d'y porter rémède."

[1] The eleventh congress was to have taken place in Frankfort a./M. in 1911, but has been postponed to 1912.

[2] The most important of these will be noted in the bibliography at the end of this volume.

[3] *Bulletin Abolitionniste, Organe Central de la Fédération Abolitionniste Internationale*.   Geneva, Switzerland.   The accomplished Secretary of the International Federation is M. Henry Minod.

and M. Louis Fiaux, the most voluminous living writer on the subject.[1] The French committee does not publish a journal of its own, as the international journal is published in French and circulates in France. There is, however, a French League of Public Morality, which issues a periodical with a special supplement devoted to the abolitionist cause.[2] One of the important offshoots of the French committee is the so-called *L'Œuvre Libératrice*, or Rescue Home, which was founded in 1900 by Madame de Sainte-Croix under distinguished auspices, and which has extended its beneficent operations to many unfortunate women.[3]

In England after the death of Mrs. Butler the most prominent members of the committee were the Right Hon. James Stuart, Hon. Henry J. Wilson, M. P., Mr. W. A. Coote, and Dr. H. M. Wilson. The English committee publishes its own periodical, *The Shield*,[4] and issues a large

[1] For a complete list of Mr. Fiaux's contributions see the bibliography to this work.

[2] *Le Relèvement Social, Organe de la Ligue Française de la Moralité Publique*, edited by M. Louis Comte.

[3] *L'Œuvre Libératrice* publishes an annual pamphlet giving an account of its work. The record for the tenth year was published in 1911. During the decade of its existence 755 women have been put in hospitals or other establishments, and 1255 other women have been otherwise aided. Quite a goodly number of young girls who had been rescued in this way have now become industrious working women, good servants, and excellent mothers.

[4] *The Shield, the Official Organ of the British Committeee of the International Federation for the Abolition of State Regulation of Vice.* This is a monthly, the present volume being volume xiii. of a new series.

number of pamphlets. In both the English and the French societies men have been equally interested with women.

In Germany, on the other hand, the society is composed more largely of women, and the male members, with the exception of a few distinguished physicians, consist chiefly of clergymen. The head of the German committee is Frau Katharina Scheven and its journal is called *Der Abolitionist*.[1] The German committee, however, has no less than eighteen branches in the most important German cities, and holds interesting annual conferences. The last meeting took place at Dresden in June, 1911, and devoted especial attention to the evils of the so-called *Animier-Kneipen*, or drinking places, which are open all night and are served by young women who are supposed to amuse the customers, to drink with them, and incite them to drink more. The German branch also publishes a large number of tracts and monographs which are now beginning to produce some influence.

In the other European countries, each of the branches is doing effective work and furnishes every year fresh and distinguished recruits to the cause of abolitionism.[2] The greater part of

---

[1] *Der Abolitionist. Organ des Deutschen Zweiges der I. A. Föderation.* Herausgegeben und begründet von Katharina Scheven. This is published in Dresden, and is now in its tenth volume.

[2] A complete list of all the periodicals in other countries that are in

the reform movement described in the following sections is due directly or indirectly to the unceasing efforts and the continual vigilance of the international association.   The real meaning of the movement can best be summarised in the following recent words of an eminent British physician:

"The Abolitionist Federation has always been convinced of the futility of regulation as a hygienic measure, a conviction which is now shared by most of those whose experience entitles them to speak with authority.   But the Federation goes further, and maintains that regulation is not merely futile, but mischievous; that its tendency is to aggravate the evils which it is designed to prevent.   It does not fulfil the first conditions of sound prophylaxis; it does nothing whatever to check the *causes* of disease;   on the contrary, it tends, in greater or lesser degree, to foster those habits of thought and action which are the source of disease.   It may exist side by side with efforts to diminish vice by raising the moral tone, by inculcating self-control, by spreading knowledge as to the dangers of disease, or by providing counter attractions; but it can never assist those efforts and tends rather to divert attention from them and to weaken them.

"The knowledge that the authorities try to

---

harmony with the work of the International Federation is published in its monthly *Bulletin*.

provide safety in indulgence maintains on the part of young men a false confidence which the more diffused knowledge of the dangers of disease would otherwise counteract; moreover, it bolsters up the belief that sexual indulgence is necessary for a man's health. Nowadays every medical man knows that this belief has no foundation, but it lingers persistently among the uneducated, who are apt to regard the continued existence of government 'protection' as a proof of the necessity. In every way regulation works to undermine that resolute and purposeful self-control which is the only reliable safeguard.

"In many quarters there is a curious misapprehension on the objects and motives of abolitionists. They are supposed to object to regulation on some obscure theological ground, or with the fantastic idea that venereal disease being a punishment for sin ought to be encouraged. Nothing is farther from the truth. Abolitionists believe that all diseases should be treated, that all sufferers should be cared for, and, if possible, cured, and that reasonable precautions should be taken to prevent the spread of disease. But regulation is not a reasonable precaution; firstly, because it deals only with a particular section of infected persons, leaving a much larger number at liberty to spread the contagion; and secondly, because it fosters the immorality which is the ultimate cause of disease.

"More than thirty years ago, when the majority of the medical profession were solidly in favour of regulation, the International Abolitionist Federation was founded to combat a system which is based on injustice, and which, wherever it exists, lowers respect for women, and undermines the foundations of personal liberty The Federation maintains that the basis of hygienic legislation as of all other legislation must be righteousness, and that if founded on any other basis failure is inevitable; the progress of medical science has justified this contention. This Federation is not, and never has been, primarily an organisation for promoting hygiene. Its business is to secure the abolition of an immoral and unjust system. But it claims that by destroying reliance on a false system it has cleared the way for the discovery of better methods for dealing with the curse of prostitution and its attendant evils."[1]

3. *The Brussels International Conferences*

The system of regulation in Brussels was, as stated above, long considered a model. At the end of the seventies, however, a series of most outrageous scandals occurred, showing an astounding condition of corruption among police officials, and direct complicity between the chief of police and

---

[1] *Notes on Administrative Measures against Enthetic Disease.* By H. M. Wilson, M.D. London, 1910.

12

the houses of ill-fame. These revelations which confounded all Europe, somewhat abated the zeal of the enthusiasts for the Brussels system, and doubts now began to be heard. The subject was energetically taken up by the international federation, and during the nineties a distinguished Belgian specialist, Dr. Dubois-Havenith, organised a committee to arrange for an international conference to consider the whole problem of regulation. The conference was held in Brussels, in 1899, under the presidency of the Belgian Minister of Health and the Burgomaster of Brussels. It was composed of 360 members, representing 33 nationalities, 107 being government delegates and 295 being distinguished physicians. In order that the discussions might not wax too warm, however, some of the extreme abolitionists, like M. Yves Guyot, were not invited. The Brussels conference lasted five days and considered six questions, which were as follows:

1. Have the systems of regulation now in force had any influence upon the prevalence of disease?

2. Is the present organisation of medical supervision susceptible of improvement?

3. Is it desirable, from a medical point of view, to maintain or to suppress the licensed houses?

4. Can the administrative organisation of police supervision be improved?

5. By what legal measures can the number of

women earning their living by immorality be diminished?

6. What preventive measures bearing on the population generally are to be recommended?[1]

The chief discussion centred around the first question. Although the regulationists, or reglementationists, were naturally in the great majority, the most significant occurrence in the entire congress was that the physicians were no longer, as a generation before, unanimous in their opinion. In fact some of the most prominent continental as well as English physicians now utterly denied the value of regulation, and even the medical advocates of regulation conceded that entirely too much had been claimed for it. The very first morning was one of surprises, for three out of the first four speakers—all prominent continental physicians—condemned the existing system.

[1] The official report is published in six large volumes of some 3000 pages, under the following title: *Rapports, Enquêtes, et Compte Rendu des Débats de la Conférence Internationale de Prophylaxie des Maladies Vénériennes.* Publiés par le Dr. Dubois-Havenith, agrégé à l'Université de Bruxelles, Secrétaire-général de la Conférence. T. I. Première partie, *Rapports Préliminaires;* Seconde partie, *Enquêtes sur l'État de la Prostitution et la Fréquence de la Syphilis et des Maladies Vénériennes dans les différents Pays;* T. I., Appendice, *Communications relatives aux six Questions à l'Éude.*—T. II.: Première partie, *Compte Rendu des Séances;* Seconde partie, *Appendice aux Enquêtes et Communications Documentaires.* H. Lamertin, edit., Bruxelles, 1899–1900.

An excellent, full, and critical account of the Congress will be found in Louis Fiaux, *L' Intégrité Intersexuelle des Peuples et des Gouvernements.* Paris, 1910, 811 pp. A very abbreviated account in English will be found in *Preventive Hygiene. The International Conference at Brussels,* Sept., 1899. *By one who was there.* London, 1900.

These were Dr. Blaschko of Berlin, Dr. Augagneur, of Lyons, and afterwards governor-general of Madagascar, and Dr. Barthélemy, one of the medical chiefs of St. Lazare, the great hospital prison in Paris. Perhaps the most distinguished member of the congress, Professor Fournier, the head of the French delegation, who still declared himself an advocate of the system, conceded that it did very little good. "You ask me," he said, "am I content with the regulation as it is? No, I am not. Yet I approve it, yes, because it does a little good ('un peu de bien'). It controls but a small number of women, but at least it controls those few." In addition to the physicians who had now become skeptical of the whole scheme, there was a small band of abolitionists pure and simple, whose speeches were marked by conspicuous ability and restraint. One of the most impressive speeches was made by a Dutch delegate who, referring to the plea of Professor Fournier that they be allowed to do "a little good," pointed out that in order to do this "little good" they were compelled to do incalculable harm.

On the main question of state regulation, opinions were so divided that the conference was unable to adopt any resolution. On the other points, however, it was possible to secure unanimous approval for the following recommendations:

1. That the governments should use their

utmost efforts to suppress the prostitution of girls under age.

2. That a permanent international society of sanitary and moral prophylaxis (prevention) should be constituted, with its headquarters in Brussels; that it issue a quarterly journal in French, English, and German; and that it hold congresses from time to time, the next congress to meet at Brussels, in 1902.

3. That complete and compulsory courses of instruction in venereology should be instituted in every university.

4. That all those charged with the education of the young should use every effort to promote their moral development and to teach them temperance and respect for women of all classes.

5. That the utmost rigour of the law should be enforced against *souteneurs* (that is, men who live upon the earnings of prostitutes, and who in New York are ordinarily called "cadets.)"

6. That the government should appoint in each country a commission to study the best means of preventing the dissemination of venereal diseases.

7. That the governments should find means to warn the public, and especially young persons, of the dangers attending an immoral life.

8. That the statistics of disease should be drawn up in all countries on a common basis.

As most of the important points brought out

in the first Brussels conference have been touched
upon in the body of this book, we may pass them
by here. The general impression created by the
discussions may be inferred from the statement of
an American delegate, to one of the German doctors:
"We are waiting to see how you get on in Europe,"
said he. "After a hundred years of it you do not
seem much better off than ourselves. At present
we are not much tempted to copy you." A few
weeks later Professor Fournier read a paper at
the Paris Academy of Medicine, in which he
pointed out "the inadequacy of the whole system
of our administrative measures. Without ignoring
their advantages (which would be an ingratitude
and an error), we must admit their insufficiency.
I will add that they are likely to become even less
useful as time goes on." And even Professor
Neisser, the distinguished German advocate of
regulation, said: "The question of prostitution
is essentially and primarily a man's question,
rather than a woman's question. I personally
do not believe in the alleged physical necessity
argument, nor in the harmfulness of abstention."

Shortly after the disbanding of the Brussels
conference the International Society of Sanitary
and Moral Prophylaxis was founded. Its quarterly
Bulletins, which have continued to this date,
abound in the most interesting and valuable
discussions. National societies with the same
name were now also instituted. France, under

the leadership of Professor Fournier, was the first
to have its own society, founded in 1900.[1] The
United States, as we shall see later on,[2] followed
before long under the leadership of Dr. Prince A.
Morrow, who was one of the sixteen American
members of the first Brussels conference.

In September, 1902, the second conference,
provided for in the second resolution above, was
held, again in Brussels and under the same auspices as before.[3] Perhaps the most significant difference was the presence of a larger number of invited
abolitionists, and especially M. Yves Guyot, who took
a prominent part in the discussion. The abolitionist
movement was now headed by four leading Paris
doctors; Dr. D. Gailleton, the head of the French
government delegation, Dr. Gaucher, the successor
of Professor Fournier, Dr. Queyrat, the head of
one of the leading hospitals, and Dr. Landouzy,
who represented the French ministry of public
instruction. These physicians condemned the
existing system as absolutely valueless ("Il ne

---

[1] As to the admirable work accomplished by the French society see
the article by Dr. Keyes in *Transactions of the American Society of
Sanitary and Moral Prophylaxis*, vol. i. (1906), pp. 80 *et seq.*

[2] Page 222 *infra*.

[3] The proceedings of this conference were published in two large
volumes under the title of *Seconde Conférence Internationale pour la
Prophylaxie de la Syphilis et des Maladies Vénériennes, sous le patronage
du Gouvernement Belge (Septembre, 1902)*. Publié par le Dr. Dubois
Havenith, Secrétaire-général. 2 thick volumes, not paged consecutively.
Tome premier, *Rapports Préliminaires;* Tome second, *Compte Rendu
des Séances.* Henri Lamertin, editeur, Bruxelles, 1902–1903.

sert absolument à rien'') and moved a resolution
that it ought to be abandoned.   Of course, it was
impossible to hope for unanimity on such a
resolution and it was therefore withdrawn.   Much
new material was now presented and some admirable reports were made, especially on the problems
of individual prophylaxis.

Professor Neisser, the distinguished German
specialist, presented a scheme for what soon came
to be called Neo-regulation, a regulation through
a standing sanitary commission with plenary
powers to place all patients, male and female, under medical supervision, and to compel obedience
to all the restrictions imposed.   But the conference
refused to consider it seriously.   There is no
doubt that the current against any form of
regulation which involved compulsory examination
was flowing more and more strongly.

The debates were largely an echo of those in
the preceding conference and at the close several
resolutions were unanimously passed.   The most
important of these were the following:

1.   That all persons suffering from venereal
maladies should have easy access to gratuitous
treatment, with no unnecessary publicity.

2.   That prostitutes suffering from venereal
maladies ought to be considered not as criminals
but as patients.

3.   That all military recruits should receive
printed instructions of the danger of disease, and

should take these with them when they leave the service.

4. That the most important and most effectual means for combating the diffusion of venereal maladies consists in widespread information as to the importance of these maladies and the very grave dangers attending them. It is especially necessary to teach young men not only that chastity and continence are not injurious, but that these practices are wholly recommended from the medical point of view.

This last resolution—the unanimous pronouncement of all the physicians present—that chastity is not injurious to young men, but on the contrary beneficial—is one of extraordinary significance.

Before the conference met, it had been intended to hold a third congress within a few years. Now, however, it was decided that during the next decade or two probably the best work could be done by the separate national committees formed or to be formed and each working in its own country.

If we were to sum up the results of the two Brussels conferences, the conclusion would be that they were more important from the negative than from the positive point of view. It had originally been hoped especially by the "reglementationists" that some form of international regulation might be proposed. It was soon recognised, however, that any attempt to spread the existing system of regulation was hopeless. From this point of view the conclusions of the conferences were essentially negative. On the other hand, the emphasis was laid, in all the discussions and in many of the resolutions, upon constructive methods of dealing with the problem, not indeed through "reglementation," but in other ways that would be in consonance with modern social and moral demands. Taking it all in all, therefore, the Brussels conferences showed the beginning of a decided change of heart on the part of the continental thinkers, and in this way marked a decided step in advance in the solution of the problem.

4. *The French Extra-Parliamentary Commission*

The Brussels conferences, as we have seen, brought about a distinct change not only in public opinion, but also in medical opinion in France, as to the excellence of their long-continued policy of regulation. Now, in the early years of the new century, confidence in the system was still more rudely shattered by some outrageous mistakes on the part of the Morals Police, both in Paris and in Rennes. As a result of the interpellations in Parliament on these outrages, an Extra-Parliamentary Commission was appointed on July 18, 1903, to consider the whole subject. It was composed of about seventy-five members, deemed to represent the various classes of experts. About one third of the members were legislators, that is senators and deputies; another third was composed of important administrative officials connected with the government departments, as well as some important prefects and mayors; and the remaining third comprised about a dozen of the foremost physicians and about the same number of publicists and professors of social economy, including M. Yves Guyot, Professor Gide, and Mme. Avril de Sainte-Croix. The sessions lasted almost three years and were full of the most interesting discussions.[1]

In order to insure absolute impartiality, preliminary reports were invited from the leaders of the two parties—those who still believed in the policy of regulation and those who were opposed to it. The argument in favour of regulation was presented by Professor Fournier, the opposed argument by M. Augagneur, who later became a member of the

[1] The most convenient account of the labours of the commission will be found in the report by the secretary: *Rapport Général sur les Travaux de la Commission Extraparlémentaire du Régime des Mœurs*, Présenté par M. F. Hennequin, Sous-Directeur au Ministère de l'Intérieur, Secrétaire-général de la Commission. Melun, Imprimerie Administrative, 1908, 4to, 285 pp.

There was also a thick volume of *Annexes au Rapport Général* giving all the important reports presented to the commission. A critical and full study of these reports was made by M. Louis Fiaux, one of the members, in a three-volume work entitled *La Police des Mœurs devant la Commission Extraparlémentaire du Régime des Mœurs*. Vols. i. and ii., each of 1000 pages, were published in 1907; volume iii., a book of 744 pages, was published in 1910.

French cabinet of 1911. Each report was followed by long discussions.

Although the abolitionists were originally in the minority, the force of the arguments and the facts presented by them was such that at the end of its deliberations the commission voted by a considerable majority that the entire system of regulation, as practised in France, was so defective, and on the whole so immoral, that it ought to be entirely abandoned. Thus, after an experience of more than a century, the French experts came to the conclusion that the whole *régime des mœurs* had outlived its usefulness. The importance of this pronouncement cannot well be overestimated.

The commission, however, was not satisfied merely with negation. It considered somewhat at length the so-called neo-regulation scheme and the Scandinavian scheme. The neo-regulationist proposals were, in short, as follows: abolition of compulsory registration except after a proper trial and judicial decision; the appointment of women as police and as doctors; the prohibition of the sale of intoxicants in disorderly houses; the exclusion of minors from these houses; and the prohibition of licensed houses. The neo-regulation scheme, however, was considered to be an unsatisfactory modification of the present system, and was not approved.[1]

[1] A fuller discussion of neo-reglementation will be found in a mono-

The Scandinavian scheme had for its chief feature the placing of venereal diseases among the infectious diseases for which compulsory notification is required, and which the law insists upon placing under proper medical treatment, with the imposition of penalties for neglect.

The system which the commission finally recommended was what it called "indirect" regulation. It provided for a careful organisation for the treatment of disease, with the exclusion of all one-sided provisions affecting only women. It included provisions for protecting minors from corruption, and comprised also a general scheme of education in sexual matters. It prohibited all tolerated or licensed houses and recommended punishment for all incitement to immorality, or what it called "public provocations to debauchery" and for all infractions of public order. Finally, it recommended some important provisions for the prophylaxis of venereal diseases. As the secretary put it in his report, summing up the general conclusions: "In suppressing a century-old system

---

graph written by Mr. B. Leppington, of London. The official French edition is *Le Néo-Réglementarisme. Ses Principes, son Application, ses Perspectives.* Published at Geneva, 1904, by the International Abolitionist Federation.

A most remarkable suggestion was made by Dr. Sperk of St. Petersburg, who proposed that there be two classes of houses, one where certified healthy women might be found, and to which none but healthy men should resort; another to be occupied by infected women, to which infected men might go. This monstrous proposition, of course, received no consideration whatsoever.

which is not unanimously condemned, and in objecting to any form of reglementation as such, the commission has not sacrificed important interests to any ideal of justice, nor has it accomplished an utterly destructive work. On the ruins of the old system, in fact, it has built a new, in recommending, with the greatest care, all those measures, which are deemed necessary and adequate for the defence of public order and for the maintenance of public health."[1]

The first fruit of the work of the extra-parliamentary commission was the law of 1908, designed to afford more adequate protection to young girls under eighteen. The main recommendation of the report—namely, the complete abolition of the whole system of *régime des mœurs*—was not so easy to accomplish. The matter has been taken up several times in Parliament, but public opinion is not yet sufficiently educated to force the contest to a victorious issue. So strong is the opposition to any sudden break with methods that have lasted for over a century, and so obstinate are the administrative forces arrayed against any such complete overthrow, that it will probably take a somewhat longer period of agitation and education before France abandons her present methods. But the battle has been at least half won when a majority not only of the leading

[1] *Rapport Général*, p. 269.

French physicians but also of the most important administrative officials have recognised that their present system does more harm than good. It is only a question of time before the opinion of the expert minority will become the public opinion of the great majority. It must not be forgotten that in England it took an agitation of almost twenty years to overcome a system which had been in operation only a few years before the opposition began. In France we have to deal with a method which has been in force for over a century, and which has spread to the entire European continent, and to other continents as well. But the remarkable and unexpected conclusions of the extra-parliamentary commission have given fresh hope to the defenders of liberty and to the advocates of moral and social progress. Two members of the French government in 1911, M. Cruppi, minister of justice, and M. Augagneur, minister of public works, were abolitionists; a parliamentary group of not less than eighty abolitionists was formed in 1911; and we are told that "all the great chiefs of the medical faculties and all the important heads of hospitals have now become converted to abolitionism."[1] It is, thus, perhaps not too much to say that the beginning of the end can already be discerned.

If, therefore, we sum up the movement of the

[1] See the report at the Colmar Congress, 1911.

last few decades in Europe, we find that considerable progress has been made. In Sweden the change of opinion has been scarcely less marked than in France. In 1903, after the second Brussels conference, Mr. Otto Westerberg and Mr. Hugo Tamm, who had been converted to abolitionism, persuaded the Swedish parliament to ask the King to appoint a royal commission to study the subject. The commission was formed with nine members, seven of whom were regulationists. During the course of the discussion, however, all seven were converted to the other side. After several years' work the commission made its report in 1911. The members unanimously agreed in recommending an abandonment of the existing system of regulation, while their constructive recommendations included the compulsory notification of venereal disease, and the subjection of confirmed prostitutes to the provisions of the law governing vagrants.[1]

In Norway and Denmark the *police des mœurs* has been abolished, and while some of its powers have been transferred to the ordinary police, the provision with reference to compulsory treatment has become a dead letter.[2]

[1] The report is published in four large volumes, edited by the secretary, Dr. Carl Malmroth. A short account will be found in the *Bulletin Abolitionniste* for February, 1911.

[2] Professor Erik Pontoppidan, *What Venereal Diseases mean, and how to prevent them* (1909). For the changes instituted in Denmark and in Norway, see *The Shield* for June, July, and August, 1911.

In Italy a complete system of gratuitous treatment in dispensaries for all venereal patients, that was developed in the eighties and the nineties, paved the way for the abolition of the entire system of police control over women. In 1904, this system was rescinded by administrative ordinance on the ground that "every sort of direct compulsion for the ascertainment and cure of venereal diseases is injurious to public prophylaxis, as it increases the number of persons impelled to conceal their malady and to avoid the means of cure." But some features of the old system are preserved in the *Regolamento sul Meretricio* in that the government still recognises tolerated houses. The inmates, however, are entirely free to leave at any time.[1]

In Germany, with its fondness for administrative regulation of every kind, the abolitionist movement has made perhaps less headway than anywhere else, although not a few prominent physicians and officials have now been brought around to the other side;[2] and more recently several of the national organisations, like the evangelical

[1] See *Fédération Abolitionniste. Dixième Congrès tenu à Genève les 7–11 Septembre, 1908. Compte Rendu des Travaux.* Geneva, 1909, p. 283.

[2] A good indication of the prevalent view in Germany may be found in the two articles by Kurt Woltzendorff, entitled "Polizei und Prostitution; eine Studie," in the *Zeitschrift für die Gesammte Staatswissenschaft*, vol. lxvii, 1911, Erstes und Zweites Heft. It is significant, however, that Dr. Woltzendorff desires to have the regulations apply to men as well as to women.

13

association and the white slave committee, to be mentioned in the next chapter, have been converted to the abolitionist point of view. The controversy between the "regulators" and the "abolitionists" has become a bitter one, with much exaggeration on both sides.[1]

In Germany, however, excellent constructive work has been accomplished by the Society for the Prevention of Venereal Diseases, which was founded in 1902. Far better facilities have been provided for venereal patients, chairs for the teaching of venereology have been established in the universities, courses in sex pedagogy have been instituted in the high schools, and millions of leaflets have been issued to enlighten the public on the dangers. The result has been a complete change of front in the attitude of the periodicals and the daily press to the subject.

In far-away Australia, also, a commission has recently been instituted in the state of Victoria to investigate the subject; and as a result syphilis was made a notifiable disease in May, 1911. The government now proposes to bring in a bill providing for accessible treatment for those afflicted with venereal diseases, and to inaugu-

[1] An excellent summary of the opposing arguments will be found in *Freiheit oder gesundheitliche Ueberwachung der Gewerbsunzucht. Eine zeitgemässe Betrachtung.* Von Dr. med. Gaston Verberg. Munich, 1907. *Cf.* the article by Dr. Henry B. DeForest, in *Transactions of the American Society of Sanitary and Moral Prophylaxis*, vol. ii., 1908, pp. 141 *et seq.*

rate a campaign of public education on the whole question.

Even in Japan, where the celebrated segregated quarter, the Yoshiwara, was destroyed by fire a year ago, a movement has been inaugurated, with the co-operation of no less important a personage than ex-Premier Count Okuma, to abolish the system of government regulation. A new society, called the *Kakusei Kai*, is now vigorously at work and is publishing its own journal. Thus, slowly but surely, breaches are being made in the solid ranks of those who, until a generation ago, had no doubt as to the effectiveness and beneficence of regulation.

CHAPTER II

THE WHITE-SLAVE TRAFFIC IN EUROPE AND AMERICA

So far as we can learn, the term "White Slaves," in its present connotation, is due to Victor Hugo. In the English labour struggle of the thirties, when the anti-slavery movement in the colonies was coming to a head, some of the labour leaders used the term "White Slavery" to designate the condition of the factory operatives in Great Britain. The term spread to the United States, where a work on the subject was published in 1853.[1] After the enactment of the ten-hour factory law, however, this term fell into disuse. But in 1870, in a letter written to Mrs. Josephine Butler, to cheer her in the struggle against the Contagious Diseases Acts, Victor Hugo wrote: "The slavery of black women is abolished in America; but the slavery of white women continues in Europe."[2] It was not long before the phrase became common in this newer connotation.

[1] *The White Slaves of England, compiled from Official Documents.* By John C. Cobden. Auburn, Buffalo, and Cincinnati, 1853. 498 pp.

[2] Josephine E. Butler, *Personal Reminiscences of a Great Crusade,* 1896, p. 7.

1. *The White-Slave Traffic in Europe*

The existence of an organised traffic to supply houses of ill-fame was for a long time neither suspected nor acknowledged. The earliest inkling of such a nefarious traffic came to the ears of the public at the time of the first congress of the international abolitionist federation at Geneva, in 1877. It was there pointed out that under the pretext of providing governesses or maids for private families in Austria and Hungary, sometimes whole carloads of young women were being sent by different agencies to recruit the houses of ill-fame. So great, in fact, did the scandal become that in 1875 certain Swiss cantons formed an agreement designed to check the traffic, but without much result. A few years later similar scandals arose in Brussels, and the complicity of the chief of police in the matter was proven.[1] The matter was taken up at the second congress of the international federation at Geneva, in 1880, at which Mrs. Josephine Butler delivered a remarkable address. After some discussion the following resolution was adopted:

"The Second Congress after having acquired proof of the fact that there exists a wide and permanent traffic designed to keep alive legalised prostitution in Belgium and elsewhere;

"Convinced by the facts brought to its attention

[1] See above, pages 177–178.

that the *police des mœurs* contributed in certain cases in no small measure to this traffic;

"Approves of everything that has thus far been done by the Federation in its endeavour to repress this international traffic, and instructs the executive committee to proceed energetically along the same line."

In the ensuing conventions held at London in 1881 and at Neuchâtel in 1882 this matter again formed the centre of discussion, and memoirs on the subject were published by several writers. At the third international congress held at The Hague, in 1883, attention was called to the correspondence between the Dutch lower house and the former minister of justice, M. Modderman, who had proposed an international conference on the subject. In the following year, however, a far wider public was reached. In England, after the Contagious Diseases Acts had been repealed, a movement was initiated to add an amendment to the criminal law designed to afford more adequate protection to young girls; and when the disclosures were made by Messrs. Dyer and Gillett as to the Belgian abuses[1] and the traffic in young women between Belgium and England a commission was appointed. Although the commission reported in favour of some amendment of the criminal law, nothing was done by Parliament.

[1] See above, p. 177.

It was now that Mrs. Josephine Butler and Mrs. Booth, of the Salvation Army, approached Mr. W. P. Stead, the editor of the *Pall Mall Gazette*, and begged him to publish a complete exposure of the facts as they existed in London. Mr. Stead investigated the subject and, in 1885, stirred all England by the graphic account that he published in his paper. The public outcry was so loud and vehement that it led to the passage of a Criminal Law Amendment Act, and to the indictment and conviction of the famous Jeffries. At the congress of London, in 1886, the subject of an international agreement was further considered. The first successful attempt in this direction was realised on December 18, 1886, when Belgium and Holland contracted a treaty, each delegating the other to aid in suppressing the traffic. At the succeeding conferences at Lausanne, in 1887, and at Copenhagen, in 1888, the matter was again brought forward. It was now that Mr. William Alexander Coote reported to the conference the creation of the British National Vigilance Association, of which he was secretary, and which was formed especially to combat the white-slave traffic. Mr. Coote recommended the institution of similar societies elsewhere.[1] At the end of 1888, the Netherlands and Austro-Hungary entered

---

[1] The British association soon began the publication of a monthly periodical, *The Vigilance Record*, which is still edited by Mr. Coote. The head office is at St. Mary's Chambers, 161a Strand, London.

into a treaty similar to the existing treaty between Belgium and the Netherlands. Passing over the intervening years, the matter was taken up anew in 1895, by the international prison congress, at Paris, which went on record as demanding an international commission to study the whole subject. Partly as a result of this recommendation but chiefly owing to the indefatigable efforts of Mr. Coote, the secretary of the British National Vigilance Society, arrangements were made for the holding of an international congress.[1]

The first international congress for the suppression of the white-slave traffic was held in London, in June, 1899, with 120 delegates from various nations. Important speeches were made by Sir Percy Bunting, the editor of the *Contemporary Review*, and by many other distinguished persons. Resolutions were adopted for a permanent organisation, to be known as the International Congress and to be composed of the national committees, of which there should be one in each country. The representatives from each national committee were to form the international committee, and the management was to

---

[1] In a work entitled *A Vision and its Fulfilment, being the History of the Origin of the Work of the National Vigilance Association for the Suppression of the White-Slave Traffic. With a record of visits paid to the capitals of Europe, America, Egypt, and South Africa for the purpose of organising national committees for the suppression of the traffic* (London, 1911), Mr. Coote gives a graphic account of his remarkable success.

be entrusted to an international bureau of five (later seven) members.

The international committee now set to work vigorously and in the next few years a number of conferences and congresses were held—the second international congress at Frankfort a./M. in 1902, the second preliminary conference at Zürich, in 1904, and the third international congress at Paris, in 1906. The preliminary conferences always prepared the way for the subsequent more formal congresses where reports were made and resolutions adopted. In the meantime the governments of the various countries themselves had been awakened by their national committees to the necessity of action, and in 1902 an international congress was called to meet in Paris that year. At the Paris congress fifteen European states were represented by official government delegates. It did not take long for the main lines of an international treaty to be framed, but it was thought best to defer the signing of the treaty until after each of the signatory powers could have an opportunity to study the problem in detail. The matter was therefore adjourned for two years. When the official congress reconvened in 1904, an international treaty for the suppression and prevention of the white-slave traffic, binding the signatory powers to unite in the various measures that were taken, was signed on May 18, 1904, by the representatives of thirteen states. These were France, Germany, Great Britain, Italy, Russia, Sweden, Denmark, Belgium, Holland, Spain, Portugal, Norway, and Switzerland; a little later Austro-Hungary and Brazil signified their adhesion to the treaty.[1]

[1] The terms of the International White Slave Treaty are as follows:

Article 1. Each of the contracting governments agrees to establish or designate an authority who will be directed to centralise all information concerning the procuration of women or girls with a view to their debauchery in a foreign country; that authority shall have the right to correspond directly with the similar service established in each of the other contracting states.

Article 2. Each of the governments agrees to exercise a supervision, for the purpose of finding out, particularly in the stations, harbours of embarkation, and on the journey, the conductors of women or girls intended for debauchery. Instruction shall be sent for that purpose to the officials or to any other qualified persons, in order to procure, within the limits of the laws, all information of a nature to discover a criminal traffic.

The arrival of persons appearing evidently to be the authors, the accomplices, or the victims of such a traffic will be notified, in each case, either to the authorities of the place of destination or to the interested diplomatic or consular agents, or to any other competent authorities.

Article 3. The governments agree to receive, in each case, within the limits of the laws, the declarations of women and girls of foreign nationality who surrender themselves to prostitution, with a view to establish their identity and their civil status and to ascertain who has induced them to leave their country. The information received will be communicated to the authorities of the country of origin of the said women or girls, with a view to their eventual return.

The governments agree, within the limits of the laws and as far as possible, to confide temporarily and with a view to their eventual return, the victims of criminal traffic when they are without any resources, to some institutions of public or private charity or to private individuals furnishing the necessary guaranties.

The governments agree also, within the limits of the laws, to return to their country of origin, those women or girls who ask their return or who may be claimed by persons having authority over them. Return will be made only after reaching an understanding as to their

In each of the signatory states national committees have been formed in order to second
the efforts of the respective governments.[1] In

---

identity and nationality, as well as to the place and date of their arrival
at the frontiers.   Each of the contracting parties will facilitate the
transit on its territory.

The correspondence relative to the return will be made, as far as
possible, through the direct channel.

Article 4.   In case the woman or girl to be sent back cannot herself pay the expenses of her transportation and has neither husband,
nor relations, nor guardians to pay for her the expenses occasioned by
her return, they shall be borne by the country on the territory of which
she resides, as far as the nearest frontier or port of embarkation in
the direction of the country of origin, and by the country of origin
for the remainder.

Article 5.   The provisions of the above articles 3 and 4 shall not
infringe upon the provisions of special conventions which may exist
between the contracting governments.

Article 6.   The contracting governments agree, within the limits of
the laws, to exercise as far as possible a supervision over the bureaus
or agencies which occupy themselves with finding places for women or
girls in foreign countries.

Article 7.   The non-signatory states are admitted to adhere to
the present arrangement.   For this purpose, they shall notify their
intention, through the diplomatic channel, to the French government,
which shall inform all the contracting states.

Article 8.   The present arrangement shall take effect six months
after the date of the exchange of ratifications.   In case one of the
contracting parties shall denounce it, that denunciation shall take
effect only as regards that party and then twelve months only from
the date of the said denunciation.

Article 9.   The present arrangement shall be ratified and the ratifications shall be exchanged at Paris, as soon as possible.

In faith whereof the respective plenipotentiaries have signed the
present agreement, and thereunto affixed their seals.

Done at Paris, the 18th May, 1904, in single copy, which shall be
deposited in the archives of the Ministry of Foreign Affairs of the
French Republic, and of which one copy, certified correct, shall be sent
to each contracting party.

[1] A complete list of these national committees, with the name and

Spain the matter was even taken up by the throne and a *Patronato Real* was formed under the highest official auspices to aid. Notwithstanding the treaty, however, the organised traffic seemed to increase rather than diminish, and as a consequence the international abolitionist federation, which, after giving the original impetus to the whole movement, had left the matter in the hands of the English vigilance committee and the international committee, now again took up the subject with energy. It decided to devote its international congress at Geneva in 1908 entirely to this topic. In the proceedings of that congress,[1] will be found most valuable reports showing that in most of the continental states, at least, there is a very close relation between the white-slave traffic and the special Morals Police, and that this police force, which is a necessary adjunct to the system of state regulation of vice, has actually become a part of the white-slave system.

Partly as a result of the Geneva congress of the international abolitionist society, and partly owing to the inauguration of the *Patronato Real* in Spain, a third preliminary international white-slave conference was held in Vienna in

addresses of the secretaries, will be found in Coote, *A Vision and its Fulfilment* (1911), p. 165.

[1] *Fédération Abolitionniste Internationale. Dixième Congrès tenu à Genève les 7–11 Septembre, 1908. Compte rendu des Travaux.* Geneva, 1909, 407 pp.

October, 1909, to prepare for a great international congress, to be held in Madrid in 1910. The discussions in Vienna were participated in by representatives of sixteen nations, and occupied three days,[1] incidentally giving an excellent account of what had been accomplished up to that date by the national committees.

In the following year the fourth international white-slave congress duly took place at Madrid, lasting from the 24th to the 28th of October. It was attended by official representatives of fifteen governments and by delegates from the national committees of twenty-one countries. The chief subjects that came up for discussion were the need of more effective police measures, the necessity of more uniform laws, a study of the sources of the white-slave traffic, the need of safeguarding women looking for employment, and the extension to adults of the laws governing the white-slave traffic in minors. Incidentally, the whole question of regulation came up, and a sensation was created by the announcement of Dr. Costello, the head of the special hospital in Madrid, that he had become thoroughly convinced of the inefficacy of regulation, and had become converted to the abolitionist programme.[2]

[1] *La Répression de la Traite des Blanches. Rapport Officiel de la Conférence Internationale. Tenue les 5, 6, et 7 Octobre, 1909.* Vienna, 1909, 231 pp.

[2] An account of this and similar incidents at the congress at Madrid will be found in the *Bulletin Abolitionniste* for November, 1910.

The Spanish national committee presented to the congress a volume containing a compilation of the legislation of all countries on the general question, and it was decided to hold the next international congress in London, 1913. Some of the recommendations of the Madrid congress were incorporated into the international agreement by the amendments of May, 1911, to the international white-slave treaty.

Since the great congress at Madrid, both the international association and the various committees are pursuing the subject energetically. The international association publishes a monthly devoted entirely to the subject.[1] Great activity has recently been displayed by the Austrian league whose annual reports are a model of their kind.[2] The British committee has branches in many of the large cities and possesses a considerable staff of women watchers who within the last seven years have dealt with no less than 17,550 cases.[3] The other national committees also publish annual

For a fuller report of the congress see *The Vigilance Record* for November, 1910, and *The Shield* for December, 1910.

[1] *La Traite des Blanches. Bulletin du Bureau International.* This is published in London at the same office as *The Vigilance Record* (see *supra*, p. 199).

[2] The last report, published in 1911, is entitled: *Bericht des Vereins " Oesterreichische Mädchen- und Kinderschutz Liga " (Oesterreichische Liga zur Bekämpfung des Mädchenhandels), über das Vereinsjahr 1910, und Generalversammlungs-Protokolle vom 30 Mai und 26 Juni, 1911.* Vienna, 1911, 100 pp.

[3] See the publication entitled *The White-Slave Traffic.* Published at the offices of the M. A. P. London (1909).

reports and pamphlets.[1]   The movement has spread
to South America where the Argentine *Société de
Protection et de Secours aux Femmes* is the most
prominent of the national associations.

2.   *The White-Slave Traffic in America*

In the United States the movement came a little
later.   The investigations of the Committee of
Fifteen had disclosed the existence of a similar
shameful traffic in New York City; but it was not
until 1906 that a national vigilance committee was
formed in the United States.   Mr. W. A. Coote,
who, we know, had been largely instrumental
in organising the international committees in
Europe, came to help and did much to arouse
enthusiasm in the various cities in which he spoke.
The American National Vigilance Committee now
has members in every state of the Union, with
state vigilance committees in many of the separate
commonwealths.[2]

Partly as a result of the work accomplished by

[1] *Cf., e. g.*, the French *Association pour la Répression de la Traite des
Blanches et de la Préservation de la Jeune Fille.   Assemblée Générale du
13 Juin, 1911.*   Paris, 1911.

[2] The National Vigilance Committee publishes a monthly called, since
1910, *Vigilance*, which gives an account of the progress of the movement throughout the country and in Europe.   It is on the whole a
more valuable periodical than the English *Vigilance Record*.   Early in
1912 the committee was reorganised under the name of the American
Vigilance Association with Dr. David Starr Jordan as president and
Mr. Clifford G. Roe as executive secretary.

this committee, the national government decided to join the international union, and on June 6, 1908, President Roosevelt issued a proclamation declaring the adhesion of the United States to the white-slave treaty. Since that time the work of breaking up the white-slave traffic has been actively pursued by both national and state governments, the federal government seeking to look after the immigrants, and the separate states dealing with the internal or domestic traffic. Federal legislation began with the Howard-Bennett Act of 1907, but more effective laws were due in large measure to the investigations instituted by the commissioner-general of immigration, as well as to the reports of the state immigration commission of New York and of the federal immigration commission. The preliminary report of the federal commission in 1909 discloses, in some detail, the existence of this nefarious traffic.[1]

The national immigration act of 1908 sought to provide for adequate punishment of the malefactors, and in the successive reports of the commissioner-general of immigration will be found a full discussion of the progress made each year. Since the decision, in 1909, by the

[1] See *Immigration Report. Importing Women for Immoral Purposes. A Partial Report to Congress on the Importation and Harboring of Women for Immoral Purposes.* Senate Document 196, 61st Congress, 2d Session, 61 pp.

United States supreme court in the Keller case[1]
which declared certain sections of the federal
immigration law unconstitutional, as infringing
on the reserved rights of the states, it became
necessary to connect any person whom it was
proposed to punish under the national law for
harbouring and concealing in houses of ill-fame
with the actual importation. As this, however,
was almost impossible to prove in most cases,
an effective co-operation on the part of the
separate states has become indispensable. The
federal government attempted to remedy the
weakness of the act of 1908 by enacting in 1910
a new and comprehensive law known as the White-
Slave Traffic act, or Mann act, which regulates
not only foreign traffic in women, but interstate
traffic as well.[2] Under this law successful prosecution has become possible.

A notable advance, however, has more recently
been made in the separate states. In each of
the last three years, ten or fifteen states have
enacted stringent laws designed to cope with the
evil, so that to-day the great majority of the states
have fairly satisfactory laws on the subject. Illinois was the first state to pass (in July, 1908)
the so-called "pandering law," and under this

[1] 213 U. S., 138.
[2] The exact title of the law of June 25, 1910, is "An Act to further
regulate interstate and foreign commerce by prohibiting the transportation thereunder for immoral purposes of women and girls and for
other purposes."

14

act, as amended later, considerable progress has been made in bringing the malefactors to the bar. In Chicago, for example, where Mr. E. W. Sims, the federal district attorney, took up in 1908 the policy initiated two years before by Mr. Clifford G. Roe, an assistant state district attorney, the latter was now put in charge of a special fund provided by public-spirited citizens, and met with remarkable success in prosecuting offenders. The other states followed rapidly with their pandering laws and many convictions have been secured and many organised gangs of traders broken up.[1]

In New York City the matter has recently been brought to a head by the swearing in, on January, 1910, of a special grand jury, charged to investigate the alleged existence in New York of such organised traffic. Additional interest was lent to the matter by the fact that Mr. John D. Rockefeller, Jr., was selected as foreman. For six months this jury made a careful study of existing conditions and employed various agents through the district

[1] A good account of the whole subject will be found in *The White-Slave Traffic in America*, by O. Edward Janney, New York, 1911. Of less value although containing some useful information, is *The Great War on White Slavery; Horrors of the White-Slave Traffic*, by Clifford G. Roe, Chicago, 1911. The same work was later issued, without illustrations, under the title, *The Prodigal Daughter: The White-Slave Evil and the Remedy*. An earlier work by Mr. Roe is *Panders and their White Slaves*. An admirable treatment of the subject will be found in a series of articles by Miss Jane Addams in *McClure's Magazine*, beginning with November, 1911, entitled "A New Conscience and an Ancient Evil." This is to be published as a book in 1912.

attorney's office, for the detection of crime, a special appropriation of \$25,000 having been made by the board of estimate and apportionment to cover the expenses of the investigation. The jury rendered its presentment in June, 1910.[1] They reported that while they had not been able to find any evidence of organisations engaged in the traffic, they had discovered "that a trafficking in the bodies of women does exist and is carried on by individuals acting for their own individual benefit, and that these persons are known to each other and are more or less informally associated."

The grand jury further reported that they also found that associations and clubs, composed mainly or wholly of those profiting from vice, have existed, and that one such association still exists. These associations and clubs are analogous to commercial bodies in other fields, which, while not directly engaged in commerce, are composed of individuals all of whom as individuals are so engaged. The grand jury also declared that the "incorporated syndicates" and "international bands" referred to in published statements are really more or less informal relations, and that the "international headquarters," "clearing-houses," and pretentious "club-houses" often spoken of

[1] *White-Slave Traffic. Presentment of the Additional Grand Jury for the January Term of the Court of Special Sessions in the County of New York, as to the Alleged Existence in the County of New York of an Organised Traffic in Women for Immoral Purposes. Filed June 29, 1910.*—New York, 1910, 16 pp.

are in reality cafés or other so-called "hangouts" where people interested in the various branches of the business resort. These and the houses of prostitution are also referred to as "markets." In the language of the New York market, the "dealers" and "operators" are the so-called "pimps" and "procurers," the "pimp" being referred to as the "retailer" and the manager of houses as the "wholesaler."

After a significant and thorough discussion of the subject, the grand jury made the following recommendations:

1. That no effort be spared in bringing to justice the so-called "pimp." When the character and prevalence of these creatures are more fully realised and public sentiment aroused regarding them, the inadequate punishment now imposed should be increased and every legitimate means devised and put into execution to exterminate them.

2. That the existing laws be more rigidly enforced to safeguard the patrons of the moving-picture shows, and that parents and guardians exercise more careful supervision over their children in connection with their attendance upon these shows.

3. That vigorous efforts be made to minimise the possibility of the Raines-Law hotel becoming a disorderly house, and that where necessary proper supervision and inspection looking toward that end be provided.

4. That the so-called massage and manicure parlours be put under the control of the Health Department; that a license from this department be required for their operation; that certificates be granted to operators only by some approved medical authority, and that proper measures be taken to enforce these laws.

5. That the laws relating to prostitution in apartment and tenement houses be rigidly enforced, and that the present laws be supplemented if necessary.

6. That a commission be appointed by the mayor to make a careful study of the laws relating to, and the methods of dealing with, the social evil in the leading cities of this country and of Europe, with a view to devising the most effective means of minimising the evil in this city.

In line with the last recommendation in the presentment, the mayor asked the foreman of the grand jury to suggest suitable commissioners, although expressing doubt as to the wisdom of appointing such a commission. For a number of months the foreman, Mr. Rockefeller, devoted himself to the study of the field for such a commission, having personal conferences with numerous representative men and women in the city in all walks of life. The result, however, was to the effect that an unofficial rather than an official organisation seemed desirable. This view was presented to the mayor, who cordially agreed with the conclusions reached. It was clear to those who had studied the problem that two things were necessary to the success of any movement looking towards the reduction of commercialised vice:

1. That the warfare against evil-doers should be permanent—that is, that the organisation taking up the work should be a permanent rather than a temporary one.

2. That the work in its initial and experimental stages should be carried on entirely apart from publicity; that it should begin in a small way and develop as the problem was grasped and as wise methods of attack presented themselves.

It is understood that a small and informal committee has been formed, which is to be the nucleus of a permanent organisation, the purpose of which is to deal eventually with the larger question involved, the committee addressing itself for the present to a careful study of the problem and the working out of wise lines of attack.

In the light of what has been stated in the preceding pages, it is clear that public opinion throughout the United States is now gradually being aroused to the enormities of this infamous traffic, and that during the next few years we may expect to see a decided progress made in the checking of what has become the most shameful species of business enterprise in modern times.

CHAPTER III

THE immediate results of the work of the Committee of Fifteen have been recounted above in the preceding portions of this book. Having accomplished its chief object, in part at least, and for the time being, the committee dissolved. But it was not long before the need was felt for taking up the work anew along several different lines. The three chief manifestations of this newer movement were: The inauguration of the Committee of Fourteen; the formation of the American Society of Sanitary and Moral Prophylaxis, followed by similar societies elsewhere; and the creation of vice commissions in several cities, notably Chicago and Minneapolis.

We shall deal with each of these in order.

1. *The Committee of Fourteen*

In its original report the Committee of Fifteen had called especial attention to the evils connected with the Raines-Law hotels. As these evils seemed to increase rather than diminish, a committee of fourteen citizens of New York was organised in 1905, for the express purpose of suppressing these hotels. The committee included in its membership a few of the old Committee of Fifteen, as well as the widow of its lamented chairman, who had in the meantime passed away. It was soon recognised, however, that many other evils were connected with the existing laws. Accordingly a sub-committee was created in 1907, for the closer investigation of these other phases of the social evil, and before long assumed the name of the Research Committee of the Committee of Fourteen. Its first work was to investigate the relation of the magistrates' courts to the women of the street in New York City, and also the disposition of disorderly-house cases of all kinds, and in the care of special associations. This report was submitted to Governor Hughes, and had no little influence in the creation of the Page commission (so-called from its chairman, Mr. Alfred R. Page), formed to investigate the courts of minor criminal jurisdiction in New York.

The report[1] of that commission resulted in the passage of the famous Page law,[2] which revolutionised the procedure in the New York city magis-

[1] *Final Report of the Commission to inquire into Courts of Inferior Criminal Jurisdiction in Cities of the First Class*, Albany, 1910, pp. 81. The proceedings were published in 1909 in two thick volumes.

[2] Act of June 25, 1910, ch. 659, with short title: "Inferior Criminal Courts Act of the City of New York."

trates' courts and which introduced a host of other beneficent changes. In the meantime the research committee had begun in 1908 their larger investigation into the administration of all the laws which had any direct reference to the social evil and after two years of close investigation published their report in 1910.[1]

As the report was confined to the problem of law enforcement, the committee did not attempt to ascertain the causes of the extent of the social evil, or to deal with the various systems of regulation, or with the arguments for or against its existence. They limited their efforts to the study of each particular law, and to a presentation of so much of the prevailing conditions as might fairly represent the effectiveness of the law. The report classified the laws into seven groups, according as they affected the following points:

1. Social conditions, embracing the places where prostitution is carried on or facilitated, such as tenement houses, disorderly houses, Raines-Law hotels, and dance halls.

2. The protection of women, covering such topics as seduction under promise of marriage, compulsory marriage, compulsory prostitution of wives, vagrancy, and disorderly conduct.

3. The modification of penalties and procedure

[1] *The Social Evil in New York City: A Study of Law Enforcement by the Research Committee of the Committee of Fourteen.* New York, 1910, pp. 268.

in the attempt to better the conditions of the unfortunate women. Under this head special attention was paid to prohibition laws and to the night courts.

4. Special education, especially the matters connected with obscene prints and articles, the display of immoral pictures, and the presentation of immoral plays and exhibitions.

5. The protection of the family. Under this head fell the laws connected with marriage licenses, false personation, adultery, abortion, and midwifery.

6. The protection of children, more especially the problems of rape, of abduction, of kidnapping, of child labour, and the children's court.

7. The protection of those seeking work, covering investigation of the employment agencies.

On each of those points the committee presented a mass of information which it would be hopeless to attempt to summarise here. The conclusion to which the committee came was that the social evil in New York City is an elaborate system systematically fostered by business interests rather than a consequence of emotional demand. What reformers have to deal with, they tell us, is not simply vice as such, but vice as a business conducted for profit, with various beneficiaries in all walks of life. The committee understated rather than overstated the evils of the situation, and rigidly eliminated from the report all sensational matter.

The committee tell us that they began the investigation with the expectation of finding the laws fairly well-enforced.   They declare that the truth has been a painful surprise, but that nevertheless, sombre as is the picture, it is not without hopeful features; that the first step toward improvement cannot be taken until existing conditions are fully realised.   They put the main emphasis, however, not upon the enactment of new laws, but upon the enforcement of existing laws, which in itself would bring about a notable improvement.   "It is entirely possible for public opinion to demand and secure the appointment of officials who shall be free from political and financial influence, and who shall administer the laws with intelligence and even-handed justice.   It is entirely possible directly to rid our streets and tenements of the social evil; possible to force its withdrawal from the conspicuous place which it occupies in the community to-day; possible to surround with wholesome influences the places to which young people go for innocent amusement, and to separate them from association with the liquor traffic and the social evil; possible to protect our children, by enforcement of the child-labour, education, and similar laws, from daily exposure to the moral contamination to which many of them are subjected; possible to hunt to their undoing the unscrupulous or indifferent business interests which profit from the exploitation of vice, unwitting that their cupidity is a baser sin than the lust on which it profits."

As a result of the careful investigation, the committee made the following recommendations:

1. The appointment of a non-salaried commission to make a further study of the problem, to look after the enforcement of existing laws, and to recommend changes whenever desirable.

2. A change in the attitude of the magistrates, and an improvement in their personnel.

3. Instead of punishment for the unfortunate women, the weight of public opinion should be brought to bear upon the profit-sharers—the men higher up.

4. The separation of recreation from vice.

5. Co-operation between the officials charged with the enforcement of the various laws.

6. The burden of punishment should not fall alone upon women.

7. The development of local improvement boards.

8. The abolition of the system of fine for repeated offences and the establishment of accurate records and means of identification.

9. The publication in code form of all the laws governing the social evil and a digest of the decisions.

The chief results of the work of the Committee

of Fourteen, outside of the impetus given to the movement which resulted in the passage of the Page law, have been some notable improvements in the New York excise law, and more efficient administration of the laws, not only by the state excise department but by the local authorities, such as the courts, the district attorney, and the police. In 1905, there were over twelve hundred Raines-Law hotels in Manhattan and the Bronx; in 1911, this number has been reduced to 87—a remarkable showing. This result could not have been attained without the co-operation of the brewers and of the surety companies writing excise bonds, without which no hotel can secure a license.

The programme of the committee for the immediate future is declared to be as follows: constant supervision of probationary places to maintain proper conditions; active efforts to secure improved conditions in saloons and hotels through the co-operation of the brewers; aggressive fighting of the incorrigibly bad places; effective opposition to any attempt to weaken the restrictive sections of the excise law; cordial co-operation with other organisations to secure a broad and effective movement against all phases of commercialised sexual vice; and extension of the work to the Bronx and Brooklyn, where conditions, however, have been shown to be different from Manhattan, in that there is much less commercialism.

2.   The Societies Formed to Combat the Social Evil

A few months after the institution of the Committee of Fifteen the New York Medical Society
appointed a committee to study measures to
reduce the spread of venereal deseases.   The
chairman of this committee was Dr. Prince A.
Morrow, a distinguished specialist who had been a
delegate to the international Brussels conference.
The committee became known as the Committee
of Seven and its report,[1] which for the first time
in America gathered statistics on the subject,
attracted great attention, but chiefly among physicians.   On May 23, 1904, however, Dr. Morrow
read a paper in which he advanced the proposition
to form in this country a society of sanitary and
moral prophylaxis, similar to those abroad.   The
facts to which attention was especially invited
were the following[2]:

1.   The enormous prevalence of the venereal
diseases, and their significance as a danger to
public health.   It was declared to be a conservative
estimate that fully one-eighth of all diseases and
suffering are due to this source, and that the incidence of the diseases falls most heavily upon

[1] *Report of the Committee of Seven on the Prophylaxis of Venereal Disease in New York City.*   By the chairman.   Reprinted from the
Medical News, Dec. 21, 1901.

[2] *Cf.* the pamphlet entitled *Society of Sanitary and Moral Prophylaxis:
Origin of this Movement.   Its Objects, Means, and Methods of Work.*
By Prince A. Morrow, M.D.   New York, 1908.

the young, during the most active and productive period of life.

2. Dangers to the innocent members of society. Of the large proportion of men who contract such diseases, many of them carry this infection into the family. It was stated that eighty per cent. of the deaths from inflammatory diseases peculiar to women, seventy-five per cent. of all special surgical operations performed on women, and over sixty per cent. of all the work done by specialists in diseases of women are the result of infection of innocent women. Moreover, fifty per cent. or more of these infected women are rendered irremediably sterile, and many are condemned to life-long invalidism.

3. Dangers to the offspring. Fully eighty per cent. of the ophthalmia which blots out the eyes of babies, and twenty to twenty-five per cent. of all blindness, are caused by what is known as gonococcus infection. Sixty to eighty per cent. of infected children die before being born, or come into the world with the mark of death upon them. Those that finally survive—one in four or five—are the subjects of degenerative changes and organic defects, which may be transmitted to the third generation. It is for this reason that these diseases have sometimes been designated in recent years as "the great black plague" whose ravages have always been covered up and concealed from the public.

4. The economic significance of the fact that these diseases constitute the most potent factor in the causation of blindness, deaf-mutism, idiocy, insanity, paralysis, locomotor ataxia, and other incurable afflictions that impose an enormous charge upon the community.

5. Relation to tuberculosis. It is well recognised by the medical profession that venereal diseases, by lowering the vitality and weakening resistance, produce a condition favourable to the development of tuberculosis. Until the spread of syphilis is effectively checked, the fight against tuberculosis will be but partially successful.

The founders of the movement declared that the most lamentable fact about the whole situation is the ignorance of the general public. An essential part of the society's programme, therefore, was destined to be educational in character, and this education was to embrace the following factors:

First, the general dissemination of knowledge among the public, in a proper and discreet manner, of the extent and danger of these diseases, and their modes of contagion, direct and indirect.

Secondly, the enlightenment of the public respecting the social danger of these diseases, especially to the innocent members of society, through their introduction into marriage.

Thirdly, the education of young people in a knowledge of their physical selves, and of the laws and hygiene of sex.

The invitations found a ready response, especially as Dr. Morrow had in the meantime published his admirable work *Social Diseases and Marriage*, written to create a professional sentiment in favour of the movement.   In this it succeeded beyond expectation, and in the beginning of 1905 the American Society of Social and Moral Prophylaxis came into existence, with several members of the old Committee of Fifteen on its governing board and in the membership lists.   The society held frequent meetings, at which all manner of topics connected with the general subject were discussed, on the basis of scientific investigation and accurate presentation.   In this way the end was attained of gradually accustoming the public to a discussion of the topic which had been so long tabooed.   Most of the papers presented dealt with the problem of preventive medicine, chiefly in its educational aspects.   The educational work of the society consisted of public meetings and conferences, of lectures, and of the circulation of educational literature and pamphlets.   The public meetings and conferences were reported in volumes of transactions published every two years, forming a valuable arsenal of facts and a well-digested set of conclusions.[1]

---

[1] *Transactions of the American Society of Sanitary and Moral Prophylaxis*.   Vol. i., 1906, 166 pp.; vol. ii., 1908, 246 pp.; vol. iii., 1910, 211 pp. The office of the Secretary is at 29 West 42d Street, New York City.

The efforts connected with educational literature consisted largely of the preparation and dissemination of the so-called "educational pamphlets." Some of these have been distributed by the tens of thousands and constitute in many respects the best available literature on the subject that is to be found in English.[1] In fact, one notable feature of the work accomplished by the New York society has been the accustoming of the public to the discussion of these topics. As the president of the society has said: "The real difficulty is that we have been unable to reach the great masses of the public to any effective extent. The public press and periodicals which serve for the enlightenment of the masses, and which have rendered such signal service in the campaign against tuberculosis and other infectious diseases through the popularising of hygienic knowledge, are absolutely barred to the mention even of the diseases which we wish to prevent. I believe that with publicity for a fulcrum we have in our facts a sufficiently strong lever to move the world. . . . Once the crust of conventional prejudice is broken by a courageous

[1] The educational pamphlets are as follows:

1. *The Young Man's Problem*, 32 pp. 2. *Instruction in Physiology and Hygiene of Sex*, 24 pp. 3. *The Relations of Social Diseases with Marriage and their Prophylaxis*, 72 pp. 4. *The Boy Problem for Parents and Teachers*, 32 pp. 5. *How my Uncle, the Doctor, Instructed me in Matters of Sex.*, 32 pp. 6. *Health and the Hygiene of Sex, for College Students*, 32 pp. 7. *Sex Instruction for Little Girls* (in preparation). 8. *Instruction for 'Unprotected Young Women* (in preparation).

leader, there is no doubt that other progressive periodicals will fall into line."[1]

Not only has the society had some measure of success in accomplishing this end, but it has prepared the way for the construction in New York of a large special hospital for venereal patients, and it has given considerable strength to the movement for securing a national census of venereal morbidity and mortality in the United States.

It was not long before branches of the American Society, or associations with similar aims and purposes, were started. Beginning in the year 1906, and rapidly following in the succeeding years, such societies were formed in Syracuse, Buffalo, Baltimore, Philadelphia, St. Louis, Hartford, Milwaukee, Detroit, Oakland, Denver, Chicago, Indianapolis, Portland (Ore.), Spokane, Elkins (W. Va.), San Antonio, Providence, Seattle, and East Orange.[2] Of these eighteen societies one-half (California, Colorado, Connecticut, Indiana, Maryland, New Jersey, Rhode Island, Texas, and West Virginia) are state, the

[1] *Social Diseases*, January 1910, p. 11.   The hope here expressed has been in part realised by the appearance of the articles on the subject by Miss Jane Addams, mentioned above on p. 210.

[2] There is also a society in the city of Mexico.   The names of these societies vary slightly, including such differences as: Society for the Prevention of Social Diseases, Society of Social Hygiene, Society of Sex Hygiene, Society of Sanitary and Moral Education, Society of Social and Moral Hygiene, Society for the Study and Prevention of Gonorrhœa and Syphilis, Sanitary Association and Society for Social Health.

remainder local associations. Many of these societies publish literature of their own, and are aiding materially in spreading a knowledge of the movement throughout the country, co-operating also with the vigilance committees mentioned in the preceding chapter and designed to suppress the white-slave traffic.[1] In several states, notably California, Florida, Idaho, Indiana, Iowa, Kentucky, Michigan, Ohio, North Dakota, and Rhode Island, the state board of health has been induced to take up the matter and spread broadcast suitable literature.[2]

At the beginning of the year 1910, the interest in the subject had become so great that a general demand arose for a bulletin or journal to serve as the official organ of the various societies throughout this country. In order to satisfy this demand, a quarterly periodical was started, entitled *Social*

[1] *Cf.* especially the publications of the Chicago and Spokane societies, of which the most important have been: (1) *Sexual Hygiene for Young Men;* (2) *Family Protection;* (3) *Community Protection;* (4) *Comments on the Aims and Efforts of the Society of Social Hygiene.*

[2] Among such information are the following sex hygiene circulars, issued by the Rhode Island state board of health: (1) *For Young Men;* (2) *Information for Persons having Syphilitic and Gonorrhœal Diseases;* (3) *Infection for Young Women; Ophthalmia Neonatorum: Preventive Treatment, Suggestions, and Treatment of the Disease. Cf.* also the excellent health circular issued by the Indiana state board of health: *Social Hygiene vs. The Sexual Plagues, with their Rapid Invasion of the American Home; The Horrible Consequences of Sex Secrecy and the Obligation of Parents in the State to Protect the Rising Generation.* Indianapolis (1910), 38 pp.

Diseases: Report of the Progress of the Movement for their Prevention. This did its work so well that in June of the same year a meeting of the delegates from the various societies was held in St. Louis, and a national organisation was formed under the name of the American Federation for Sex Hygiene. The purpose of this federation was declared to be the education of the public in the physiology and hygiene of the sex, and the study and application of every means—educational, sanitary, moral, and legislative—for the prevention of syphilis and of gonococcus infection. Dr. Morrow was elected president, and emeritus president Eliot of Harvard University was made honorary president, with a distinguished list of vice-presidents of national reputation. The following resolutions offered by a noted physician were adopted for presentation to the American Medical Association, with the request that they be accepted as the public attitude of that body also:

"*Whereas*, there is ample evidence of a belief, deeply grounded, among the laity, that sexual indulgence is necessary to the health of the normal man: and,

"*Whereas*, there exists, in consequence, widely differing and double standards of moral and of physical health for the male and female sexes, that lead directly to the disease and death of many women and children:

"*Be it resolved*, that the American Medical

Association, through its House of Delegates, hereby presents for the instruction and protection of the lay public the unqualified declaration that illicit sexual intercourse is not only unnecessary to health, but that its direct consequence in terms of infectious disease constitutes a grave menace to the physical integrity of the individual and the nation."

The objects of the national society are, therefore, primarily educational. That there is need of this can scarcely be doubted. We are told that, in consequence of the awakening of public interest in the sex problem, a deluge of so-called sex books is now flooding the country—a few of them good, more of them indifferent, and most of them positively bad. This multiplication of harmful literature constitutes a real danger. It is important to separate the wheat from the chaff—to recommend what is good and to condemn what is bad. Furthermore, many persons have entered the lecture field who are not qualified by either knowledge or experience to undertake this difficult and delicate work, and who by their injudicious utterances offend rather than educate the public. Another danger, we are told, consists in the precipitancy and haste with which the introduction of sex instruction in the public schools has been urged by many who do not fully appreciate the difficulties. As a matter of fact, there is at present an utter lack of preparation on the part of teachers, and also a want of elementary text-books. What the new society has primarily in view is the organisation of an influential central body, composed of wise and experienced educators, who shall co-ordinate and standardise the work of sex instruction, formulate the matter and method of this instruction, prepare suitable text-books, and establish special courses for the education of teachers for this delicate and difficult task.[1]

The formation of the national society will probably form a turning point in the history of the whole movement in America.

3. *The Page Law in New York and the Vice Commissions in Chicago and Minneapolis*

The years 1910–11 have witnessed the culmination of the new interest in the general problem as manifested not only in the formation of the national society, but in the defeat of the attempt to introduce the beginnings of reglementation in New York City, and in the remarkable reports of the Chicago and Minneapolis commissions.

The discussion as to the best methods of dealing with the social evil as a whole was precipitated in an acute form in New York City by the controversy over the famous section 79 of the Page law. The Page law, to which reference has already been

[1] *Social Diseases*, July, 1911, p. 2.

made above,[1] was admirable in almost all its features. It included, however, one section which had been slipped into it without adequate discussion, largely through the efforts of a New York physician who had been much influenced by the German reglementists.

This section 79, it may be said in passing, was not the first attempt to introduce the state regulation of vice by law into the United States. The short-lived St. Louis experiment of 1870–74 has been touched upon above in the body of this work.[2] But it is not generally known that in 1876 a similar attempt was made in New York City. In that year the grand jury of the court of general sessions made a presentment, closing with a resolution which requested the legislature to segregate houses of ill-fame, and to subject them at all times to the careful and vigilant supervision of the boards of health and police.[3] Mrs. Josephine E. Butler happened to be in New York at the time, and at once took the lead in starting a public agitation, which culminated in the formation of the New York committee for the prevention of licensed prostitution. The activity of this society was sufficient to prevent the passage of any such law.[4]

[1] *Supra*, p. 216.   [2] *Supra*, p. 109.
[3] This presentment will be found in the *New York Evening Post* of June 2, 1876.
[4] An interesting account of the attempts made to legalise prostitution in St. Louis, New York, Philadelphia, etc., at this period will be found

In the intervening half century, up to 1910, nothing more was done until the enactment of the Page law.   Section 79 of the Page law provides for the compulsory examination of prostitutes, and their detention if found diseased, thus embodying some of the chief provisions of the French system.[1]   The law went into operation in Septem-

in Wilson and Gledstone: *Report of a Visit to the United States as Delegates from the General Federation*, etc.   Sheffield, 1876.   See also Nevins, *An Address to Members of the American Legislature.*   London, 1877. For full titles see the Bibliography.   *Cf.* also the appendix to Sanger's *History of Prostitution*, new ed., 1906.

[1] The full text of Section 79 is as follows:

" SECTION 79.   Medical Examination of Prostitutes.   On and after the first day of September, nineteen hundred and ten, any person who is a vagrant, as defined in subdivision four of section eight hundred and eighty-seven of the code of criminal procedure, or who is convicted of a violation of subdivision two of section fourteen hundred and fifty-eight of the consolidation act, or of section one hundred and fifty of the tenement-house law, shall after conviction be taken to a room adjacent to the court room, and there be physically examined by a woman physician of the department of health detailed for such purpose. After such examination the physician making the same shall promptly prepare and sign a written report to the Court of the prisoner's physical condition, and if it thereby appears that the prisoner is afflicted with any venereal disease which is contagious, infectious, or communicable, the magistrate shall commit her to a public hospital having a ward or wards for the treatment of the disease with which she is afflicted, for detention and treatment for a minimum period fixed by him in the commitment and for a maximum period of not more than one year; provided, that in case a prisoner so committed to any institution shall be cured of her venereal disease, which is contagious, infectious, or communicable, after the expiration of the minimum period and before the expiration of the maximum period for which she was committed to such institution, she shall be discharged and released from custody upon the written order of the officer in charge of the institution to which she was committed, upon the certificate of a physician of such institution or of the department of health that the prisoner is free of any venereal

ber, 1910, and at once gave rise to a spirited protest. In this movement, the Society for Social and Moral Prophylaxis took a prominent part, under the able leadership of its president, and devoted several sessions to the discussion.[1] It was at one of these sessions that the present writer, as the former secretary of the Committee of Fifteen, delivered an address, which is printed in the appendix.

Under the auspices of the Women's Prison Association and allied societies, a mass meeting of protest was held at Cooper Union on January 19, 1911, and resolutions were adopted, calling on the legislature to repeal the law, and upon the board of health to establish a method of broad treatment for venereal diseases. In the meantime, a suit had been brought to test the constitutionality of the law, and Justice Bischoff had declared section 79 unconstitutional. Pending the appeal, the enforcement of the clause was discontinued after eighty-four days of actual life. On May 1, 1911, the appellate division reversed the decision

---

disease which is contagious, infectious, or communicable. If, however, such prisoner shall be cured prior to the expiration of the minimum period for which she was committed, she shall be forthwith transferred to the workhouse and discharged at the expiration of said minimum period. Nothing herein contained shall be construed to limit the authority of a city magistrate to commit any prisoner for an indeterminate period to any institution now having authority by law to receive inmates for detention for a period of more than one year.

[1] See, especially, *Social Diseases*, October, 1910, and January, 1911. The arguments of the reglementists were marshalled by Dr. Bierhoff, in four articles in the *Medical Record* for November 12th and December 3d, 1910, and March 15th and April 1st, 1911.

of Judge Bischoff by a vote of two to one; but on June 15th of the same year the court of appeals reversed the appellate division by a vote of six to one, declaring clause 79 unconstitutional on the ground that the nature of the sentence for conviction was made to depend upon the report of a physical examination, without an opportunity for a hearing upon the facts entering into the report. Thus came to an end, probably for many years, the effort to introduce by law into any American city the European system of reglementation.

At about the same time as the passage of the Page law in New York, the subject had also come to a head in Chicago. The Chicago commission owed its origin to a meeting held by the church federation, at the beginning of the year 1910. In March of that year, the mayor appointed a so-called Vice Commission of thirty members, which undertook an exhaustive investigation into the whole problem of the social evil in Chicago, and which brought in its report a year later.[1] The report is comprehensive, and the recommendations are so numerous that they almost defy condensation. The commission found that prostitution in Chicago had become a vast commercialised business, that the present laws were

[1] *The Social Evil in Chicago: A Study of Existing Conditions with Recommendations by the Vice Commission of Chicago.* Chicago, 1911, 399 pp.

not enforced, and that there was a lamentable
ignorance of the existing conditions on the part
of the public. The body of the report contains
a disclosure of the facts as they were found to
exist; and this plain, unvarnished, sedulously
calm statement of the situation was in itself sufficient to arouse and to startle the public. The
commission unanimously concluded that the
continental system of reglementation was not to
be recommended. "One has but to read scientific
works on the subject; to study the reports of international conferences held in Europe, and to hear
the reports of careful investigators, to see the unreli-
ability and futility of such a system, and to learn
of its failure as a permanent institution wherever it
has been undertaken in this country or abroad."

The commission did not close their eyes to the
fundamental facts. "So long as there is lust in
the hearts of men," they tell us, "it will seek out
some method of expression. Until the hearts of
men are changed, we cannot hope for any absolute
annihilation of the Social Evil." They contend,
however, that the social evil, in its worst phase,
may be checked if only the public conscience can
be aroused. "We may enact laws; we may
appoint commissions; we may abuse civic administrations for their handling of the problem,
but the problem will remain just as long as the
public conscience is dead to the issue, or is indifferent to its solution "

The chief recommendation of the commission was the appointment of a morals commission and the establishment of a morals court.   From among the no less than ninety-three other recommendations, the following may be selected as the most important:

1.   The establishment of a federal bureau of immigration at Chicago and greater control of the lake steamers;

2.   The enactment of a law whereby houses of ill-fame may be declared public nuisances;

3.   The abandonment of fines and the substitution of imprisonment or the probation system;

4.   A supervision of the employment agencies;

5.   A stricter enforcement of the city ordinances governing the saloons and dance halls;

6.   The provision of more ample hospital facilities;

7.   Better statistics as to the extent of venereal diseases;

8.   A comprehensive system of education in sex;

9.   A better control of the parks and playgrounds;

10.   An industrial home for prostitutes;

11.   The separation of semi-delinquent from delinquent girls;

12.   The prohibition of women without male escorts in saloons;

13.   More homes and hotels for working girls; and

14. A curtailment of the extreme liberty given by parents to young children.

If any criticism is to be urged against the Chicago report, it is that it attempted too much To make ninety-five recommendations, with any hope of having them adopted, is to expect more than is reasonable from human nature. Greater success would probably have been achieved if the commission had contented themselves with a less ambitious programme. As a portrayal, however of existing conditions in a large city, the Chicago report will long remain unexcelled.

At the end of the same year, 1910, a similar commission was appointed in Minneapolis, and in July, 1911, its report was issued.[1] The Minneapolis commission had, naturally, a far less difficult work to perform than that of Chicago Its report is, however, more valuable than that of the Chicago commission in several respects: it is more compact; its conclusions are presented in better form; and its recommendations are based upon a comparative survey of the problem. Moreover, the report does not contain a statement of all the detailed facts upon which the conclusions were based. The commission tell us that the materials upon which the report was founded would in their opinion more fittingly adorn a safety-deposit box than a public document. The Min-

[1] *Report of the Vice Commission of Minneapolis to his Honor, James C. Haynes.* Minneapolis, 1911, 12mo, 134 pp.

neapolis commission, therefore, contented themselves with presenting their conclusions, together
with the chief reasons upon which the recommendations were founded.

It is interesting to observe that, precisely as
in the case of the Committee of Fifteen,[1] the
great majority of the Minneapolis commission
were, at the outset, in favour of some system of
regulation or segregation, and that at the conclusion of this study they came unanimously to
the opposite opinion. We are told that, "the
chairman himself has yielded the theory which he
held on becoming a member of this committee,
to the overwhelming mass of evidence which he
discovered against it."[2]   The commission report
that "legalising and licensing prostitution is a
method foreign to the sentiment and feelings
of the American people and repugnant to their
high moral sense," and they call attention to
the fact that the system has actually broken
down throughout Europe. With reference to
segregation—which, as they point out, contrary to
ordinary opinion, is not the usual practice in
Europe, but is found in only a very few cities—the
commission maintain that segregation does not
segregate, and that it complicates rather than
simplifies the problem for the police.

The chief recommendations of the commission
are the policy of strict law enforcement and of

[1] See below, page 247.   [2] *Report*, p. 107.

increased police vigilance under existing ordinances. But they also lay stress upon remedial and preventive measures. Among these are more adequate hospital facilities, and improvements in sex education, in recreation facilities, in economic conditions, and in provision for institutional care. They approve, finally, a recommendation for a permanent commission whose immediate functions shall be to assist in carrying out the policy of suppressing the social evil and of attacking its causes.

Taking them together, the reports of the Chicago and Minneapolis commissions are so exhaustive, so sensible, and so stimulating that they may well serve as models to the other American cities. That they agree in the main with the conclusions formulated by the Committee of Fifteen in 1902, recited in the earlier part of this book, is a subject of no little congratulation.

While it is a cheering evidence of the times that expert opinion in the United States, like that in Europe, is tending in the same direction, actual practice, as is to be expected, has not made the same progress. The conditions of police control of the social evil in the American cities at present vary widely, and in but few of them has the modern or constructive point of view been adopted. A recent census of seventy-two of the leading cities in this country has disclosed the fact that while there is no legal licensing of prostitution in any of the cities, it exists, in fact, in two, namely Atlantic City and Cheyenne.[1] In those two cities there is segregation of prostitution, medical examination, and a system of fines for houses of ill-fame and their inmates. In thirty-two of the cities, the police declare there is a system of regulation, by which fact, however, is simply meant that the police take an active part in dealing with the problem. In thirty-three of the cities the policy of segregation is followed, while in most of the others that policy has been abandoned as unsuccessful. In this respect, the recent experience of Winnipeg, Canada, is noteworthy. An earlier experiment had failed and had been abandoned. In 1909, the scheme was again introduced, but we are told that "the grave abuses, the flaunting of vice, the demoralising influence on childhood and youth, the exhibitions of obscenity and bestiality" led to such an outbreak of public criticism as to result in the appointment of a commission and the final abandonment of the whole policy.

Interesting in this respect also, as indicating the trend of American legislation, is the passage in 1909 of the "Injunction and Abatement Law" in Iowa. This is definitely opposed to the policy of segregation, and declares a house of ill-fame to be a public nuisance.

[1] A circular containing eleven questions was sent by the National Vigilance Committee to seventy-two cities, and the answers are given in detail in *Vigilance* for May, 1911.

The director of the department of public safety in Des Moines has recently called attention to the fact that the success of the law has been such as to convert those who had previously upheld the policy of segregation. A similar law is now in force in Nebraska.

It is unfortunately true that the heads of police not infrequently proclaim segregation as a panacea. Even so admirable a man as the late head of the police force of New York has advanced this idea.[1] Such a position, however, is not only indefensible in the light of both American and European experience, but is abandoned by the most discerning police officials themselves. In a recent interesting document issued by the police commissioner of Boston, Mr. Stephen O'Meara, we find, for instance, the following passage[2]:

"Total extinction of public and semi-public sexual immorality in a city of the size of Boston cannot be hoped for, can hardly be imagined; but effectual restraint can be applied. I do not mean restraint by license, as practised in the cities of other continents the world over, and as tried at times in this country; and neither do I mean the restraint common to almost all cities of the

[1] *The Girl that Disappears*, by Theodore A. Bingham, New York, 1911.
[2] *Police Department of the City of Boston: A Record of the Enforcement of the Laws against Sexual Immorality since December 1, 1909, as contained in the Information relating thereto embodied in the Reports to the Governor of Massachusetts, made annually by the Police Commissioner of the City of Boston.* Boston, n. d. (1911), 50 pp.

United States with populations large enough to raise the question—the restraint which attempts to confine vice to particular localities, which says to brothel keepers that within territories bounded by certain streets they may carry on their business untroubled, or at worst with no greater inconvenience than a fine imposed with such regularity and moderation as to become practically a license fee; which guarantees prostitutes in houses or out of doors within designated sections against the danger of prosecution; which assures licentious men that for breaches of the law committed within certain territorial limits there is neither punishment nor exposure.

"Restraint by license is a surrender to vice under authority of law; restraint by segregation is a compromise with vice, illegally made, and a nullification of laws by public officers appointed to enforce them. Either license or segregation condemns whole neighbourhoods, in which the vicious are but a minority, to the common brand of infamy, and fails, nevertheless, to save other neighbourhoods from incursions of vice.

"When I speak of restraint, therefore, I mean the restraint which is founded on the effective laws, the vigilant performance of police duty, and that responsive action by courts and juries without which both laws and police are powerless."

After giving a detailed account of what the department has been attempting to accomplish, the police commissioner closes with a paragraph which shows with remarkable clearness the difficulties of the problem:

"The Police Department regards the business of vice as a social tragedy, which has gone on from the beginning and presumably will go on to the end; but police action against it is confined, of necessity, to the attempted enforcement of the laws. The police have no other mission or authority. But the efforts to reduce the profits of the business, to secure the adequate punishment of those who engage in it and thus check its growth, have met with practically no helpful or appreciative response from any direction. If a future police commissioner were intending to pursue the same course with respect to the business of vice that has been followed for four years I should advise him that he might expect loyal support from the police when once he has convinced them that he was in earnest; little encouragement from courts; bitter hostility from persons whose profits were curtailed; indifference from the public; and from a few enthusiasts in the cause of social purity whose admirable purposes are not sustained by straight and intelligent thinking, he would be sure to receive some measure of abusive criticism. I should advise him that unless he held his oath of office in high regard, and cared for no reward other than the consciousness that he had done his duty faithfully, and with some benefit to the community, it would be better for him personally that he should follow the easy road of indifference, which is always chosen by those who are officially blind." [1]

It is the public indifference, referred to by the police commissioner, that is really at the root of the problem. The secret of all the efforts that have been recounted in the preceding pages is to overcome and to break down this public indifference. With publicity, with awakening interest, and with the determination to do what is at once right and practicable, the first steps in the solution of the problem will have been taken. At no time in the history of the world has the outlook for such progress been so bright as it is at present.

[1] *A Record*, etc., pp. 49–50.

APPENDIX

THE SANITARY SUPERVISION OF PROSTITUTION.   AN ADDRESS ON SECTION 79 OF THE PAGE LAW [1]

WHEN your President asked me to appear before this Society, I told him that I should not have time to prepare a set paper, but that, as the result of my efforts in connection with the Committee of Fifteen some years ago, I had formed certain opinions which reflection has confirmed, and that I should be glad to say a few words on the subject to-night.

As I take it, in such a question as this, where good men differ so fundamentally—and good women too—it is perhaps wise to approach the subject from a somewhat broader point of view.   Some who are in favour of section 79 of the Page law support it frankly and avowedly as the first step—as an entering wedge to some system of reglementation.   If I am not mistaken, the gentleman who addressed the Society at its last meeting, Dr. Bierhoff, quite openly stated that this was his opinion.   On the other hand, others like Mr. Homer Folks, and perhaps Mr. Mayer, desire to draw a sharp line between reglementation or regulation on the one hand, and the Page law on the other.   In the first part of my remarks, therefore, I shall address myself to those who in one way or another favour reglementation; and, secondly, I shall speak to those who, while theoretically opposed to regulation, are nevertheless in favour of the Page law.

[1] This address was delivered by the author at a meeting of the Society of Sanitary and Moral Prophylaxis, on December 22, 1910.

This is not the place to call your attention to the historical aspects of the subject. There is only one point I should like to emphasise, as leading up to the position which I take— and, I may say in this respect, it is the position which, so far as I know, is taken to-day by all the surviving members of the Committee of Fifteen. It is a remarkable fact, that when we came together to investigate the problem, knowing very little about it—just about as much or as little as does the ordinary man or woman,—the great majority of us were in favour of regulation on the principle that it could do no harm and might do some good. It was only after a prolonged study of the situation as regards both the facts and the general principles involved, that the committee came unanimously to the conclusion that regulation or reglementation was inadvisable and inadmissible. Let me then devote a few remarks to an endeavour to point out why we came to that conclusion; for the arguments that held then would hold with most of us to-day.

The method used in ancient times in dealing with this subject was to regard it from the religious, or political, or even the fiscal point of view. We all know that prostitution was subject to various forms of regulation in Greek and Roman times, and that it was made subservient to the political ends just as was the marriage relation itself; and we know, furthermore, that the government in many cases secured large revenues from the quasi-religious organisations under whose ægis these practices were carried on. In the Middle Ages the situation was entirely different. Partly as a result of the Christian doctrine, but chiefly under the influence of the newer civilisation of Germanic type as against the old Romanic type, an effort was made to repress this hideous evil as far as possible. It is only with the spread of commerce and industry in the twelfth and thirteenth centuries that we find in the various Italian,

German, and French towns a different attitude taken to it. It was then that the importance of the earlier religious objections diminished, and these unfortunate women were formed into guilds, very much like the other classes of artisans and craftsmen in those days, whose organisations were made to minister to the fancied ends of the communal welfare. Only the other day I was reading in a work on Japan that, in one of the inland towns, they have every five years a great civic procession, headed by all the loose women of the town garbed in beautiful costumes, and every man, woman, and child goes out to see the spectacle. How many realise that this was an early quasi-religious custom throughout Europe? It was a feudal idea which gave rise to this custom in Europe, just as it is a survival of feudalism which explains its continuance in Japan to-day. It does not argue that the Japanese are less good or less wise than we, but simply that they still have survivals of a feudal civilisation which with us has passed away. In so far as any effort was made by mediæval governments to regulate the institution, it was chiefly to maintain public order. Only after the outbreak of the syphilitic scourge in the sixteenth and seventeenth centuries throughout all the European countries was a different attitude assumed.

In modern times, however, has come the evolution of the true democratic and social way of regarding the problem; and the modern way of looking at the problem differs from the mediæval in three respects:

First, in former times the loose women were treated as outcasts and aliens and they were compelled to wear a different garb or costume. Now, with the economic development of modern times, we have gotten over the idea of the alien character of these women, and with the growth of the democratic spirit we feel that they are with us and of us. They may form a separate class, indeed, we may pity them or hold them in contempt, but in the larger sense they are a part of us.

The second distinction is the emergence of the ethical or moral ideal. This had never—or almost never—been realised before. Nowadays every one feels that whatever may be the method of dealing with these unfortunates, any scheme which has not directly or indirectly, purposely or incidentally, a moral connotation, is bound to fail.

Third, above all, with the growth of modern medicine and modern science, we have learned to emphasise the sanitary aspect of the problem. In fact, this is the one which really confronts us at present. By regulation in modern times, we mean sanitary regulation, and this brings us to the objections to the system of reglementation as a whole. These may be summed up as follows:

In the first place, there is always a conflict between sanitary and moral ends. I do not mean to say that sanitary precautions may not go hand in hand with ethical ends, and that certain moral ends may not also involve sanitary precautions; but in these points of contact there is apt to be far less of harmony than of conflict. We find a difference of opinion, for instance, between the doctors' point of view and that of the police. This has been brought out fully in the history of the Parisian, the Viennese, and the German systems; and you all see, of course, why it should be so. The sanitary point of view does not look at all to the chances of reformation. The moral point of view always holds up, as an ideal, at least, the opportunity for reformation—that those women who really are unfortunate rather than perverted, those who are, if you will, occasional rather that professional prostitutes, and who wish to reform, may have a chance to do so. It is because of this conflict between the ethical and the sanitary purposes of regulation that we find such an opposition between those who look at it only from the sanitary point of view, and those who regard it from the larger and more social point of view. Sanitary regulation may tend, and has frequently tended, to convert a woman from a temporary into a permanent prostitute.

Second, regulation is apt to strengthen the belief that it is for ever inevitable, and that, in so far as it responds to a general need, prostitution is something not only inevitable but beneficial. That is a point upon which the physician can speak more authoritatively than those who look at it from the moral, economic, or ethical point of view. Not a few physicians, however, take issue with the older doctrine which believes in the imperative necessity of sexual intercourse for the young man. To the extent that a system of reglementation impliedly recognises this function of prostitution. it runs counter to the newer doctrine.

Third, every system of reglementation tends to make men believe that they may indulge in these practices with comparative safety. Anything that tends to render vice innocuous tends to incite to debauch. To the extent that the state whitewashes the situation—and it can scarcely fail to do so when it officially regulates the practice,—to that extent it tends to augment the increase of the demand itself. It is for this reason that many who would perhaps otherwise be lukewarm, or disinclined to take any definite attitude on the subject, are disposed to oppose the system.

In the fourth place, the system of reglementation, especially in the Romance countries, shows that regulation is scarcely of any use at all, unless it tolerates and even favours the houses of ill-fame. You cannot get at the clandestine prostitute; you can, to a certain extent, reach the houses of ill-fame. Consequently, in the very country which has done the most in this direction, we find that the indirect result of the system is to encourage such houses, because it enables the police to regulate with a little more success. Not alone does it encourage houses of ill-fame, but it has also tended—in these Romance countries, at all events—to increase the subordinate and ancillary features—the dance-houses, the giving of liquor in the brothels, etc., making them veritable palaces of delight, as they have been called.

In the fifth place, the chief objection to regulation is that the state cannot regulate anything without recognising it; and that the state in modern times has no business to lend its active support to prostitution through recognition. In modern times, for instance, we have no state lotteries. Whereas in years past churches and other laudable institutions were built and aided by lotteries—Columbia University, for instance, was started by a lottery,—in modern times the state no longer lends its support to lotteries. At least, our own country, as well as most other civilised countries—with the surprising exception of some of the German states,—has abandoned state lotteries altogether. In the same way, we in America and other English-speaking countries believe that by legalising vice the state identifies itself more or less with immorality, and that by helping to maintain a class of such unfortunate women the state tends to outrage the decent element of society, and discriminates between men and women offenders. I can but sympathise with those women who maintain that this is, to that extent, an insult to womankind.

Finally, we do not believe in reglementation, because regulation does not regulate. Even in those countries where they have regulation, the most recent opinion, even among its advocates, is that if it does any good at all, it accomplishes so little as to be negligible; while, on the other hand, there is an increasing number of scientific men in France, Germany, Holland, and other countries on the continent who are assuming an attitude of dissent and opposition.

We need, therefore, not spend any more time on the problem of reglementation as such. It may appeal to certain of the European countries, which are accustomed to the continual interference of government in the smallest and most detailed affairs of daily life; but it may safely be affirmed that reglementation as such will not appeal to the American public.

Let us come, then, to the Page law. Some say: It is not regulation; we don't want regulation, but we favour the Page law because it is simply an attempt to protect the community from a sanitary point of view—not to regulate the traffic. As regards this point, I must say that after reading the colloquy between our respected chairman and Mr. Folks, it seems to me that the distinctions Mr. Folks makes between the Page law and the French system of reglementation are exceedingly tenuous. I think Dr. Morrow is quite right in saying that it is a distinction without a difference. Mr. Folks makes a great deal of the point that in the one case we deal only with vagrants, with criminals, whereas, in France, they deal with any person found walking the streets. But is that really a distinction? Is not every one who is found walking the streets in this city to-day considered a vagrant? Is there really any distinction between the details of the French system and those of the Page law, so far as that is concerned? I fail to see it.

Secondly, it may be said—and that is an opinion that deserves respectful consideration—that the Page law is a measure of beneficence in that it provides humane treatment for the unfortunate women who happen to be diseased. Here, however, we must remember that the number who are affected by the Page law are so few, so infinitesimal—perhaps a few dozen or a few hundreds, as compared with the tens of thousands of prostitutes in the city—as to be negligible. *De minimis non curat lex.* But even conceding that we do deal with a large number, is it necessary to have a law so degrading and humiliating as the Page law in order to give these unfortunate women the benefits of medical treatment? No one would object to an increase in our facilities for treatment, hospital, reformatory, or otherwise, designed to give these women a chance to regain their health. But to say that we need the Page law with its system of finger-print identification, and its degrading and compulsory examination in the police court in order to effect that result, is a very different matter. The end may be desirable, but the particular methods employed to reach that end are, in my opinion, exceedingly undesirable.

In the third place, the Page law makes use of the ordinary policeman and the ordinary police court. Now, if there is one thing on which most scientists and experts who have dealt with the problem abroad agree, it is that of all the people in the world the most unsuitable to administer such a system are the ordinary police and the ordinary police court. For that reason, France, which has led the way in this respect, has a separate body known as the *police des mœurs*, quite distinct from the ordinary police and not subject by any means to the same temptations and weaknesses. Even assuming that everything else about the Page law was good, this one fact would, in my opinion, be sufficient to convict it.

Fourthly, the Page law, as I take it, seeks to achieve one end and yet confuses it with another. Its object is sanitary control; it desires, to a certain extent, reformation; and it attempts to accomplish these things by punishment. The confusion between the punitive and the reformatory ideas is a gross one. While one may sometimes kill two birds with one stone, you generally have to choose between them.

And in this case a choice is necessary. The kind of punishment meted out by the Page law is not calculated to reform.

We come now to the principal indictment against the law. I should say that the chief aim of the Page law, which is to protect the health of the community—and let us frankly confess it: primarily, the health of the patrons, the health of the male sex,—is not attained and cannot be attained, because the sanitary protection turns out to be illusory. It is here, perhaps, that I may venture to speak with a little more assurance than in those other domains which are those of the expert physician or even the sociologist. For it is here that certain economic considerations come into play. After all, we are dealing here with services which have a price, and like everything else which has a price it is an economic problem. It has, of course, its sanitary, moral, and social aspects, but none the less there is a decided economic aspect to it. Now when we say that it is regulated by demand and supply we don't say much about it, for the province of the economist is to study in detail the forces which affect demand and supply. Mr. Folks —so far as I can learn from the report of the last session of the Society—says that it is a simple arithmetical problem: that if you take away a certain number, the total will be less than before.

I should say yes; if you have a lake of water and you take out a bucketful, of course, arithmetically, there is less water in the lake than before: but practically is there not the same amount as before? Removing ten or twenty or a hundred from the tens of thousands of these unfortunates is so insignificant that you may virtually disregard it. But even if we grant that you do remove a large number of women in this way through the Page law, what would be the result? If there is one thing definitely fixed in economic science, it is that when you are dealing with reproducible goods, things manufactured at practically the same cost, the chief point is not the supply but the demand; *i. e.*, the supply always adjusts itself to the demand. When you do nothing to affect the demand, and when you affect the supply only at one end, you are really not changing the situation. Take a mill-race with the water running in at one end and going out at the other. If you take water out of the lower end but do not change the inflow—the upper end—the level remains the same. The Page law at best takes out some of the supply at the lower end, but that does not prevent a corresponding change in the supply at the upper end; and as long as you do not change the total supply the situation remains the same. In other words, the supply of these unfortunate women on the streets will be made good from other sources. I concede that if you were to stop the water at the upper end you might do some good; but I am not sure how much, because there is another accepted economic principle: *i. e.*, that by diminishing the supply you do not diminish the demand unless the point of saturation has been reached. Suppose that you have a large number of liquor saloons, and that you diminish the number by a tenth or a quarter. Are you checking the supply? Will not the only result be that you will increase the patronage of the remaining liquor saloons? It is not until the saloons become uncomfortably crowded that the patrons would be tempted to go somewhere else, and then, indeed, if there were nowhere else to go to, the effect would be felt. Therefore, even the diminution of the supply through a police regulation which would prevent street-walking, would attain the desired result only if it brought about a decided diminution in numbers.

The Page law, however, not only fails to affect the supply at all, leaving the demand as before—but it affects the demand the wrong way   The only way in which supply can affect demand is through a change in the quantity or quality of the supply. The quantity of the supply now is, as we have just seen, not changed by the Page law, but the quality is changed. To the extent that people will get the idea that the street-walkers are not diseased either after they have been treated or when they have been discharged as not in need of treatment, the imagined improvement in the quality of the services offered for sale will tend to attract purchasers who would otherwise be somewhat suspicious or on their guard. It will tend, in other words, to augment the demand. At all events, it is reasonably sure that as an economic proposition the Page law is illusory, in so far as concerns the hope that it would bring about a decided diminution in prostitution.

But, finally, if I do not believe in regulation and if I do not believe in the Page law, in what do I believe? I think that that is a fair question. Every one has a right to object to a man or a woman who says "Hands off"; or, like the ostrich, puts his head in the sand and says: "Don't let us talk about it, it does not exist." The way to deal with the problem is to influence both supply and demand. You can affect the supply in several ways. One of these is to secure the introduction of general economic and social measures which tend to raise the whole plane of the standard of life. For the problem is, nowadays, primarily a social and economic one. It is, in large measure, the problem not of the moral pervert but of the woman who has not enough to live on and who, therefore, takes to this practice as a means of livelihood. You can affect the supply by doing what is needful in connection with the white-slave traffic. Furthermore, you can change the character as well as the quantity of the supply. You can accomplish this by regulating and improving the dance halls and the Raines-Law hotels, and by checking the other things that tend to convert the occasional into the professional prostitute. On the other hand, you can affect the demand in many ways, some of which have been emphasised so magnificently by this society under whose auspices we are meeting to-night. You can affect the demand by proper education; you can provide the opportunity of securing knowledge, and do much to make the situation very different from what it is to-day. You can change the demand by requiring a license of good health and freedom from these diseases before marriage—a by no means impracticable or visionary scheme, and one the necessity of which is already beginning to be recognised in some of our states. You can alter both demand and supply in many other ways which it is not my province to point out, for it has been a critical rather than a constructive thought which I wish to present to-night.

The great trouble with all our efforts has been the lack of continuity of effort. The Committee of Fifteen did what it could, but the community soon lapsed from the stage of enthusiasm and high moral force; the flame which burned so brilliantly for a time died out—and so it is with most of our efforts at reform. This society takes up one phase of the subject—only one little phase, and yet in itself large enough, for without this society it would have been impossible to speak to you to-night as I have done. To have accomplished merely the possibility of a free discussion of such subjects is no mean result.

I want to plead for an organisation which will remain constantly in operation, which will study these questions, which will not take a mere snap-shot at them, as did those worthy gentlemen who enacted this particular provision of the Page law, but which will study the whole problem from the medical standpoint, the social standpoint, the economic standpoint, and the moral standpoint; and which will not alone prepare legislation, but will help the government in administering whatever laws or ordinances may be

17

found to be desirable. If the result of a discussion like this is to bring into existence an organisation of permanent character which will create and maintain a continuity of effort, we may look forward to the time not indeed when we can extirpate prostitution—for that will not come very easily nor very quickly; not to the time when we can discover a panacea for the trouble; but to the time when, even if we shall not be able to attack the evil in front, we may be able to effect a breach in the side, which will gradually but surely expose and lay bare more and more of the hideous enemy which constitutes, perhaps, the worst of our modern evils.

BIBLIOGRAPHY

(Exclusive of the Technical Medical Literature)

GENERAL

UNITED STATES

A. *Signed Works.*

Andrews, Edmund. *Prostitution and its Sanitary Management.* Chicago, 1871.

Andrews, Elizabeth, and Bushnell, Katherine. *Heathen Slaves and Christian Rulers.* Oakland (Cal.), 1907.

Backus, Wilson M. *The Social Evil; an address.* Minneapolis, 1910.

Bell, Ernest A. *War on the White Slave Trade.* Chicago, 1909.

Bingham, Theodore A. *The Girl that Disappears; the Real Facts about the White Slave Traffic.* Boston, 1911.

Blackwell, Antoinette B. *Sex Injustice; an address.* New York, n. d.

Burnett, John L. *White Slave Traffic;* a speech in the House of Representatives, Jan., 1910.

Cobden, John C. *The White Slaves of England; compiled from Official Documents.* Auburn, Buffalo, and Cincinnati, 1853.

Currier, Andrew F. *The Unrestricted Evil of Prostitution; a Paper.* (Reprint from *Philanthropist*, May, 1891.)

Day, Mrs. Helen Gardiner. *Have Children a Right to Legal Protection?* Boston, 1895.

Dock, Lavinia L. *Hygiene and Morality; a Manual for Nurses and others, giving an Outline of the medical, social, and legal Aspects of the venereal Diseases.* New York, 1910.

Edholm, Charlton. *Traffic in Girls and Rescue Missions.* Los Angeles, 1907.

Eliot, Wm. G. *A Practical Discussion of the Great Social Question of the Day.* New York, 1879.

[1] In the preparation of this part of the bibliography the editor received much aid from Miss Marion Dodd, the secretary of the American Vigilance Association, who generously provided duplicate cards of all the numerous items in the Association library.

Forbush, Wm. Bryon. *The Boy Problem.* New York, 1907.

Forel, August. *The Sexual Question; a scientific, psychological, hygienic, and sociological Study for the cultured classes.* (English adaptation by C. F. Marshall.) New York, 1908.

Fuld, Leonhard F. *Police Administration; a critical Study of Police Organizations in the United States and abroad.* New York, 1909.

Gerrish, Dr. Frederick Henry. *The Duties of the Medical Profession Concerning Prostitution and its Allied Vices;* being the oration before the Maine Medical Association. 2d. ed. Portland, 1879.

Goodnow, Elizabeth. *The Market for Souls.* New York, 1910.

Hall, G. Stanley. *Youth, its Education, Regimen, and Hygiene.* New York, 1908.

Hall, Dr. Winfield Scott. *Reproduction and Sexual Hygiene.* n. d.

Hall, Dr. Winfield Scott. *The Strength of Ten.* n. d.

Hall, Dr. Winfield Scott. *From Youth into Manhood.* New York, 1910.

Hamery, J. L. *Address . . . at the annual meeting of the Illinois Vigilance Association,* Feb. 14, 1910.

Howard, Dr. Wm. Lee. *Plain Facts on Sex Hygiene.* New York, 1910.

Janney, Dr. O. Edward. *The White Slave Traffic in America.* New York, 1911.

Kauffman, Reginald Wright. *The House of Bondage.* New York, 1910.

Kelso, Tessa L. *Report to the Committee of the Women's Municipal League on Clause 79.* New York, 1911.

Lowell, Josephine Shaw. *Municipalities and Vice.* (Reprint from *Municipal Affairs,* June, 1901.)

Lyttelton, E. *Training of the Young in Laws of Sex.* New York, 1906.

Morrow, Dr. Prince A. *Social Diseases and Marriage. Social Prophylaxis.* New York, 1904.

Morrow, Dr. Prince A. *Society of Sanitary and Moral Prophylaxis: Origin of this Movement, its Objects, Means and Methods of Work.* New York, 1910.

Morrow, Dr. Prince A. *The Prophylaxis of Venereal Disease.* New York. n. d.

Nascher, I. L. *The Social Evil, a Plea.* 1909.

Peters, John D. *Suppression of the "Raines Law Hotels."* Philadelphia, 1908. (Publication No. 569 of the American Academy of Political and Social Science.)

Powell, Aaron M. *Regulation of Prostitution; an open Letter to the President of the N. Y. Academy of Medicine.* New York, 1883.

Bibliography

Powell, Aaron M. *The State and Prostitution; a Paper read before the section on Public Health of the N. Y. Academy of Medicine.* New York, 1894.

Powell, Aaron M. *State Regulation of Vice, Regulation Efforts in America: the Geneva Congress.* New York, 1878.

Powell, Anna Rice. *The New Abolitionists: The International Federation for the Abolition of State Regulation of Vice and the Promotion of Social Purity;* a paper read at the International Council of Women. New York, 1888.

Reynolds, James B. *Prostitution as a Tenement House Evil.* (In DeForest & Veiller: *The Tenement House Problem.*)

Roe, Clifford G. *Panders and their White Slaves.* New York, n. d. [1910].

Roe, Clifford G. *The Great War on White Slavery.* n. p. 1911.

Roe, Clifford G. *The Prodigal Daughter. The White-Slave Evil and the Remedy.* Chicago, n. d. [1911]. [This is the same book as the preceding one, minus the illustrations.]

Saleeby, Caleb Williams. *Parenthood and Race Culture;* an Outline of *Eugenics.* New York, 1909.

Sanger, W. W. *The History of Prostitution, its Extent, Causes and Effects throughout the World.* New ed. New York, 1906.

Seay, Harry L. *Letter to the Committee of Ten advocating Segregation.* Dallas, 1910.

Shearer, J. G. *Social Vice and how to deal with it; an Address before the International Purity Congress,* Burlington, Iowa, 1909.

Shearer, J. G. *Canada's War on the White Slave Trade.* n. d.

Sims, J. Marion. *Legislation and Contagious Diseases;* an extract from the inaugural address delivered before the American Medical Association at its 27th annual meeting in Philadelphia, June 6, 1876. New York, 1876.

Spencer, Anna Garlin. *Women and Regulation; the Relation of Lady Henry Somerset and other English Women to State Regulation of Vice in India.* New York. n. d.

Sutherland, D. F. *The Black Plague of the American Continent.* Quitman (Texas).

Taschereau, Justice Henri T. *The Crime of Prostitution.* Part of a report of the City Council of Montreal. Montreal, n. d.

Walker, E. C. *Vice, its Friends and Foes.* New York, 1901.

Warren, John H., Jr. *Thirty Years Battle with Crime; or the Crying Shame of New York as seen in the Broad Glare of an Old Detective's Lantern.* Poughkeepsie, 1874.

Weir, Recorder S. *The Social Evil. Toleration Condemned.* Reprinted New York, 1909.

Willson, Robert N. *The American Boy and the Social Evil. From a Physician's Standpoint.* Philadelphia, 1905.

Zenner, Dr. Philip. *Education in Sexual Physiology and Hygiene.* Cincinnati, 1910.

B. *Anonymous Works* (arranged chronologically).

Facts for Fathers and Mothers, Conditions that are not to be endured. (Women's Municipal League.) New York, 1901.

Agreement between the United States and other Powers for the Repression of the Trade in White Women. Washington, 1908.

A Record of the Enforcement of the Laws against Sexual Immorality since December 1, 1907. Boston Police Department. Boston, 1908.

Proceedings of the First Conference of City Magistrates (outside of New York City), held at Albany, Dec. 10, 1909.

Report from the Immigration Commission on importing Women for Immoral Purposes, Dec. 10, 1909.

The Social Evil in New York City. A Study of Law Enforcement by the Research Committee of the Committee of Fourteen. New York, 1910.

Final Report of the Commission to inquire into Courts of Inferior Criminal Jurisdiction in Cities of the First Class. Albany, 1910.

Social Hygiene vs. The Sexual Plagues with their Rapid Invasion of the American Home; The Horrible Consequences of Sex Secrecy and the Obligation of Parents in the State to Protect the Rising Generation. Indiana State Board of Health. Indianapolis, 1910.

Message from the President of the United States, transmitting in further response to the Senate Resolution No. 86 of Dec. 7, 1909, Information concerning the Repression of the Trade in White Women. January 31, 1910.

White Slave Traffic, Views of the Minority, to accompany H. R. 12,315, January 5, 1910.

White Slave Traffic. Presentment of the additional Grand Jury for the January Term of the Court of Special Sessions in the County of New York, as to the alleged existence in the County of New York of an Organised Traffic in Women for Immoral Purposes. Filed June 29, 1910. New York, 1910.

Report of the Vice-Commission of Minneapolis, to his Honor, James C. Haynes, Mayor. Minneapolis, 1911.

Immigration Report. Importing Women for Immoral Purposes. A partial Report to Congress on the Importation and Harboring of Women for Immoral Purposes. Senate Document 196, 61st Congress, 2nd Session. Washington, 1911.

The Social Evil in Chicago. Vice Commission of Chicago. Chicago, 1911.

Department of Commerce and Labor, Commissioner-General of Immigration. *Annual Report,* years ending June 30, 1908–1911.

The Third International Congress for the Suppression of the White Slave Traffic. Baltimore, n. d.

Chicago and Spokane Societies, Publications of:
1. *Sexual Hygiene for Young Men.*
2. *Family Protection.*
3. *Community Protection.*
4. *Comments on the Aims and Efforts of the Society of Social Hygiene.*

Rhode Island State Board of Health. Circulars on Sex Hygiene:
1. *Sex Hygiene.* For Young Men.
2. *Sex Hygiene.* Information for Persons having Syphilitic or Gonorrhœal Infection.
3. *Sex Hygiene.* Information for Young Women.
4. *Ophthalmia Neonatorum.* Preventive Treatment, Suggestions, and Treatment of the Disease.

Society for Sanitary and Moral Prophylaxis, Papers issued by:
1. *The Young Men's Problem.* 32 pp.
2. *Instruction in Physiology and Hygiene of Sex.*
3. *The Relations of Social Diseases with Marriage and their Prophylaxis.*
4. *The Boy Problem. For Parents and Teachers.* 32 pp.
5. *How my Uncle, the Doctor, instructed me in Matters of Sex*
6. *Health and the Hygiene of Sex.* For College Students.
7. *Sex Instructions for Little Girls.* (In preparation.)
8. *Instruction for Unprotected Young Women.* (In preparation.)
Published in New York.

ENGLAND.

A. *Signed Works.*

Acton, William. *Prostitution considered in its Moral, Social, and Sanitary Aspects in London and Other Large Cities.* London, 1857.

Amos, Sheldon. *A Comparative Survey of the Laws in Force for the Prohibition, Regulation, and Licensing of Vice in England and Other Countries.* London, 1877.

Bebel, August. *Woman in the Past, Present, and Future.* Translated from the German by H. B. A. Walther. London, n. d.

Blackwell, Elizabeth. *Purchase of Women: the Great Economic Blunder.* 2d edition. London, 1887.

Blackwell, Elizabeth. *Rescue Work in Relation to Prostitution and Disease.* London, 1881.

Borel, Pastor T. *The White Slavery of Europe* (translated from the French). London, n. d.

Collingwood, C. S. *The French Regulation of Immorality at the Bar of Public Opinion.* London, 1877.

Coote, Wm. Alexander. *A Vision and its Fulfilment; being the History of the Origin of the work of the National Vigilance Association for the Suppression of the White Slave Traffic.* London, 1910.

Daubie, Mlle. J. *French Morality under the Regulation System.* Translated from the French. London, 1870.

De Graaf, Dr. *Sources of the White Slave Traffic;* paper at the Madrid Congress, 1910.

Drysdale, Dr. Charles. *Prostitution medically considered, with Some of its Social Aspects.* London, 1886.

Dyer, Alfred S. *The European Slave Trade in English Girls.* London, 1880.

Dyer, Alfred S. *Slavery under the British Flag.* London, 1886.

Lecky, Wm. E. H. *History of European Morals.* London, 1869, and many later editions.

Miller, James. *Prostitution considered in Relation to its Cause and Cure.* London.

Pontoppidan, (Professor) Erik. *What Venereal Diseases Mean, and How to Prevent Them.* London, n. d.

Powell, A. M. *State Regulation of Vice.* London, 1877.

Pressensé, Ed. de. *Speech in London, May 19th, 1876.* London, 1876.

Richardson, H. M. *The Outcasts.* London, 1909.

Roberts, Ursula. *The Cause of Purity and Woman's Suffrage.* London, n. d.

Scott, Benjamin. *State Regulated Vice as it existed anciently in London.* London, 1886.

Scott, Benjamin. *Six Years' Labour and Sorrow, in reference to the Traffic in English Girls.* London, 1885.

Scott, Benjamin. *Is London more Immoral than Paris or Brussels?* London, 1881.

Scott, J. F. *The Sexual Instinct, its Use and Dangers as affecting Heredity and Morals.* New York, 1907.

Stead, William T. *Josephine Butler, a Life Sketch.* London, 1887.

Stead, William T. *The Right and Wrong Relations between Men and Women.* London, 1888.

Tod, Isabella M. S. *The Necessity of Stronger Representation in*

Parliament of the Religious Feeling against State Regulation of Vice. Abstract of a paper read at the International Congress at Geneva. London, n. d.

Wilson, Henry J. *The History of a Sanitary Failure; Extracts (mainly from official sources) showing the Results of 90 years' Experiments in the Hygienic Regulation of Prostitution in India.* 5th ed., rev. London, 1900.

Wilson, H. J., and Gledstone, J. P. *Report of a Visit to the United States as Delegates from the British, Continental, and General Federation for the Abolition of Government Regulation of Prostitution.* Sheffield, 1876.

Wilson, Dr. H. M. *Law and Administration in Regard to the Social Evil; an Outline of Existing Conditions and Projected Reforms in the Principal Civilised States.* London, 1911.

Wilson, Dr. H. M. *Notes on Administrative Measures against Enthetic Disease.* London, 1910.

Wilson, Dr. H. M. *Sanitary Principles applied to the Prevention of Venereal Diseases.* n. p., n. d. (1911).

B. *Anonymous Works* (arranged chronologically).

An Address to Members of the American Legislature and of the Medical Profession, from the British, Continental, and General Federation for the Abolition of State Regulation of Prostitution . . . on recent Proposals to introduce the System of regulating or licensing Prostitution in the U. S., with the History and Results of such Legislation on the continent of Europe and in England. London, 1877.

The Geneva Congress on Public Morality. London, 1877.

Revelations of an Ex-Agent of the Paris Morals Police. London, 1878.

Regulations of Prostitution in the City of Brussels. (Private circulation only.) London, 1880.

A White Slave Rescued; an Authentic Narrative. By an English Barrister of Twenty Years' Standing. London, 1885.

Revelations of the Pall Mall Gazette. 1886.

The Exact Legal Position of the Regulation of Prostitution in India, as set forth in the new Cantonment Code of Oct. 1, 1899. London 1899.

Preventive Hygiene, the International Conference at Brussels, Sept., 1899. By one who was there. London, 1900.

The Failure of a Century of Regulated Vice in France. By Friends' Association for abolishing State Regulation of Vice. London, 1901.

The Recent Revival of Military Imperialism and its Effect upon the

Abolitionist Cause.   By Friends' Association for abolishing State Regulation of Vice. London, 1901.

An Account of the Brussels International Conferences. London, 1909.

Preventive Hygiene. An account of the Brussels International Conferences, 1899 and 1902. By an English member. 3d ed. London, 1909, 31 pp.

Hygiene in Relation to Rescue Work. The Papers read at a Private Conference held at Caxton Hall. Westminster, Nov. 24, 1910. London, 1910.

The White Slave Traffic. London, 1910. 115 pp.

Should Syphilis be made notifiable? 2d ed. (London), 1911.

A Warning Voice from Old England. London, n. d.

Fourth International Conference for the Suppression of the White Slave Traffic at Madrid. London, n.d.

The European Revolt Against White Slavery. London, n. d.

FRANCE.

A. *Signed Works.*

Bebel, August. *Le Socialisme et la Réglementation. Discours . . . au Reichstag Allemand.* Genève, 1893. 23 pp.

Bell-Taylor, Dr. Ch. *Dangers de la Réglementation.* n. d.

Bérenger, R. *La Traite des Blanches et le Commerce de l'Obscénité; Conférences Diplomatiques Internationales du 15 Juillet, 1902, et du 18 Avril, 1910.*

Bertani, A. *La Prostituzione Patentata e il Regolamento Sanatorio.* Milano, 1881.

Bovet, Felix. *La Prostitution au point de vue Légal.* n. d.

Bridel, Louis. *Mesures Légales propres à restreindre la Prostitution.* (Extrait de la *Revue de Morale Progressive.*) Genève, 1893.

Bureau, Paul. *La Crise Morale des Temps Nouveaux,* Préface de M. Alfred Croiset. Paris, 1908.

Butler, Josephine E. *Une Voix dans le Désert.* Paris, n. d. (1910).

Butler, Josephine E. *Avant l'Aurore; Appel aux Hommes.* Préface de Paul Bureau, 2d éd. Sainte-Blaise, 1911.

Butler, Josephine E. *Souvenirs et Pensées.* Geneva, n. d.

Carlier, F. Études de Pathologie Sociale. *Les Deux Prostitutions.* Paris, 1837.

Chanfleury van Ijsselstein, J. L. *La Visite des Prostituées au point de vue d'Hygiène Publique.* Genève, 1889.

Decante, R. *La Lutte contre la Prostitution.* Préface par Henri Turot. Paris, 1909.

De Meuron, Alf. *La Fédération et le Christianisme.* Genève, 1905.

De Meuron, Alf. *L'Influence Morale et Sociale du Régime de la Police des Mœurs.* Genève, 1898.

De Meuron, Alf. *La Traite des Blanches.* Genève, 1896.

De Morsier, A. *Les Maisons de Tolérance devant le Grand Conseil de Genève. Notes et documents.* Genève, 1909.

De Plauzoles, Sicard. *La Police des Mœurs et la Santé Publique.* Genève, 1907.

Dupouy, Dr. E. *La Prostitution dans l'Antiquité dans ses Rapports avec les Maladies Vénériennes.* 5th ed. Paris, 1906.

Fallot, T. *La Femme Esclave. Conférence.* Neuchatel, 1884.

Fiaux, Louis. *La Police des Mœurs en France et dans les Principaux Pays de l' Europe.* 2d ed. Paris, 1888.

Fiaux, Louis. *Les Maisons Tolérées, leur Fermeture.* Paris, 1896.

Fiaux, Louis. *La Prostitution Cloîtrée.* Paris, 1902.

Fiaux, Louis. *La Police des Mœurs devant la Commission Extraparlémentaire du Régime des Mœurs. Introduction, Rapports, Débats. Abolition de la Police des Mœurs, le Régime de la Loi. Documents inédits.* 3 vols. Paris, 1907–1910.

Fiaux, Louis. *Le Délit Pénal de Contamination Intersexuelle.* Paris, 1907.

Fiaux, Louis. *Enseignement Populaire de la Moralité Sexuelle.* Paris, 1908.

Fiaux, Louis. *Un Nouveau Régime des Mœurs.* Paris, 1908.

Fiaux, Louis. *La Prostitution Réglementée et les Pouvoirs Publics dans les Principaux États des Deux Mondes.* Paris, 1909. (Vol. I of a work to be completed in 6 vols., entitled: *Histoire Générale du Mouvement pour l' Abolition de la Police des Mœurs.*)

Fiaux, Louis. *L'Intégrité Intersexuelle des Peuples et des Gouvernements (La Conférence Internationale de Bruxelles).* Paris, 1910.

Guillot, Alexandre. *L'État et la Moralité Publique.* Genève, 1896.

Guillot, A. *La Lutte contre l'Exploitation et la Réglementation du Vice à Genève. Histoire et Documents.* n. d.

Guyot, Yves. *Études de Physiologie Sociale. La Prostitution.* Paris, 1883.

Herzen, M. A. *La Question des Mœurs.* Genève, 1894.

Hoffet, E. *De l'Influence de l'Esprit Réglementariste sur la Vie Morale.* Saint-Étienne, 1908.

Homo, Dr. H. *Étude sur la Prostitution.* London. 1872.

Jeannel, J. F. *La Prostitution dans les Grandes Villes au Dix-neuvième Siècle, et de l'Extinction des Maladies Vénériennes.* 2d ed. Paris, 1874.

Ladame, Paul. *Discours sur les Remèdes Secrets et Annonces Immorales dans leurs Rapports avec la Prostitution.* Neuchatel, n. d.

Ladame, Paul. *Les Maisons de Tolérance au point de vue de l'Hygiène.* New ed. Genève, n. d.

Ladame, Paul. *L'Hygiène Sexuelle et la Prostitution.* Genève, 1905.

Ladame, Paul. *L'Institution de la Police des Mœurs au point de vue de l'Hygiène.* Neuchatel, 1882.

Ladame, Paul. *Prostitution, Police des Mœurs et Santé Publique.* Genève, 1907.

Lecour, C. J. *La Prostitution à Paris et à Londres, 1789–1877.* 3d ed. Paris, 1882.

Lenoble, Jules. *La Traite des Blanches et le Congrès de Londres de 1899.* Paris, 1900.

Leppington, B. *Le Néo-Réglementarisme. Ses Principes, son Application, ses Perspectives.* Genève, 1904.

Lutaud, A. J. *La Prostitution et la Traite des Blanches à Londres et à Paris.* Paris, 1886.

Minod, Henri. *Rapport. Protection de la Jeune Fille en Danger. IV Congrès International d'Assistance Publique et Privée.* Milan, 1906.

Minod, Henri. *La Lutte contre la Prostitution. Rapport.* Genève, 1905.

Minod, Henri. *Origines et Développement de l'Œuvre, les Principes. Exposé historique.* Genève, 1905.

Minod, Henri. *Simple Exposé du But et des Principes de la Fédération Abolitionniste Internationale.* Genève, 1905.

Minod, Henri. *La Prostitution est-elle delictueuse en soi? Rapport au Congrès de la Fédération à Dresde.* 1904.

Minod, Henri. *Les Principes de la Fédération.* n. d.

Morhardt, Paul-Emile, Dr. *Les Maladies Vénériennes et la Réglementation de la Prostitution au point de vue de l'Hygiène Sociale.* n. d.

Morsier, A. *La Police des Mœurs en France et la Campagne Abolitionniste.* Paris, 1907.

Parent-Duchatelet, A. J. B. *De la Prostitution dans la Ville de Paris, considerée sous le Rapport de l'Hygiène Publique, de la Morale et de l'Administration.* 3d ed. Paris, 1857. 2 vols.

Pieczynska, Mme. E. *La Fédération et l'Hygiène.* n. d.

Reuss, L. *La Prostitution au point de Vue de l'Hygiène et de l'Administration en France et à l'Étranger.* Paris, 1889.

Richard, Chas. *La Prostitution devant la Philosophie.* London, 1882.

Richard, Émile. *La Prostitution à Paris.* Paris, 1890.

Schlumberger, Mme. de. *Une Femme aux Femmes. Pourquoi les Femmes doivent étudier la Question des Mœurs.* n. d.

Stoukowenkoff, Dr. *La Réglementation jugée théoriquement au point de vue de la Syphilographie Moderne.* Genève, 1889.

Tammeo, Guiseppe. *La Prostituzione: Saggio di Statistica Morale.* Torino, 1890.

Taylor, Charles Bell. *Dangers de la Réglementation et Difficulté de reconnaître le Syphilis chez la Femme.* Genève, n. d.

Tommasoli, Pierleone. *Prostitution et Maladies Vénériennes en Italie.* Traduit par L. Le Peleur. Brussels, 1900.

Von Düring, Dr. *Inutilité de la Surveillance Sanitaire des Prostituées.* Genève, 1907.

B. *Anonymous Works* (arranged chronologically).

Fédération Britannique, Continentale et Générale. Cinquième Congrès International tenu Septembre, 1889 à Genève. Compte Rendu officiel des Travaux de Congrès. Genève, 1890.

Rapports, Enquêtes et Compte Rendu des Débats de la Conférence Internationale de Prophylaxie des Maladies Vénériennes. Publiés par le Dr. Dubois-Havenith, agrégé à l'Université de Bruxelles, Sécrétaire-Général de la Conférence: T. Ier. Première partie. *Rapports Préliminaires;* seconde partie, *Enquêtes sur l'État de la Prostitution et Fréquence de la Syphilis et des Maladies Vénériennes dans les Différents Pays;* Appendice: *Communications relatives aux six Questions à l'Étude.* Tome II. Première partie, *Compte Rendu des Séances:* Seconde Partie, *Appendice aux Enquêtes et Communications Documentaires.* H. Lamartin, edit., Bruxelles, 1899–1900.

Fédération Abolitionniste Internationale. Conférence de Genève. Compte Rendu des Travaux. Genève, 1900.

Fédération Abolitionniste Internationale, fondée le 19 Mars, 1875. Statuts. Genève, 1901.

Seconde Conférence Internationale pour la Prophylaxie de la Syphilis et des Maladies Vénériennes sous le Patronage du Gouvernement Belge. Rapports et Compte Rendu des Séances. Ouvrage publié par le Dr. Dubois-Havenith, Sécrétaire-Général. 2 vols. Brussels, 1903.

Fédération Abolitionniste Internationale. Notice Historique. Genève, 1904.

Fédération Abolitionniste Internationale—Branche Française. Contre la Police des Mœurs. Critiques et Rapports. Avec une préface de V. Augagneur. Paris, 1904.

Rapports au Nom de la 2 Commission sur la Prostitution et la Police des Mœurs. Presentés par Adrien Mithouard, Maurice Quentin et Henri Turot. Conseil Municipal. Paris, 1904.

Fédération Abolitionniste Internationale. Compte Rendu des Travaux du Congrès de Dresde, Septembre, 1904. Genève, 1905.

Les Maisons de Tolérance sont-elles nécessaires? Genève, 1907.

Fédération Abolitionniste Internationale. La Traite des Blanches dans ses Rapports avec le Police des Mœurs (Congrès de Genève, 7–11 Septembre, 1908).

Fédération Abolitionniste Internationale. Le Patronage Royal pour la Répression, de la Traite des Blanches (Madrid), et le Congrès de la Fédération Abolitionniste Internationale (Genève), 1908. Madrid, 1908.

Fédération Abolitionniste Internationale. Congrès de Genève, 7–11 Septembre 1908; La Traite des Blanches dans ses rapports avec le Police des Mœurs. 1908.

Rapport Général sur les Travaux de la Commission Extraparlémentaire du Régime des Mœurs. Presenté par M. F. Hennequin, sous-Directeur au Ministère de l'Intérieur; Sécrétaire-Général de la Commission. Melun, Imprimerie Administrative, 1908.

Fédération Abolitionniste Internationale. Dixième Congrès tenu à Genève, Septembre, 1908, Compte Rendu des travaux. Genève, 1909.

La Répression de la Traite des Blanches. Rapport officiel de la Conférence Internationale, tenue les 5, 6, et 7 Octobre, 1909. Vienne, 1909.

La Répression de la Traite des Blanches. Conférence Internationale Octobre, 1909, à Vienne. Rapport officiel. 1910.

Association pour la Répression de la Traite des Blanches et de la Préservation de la Jeune Fille. Assemblée Générale du 13 Juin, 1911. Paris, 1911.

Commission Extraparlémentaire du Régime des Mœurs. Rapports 1903–1908:

1. Chef de Bureau au Ministère de l'Intérieur M. Hennequin. *Réglementation de la Prostitution en France.* 1903.

2. Député Paul Meunier. *Rapport sur le Fonctionnement du Service des Mœurs à Paris.* 1904.

3. Prof. Alfred Fournier. *Rapport. Réponse à deux Questions.* 1904.

4. Préfêt de Police M. Lepine. *Rapport sur la Réglementation de la Prostitution à Paris et dans le Département de la Seine.* 1904.

5. M. André Lucas. *Rapport sur Deux Vœux ayant pour But l'Abolition de certaines Pratiques s' inspirant de la Réglementation Actuelle,* 1904.

6. Prof. Augagneur. *De l'Influence de la Réglementation de la Prostitution sur la Morbidité Vénérienne.* 1904.
7. M. Bulot. *Rapport sur les Modifications à apporter aux Articles 330 et 334 du Code Pénal.* 1904.
8. M. Bérenger. *Rapport relatif au Délit de Contamination.* 1905.
9. Dr. Butte. *Propositions relatives aux Mésures Prophylactiques contre les Maladies Vénériennes.* 1905.
10. M. Delaitre. *Rapport Sommaire résumant les Procès-verbaux de la Commission en ce qui concerne les Jeunes Mineurs se livrant habituellement à la Prostitution.* 1906.
11. Hennequin. *Rapport Général sur les Travaux de la Commission Extraparlémentaire, etc.* 1908.

GERMANY.

Bauer, M. *Das Geschlechtsleben in der Deutschen Vergangenheit.* 4. Aufl. Berlin, 1909.
Behrend, F. J. *Die Prostitution in Berlin und die gegen sie und die Syphilis zu nehmenden Massregeln.* Erlangen, 1850.
Bettman, Dr. S. *Die ärtztliche Ueberwachung der Prostituierten.* Jena, 1905.
Block, Dr. Iwan. *Das Sexualleben unserer Zeit in seinen Beziehungen zur Modernen Kultur.* 9th ed. Berlin, 1909.
Finger, Ernest und Baumgarten, A. *Oesterreichische Liga zur Bekämpfung des Mädchenhandels. Die in Betracht kommenden Oesterreichischen Gesetze, Verordnungen und Erlässe: Referat über die Regelung der Prostitution in Oesterreich.* Wien, 1909.
Flesch, Max. *Prostitution und Frauenskrankheiten: Hygienische und Volkswissenschaftliche Betrachtungen.* 2d ed. Frankfort, A. M., 1898.
Foerster, Fr. W. *Sexualethik und Sexualpädagogik.* 2d ed. Kempten, 1909.
Forel, August. *Die Sexuelle Frage; eine Naturwissenschaftliche, Psychologische, Hygienische und Soziologische Studie für Gebildete.* 9th ed. München, 1909.
Fürbringer, Dr. *Die Störungen der Geschlechtsfunctionen des Mannes.* Wien, 1895.
Gaertner, Emil. *Bericht über den in der Zeit Oktober, 1906, zu Paris abgehaltenen III Internationalen Kongress zur Bekämpfung des Mädchenhandels.* Wien, 1907.
Henne am Rhyn, Otto. *Prostitution und Mädchenhandel. Neue Enthullüngen aus dem Sklavenleben Weisser Frauen und Mädchen.* 2d ed. Leipzig, 1907.

Hoffet, Emile. *Warum bekämpfen wir die Reglementierung der Prostitution?* Dresden, 1906.

Hügel, F. J. *Zur Geschichte, Statistik und Regelung der Prostitution.* Vienna, 1865.

Lette, Frau Fischer. *Durch Kampf zum Sieg. Dem Andenken der Frau Butler gewidmet.* Hamburg, n. d.

Lux, Heinrich. *Die Prostitution, ihre Ursachen, ihre Folgen und ihre Bekämpfung.* 2d ed. Berlin, 1894.

Nudeck, W. *Geschichte der Öffentlichen Sittlichkeit in Deutschland. Moralhistorische Studien.* Jena, 1897.

Pappritz, A., und Scheven, Katharina. *Die Positiven Aufgaben und Strafrechtlichen Forderungen der Föderation.* Dresden, 1909.

Rudeck, Dr. Wilhelm. *Geschichte der Öffentlichen Sittlichkeit in Deutschland.* New ed. Berlin, 1905.

Scheven, Katharina. *Denkschrift über die in Deutschland bestehenden Verhältnisse in Bezug auf das Bordellwesen und über seine Sittlichen, Sozialen und Hygienischen Gefahren.* Dresden, 1904.

Scheven, Katharina. *Die Uebel der Reglementierung der Prostitution.* 3d ed. Dresden, 1903.

Scheven, Katharina. *Warum erachtet die Föderation die Prostitution nicht als Strafbares Vergehen!* Dresden, 1904.

Schmölder, R. *Staat und Prostitution.* Berlin, 1900.

Schmölder, R. *Die Prostituierten und das Strafrecht.* Munich, 1911.

Schneider, Camillo Karl. *Die Prostituierte und die Gesellschaft. Eine Soziologisch-ethische Studie.* Mit einen Geleitwort von A. Blaschko. Leipzig, 1908.

Schranck, J. *Die Prostitution in Wien in Historischer, Administrativer und Hygienischer Beziehung.* 2 vols. Wien, 1886.

Strömberg, C. *Die Prostitution. Ein Beitrag zur öffentlichen Sexual Hygiene und zur staatlichen Prophylaxe der Geschlechtskrankheiten.* Stuttgart, 1899.

Tarnowsky, B. *Prostitution und Abolitionismus. Briefe.* Hamburg, 1890.

Vorberg, Dr. Gaston. *Freiheit oder Gesundheitliche Ueberwachung der Gewerbsunzucht; eine zeitgemässe Betrachtung.* Munich, 1907.

Wagener, Major A. D. H. *Mädchenhandel.* Berlin, 1911.

Weyl, Dr. Theodore. *Zur Geschichte der Sozialen Hygiene.* Jena, 1904.

Wolzendorff, Kurt. *Polizei und Prostitution. Eine Studie zur Lehre von der öffentlichen Verwaltung und ihrem Recht.* "Zeitschrift für die Gesamte Staatswissenschaft." Vol. 67. Tübingen, 1911.

Zehnder, C. *Die Gefahren der Prostitution und ihre Gesetzliche Be kämpfung mit besonderer Rücksicht der Zürcherischen Verhältnisse.* Zurich, 1891.

Ethische und rechtliche Konflikte im Sexualleben in und ausserhalb der Ehe. Munich, 1909.

Deutsche Nationalkomite zur Internationalen Bekämpfung des Mädchenhandels. Protocol 63, 64, 65, 66, 68, 70, 71. Monthly reports of the German Committee for the suppression of the White Slave Traffic.

Bericht des Vereins "Oesterreichische Mädchen- und Kinderschutz Liga" (*Oesterreichische Liga zur Bekämpfung des Mädchenhandels*) *über das Vereinsjahr 1910 und Generalversammlungs-Protokolle vom 30 Mai und 26 June, 1911.* Vienna, 1911.

JAPAN.

Murphy, U. G. *The Social Evil in Japan and Allied Subjects; with Statistics.* 3d ed. Tokyo, 1908.

De Becker, J. E. *The Nightless City; or, The History of the Yoshiwara Yuwaku.* 4th ed., rev. Yokohama, 1899.

PERIODICALS.

Social Diseases. Report of progress of the movement for their prevention. Official organ of societies throughout America. New York.

Vigilance (continuing the *Philanthropist*). Published monthly by the American Purity Alliance and the National Vigilance Committee (reorganised in 1912 under the name of the American Vigilance Association). New York.

The Light. Published by the American Purity Federation.

Transactions of the American Society of Sanitary and Moral Prophylaxis. New York.

The Philanthropist. Edited by Aaron Powell. New York. Continued in 1910 as *Vigilance.*

The National League Journal. (Monthly.) London, 1875–1884.

The Shield. The Official Organ of the British Committee of the International Federation for the Abolition of State Regulation of Vice. London.

The Vigilance Record. The Organ of the National Vigilance Association. London.

The Sentinel. (Monthly.) London, 1875–1878.

Bulletin Abolitionniste. Organe Central de la Fédération Abolitionniste Internationale. (Suite au *Bulletin Continental,* fondé en 1875.) Geneva.

Bulletin Mensuel de l'Association Catholique Internationale des Œuvres de Protection de la Jeune Fille. Paris.

Bulletin de la Société Internationale de Prophylaxie Sanitaire et Morale. Paris.

La Traite des Blanches. Bulletin du Bureau International.

Le Relèvement Social. Organe de la Ligue Française de la Moralité Publique. Edited by M. Louis Comte. Paris.

Bolletino della Lega per la Moralità Pubblica. Torino.

Der Abolitionist. Organ für die Bestrebungen der Internationalen Föderation zur Bekämpfung der staatlich reglementierten Prostitution. Edited by Katharina Scheven. Dresden.

Der Deutsche Bund für Mutterschutz. Die neue Generation. Edited by Dr. Helene Stöcker. Berlin.

Sexual Probleme. Zeitschrift für Sexualwissenschaft und Sexualpolitik. Edited by Dr. Max Marcuse.

PART II

The Repeal of the English Contagious Diseases Acts [1]

A. *Signed Works.*

Amos, Sheldon. *The Present State of the Contagious Diseases Acts Controversy.* London, 1870.

Amos, Sheldon. *A Concise Statement of Some of the Objections to the Contagious Diseases Acts of 1864, '66 and '69 dealing with the Argument up to the Present Time.* London, 1876.

Amos, Sheldon. *The Policy of the Contagious Diseases Acts, 1866 and 1869.* London, n. d.

Ash, Edward. *The Contagious Diseases Acts considered in their Relation to Religion and Morals.* London, 1871.

Barcroft, W. *The Contagious Diseases Acts. Shall their Repeal be permitted?* (For private circulation only.) London. n. d.

Batchelor, Rev. Henry. *The Injustice, Inutility, and Immorality of the Contagious Diseases (Women) Acts.* (A speech delivered at Glasgow.) London, 1872.

Beales, Edmond. *A Letter on the Contagious Diseases Acts.* London, 1872.

Beggs, Thomas. *The Proposed Extension of the Contagious Diseases Acts in its Moral and Economical Aspects.* London, 1870.

Blackstone, Samuel. *Paternal Government. Whither are we Drifting?* London, 1873.

Blackwell, Elizabeth. *Wrong and Right Methods of Dealing with the Social Evil as shown by lately Published Parliamentary Evidence.* London, n. d.

Blackwell, Elizabeth. *Medical Responsibility in Relation to the Contagious Diseases Acts.* An Address. . . . 3d ed. London, 1897.

[1] This bibliography is based in part on that found in Benjamin Scott, 'Literature of the Repeal Movement," in *A State Iniquity*, London, 1890, pp. 329 *et seq.*

Blunt, Frederick. *Hindrances to the Work of the Church arising from Immorality, and Practical Suggestions for overcoming them.* London, 1871.

Bright, Jacob. *Speech delivered in the House of Commons* (with closed doors), July 20, 1870. London, 1870.

Bright, Jacob. *Speech in the Debate on the Contagious Diseases Acts, House of Commons, July 22, 1872.* London, 1872.

Bulteel, Christopher. *The Contagious Diseases Acts considered in their Moral, Social, and Sanitary Aspects.* London, 1870.

Bunting, Thomas P. *State Provision for Vice.* London, 1875.

Burgess, Wm. *Dangerous Tendencies of Medical Alarmists.* London, 1876.

Butler, Rev. George. *The Moral Duty of the Church of England in reference to Social Questions.* London, 1871.

Butler, Josephine E. *An Appeal to the People of England on the Recognition and Superintendence of Prostitution by Governments.* London, 1870.

Butler, Josephine E. *The Moral Reclaimability of Prostitutes.* London, 1870.

Butler, Josephine E. *The Duty of Women in Relation to our Great Social Evil.* An address at Carlisle, Nov. 25, 1870. London, 1870.

Butler, Josephine E. *The Contagious Diseases Acts.* Letter to the *Liverpool Mercury.* London, 1870.

Butler, Josephine E. *The Constitution Violated. An Essay.* Edinburgh, 1871.

Butler, Josephine E. *A Letter to a Meeting of Repealers at Chatham.* London, 1871.

Butler, Josephine E. *The Constitutional Iniquity. Speech at Bradford, Jan. 27, 1871.* London, 1871.

Butler, Josephine E. *Vox Populi.* A selection of letters from various persons. London, 1871.

Butler, Josephine E. *Sursum Corda.* Address to the Ladies' National Association. London, 1871.

Butler, Josephine E. *An Address delivered at Edinburgh, Feb. 24, 1871.* London, 1871.

Butler, Josephine E. *The New Era.* Containing a Retrospect of the History of the Regulation System in Berlin, etc. London, 1871.

Butler, Josephine E. *A Letter on the Subject of Mr. Bruce's Bill.* London, 1872.

Butler, Josephine E. *Reply to Dr. Sandwith's Charges.* London, 1872.

Butler, Josephine E. *A Letter to a Friend.* London, 1873.

Butler, Josephine E. *Speech at the Annual Meeting of the Vigilance Association for the Defence of Personal Rights.* London, 1873.

Butler, Josephine E. *Some Thoughts on the Present Aspect of the Crusade against the State Regulation of Vice.* London, 1874.

Butler, Josephine E. *A Letter to the Members of the Ladies' National Association.* London, 1875.

Butler, Josephine E. *Speech to Ladies at Hull.* London, 1876.

Butler, Josephine E. *Three Addresses on Public Morality.* London, 1877.

Butler, Josephine E. *A Question of Life and Death for the Nations.* (Supplement to the Second Annual Report of the Federation.) London, 1878.

Butler, Josephine E. *Letter to the Daily Western Times.* London, 1878.

Butler, Josephine E. *Address at Dublin*, November 4, 1878. London, 1878.

Butler, Josephine E. *Government by Police.* London, 1879.

Butler, Josephine E. *Social Purity. An Address.* London, 1879.

Butler, Josephine E. *Address to the Vigilance Association for Defence of Personal Rights, March 9, 1880.* London, 1880.

Butler, Josephine E. *Address on the Tenth Anniversary of the Ladies' National Association.* London, 1880.

Butler, Josephine E. *Deposition on Oath, Statement, and a Letter to the Home Secretary.* London, 1880.

Butler, Josephine E. *A Letter to the Mothers of England.* London, 1881.

Butler, Josephine E. *A Call to Action.* London, 1881.

Butler, Josephine E. *Speech at Leeds, February 7, 1881.* London, 1881.

Butler, Josephine E. *The New Godiva.* London, 1883.

Butler, Josephine E. *The Bright Side of the Question.* London, 1883.

Butler, Josephine E. *Simple Words for Simple Folk* (about the Repeal of the Contagious Diseases Acts). London, 1884.

Butler, Josephine E. *Federation. New Abolitionist Work throughout the World.* London, 1885.

Butler, Josephine E. *The Demand for Moral Members of Parliament.* London, 1885.

Butler, Josephine E. *On the Dangers of Constructive Legislation in Regard to the Social Evil.* London, 1885.

Butler, Josephine E. *Earnest Words to Men and Women.* London, 1885.

Butler, Josephine E. *The Revival and Extension of the Abolitionist Cause.* London, 1887.

Butler, Josephine E. *Letter to the International Convention of Women at Washington.* London, 1888.

Butler, Josephine E. *Personal Reminiscences of a Great Crusade.* London, 1896.

Butler, Josephine E. *The Hour Before the Dawn. An Appeal to Men.* London, n. d.

Calderwood, Prof. *The Purposes and Provisions of the Contagious Diseases Acts, and Reasons for the Total Repeal of the Same.* London, n. d.

Carpenter, R. L. *Three Articles on the Contagious Diseases Acts.* London, 1870.

Chant, Mrs. Ormeston. *Speech at Annual Meeting of the Ladies' National Association.* London, 1886.

Chapman, Dr. John. *Prostitution: Governmental Experiments in controlling it.* London, 1870.

Chapman, Dr. John. *Compulsory Medication of Prostitutes.* London, 1871.

Chesson, F. W. *Paper on how to influence Members of the House of Commons.* London, 1870.

Close, Francis, Dean of Carlisle. *On the Abominable System of Espionage, etc., under the Contagious Diseases Acts.* London, 1870.

Close, Francis. *An Examination of the Witnesses and their Evidence given before the Royal Commission upon the Administration and Operation of the "Contagious Diseases Acts, 1871."* London, 1872.

Collingwood, C. S. *To the Clergy. Some of the Religious and Moral Aspects of the Contagious Diseases Acts.* London, 1871.

Collingwood, C. S. *The Church of England, and a Great Moral Uprising.* London, 1871.

Collingwood, C. S. *Some Remarks on a Recent Contribution to the Literature of Regulated and Supervised Immorality.* London, 1874.

Collingwood, C. S. *Josephine Butler.* A Sketch. London, 1876.

Collingwood, C. S. *The Real Question.* London, 1879.

Collingwood, C. S. *A Few Leaves from the Story of the Struggle against Immoral Legislation during the Past Year.* London, 1880.

Cooper, Daniel. *The Remedy Worse than the Disease.* London, 1869.

Craigen, Jessie. *Speech at Leeds,* February 7, 1881. London, 1881.

Dawson, J. H. *The Black Acts.* London, 1870.

Dell, Barton. *An Enquiry.* London, 1874.

De Pressensé, Ed. *Speech Delivered in London, May 19, 1876.* Liverpool, 1876.

Duff, Rev. Dr. *On the Contagious Diseases Acts.* London, 1873.

Edmondson, Joseph. *Regulationists and their Policy.* A paper on the . . . prospects of the movement for the repeal of the Contagious Diseases Acts. London, 1875.

Edmondson, Joseph. *Mr. Gladstone and the Contagious Diseases Acts.* London, 1874.

Edmondson, Joseph. *The Substitutes Proposed by the Rt. Hon. H. C. E. Childers, M.P.* London, 1875.

Edmondson, Joseph. *The Regulationists' "Flank Movements" or Substitutes for the English Contagious Diseases Acts.* Sheffield, 1877.

Edmondson, Joseph. *Speech Delivered at Leeds, Feb. 7, 1881.* London, 1881.

Edmondson, Joseph. *The Moral Forces which defeat the Hygienic Regulation of Social Vice.* London, 1882.

Edmondson, Joseph. *A More Excellent Way.* London, 1883.

Edmondson, Joseph. *The House of Commons, the Ministry, and the Contagious Diseases Acts.* London, 1883.

Edmondson, Joseph. *Serious Considerations for Christian Citizens.* London, 1883.

Edmondson, J., and Rev. J. P. Gledstone. *Manifesto of the Repeal Associations in Opposition to the Substitutes Proposed by the Rt. Hon. H. C. E. Childers.* London, 1875.

Ewing, Alexander, Bishop of Argyle. *On National Morality.* London, 1873.

Fallot, M. *Speech at Neuchâtel Conference,* Sept., 1882. London, 1882.

Field, Horace B. A. *Some Thoughts on a Public Agitation.* London, 1872.

Fowle, Rev. F. W. *Aholah and Aholibah.* A Sermon having reference to recent Immoral Legislation by the British Parliament. London, 1871.

Fowler, William, M. P. *Speech in the House of Commons on May 24, 1870, on the Contagious Diseases Acts, with Notes.* London, 1870.

Garrett, Elizabeth. *An Enquiry into the Character of the Contagious Diseases Acts.* London, 1870.

Gledstone, Jas. P. *Observations on Report of Select Committee, 1882, with Reference to the "Moral" Section of Minority Report.* London, 1882.

Guthrie, Thomas. *Address to the Mothers of Our Country*. London, 1870.

Guyot, Yves. *Prostitution under the Regulation System, French and English*. Translated by Edgar Beckit Truman, M.D. London, 1884.

Guyot, Yves. *Reply to the Evidence given by Mr. Treitt and Mr. Howard Vincent before the Select Committee of the House of Lords, on the Law relating to the Protection of Young Girls*. London, 1884.

Henley, Rt. Hon. J. W. *Speech in the House of Commons, August 14, 1871*. London, 1871.

Henley, Rt. Hon. J. W. *Speech in the House of Commons, May 31, 1873*. London, 1873.

Henley, Rt. Hon. J. W. *A Conservative's Opinion on the Contagious Diseases Acts; being extracts from speeches delivered in the years from 1870 to 1876*. London, 1876.

Hennessy, Sir John Pope. *Speech on the Contagious Diseases Ordinance in Hong-Kong*. London, 1882.

Hennessy, Sir John Pope. *The Iniquity of State Regulated Vice in the British Colony of Hong-Kong*. London, n. d.

Herbert, Jesse. *The Enemy in Ambush*. London, 1878.

Herford, Brooke. *The Great Sin of Great Cities*. London, 1872.

Hill, Sarah. *Antagonism of State Regulation to Christian Teaching*. London, n. d.

Holmes, Marion. *Josephine Butler: a Cameo Life Sketch*. London, 1911.

Hooppell, R. E. *The Statistical Results of the Contagious Diseases Acts*. London, 1871.

Hume-Rothery, Mrs. *A Letter to the Right Hon. W. E. Gladstone*. London, 1873.

Hume-Rothery, Mrs. *Reply to Miss Garrett*. London, 1870.

Hume-Rothery, Mrs. *The Prayer and Humble Petition to Her Most Gracious Majesty Queen Victoria, of a Loyal Englishwoman*. London, 1870.

Judson, Rev. J. E. *A More Excellent Way*. London, 1870.

Ker, Rev. John, D.D. *The Nation's Attitude towards Prevailing Vice*. London, 1872.

Kingsford, Douglas. *A Critical Summary of the Evidence before the Royal Commission upon the Contagious Diseases Acts, 1866–69*. London n. d.

Lane, Jas. R. *Facts respecting the Contagious Diseases Acts*. London, 1870.

Laveleye, Émile de. *Regulated Vice in Relation to Morality*. London, n. d.

Malleson, Miss F. R. *On the Personal Co-operation of Men and Women.* London, 1871.

Malleson, Mrs. W. T. *A Reply to Miss Garrett's Letter on the Contagious Diseases Acts.* London, 1871.

Manning, Archbishop. *Letter on the Contagious Diseases Acts.* London, 1875.

Martindale, L. *Under the Surface.* Brighton, n. d.

Martineau, Harriet. *Four Letters on the Contagious Diseases Acts.* By "An Englishwoman." London, 1870.

Mill, John Stuart. *Evidence taken before the Royal Commission of 1870, on the Administration and Operation of the Contagious Diseases Acts of 1866 and 1869.* London, 1871.

M'Laren, Duncan, M.P. *Facts respecting the Contagious Diseases Acts. Substance of a speech delivered at Newcastle, September 27, 1870.* London, 1870.

Mundella, Rt. Hon. A. J., M.P. *Speech delivered in the House of Commons, August 14, 1871.* London, 1871.

Nevins, Dr. J. Birkbeck. *Statement of the Grounds upon which the Contagious Diseases Acts are opposed.* London, 1874.

Nevins, Dr. J. Birkbeck. *Sanitary Results of Regulated Prostitution in Great Britain and her Dependencies.* London, 1874.

Nevins, Dr. J. Birkbeck. *On the Latest Government Statement.* London, 1875.

Nevins, Dr. J. Birkbeck. *Enquiry into the Condition of Prostitution in Towns under, and not under, the Acts.* London, 1876.

Nevins, Dr. J. Birkbeck. *On the Sanitary Results of the Contagious Diseases Acts in the British Army and Navy, and among the Prostitutes registered under the Acts.* London, 1877.

Nevins, Dr. J. Birkbeck. *An Address to Members of the American Legislature and of the Medical Profession, on Recent Proposals to introduce the System of Regulating or Licensing Prostitution into the United States.* London, 1877.

Nevins, Dr. J. Birkbeck. *The Health of the Navy.* An Analysis of the Official Report for 1876. London, 1878.

Nevins, Dr. J. Birkbeck. *On Hereditary Syphilis.* London, 1878.

Nevins, Dr. J. Birkbeck. *Analysis of the Army Medical Report for 1877 and of the Navy Report for 1877.* London, 1879.

Nevins, Dr. J. Birkbeck. *What Public Measures can with Benefit be Adopted for the Diminution of Venereal Diseases?* London, 1880.

Nevins, Dr. J. Birkbeck. *Is Compulsion Necessary in order to Secure that Patients who are Suffering from Venereal Diseases will remain in Hospital until they are cured?* London, 1880.

Nevins, Dr. J. Birkbeck. *Evidence before the Select Committee of the House of Commons.* (*Medical Enquirer*, May, 1880.) London, 1880.

Nevins, Dr. J. Birkbeck. *The Contagious Diseases Acts.* Admiralty Statistics. London, 1884.

Nevins, Dr. J. Birkbeck. *Correspondence between the Admiralty and the President of the National Medical Association for the Repeal of the Contagious Diseases Acts.* London, 1884.

Nevins, Dr. J. Birkbeck. *Examination of the War Office and Admiralty Returns, as to the Amount of Venereal Disease in the Army and Navy since the Suspension of the Compulsory Examination of Women.* London, 1884.

Nevins, Dr. J. Birkbeck. *Analysis of the Navy Report for 1883.* London, 1885.

Nevins, Dr. J. Birkbeck. *Letter addressed to all Candidates for the House of Commons by the National Medical Association for Repeal.* London, 1885.

Nevins, Dr. J. Birkbeck. *Letter to Members of Parliament on the Resolution to be Proposed on June 5, 1888.* London, 1888.

Newman, F. W. *The Cure of the Great Social Evil.* London, 1869.

Newman, F. W. *Address to the London Conference, May 5, 1870.* London, 1870.

Newman, F. W. *Speech at Clifton, May 16, 1870.* London, 1870.

Newman, F. W. *The Theory and Results of the Contagious Diseases Acts.* London, 1870.

Newman, F. W. *Refutation of the Fundamental Principle of the Contagious Diseases Acts.* London, 1870.

Newman, F. W. *On the Unconstitutional and Immoral Teachings of the Acts.* London, 1870.

Newman, F. W. *On State Provision for Vice by warranting Impunity.* London, 1871.

Newman, F. W. *Syllabus of Lecture delivered at Sheffield, February 8, 1876, on Moral, Constitutional, and Sanitary Objections to the Contagious Diseases Acts.* London, 1876.

Newman, F. W. *The Coming Revolution.* London, 1882.

Newman, F. W. *Remedies for the Great Social Evil.* London, 1884.

Newman, F. W. *The New Crusade; or, Duty of the Church to the World.* London, 1886.

Patterson, Alex., M.D. *Statistics of Glasgow Lock Hospital since its Foundation in 1805, with Remarks on the Contagious Diseases Acts, and on Syphilis.* London, 1882.

Rainy, Principal. *Imperial Legislation for Regulating Vice.* London, n. d.

Rainy, Principal. *The Contagious Diseases Acts: Their Character and Necessary Tendency.* London, 1877.

Renzy, A. C. C. De. *The Contagious Diseases Acts in India.* London, 1871.

Russell, J. M. *A Cry From the Depths.* A new Abolitionist poem. London, 1868.

Scott, Benjamin. *A State Iniquity: Its Rise, Extension and Over-throw.* London, 1890.

Scott, Benjamin. *Speech on Social Purity at Exeter Hall.* London, 1885.

Scott, Benjamin. *Seven Reasons for the Repeal of the Contagious Diseases Acts, 1866–1869.* London, 1881.

Shaen, Wm. *Aid and Defence Operations.* London, 1870.

Shaen, Wm. *Suggestions on the Limits of Legitimate Legislation on the Subject of Prostitution.* London, 1877.

Shaen, Wm. *The Common Law in its Relation to Personal Liberty and the State Regulation of Vice.* London, 1880.

Shaen, Wm. *Evidence before the Select Committee.* London, 1881.

Simon, John. *Report to the Privy Council on the Proposed Extension of the Contagious Diseases Acts to the Civil Population.* London, 1869.

Simpson, W. *The New Morality.* London, 1875.

Stansfeld, Hon. J., M.P. *Speech at Bristol,* Oct. 15, 1874. London, 1874.

Stansfeld, Hon. J., M.P. *On the Validity of the Annual Government Statistics of the Operation of the Acts.* London, 1876.

Stansfeld, Hon. J., M. P. *Speech in Free Trade Hall,* Manchester, Dec. 4. London, 1877.

Stansfeld, Hon. J., M.P. *On the Hygienic Failure of the Acts, as proved by the official evidence submitted to the Select Committee of the House of Commons, 1879, 1880 and 1881.* London, 1884.

Stansfeld, Hon. J., M.P. *Introduction to a Critique on Lord Kimberley's Defence of the Government Brothel System at Hong Kong.* London, 1882.

Stansfeld, Hon. J., M.P. *Letter to Belfast Committee on the Present Position of the Warfare against Legalized Vice.* London, 1882.

Stansfeld, Hon. J., M.P. *Speech in the House of Commons, Apr. 20, 1883, in Support of Abolition of Compulsory Examination.* London, 1883.

Stansfeld, Hon. J., M.P. *The Liberal Programme and the Contagious Diseases Acts* (from the *Contemporary Review*). London, 1885.

Stansfeld, James. *Substance of His Speeches on the Contagious Diseases Acts, 1874–75.* London, n. d.

Stuart, Jas., M.P. *The New Abolitionists, a narrative of a year's work.* London, 1876.

Stuart, Jas., M.P. *Repeal of the Contagious Diseases Acts in India and the Colonies.* London, 1888.

Stuart, James, and Wilson, H. J. *Facts vs. Panic; being a Reply to certain alarmist Statements and Proposals recently made.* London, 1898.

Stuart, James, M.P. *Speeches at Annual Meetings of Ladies' National Association.* London, 1881 to 1886.

Tanner, Mrs. *A Bristol Lady at the Geneva Congress.* London, 1877.

Taylor, Charles Bell. *Observations on the Contagious Diseases Acts (Women, not Animals).* London, 1870.

Taylor, Charles Bell. *Substance of an Address to the Medical Society of London.* London, 1871.

Taylor, Charles Bell. *The Statistical Result of the Contagious Diseases Acts;* in two parts. London, 1872.

Taylor, Charles Bell. *Army Statistics and Hygiene in re the Contagious Diseases Acts.* By a Physician. London, 1872.

Taylor, Chas. Bell. *Brief Replies to Three Parliamentary Papers by* Dr. Taylor and the Rev. Dr. Hoppell. London, 1873.

Taylor, Chas. Bell. *The Contagious Diseases Acts examined* (in three parts). London, 1875.

Taylor, Chas. Bell. *Letter to the Hon. Secretary of the City of London Committee.* London, 1875.

Taylor, Chas. Bell. *Speech to the Working Men of Exeter.* London, 1879.

Taylor, Chas. Bell. *Speech to Nottingham Parliamentary Debating Society.* London, 1883.

Trestrail, Frederick. *Letter to the Baptist Union on the Contagious Diseases Acts.* London, 1874.

Varley, Henry. *Reply to Sir W. Harcourt's Speech.* London. n. d.

Vicars, Mrs. Murray. *A Letter addressed to the Chairman of the Committee of Convocation.* London. n. d.

Webb, Mary Anne. *Reprint of Evidence before the Select Committee of the House of Commons.* London, 1882.

Wheeler, Frederic. *An Authentic and Shocking Illustration of the Working of the Acts.* London, 1876.

Wheeler, Frederic. *The Working of the Contagious Diseases Acts.* London 1877.

Wheeler, Frederic. *Further Important Testimony from Chatham.* London, 1882.

Wheeler, Frederic. *The State Regulation of Vice.* London, 1882.

Wheeler, Frederic. *Facts about Chatham.* London, 1884.

Wheeler, Frederic. *Chatham Controversy.* London, 1884.

Wheeler, Frederic. *Medical Alarmists.* London, 1884.

Wheeler, Frederic. *Legalized Vice in the Colonies and Dependencies of the Queen of England with a Facsimile of a License granted to Prostitutes in India.* London. n. d.

Wheeler, Frederic. *The Remarkable History of the Contagious Diseases Acts in England for the Last Seven Years of their Operation.* London, 1887.

Williams, J. Carvell, M.P. *Speech at Annual Meeting of the Ladies' National Association.* London, 1886.

Wilson, Robert. *Prostitution Suppressible and Resistance to the Contagious Diseases Acts a Duty.* London, 1871.

Worth, Thos. *A Second Letter to the Right Hon. W. E. Gladstone.* London, 1870.

B. *Anonymous Works* (arranged chronologically).

The Contagious Diseases Acts; Letters to the Medical Press and Circular. London, 1867.

Report from the Committee appointed in 1864 by the Admiralty and the War Office to inquire into the Pathology and Treatment of Venereal Disease, etc. London, 1868.

Report from the Select Committee of the House of Lords on the Contagious Diseases Acts, 1866. London, 1868.

Licensing Prostitution. London, 1869.

Report from the Select Committee of the House of Commons on the Contagious Diseases Act, 1866. London, 1869.

The Remedy Worse than the Disease. London, 1869.

A Grave Subject. London, 1870.

A Letter from a Medical Practitioner. London, 1870.

Letter from the Bishop of Cape Town. London, 1870.

Letters in Reply to Miss Garrett's Defence of the Contagious Diseases Acts. By Justina. London, 1870.

Memorial of a Conference to the Home Secretary. London, 1870.

The Ladies' Appeal and its Critics. London, 1870.

The Protest of the Associations for Repeal against the Appointment of the Royal Commission. London, 1870.

Facts and Arguments in favour of Voluntary Hospitals. London, 1871.

Letters I and II to my Countrymen. "*Be Not Deceived,*" *an Unspoken Address. Universal Repeal of the Contagious Diseases Acts.* By an English Lady. London, 1871.

The Contagious Diseases Acts and the Royal Commission. By Necessarian. London, 1871.

Report of the Royal Commission upon the Administration and Operation of the Contagious Diseases Acts, with Evidence. Vols. I and II. London, 1871.

The Contagious Diseases Acts, and the Necessarian Philosophy. London, 1871.

The Royal Commission as a Court of Justice. London, 1871.

Alleged Moral Results of the Acts. London, 1872.

The Contagious Diseases Acts, and the Contagious Diseases Preventive Bill. By "Anthropos." London, 1872.

What Are the Contagious Diseases Acts? and Reasons for their Repeal. London, 1872.

Exposure of the False Statistics of the Contagious Diseases Acts. By the Managers of Metropolitan Female Reformatories. London. 1873.

Influence of Legislation on Public Morals. London, 1873.

The Advantages of Military Life. London, 1873.

The Contagious Diseases Acts. London, 1873.

What I Saw at the Royal Albert Hospital, Devonport. By a member of the Ladies' National Association. London, 1873.

Statement respecting Certain Immoral Laws. London, 1874.

The Liberal Party and the Contagious Diseases Acts; a political Catechism. London, 1874.

An Address to Working Men and Women relating to a Recent Distressing Case of Suicide at Aldershot. London, 1875.

Congregational Committee for the Abolition of State Protection and Patronage of Vice. Report of the Speeches at the Meeting held in Pillar Hall . . . on Wednesday, May 12, 1875. London, 1875.

Contagious Diseases Acts. Observations suggested by the queries: 1. *Are the Contagious Diseases Acts Necessary in England?* 2. *Do they Succeed?* 3. *Would no less Objectionable Measures suffice?* London, 1875.

The Substitutes Proposed by the Rt. Hon. H. C. E. Childers, M.P. Manifesto of Repeal Associations. London, 1875.

Wesleyan Society for Securing the Repeal of the Contagious Diseases Acts. Report of the speeches . . . on Friday, March 5, 1875. London, 1875.

Three Addresses on Public Morality. London, 1877.

State Legalisation of Vice. London, 1878.

The Address of the Belfast Committee. London, 1878.

An Idea of the Extent of the Agitation for Repeal. London, 1880.

Immoral Legislation; a few Facts for the consideration of the Irish Clergy. London, 1880.

The Choice between Personal Freedom and State Protection. London, 1880.

At Home and Abroad; a Comparison of certain British and Continental Regulations. London, 1881.

Report of the Discussion of the Acts of the International Congress, with Comments. London, 1881.

A Memorial to Sir John Pope Hennessy, K. C. M. G., on the Contagious Diseases Ordinance in Hong Kong. London, 1882.

Petition to Parliament for Total Repeal of the Contagious Diseases Acts. By Belfast Medical Men. London, 1882.

Report of Parliamentary Committee on the Contagious Diseases Acts. London, 1882.

The Minority Report of the Select Committee of the House of Commons. London, 1882.

A Letter respecting the Report of the Select Committee. By E. London, 1883.

An Imminent Danger. London, 1884.

Mendacious Statistics. Issued by the Working Men's League. London, 1884.

On the Moral Condition of the Subjected Districts since the Suspension of Compulsory Examination. London, 1884.

Memorial of the National Association for Repeal of the Contagious Diseases Acts addressed to both Houses of the Legislature, 1886. London, 1886.

Friends' Association for Abolishing State Regulation of Vice; a short Summary of the History of State regulated Vice in the United Kingdom. London, 1900.

Copy of a Rough Record of Events and Incidents connected with the Repeal of the Contagious Diseases Acts, 1864-6-9, in the United Kingdom, and of the Movement against State Regulation of Vice in India and the Colonies, 1856-1906. Sheffield, 1907.

A Collection of Opinions on English, Colonial and Continental Laws and Police Regulations for the Sanitary Supervision of Vice. London. n. d.

City of London Committee for Obtaining the Repeal of the Contagious Diseases Acts. London. n. d.

Compulsory Medication of Prostitutes by the State. (Reprint from the *Westminster Review*, July, 1876.) London. n. d.

Condition of the Subjected Districts since the Suspension of Compulsory Periodical Examinations. London. n. d.

English and Continental Laws and Regulations concerning Prostitution. London. n. d.

Manifesto of the Association formed to secure the Repeal of the Contagious Diseases Acts; called forth by the Debate in the House of Commons on June 23, 1875. London. n. d.

Report of the Commission appointed by H. E. J. Pope Hennessy, Governor, etc., of Hong Kong, to inquire into the Working of the Contagious Diseases Acts. Printed by House of Commons. London. n. d.

Testimony in Favour of Repeal. London. n. d.

The Greatest Moral Hypocrisy of the Day. London. n. d.

To Women Suffering under the System of the Contagious Diseases Acts. London. n. d.

Why Should I Attend a Meeting for Repeal? London. n. d.

INDEX

A

Abduction, 63

Abolitionist, Der, quoted, note, 174

Abolitionist movement, 163 *et seq.*; in England, 163 *et seq.*; in France, 182 *et seq.*; in Germany, 193; in Italy, 193; International Federation at Geneva, 197; a convert to, 205; in South America, 207

Addams, Miss Jane, article by, quoted, note, 210

African tribes, 1

Age limitation for prostitutes, 38

America, prostitution in, 9; objections to "regulation" in, 77, 78; constitutional law in, 115; difficulties before police in, 119; puritanical sentiment in, 147; white-slave traffic in, 207 *et seq.*; Nat. Vigilance Committee, 207; United States joins International Treaty, 208; breaking up white-slave traffic in, 208; federal laws or white-slave traffic, 209; state laws concerning white-slave traffic, 209; societies formed for repressing social evil, 222 *et seq.*

American Federation for Sex Hygiene, foundation of, 229; resolutions of, 229 ff.

American Medical Association, resolutions presented to, 229

American Society of Sanitary and Moral Prophylaxis, cited, 183; 215; aims of, 224; founding of the, 225; work of, 225; list of educational pamphlets of, 226; branches of, 227; and the Page law, 234 address before, 246 *et seq.*

Amos, Professor Sheldon, quoted, iii; *Regulation of Vice,* quoted, note, 70; 167

Amusement, better forms of, needed, 149

An der Königsmauer, a haunt of vice in Berlin, 39

Ancient Regulations, 12 ff.

Animien-Kneipen, 174

Annexes au Rapport Général, cited note, 187

Argentine *Société de Protection,* 207

Armies, veneral disease in, statistics on, 53

Asia Minor, prostitution in, 2

Atlantic City, licensing of prostitutes in, 241

Augagneur, M., *Conf. Inter.,* quoted, note, 87, note, 107; note, 113; 180; opposed to regulation, 187; 191

Australia, 165, 194

Austria, regulation in, 48; venereal disease in, 53; 65; national committees formed in, 172; white-slave traffic to, 197; league in, 206; *see* Vienna

Austro-Hungary, enters into treaty with the Netherlands, 199; 202

Avignon, public houses established in, 16; regulations in, note, 21

B

Baltimore, society started in, 227

Barmaids, 116

Index

THE SOCIAL EVIL
IN SYRACUSE

BEING THE REPORT OF AN INVESTI-
GATION OF THE MORAL CONDITION
OF THE CITY CONDUCTED BY A COM-
MITTEE OF EIGHTEEN CITIZENS

*"Constant and persistent repression of
prostitution the immediate method: Absolute annihilation the ultimate ideal."*
REPORT OF THE CHICAGO VICE COMMISSION.

SYRACUSE, N. Y.
1913

A Work of Appreciation

The Moral Survey Committee of Syracuse wishes to make special mention of the services rendered to the Committee by Mr. George J. Kneeland, Director of Investigations of the American Vigilance Association. Without his faithful and intelligent supervision and co-operation in all the details of the investigation reported in this book, our work would have been impossible.

F. W. BETTS, Chairman
P. E. ILLMAN, Secretary

CONTENTS

THE COMMITTEE OF EIGHTEEN

FREDERICK W. BETTS, *Chairman*
PAUL E. ILLMAN, *Secretary*
JOHN H. APPLEBEE
MRS. CHARLES J. BARNARD
HENRY L. ELSNER
JAMES EMPRINGHAM
CHARLES S. ESTABROOK
ALBERT C. FULTON
H. J. GORKE
THOMAS H. HALSTED
CHARLES W. HARGITT
FREDERICK R. HAZARD
MRS. FREDERICK R. HAZARD
MISS ARRIA S. HUNTINGTON
SALEM HYDE
H. W. JORDAN
MRS. EDWARD B. JUDSON, JR.
MRS. IRVING G. VANN

PREFACE

The responsibility for the publication of this report of the moral survey of Syracuse is assumed by the Committee of Eighteen. The judgment of the committee has been fortified and strengthened by that of more than fifty other men and women who have read the report and approve its publication.

The work was conducted under the direction of the executive officers of the American Vigilance Association, and the actual investigation of conditions was made by its expert investigators, in whose moral character the Committee has every confidence. They have performed a difficult and disagreeable task with commendable thoroughness and discretion. The Committee of Eighteen assures the citizens of Syracuse that every statement made in the report is borne out by the facts. Indeed, understatement has been the constant policy of the Committee.

The purposes of this report are, first, to inform the citizens of Syracuse of the actual conditions relative to vice and prostitution; second, to awaken the conscience of the city and arouse a public sentiment that shall compel the present and all future administrations thoroughly and insistently to enforce the laws relative to prostitution and the liquor traffic; and third, to suggest means of reducing prostitution that have been adopted in other cities and states with marked success. In this way Syracuse may be freed from the horde of men and women who make a business of commercializing vice, and who resort to every means to lure the youth of both sexes into their toils.

The light having been thrown upon the social evil by the publication of this report, the responsibility for its continued permission rests squarely upon the citizenship of Syracuse. The committee has faith that the citizens can be relied upon to make Syracuse cleaner, healthier and more moral.

SYRACUSE MORAL SURVEY COMMITTEE

"Our own task is absolutely simple and clear. It is that of turning on the light, and of guiding the present hopeful movement as wisely as we can. To an enlightened public opinion and a growing conscience this ancient evil is rapidly becoming 'a moral affront and an utter impossibility.'"

JANE ADDAMS.

INTRODUCTION

Herewith is presented to the citizens of Syracuse the report of a moral survey of the city undertaken by a committee of citizens. In it are detailed facts as to the extent of prostitution and its attendant evils in the city. The committee has every reason to believe that these facts are authentic, and present an understatement of the actual existing conditions. The report is offered in the hope and expectation that it will be the first step in an earnest and persistent effort at least materially to reduce, if not actually abolish the evil of prostitution in the city.

The first step in any reform is to know the actual conditions as they are. The next is to awaken an indignant public conscience that shall insist upon the evil being reduced to the lowest possible point. The third step is to devise and put in practice means to that end. In this report the first step is taken, and the third is suggested.

Everyone recognizes the direfulness of the evil of prostitution. Of all the vices that afflict society it is unquestionably the worst. Indeed it is so abhorrent to every moral sense that for generations the very mention of it has been tabooed. In the secrecy thus surrounding and fostering it the evil has grown to an appalling magnitude in every municipality of the land.

It is time that this "conspiracy of silence" should end. Prostitution should be known and understood in all its hideous manifestations and *wisely* combated if for no other reason than that it is the direct cause of the most malignant diseases from which humanity suffers, diseases scattering misery and death broadcast among the guilty and innocent alike, and leaving in their wake sterility, paralysis, infantile blindness, idiocy, insanity and an unspeakable physical degeneration. When to this is added the moral corruption and the degradation of womanhood to gratify the greed and passions of men to which it gives rise, it becomes the plain duty of all citizens to do their utmost to suppress it.

The committee believes that the social evil can be suppressed in its worst phases. It may not be possible to entirely abolish prostitution for generations. Perhaps only the slow process of moral education can do that. But it is possible to abolish its flagrant manifestation. An end

9

can be put to the *commercialized aspect* of prostitution, and its association with the sale of liquor; and thus prostitution itself, in the absence of the abnormal encouragement which it now receives, may be materially reduced. But this can be done only by an awakened public conscience that is unremitting in its vigilant efforts.

The committee feels that the public conscience of Syracuse needs only a plain, unvarnished statement of the facts as they are, such as this report contains, to awaken it to an insistent rebellion against the social evil in all its phases.

The work of this committee is the logical outcome of certain preceding events in the recent history of Syracuse. In February, 1911, The Syracuse Society for the Prevention of Social Diseases issued statistics of the venereal diseases in Syracuse. The statistics showed the startling prevalence of these diseases. In the autumn of the same year, a Social Survey of the city was made, and a "Know Your City Week" held. It was felt by many at the time that a moral survey of the city was needed to complete the work. With this thought in mind, the Ministers' Association of the city, on March 25th, 1912, authorized the appointment of a committee to make such moral survey. This committee, recognizing the importance of the work it had undertaken, and that it called for as broad a representation of the best citizenship as it was possible to secure, added fourteen laymen and women to its membership. In June, 1912, this enlarged committee called in the aid of the American Vigilance Association, and immediately began the survey.

A word as to the American Vigilance Association: The investigation of the social evil in Chicago by a commission appointed by the mayor, and the publication of its report (similar in form to that here presented) disclosed the fact that the social evil is a huge, loosely organized, but none the less efficient, national *business* for the encouragement of prostitution and the merciless exploiting of men and women for profit. In other words it is commercialized vice. One result of this discovery was the formation of the American Vigilance Association. This Association thus describes its method and purpose: "Accuracy of statement is necessary as a basis for the study of causes, methods of prevention, and law enforcement. The American Vigilance Association urges a truthful, unsensational study and presentation of conditions, and a normal attitude toward the problem as a whole. The purpose of this Association shall be to suppress and prevent commercialized vice, and to promote the highest standard of public and private morals. To accomplish this purpose, the Association shall strive for the constant, persistent and absolute repression of prostitution, and the passage and enforcement of laws for the rescue and protection of girls and women; for the promotion of knowledge of the social evil, its effects and results; and for the circulation of the best literature regarding it." The officers of the Association are President, David Starr Jordan; Vice-Presidents, His Eminence James Cardinal Gibbons, Very Reverend Dean Walter T. Sumner, and Dr. Charles W. Eliot; Treasurer, Charles H. Hutchinson; Executive Secretary and General Counsel, Clifford G. Roe. Jane Addams is a member of the Executive Board.

The field work of this Syracuse Survey was done by five investigators, men and women, of the American Vigilance Association. These are men and women of integrity, in whom the committee has full confidence. The affidavits of these investigators (for the committee has in its possession affidavits covering every statement in this report) were embodied by the American Vigilance Association in a report to this committee. This report was, in turn, edited by this committee, and is herewith published. The edited report has also been submitted to a group of more than fifty citizens for their approval; and they have signed it as witnessing their conviction that its publication would be a public service, and would constitute a basis for permanent constructive efforts towards improving the moral condition of Syracuse.

Thus it will be seen that this moral survey of Syracuse is not merely a local matter, but is part of a great national movement for the repression of prostitution with its burdensome cost in money and human souls, its corroding diseases, and its withering demoralization. As a result of these surveys, the economic efficiency and moral character of our nation may be raised to a higher plane than has hitherto been attained.

This report is not published for the purpose of criticising any persons or administration. That the appalling conditions herein described exist in Syracuse is due in part to the indifference of the citizens, and their tacit acquiescence in the existence of commercialized vice, as well as to the laxity of administrations and public officials. When public sentiment insistently demands that the segregated district where prostitution is exploited for gain be abolished it will be abolished, and not until then.

It is not the purpose of this investigation to attack the personal side of the business, but the business itself. This committee is merely an investigating committee, and not a prosecuting committee. The citizens of Syracuse must themselves deal with the conditions herein revealed.

While no special attempt was made to trace the ramifications of commercialized vice to the persons or interests who manage the business and absorb its profits, enough was revealed during the investigation to suggest where these ramifications culminate. The investigators collected data on this phase of the social evil, parts of which are published in this report, and all of which can be used, if needed, as the starting point for future investigations along these lines.

It has been said above that the third step in combating an evil is the formulating of and putting into practice means for its suppression, and special attention is called to the chapter on "Conclusions and Recommendations" where this phase of the subject is treated. The committee has carefully omitted from the report all names and addresses. These are signified by the letter X and a number following, each name and place being indicated by a specific number. In no case does this number correspond to the street number of the place.

With this foreword the committee places its report in the hands of the citizens of Syracuse. No words of ours can add to the sinister significance of the facts herein recorded. The committee is convinced that the evils they reveal can be remedied; and that the moral integrity of our citizens may be relied upon to impel them to unite in a determined attack on commercialized vice until it is permanently driven from the city. This is a duty we owe not only to the young men and women of Syracuse, but to the young men and women of the whole of central New York, who, as the report shows, furnish the steady supply of human material necessary to maintain this evil business.

What Des Moines Has Done to Reduce Prostitution

"CITY OF DES MOINES

"Department of Public Affairs

"Des Moines, Iowa, Nov. 4, 1912.

"Mr. Louis M. Quitman, Secy.,

"Chicago Protective League for Women,

"108 West Twenty-second Street,

"Chicago, Ill.

"Dear Sir:

"I have your inquiry of Oct. 31 with reference to the result of the abolition of the segregated vice district in the City of Des Moines. The inferences in your inquiry are quite incorrect. Our experience leads us to several very determined conclusions; first, that segregation is a delusion in that it was never known to segregate; second, that vice cannot be driven out by manifesto, but takes an honest, conscientious, vigilant administration of the law against prostitution; and finally, that by such an administration, conditions can be wonderfully changed.

"Somewhat over a year ago, during, and just before and after, our State Fair, we put the question of investigating and making a census of moral conditions with reference to the social evil in the city into the hands of one of our most trusted officers, one, too, who had been in the service during the time of the segregated district, and also ever since the abolition of that district. His report to me was that there were under the old regime about three hundred professional prostitutes in Des Moines. Of this number, about one hundred and fifty were in the segregated district and about one hundred and fifty were scattered all about the city, conducting their business under the cloak of one disguise or another. At the time of his report there were altogether, as nearly as he could estimate, about seventy-five professional abandoned women in Des Moines. This, too, was at the time when we have our worst trouble owing to the influx of women along with the great crowds attending the State Fair.

"At the present time, conditions are much better than at the time of this report. It will be noted that the results of his investigation show that so far from our present policy, simply scattering the vice as you suggest, and as is commonly suggested, by the opponents of our method, that there are altogether in Des Moines now less than half as many abandoned women as we formerly had in the segregated district alone, and that we then had twice as many abandoned women scattered at random throughout the city as we now have in the entire city. Our policy has not only removed a very large per cent of the evil, but it has at the same time removed the entire effrontery of it.

"Other important considerations are the fact that it has rid the community of a class of criminals and hangers-on that are always attendant upon this vice; that it has removed the temptation always flaunted in the face of our young men under the old system; and that at least, so far as Des Moines is concerned, it no longer makes us a party to the annual offering up of some scores of our young girls upon the altar of lust.

"Finally, and quite to the discomfiture of those theorists who hold that a system of prostitution is necessary to protect chaste women against rape, the abolition of the segregated district has not in the least endangered the virtue of the rest of womankind in our city.

"I shall be glad to give you any further information that may be of assistance to you in your fight against vice.

"Yours very truly,

"(Signed) JAS. R. HANNA,

"Mayor."

THE SOCIAL EVIL IN SYRACUSE

This investigation of the social evil was made during June, July and August, 1912, eleven days in the autumn, including State Fair week, and three days in November.

The entire city was not covered, the attempt being rather to make a thorough investigation of as many places as time permitted. Undoubtedly there are other immoral resorts than those covered by this report, but the places herein described we know were in existence and doing business at the time of this investigation.

The investigation of the summer dealt with actual conditions; that of the autumn more particularly with the sources of supply, and the origin, lives and revenue of the girls practicing prostitution in Syracuse.

The report of the expert investigators affords a minimum basis for estimating the amount of business in vice done regularly and continuously in the city. It affords a *minimum* basis because during June, July and August the demand for prostitution is less than other seasons of the year. For example, commercial travel falls off during these months, and many residents are away on vacations. As a result many of the girls are out of town. Thus Madame X1 had only one girl in her house during one of the visits of the investigator. She usually has three.

The totals of the investigations are, therefore, not only lower than the actual figures because no attempt was made to include every place in the city, but also because the numbers observed in the places investigated were smaller than at other seasons of the year. The report is, therefore, an under estimate of actual conditions.

Syracuse has a distinct vice district. Much of it is centered in certain blocks of houses of prostitution on Washington St., certain hotels concentrated within a few blocks and furnished rooms within a narrow radius of the so-called common center of the city.

One highly concentrated district, much of it within a half mile radius, with the Soldiers' Monument for the center of the circle, is used for houses of prostitution, disorderly hotels and saloons, furnished rooms and tenements, and for street walking.

These centrally located streets are used at all hours of the day and night by numerous women open to the approaches of men, and solicitations for prostitution by both men and women are frequent.

This vice section is situated at the very heart of the city, in the midst of hotel, business, theatre and shopping district. Business men, school

15

children, young men and women, wives and mothers shopping or marketing are compelled to pass houses, hotels and saloons and apartment houses devoted to commercialized vice, and to see and be jostled by men and women living on prostitution.

Nor is this all. In three consecutive blocks on East Washington St. there are eighteen houses of prostitution. Along this street the New York Central trains pass slowly. The character of this street is well known to traveling men. The conditions are visible from the car windows. Thus the street is a lure to the visiting man. He locates the Red Light District before he alights at the depot. Indeed the train has carried him, as in a "sight seeing car" through the very heart of the city's most vicious life. The city flaunts her vice in the face of every visitor.

For convincing testimony of the evils of this condition, see affidavit of one of the investigators who revisited the city during the Convention of Older Boys held in Syracuse, November 29th-December 1st, 1912, page 29.

Through whatever of growth, uplift, beautification and betterment Syracuse has passed, this segregated district of immorality at the civic heart of the city has remained impregnable. Citizens have come and gone, families have died out, industries have risen and fallen, but the madames of Syracuse have endured. Their houses of prostitution—dens of disease and living death—and the sporting hotels and saloons by their side are seemingly as steadfast as the Rock of Gibraltar. Shall it always be so?

THE AMERICAN VIGILANCE ASSOCIATION

"After six years' experience as a prosecutor of those who buy and sell women, I have learned that the question is one of supply and demand. There must be women and girls to fill the supply and there must be men to create the demand.

"Now, the question is, how shall we reduce this supply and demand? This brings us to the question of segregation or dispersion.

"Segregation creates a neglect on the part of the public. It fosters a 'don't care' spirit toward the question, while scattering incites the public to action, puts the public on its guard.

"This 'don't care' spirit on the part of the public allows the vice interests to overstimulate the demand and establish ways of recruiting the supply by most obnoxious methods. This recruiting has given rise to the awful white slavery of to-day.

"It is argued that repression and closing of segregated districts scatter the prostitutes into residence sections. This argument assumes that public officers and private agencies will cease their activities after dispersion of the prostitutes. The public officers if they do their duty in one case will do it in the other. And also people in residence districts will be awakened to their duty by dispersion. Many people live near the segregated districts: why should these people be singled out as victims of unwholesome neighbors? It is argued that it will be more difficult for the police to locate and drive out prostitutes in residence districts. Every patrolman on his beat knows the character of every flat and house in his district, or should know.

"But, if these people are more difficult to find, then the demand is minimized and likewise the supply.

"Why do business houses of the same trade congregate in the same streets and localities? Because by so doing trade is made easier and all are benefited. It stimulates trade and increases the business. Just so with a segregated district with blocks of vice resorts."

CLIFFORD G. ROE.

CHAPTER I

The Segregated District of Syracuse

1. HOUSES OF ILL-FAME

During this investigation twenty-seven parlor houses of prostitution, commonly known as houses of ill-fame, were found within the segregated district. Each of these houses is conducted by a "madame." The investigators visited twenty-three of these houses. They actually saw and counted one hundred and nineteen inmates in twenty-two of the houses, and estimated the total number in the twenty-three houses investigated to be one hundred and fifty-six.

The houses are readily recognized. Some of them have red lamps under their push buttons on the stoop. Others have red lights in the hall.

The rooms on the ground floor are used as reception rooms, and in some houses there is one room used as a dance hall. In each house there is an automatic piano. Liquor is sold freely. The maids who serve the drinks are generally colored. The price is $1.00 per bottle for beer, and as high as $5.00 per bottle for wine. In a few of the houses the madame herself serves the drinks. The average estimated age of the prostitutes is 20 years. They receive half of what they make. The other half goes to the madame. In addition the inmate pays a weekly board to the madame of $7.00 to $10.00. In many of the houses the inmates wear kimonas. In a few, they receive in evening dress.

The price of prostitution in houses in Syracuse is set at a low figure. In over half the houses it is $1.00. The price rises to $2.00 to "easy" strangers, and to almost all visitors during special seasons, such as Fair Week and Convention Week. One house charges $5.00, and one charges $3.00 and $5.00. Perversion was found in fifteen houses. This is generally performed by one of the inmates, who is a better money getter than the other girls.

Boys from ten to fifteen years of age are often employed in the parlor houses in such work as polishing the railings and banisters, delivering newspapers, and doing odd chores. At X3 house of prostitution one of the investigators saw a twelve year old boy at work polishing

19

a brass railing, while at the same time a girl partially clad was close at hand.

Receipts from the Business of Prostitution in the Segregated District

As before stated, twenty-seven parlor houses were found within the segregated district of Syracuse alone. One hundred and nineteen inmates were actually counted in twenty-two of these houses, and the investigators estimated that in the twenty-three houses visited there were 156 inmates. Thus there were five to six inmates actually counted and seven estimated per house. These figures are *ultra-conservative.* On the basis of the five to six per house (5½), the twenty-seven houses would contain approximately 150 inmates counted, and 190 estimated.

What, upon this basis, are the probable receipts from the business of prostitution in the houses of the segregated district?

In following out this inquiry, the investigators secured an account book which shows the daily earnings of an inmate of one of the houses during a period of six months. This is the account book of girl X39, an inmate of a dollar house of prostitution. (See Appendix No. 1.)

The figures in this book give a very accurate idea of the earnings of the inmates, and as the madames receive half of these earnings as their share, it is possible to arrive at the probable yearly receipts in these twenty-seven houses during a period of one year.

It must be remembered that these figures represent only the amounts received by the madames from the sale of the inmates' bodies, and give no idea as to how much extra money the madames take in from the sale of liquor, beer and champagne. It would be safe to say that the profits from the sale of liquor at exorbitant prices are probably as great as from the sale of the bodies of the unfortunate women. Nor is there included in this estimate the madames' profits from board, the sale of clothing, jewelry, cosmetics—in fact on everything the inmates buy.

This account book shows the gross earnings of girl X39, an inmate of a dollar house of prostitution, to have been $1,962.50 for six months. At this rate her yearly earnings would be $3,925.00. Incidentally, this means that X39 "served" men over 3,900 times during the year. It may be claimed, and perhaps justly, that X39 is an exceptional girl, and this must be taken into account. On the other hand it is to be noted that this is a dollar house, while in many houses the charge is from two to five dollars, and even higher, especially for perversion, which is common in the parlor houses.

Taking girl X39's gross yearly earnings ($3,925.00) as the basis, the 150 inmates actually counted gives a total of $588,750 as the yearly earnings of the inmates of the twenty-seven parlor houses of prostitution in the segregated district, or a yearly business for each house of $21,805.55. Of this total amount, one half, or $294,375, goes to the twenty-seven madames—a return of $10,902.77 per annum for each madame from the sale of the inmates' bodies alone. The madames' profits, however, are greatly increased through the sale of liquor, commission on articles sold to inmates at exorbitant prices, inmates' board, and overcharge for medical attendance.

Applying these figures of yearly earnings to the *estimated* number of inmates (190), gives a total of $745,750 as the annual receipts from the sale of the bodies of the inmates of the parlor houses of prostitution in the segregated district of Syracuse alone.

This estimate, showing an annual gross income of approximately three-quarters of a million dollars, reveals the appalling magnitude of the business of prostitution in the parlor houses of Syracuse.

*Illustrative Cases**

June 29, 9:30 p. m., Aug. 6, 10 p. m., X4 House, Madame X5

The price of prostitution is $5.00 and for perversion $10.00. Beer sells at $2.00 and wine at $5.00. Six inmates were counted, and eight to ten estimated. They wear evening dress, and receive half the amount paid by the man. They pay $10.00 a week board.

Aug. 1, 2 p. m., X6 House, Madame X1

The inmates wear kimonas. The price is $2.00 for prostitution and $5.00 for perversion. The madame offers to sell out the business and house, of which she is the owner, for $30,000.

---

*In an address before a committee of nine of the Chicago City Council appointed to consider Segregation and Commercialized Vice, Miss Kate Adams, at that time Secretary to the Police Commissioner, thus describes her visit to a segregated district of vice in Chicago:

"I determined to study conditions at first hand, and in December, 1909, I paid my first visit to the South Side vice district. The horrors of that afternoon are burned into my memory, and can never be effaced. I shudder when I think of God looking down on these sights, knowing that we as a city are responsible for them. There were the very young girls brazening their way through the situation; the prematurely old, faded ones nearing the span of seven years allotted them in this life, their presence tolerated, but they barely able to earn their bread and butter; the dope fiends listlessly lying back on plush-covered couches, seeking a moment's oblivion from their surroundings. The hearts of many of these girls were aching because of what they had lost, as I afterwards discovered when talking with them individually."

This house is a way-station for girls coming and going. Madame X1 apparently does a traffic in girls.

July 26, 11 p. m., X7 House, Madame X8.

Four inmates counted and six estimated. The price of a girl is $1.00, of which she receives half. The dress is a kimona.

The following are reports of certain of the houses, given in the investigator's own words:

"Visited Madame X9's parlor house, X10. Met there a girl I know. She introduced me to the madame as 'one of the boys.' I stated my errand to Syracuse—to open a house, if possible, as New York is now so 'tight.' She discouraged me by informing me that 'they' will not stand for Jews,* that the minute a Jew opens up they get to Citizen X11, who gets to Official X12 and has them driven from the town. I explained to her that my 'woman' is a Gentile and that I wouldn't mix in.

"She then said, 'You can't mix in, "they" wouldn't let men mix in nohow.'

"She told me to try and 'get to' Official X13 and talk to him about it. She freely discussed her business and said she read in the papers that New York protection was $600 a month. It hardly costs her that much a whole year she said. Neither she, nor anyone else in Syracuse could pay that much because 'the money isn't here.' Her girls average $20 a week for 'themselves.' The girls buy all of their 'house stuff' of her. One girl had on a velvet-like wrapper for which she paid the madame $36. I don't think the wrapper cost more than $12. The house physician visits once a week and gets $1 from each girl he examines. His attendance is compulsory. The madame sells drinks, to the patrons a very thin wine glass of beer, and to the inmates a small glass of soda, for which she charges $1. The house is well-furnished and clean. She has a player piano, which she 'shuts up' at 12 p. m.

"At House X14, Madame X15 was sitting in her doorway in a semi-nude condition and solicited me.

"On September 6th, I visited Madame X16's, a $3 and $5 house (X17) (creole). After buying a round of drinks and a pack of Pall Malls for an inmate, I succeeded in getting some information from her. She is 18 years old, and comes from Rochester. She claims to have been ruined at the age of 14 years by a 'big man' in Rochester. Her earnings are about $25 a week, none of the girls earning more.† She has no

---

*This investigator was Jewish.

†This $25.00 is the inmate's share of her total earnings. The madame receives the same amount in addition to board, making the inmate's total earnings approximately $60.00. This is true in every case where the girl speaks of what she makes or earns.

lover. Asked what she does with the money she earns, she said she put it on her back. The madame buys all her clothes and some of the other girls'. While talking to her she freely snuffed cocaine. The madame then urged me to go upstairs and told me '$3 "straight" and $5 "French" (perversion).' I told her I came from New York. She then began to talk of the Rosenthal affair, the raids in the parlor houses, etc. She hates New York because 'you've got to submit to the police there.'

" 'In Syracuse it's different,' she said, 'if it wasn't for Official X13, Syracuse wouldn't be on the map.' I told her that I had heard that the New York housekeepers made fortunes in the last one and one-half years; she said she is satisfied with what she makes; that she need not be afraid of anybody and doesn't have to worry about any raids. She has the 'best' people in town for patrons and wouldn't cater to the 'riff-raff.'

"I next visited Madame X18's, House X19. An inmate was willing to talk. I spoke to her in Yiddish. She said she came from ———, is 19 years old, and has been two years in 'the business.' She said business was bad, that she used to make in Albany twice as much, and that she expected to stay only over the fair. She has been here seven weeks and never earned over $20, and at that she 'done well,' as some of the other girls earn only $10 and $15 per week. She said there was too much competition for a small town. She has been in two other houses since she came here and didn't 'make out' any better than she does here.

"September 7th, I visited House X19, Madame X20's, a $1 house. (Price raised to $2 for the Fair.) Met there a young girl, formerly an inmate of House X37, New York City. She came here two weeks ago when the houses in New York closed. She introduced me to Madame X20. I told the madame I was looking for an opportunity to open a house, and she promptly informed me that I was 'wasting time,' that New York people are not wanted and I should just try it. She then asked me if I had seen Official X13 about it or intended to. I pretended not to know and asked her to 'put me wise.' She then told me to try and connect with Official X13. 'But it's no use,' she said, she couldn't think of introducing me to him. The doctor's exhibit, attached to house card belongs to the girl from a New York house. This girl informed me that in the two weeks she has been in this house she earned $43, less than she earned in Big X38's house in New York in a week. The best money maker in the house, a perverter, makes only $35 at the most. Other girls make as low as $10 and $12 a week. They don't care, however, as most of them have no cadets, according to this girl.

"September 9th, I visited Madame X21, House X22. The madame sold two chemises to two girls for $8.50 apiece. The chemises can be bought in any store for $3. I found here two New York girls who came to Syracuse two weeks ago. They would not have come if New York was 'open.' Business is 'rotten' here they said. Girl X68 'made only $18 over my board' during the week.

" 'Why, the highest number Saturday night was fourteen checks,' she said. 'X185 made $21 over her board last week, which was supposed to have been a good week with the convention crowd here.'

"September 10th, a cadet brought me to Madame X26's, House X27, to see if she couldn't 'fix me up.' Madame X26 was in a very receptive mood and laid bare secrets of the Syracuse tenderloin. She informed me that I would have to get to Citizen X28 for he is the only man to see now, if that is possible for a new comer.

"The madame, discussing New York, said, 'I bet I got as much left out of my 400 men a week as any New York house.' I prompted that remark by telling her how good the houses were working in New York before 'we' were closed. She claims she has the 'best working house' on the block.

"Her receipts are about $400, but during this, the Fair Week, she, like every other madame, raised the price to $2, but only to strangers. She can clear her $200 a week, she said. She is not 'hoggish' and treats the girls well, feeds them well, and does not overcharge for wearing apparel. 'I was a "boarder" myself and know what it means,' she said.

"On September 11th I visited Madame X26's house again. I asked her whether she would consider a partner. She 'might' but not for the next few weeks to come, or until after the Democratic Convention. She told me to 'go easy' as I shouldn't get burned. 'This is not New York, you know, where any fool can open a joint as long as he's got the money.'

"September 8th, I visited Madame X8's parlor house X7. Two of the inmates came up from New York a couple of weeks ago. They will leave for the West, however, after the Fair, as there is no money here. The best they can make here is $20 a week, and the madame is trying to 'bleed' them into the bargain.

"I visited Madame X32's, House X33. Found there a Sixth Ave. girl, who promptly introduced me to the madame (who had just come in from her doorway in a semi-nude condition) as 'one of the boys' from New York. Of course the New York scandal was the topic. Madame X32 couldn't think of running a house in New York with such big rents, protection, etc. 'Here in Syracuse it's a lot different. You don't do the business that you do in New York, that's true, but you've got as much left. If I have 300 men a week and sell a few drinks, I've got my $125 to $150 a week. I get it nice and quiet and don't have to be afraid of anybody.' "

*Analysis of the Account Book of Girl X39, Inmate of a Dollar House of Prostitution, Showing how the Inmates are Kept in Debt to the Madames, their Earnings, Expenditures, etc.**

The account book of Girl X39 (See Appendix No. 1), an inmate of a dollar house of prostitution, shows that she began the year 1912 $96 in debt to the Madame X26. These accounts show how this debt was increased to $109.50 on January 2d by the purchase of a ring through the madame. The daily earnings of the inmate—half of the total daily earnings made by her, with the exception of Sunday, when board is deducted —are applied to reduce this debt each day, while expenses incurred and articles purchased through the madame increase it. On January 13th, this inmate owed the Madame $135.18 (the greatest amount owed during the six months). This debt she gradually reduced, through applying her total share of the earnings, to $78.01 on January 28th, when she bought a ring from the madame for $25. The debt was again reduced gradually to $1.16 on February 24th, when another $25 ring was sold to this inmate by the madame. On March 18th, business being exceptionally good this month, the inmate had not only entirely reduced the debt but carried a balance due her from the madame of $25.74. This figure, the highwater mark of her credit during these six months, was unendurable, for on the next day a $37.50 suit and later other articles for the new spring outfit, probably suggested by the madame, put the inmate well in debt again. On March 25th her debt stood at $33.89.

Further study of the figures shows that the madame sold the inmate clothes on April 11th, putting her $65.89 in debt. This was reduced to $41.64 on April 22, when the madame sold the girl a ring for $30 and a coat for $15, bringing the debt to $86.64. A new dress on the 24th raised the debt to $92.64. On May 9th the girl owed $107.99, which was

---

*"Once enticed into a house their street clothes are taken from them, and they are supplied instead with short dresses or flimsy finery in which they cannot appear on the streets. These garments, and the jewelry with which they are provided, are charged to them at exorbitant rates, and they are told—and believe—that they cannot leave the house until these things are paid for. When, however, the money is raised to pay for these clothes and jewelry, the victim finds that by some means or another a heavier debt has been charged to her. . . . Intimidated by threats and ill treatment, conscious of her degradation, she in time accepts the conditions and continues a life of vice."

DR. O. EDWARD JANNEY.

gradually reduced until June 5th. On June 22d, the inmate had $1.51 due her from the madame. Heavy purchases followed and the month and period ended June 30th with the girl $31.49 in debt to the madame.

This account book of X39's states that she came to Madame X26's house of prostitution on August 18th, 1911. During the remainder of August her total earnings as given were $137, during September $223, October $357, November $300, December $320. These figures substantiate the statement that prostitution as a business, especially in parlor houses, flourishes best through the winter, and that earnings fall off during the hot weather of the summer months.

The classification of expenses of this inmate shows that almost one-third of her share of earnings goes for various articles of dress, and about one-fourth for jewelry. Doctor bills constitute a regularly occurring item of importance. It appears that money and various articles are often sent "home." During four out of the six months, the girl's expenses (incurred through the madame) *exceeded her earnings*.

The total earnings of X39 from January 1st to June 30th, 1912, were $1,962.50. The madame received half of this, or $981.25 and the inmate $908.75, according to her figures after deducting the board. During these six months the girl worked 165 days and laid off seventeen days. Her average total earnings for a working day were $11.90, or at the rate or $83.30 per week. For a year at this rate her total earnings for herself and the madame would amount to $4,331.60. As this was a $1 house of prostitution, this inmate is shown to have served approximately twelve men each day. Dividing the total receipts between the madame and herself, each would receive $2,165.80. The madame would make this amount clear, while board is deducted from the inmate's earnings before she is credited with her share. Besides her profits from the sale of the inmate's body, the madame also receives substantial commissions on the majority of the inmate's purchases, at exorbitant prices, of clothes, jewelry, doctor's expenses, etc. From this it appears that the inmate's real purchasing power received from her earnings, dwindles to a third or nearly a quarter of her gross receipts, while the madame is enriched accordingly.

2. PROCURERS, ETC.*

The report of the Chicago Vice Commission thus describes the "cadet":† "He is the lowest specimen of humanity, and whenever apprehended should be dealt with to the fullest extent of the law. The 'cadet' is usually a young man, averaging from eighteen to twenty-five years, who has secured a girl or staff of girls, and lives upon their earnings. His occupation is professional seduction. He is the agent through whom business is directed towards his own woman or the house for which she works. In many cases he is the lover or 'sweetheart' of the girl, and by some power so attaches her to himself that she will never betray him, no matter if he has beaten and abused her. This strange paradox often prevents justice being meted out to this outcast from society, for in many cases he can only be convicted on her testimony."

Facts secured during the investigation suggest that procurers and cadets in Syracuse do not make as much money from their women as do those in some other cities. In the first place, the amount of money made by the inmates of houses of prostitution is smaller than in larger communities. Besides this, the money the girls make is largely taken away from them in board, rentals, and excessive prices for dress goods, jewelry, millinery and toilet articles, etc. Therefore, there is not much surplus left for the cadet and they are a starved lot for the most part.

The following are illustrative cases of cadets reported by the investigators:

"Cadet X40 lives off and with a woman named X186 on Grape St. I told him my girl was coming on, and he said that he would let us

---

*"The traffic in girls simply means the procuring of girls for immoral lives. That life of open shame, of public prostitution, is so naturally abhorrent to nearly every girl that none go into it except in one of two ways; either they gravitate into it, or they are tricked or trapped into it. Very few young, unmarried girls walk into a house of shame and say, 'Here I am; I want to be a prostitute.' Therefore the number of girls going voluntarily into this life is far too small to meet the demand; hence the necessity of tricking into the life large numbers of girls who would not come willingly. A resort owner in the vice district of Chicago admitted under oath to United States District Attorney Sims that it had cost the 'houses' of the vicinity thirty thousand dollars in one year to hire procurers to get girls."

CLIFFORD G. ROE.

†The term "cadet" is now generally used in place of male "procurer" or "pimp."

have a room with him but the 'cops' would kick. I understand that he has lived here for five years, and has never worked."

Cadet X42, a waiter in the X43 Cafe, told the investigator that he brought his girl, X187, from Buffalo, but that she is diseased and had infected him. Therefore he left her. "She could hardly walk," he said, "so what was the use of living with her, when she could not bring in any dough."

Cadet X44 is 19 years of age. His father had him arrested and proposed to send him away. He promised to be good, however, and his father relented and got him a position. He ran away that same night, came back the next day, and married a prostitute from house X45. She has consumption.

The following reports of two investigators detail their experience with Cadet X25. This is a typical case:

"September 9th, while with Miss ———— (an investigator) I met the cadet, X25. He had asked me the other day to get my girl (represented by Miss ————) to educate his girl. He told Miss ———— that his girl went to work at X46 store and that he cannot get her to do 'business.' He also told me that he is the first fellow she has done 'business' with."

Of this conversation with X25, Miss ———— reports, "Cadet X25 approached us. He said, 'My girl is getting too lazy. I educated her up to the point of making money, but she ain't got the nerve. You see, she was raised in a convent in X47, N. J. (her birthplace), for seven years.' Cadet X25 'picked her up' six months ago. 'I know what a girl can make,' he said, 'I have four, but this is a dead one. I brought her here and then she wanted to go home. I put up forty dollars, sent her here, and she has not made it. That's what has me broke. When she's fixed up, nothing on Sixth Ave. or Broadway has anything on her. I told her she must make her expenses, so she went to work at X46's store (next door to where he is employed). 'Can you imagine anyone wanting to work like that?' "

September 12th. "I gave X25 five dollars through Miss ————. I requested her to give him this to get better acquainted with him. Later in the evening I met him with his girl. She looked no older than eighteen at the most. X25 introduced me to a man named X48 from New York. X48 is here for the Democratic Convention. He promised to make proper connections for me through X25 if I was safe, which X25 guaranteed. But to come back to X25's 'kid'—there he stood, the poor little girl alongside of him, trying to persuade her to go into a house. I am sure that he will convince her that it will be the only way to 'get a front and a little change.' "

3. THE SEGREGATED DISTRICT A MENACE TO YOUTH*

Below is the copy of the affidavit of an investigator who visited the city at the time of the conference of Older Boys, November 29th, 1912.

————, living at ————, New York, N. Y., being duly sworn, deposes and says, to wit:

"While going to Syracuse on the 8:30 a. m. Empire State Express, about 200 boys were also on their way to attend some sort of conference. As the train entered Syracuse, and went through E. Washington St., where the disorderly houses are located on both sides of the street, these boys were running from one side of the car to the other, pointing out to one another the disorderly houses, and passing remarks which prompted the conductor to order them to be quiet. They rah-rahed the conductor out of the car.

About 10:30 p. m. I saw seventeen boys with arm bands initialed ———— stand in a cluster round the City Hall. They were singing some college song, and creating quite a disturbance. They then separated in groups of three and four, and entered the district. Each one of these groups entered different houses. I followed one particularly noisy group into Madame X20's house, on E. Washington St. I had known Madame X20, having made her acquaintance on a prior visit to Syracuse. I

---

*"While a hardened prostitute, perhaps, cannot be reformed, still when you had your segregated district where everybody knew where it was, it took your young boys out of the colleges in the city. They would say, 'Boys, come on; let us go down to Whitechapel.' A young boy comes in from the country and does not believe in that sort of thing; he resists the first time. They say, 'You are a sissy; you will get used to this after a while.' He may have the invitation made to him several times, but unless he is a young man of unusual moral character, if he thinks he can go down to the district, and there is a certificate that he can go down there in safety to himself as far as physical conditions are concerned, and he knows that he may go down there without any molestation by police officers and without being found out, the chances are pretty good that unless he is an unusual young man that he will go. But if he lives in Des Moines now and sees in the paper where Chief Jenney raids this district, and where a young man (perhaps the son of some prominent man, a reckless libertine) is treated the same as the unfortunate outcast, this young man will not start like that, and you are saving the young recruits. If you don't reform the hardened libertine and prostitute, you do prevent the young man and the young girl from starting in the business. And that young man is worth the whole fight that we are making."

GEORGE COSSON, Attorney-General of Iowa.

29

asked her how she liked that noisy crowd. She said, 'It's good trade, but it is a rough bunch." She then pointed to a girl, who she said was so busy during the week the university opened that she was laid up for two weeks. The boys were dancing and carrying on like lunatics. Some of them looked to be not more than seventeen years old.

"I also visited Madame X26's house, E. Washington St., X31's, E. Washington St., and X251's, E. Washington St. I saw no patrons there whom I could say were college boys. Madame X132 told me she had quite a few friends calling on her from these boys. Madame X8 said that while she has the trade she is not very anxious for it, as they are a nuisance.

"In company with a gambler named X188, who keeps a gambling house, I visited the X117 Hotel. There I was introduced to Mrs. X189. I am supposed to buy this place, and the madame readily explained the workings of the hotel. She said, 'Now, last night this piano (pointing to a self-playing piano) earned eleven dollars; two rooms with two girls brought me twenty-six dollars, all from these boys who reached here for some sort of a meeting they are holding. There was an awful racket here, and I was glad when they left.' "

4. "HIGHER UP"*

While it was not the purpose of this investigation to demonstrate the intimate relationship, if any, between persons claiming to exercise power through the so-called political machine and the segregated vice district of the city, the investigators met many intimations that such a relationship actually exists. The investigators report that in their opinion the organization of the underworld in Syracuse is highly concentrated in a few hands.

This is a field where it is of the utmost importance to get at the facts. And as it is always excessively difficult, and often impossible, to secure specific evidence except through the power to subpoena and examine witnesses, it seems necessary to confine our treatment of this subject to a recommendation for an official investigation which shall unearth the facts.

---

*"If the public officials of the various cities throughout the country will entirely eliminate blackmailing and grafting upon the female keepers of houses of prostitution, and rid their communities of those despicable human beings known as 'white-slavers,' of the male sex, it would be difficult to find houses of this character."

DETECTIVE WILLIAM J. BURNS.

"There is not enough depravity in human nature to keep alive this very large business (commercialized vice). The immorality of women and the brutishness of men have to be persuaded, coaxed and constantly stimulated to keep the social evil in its present state of business prosperity."

GENERAL BINGHAM, former Police Commissioner of New York.

"To the civilized man the ready presence of ideas which exhibit sexual desire is of distinct import. The moral freedom of the individual, and the decision whether, under certain circumstances, excesses and even crimes be committed or not, depend, on the one hand, on the strength of the instinctive impulses and the accompanying organic sensations, and on the other on the power of the inhibitory ideas.

"The exciting and inhibitory powers are variable quantities. For instance, over-indulgence in alcohol is very fatal in this respect, since it awakens and increases sexual desire, while at the same time it weakens moral resistance."

PROF. VON KRAFFT-EBING, M. D.

CHAPTER II

Hotels and Saloons and the Social Evil

1. HOTELS

Thirty-two disorderly hotels were counted and investigated. The girls who take the men to the hotels accosted the investigators on the street, in the rear rooms of saloons and in hotel grills. The price of the hotel rooms are $1 and $2. In several of the hotels no registration is necessary. During the summer investigation four such hotels were found, where the couples could enter and proceed upstairs with no delay, no publicity and no registration. The girls using these hotels charge $1 and $2.

The worst feature of these disorderly hotels is their wine rooms which are screened off as separated rooms. In certain of the places a bedroom is assigned to drink in and no extra charge for its use unless slept in. Such is the X79 Hotel. Some of the hotels are fairly clean, but most are dirty, and the rooms are used by different couples time and time again without changing the linen. In the X80 Hotel, two couples can simultaneously use the same room. The excellent external appearance of the hotels, their noisy, well-lighted, wide-open character, making for ease of access, the wine rooms and the bedrooms close to each other, make sexual vice safe and easy for both the man and the woman. The hotel looks inviting to the semi-innocent but ripe girl who goes "just for a drink." All the machinery for vice is there ready in smooth working order—the bedroom close at hand, the absence of publicity, the effects of the liquor, the urging applied at the right moment. These hotels are perhaps the most blatant as well as one of the most insidious features of the social evil in Syracuse. With them must be grouped in this characterization certain of the saloons, which conduct rooms overhead, where there are the same opportunities for immorality without inconvenience, and with perfect security from observation.

Here is an instance of how this hotel system wrecks a girl, and takes her over from an honest life into the life of a professional prostitute in a house:

A prostitute in X22, a parlor house of prostitution, said that she lived in Syracuse with a sister previous to entering the house. Some trouble came up and she left her sister's place without any money. She

33

said she had been going out with different fellows, but was too proud t
ask for money. She went with a fellow to X80 Hotel and afterwards t
X81 Hotel, N. Salina St. She knew a girl at the X180 Hotel news
stand. She met a man there and went to his room in the hotel. Thi
man gave her $2 in the morning. She lived sometimes like this, some
times having no place to sleep, as asking for money was distasteful t
her. She then went to the disorderly house, having met the madam
outside in a friendly way several times before entering.

Illustrative Cases

June 21, 10 p. m., July 23, 9 p. m., August 5, 11 p. m., Hotel X82

This hotel has twenty-five rooms rented for prostitution purposes a
$1. The price of the girls patronizing this hotel is generally $2. Ther
is a saloon downstairs. Upstairs there are wine rooms, separate room
and different sections of the main room are screened off. The regula
bar prices are charged for drinks. On July 1st one of the investigator
counted six couples going in for rooms. On July 7th, at 11:45 p. m
he counted four couples going into rooms in a space of twenty minute

July 5, 5:30 p. m., September 5, 7:45 p. m., Hotel X80

The cost of a room is $1, and the price of a girl is $2. In the gri
of this place our investigators met fast women who, in certain instance
suggested going to some other hotels. At other times, they met fas
women in other saloons who suggested coming here for a room.

The investigators found the Hotel X80 to be one of the most popula
and notorious rendezvous in Syracuse. The wine room is frequented b
young, semi-professional prostitutes, who are developing under the in
fluences there into professional money getters. Girls bring their me
to the X80 House from restaurants, saloons and grill rooms. We giv
the two reports of one of the investigators (a woman), concerning thi
hotel:

"In company with girls X66, X67 and X68, the three girls whom
met on September 4th at the X83 cafe, I visited this place. The en
trance is through the cafe and hall, and a stairway in this passage lead
to rooms upstairs. As we entered, a young girl was going upstairs with
drunken man. The man turned to look and the girl used very suggestiv
language as to his coming on. Found two rooms—the one in front a
ranged as a dining room, the rear room, connected by a door, used as
drinking room. In it were a piano and a man singer. The singer, wh
was about 33 years old, sang three vulgar songs accompanied by di
gusting movements. He gave every indication of being a degenerat

There were four unescorted women besides ourselves and three with escorts in the front room where we were ushered. Men kept passing in and out. The rear room was so crowded I was unable to count, and could not see the entire room from where I sat, but had a full view of part of the hallway where they passed in and out. Some of the girls were about 22 to 25 years of age. Some appeared of the type who work during the day. I had no opportunity of speaking to any. I heard one girl at the opposite table make this proposition to the man she was with: 'Leave a dollar to the singer and fifty cents to the waiter and come upstairs with me.' She arranged to stay all night. This man was a visitor wearing badges. He had been buying champagne, and his drinking bill was over $8 at the table. This is how she came to suggest the amount to be left to waiter and singer from the $10 bill. I saw them go up the stairway. Another couple were drinking and talking seriously. He said, 'Well, you go fix it up and I will take you up.' He was a stranger. She left the table and in a few minutes returned. They left the room, but were still arguing as to the amount the girl wanted when we passed them in the hallway. The waiter, who attended to us, knew these women with me very well, and said, 'Stick, girls, plenty doing.' These girls invited him to come up when they were fixed up.

September 10th

"Entered Hotel X80 at 11 p. m. and found both rooms crowded. Two men were at the doors to keep the crowd moving, and one was stationed at the foot of the stairway. I passed upstairs to the ladies' room, which is at the extreme end of the hall, and used as a public room for both sexes. I found several of the bedroom doors closed (rooms on either side of the hall). Laughter and profanity were coming from some. When I entered the dining room, men invited me to sit down. This place seems to be patronized by the youngest sporting element. I met three couples entering as I left. None of the girls was twenty years of age, and all were intoxicated. A man standing in the hall, minus a hat and in his shirt sleeves, said, 'Good crowd, dear, come again —sorry you are in a hurry.'

September 5th, Hotel X84

"I met ———, an investigator, by appointment, and at 3:15 p. m. we passed this place. The outside appearance looked suspicious to me, and I suggested that we go in. The Ladies' Entrance is on the side of a saloon. We passed up a stairway, entering a large room, partitioned off with about three-quarter curtains, forming booths. I inquired of a colored woman, who was cleaning, if we could have a room there. She said, 'Sure, the price is $1.' As we were passing, I found this same

woman attending a switchboard. I inquired, 'Is there any chance of
my meeting any men here?' 'Oh yes,' she replied. I learned through
girl X66 that you can get in this place almost any time of day or night
'Most of the girls go there,' said she.

September 5th, X2 Hotel

"I asked Mr. ———— (one of the investigators) to step into this
place with me. I inquired for an actor, who had roomed at this place
one year ago. I asked concerning transient rooms, saying that Mr.
————, the actor, had suggested this place as being all right. 'You could
not have a single room for no price,' the clerk replied. 'I don't mean
that way, I mean for a little while,' I said, with a wink. 'Not now, we
are filled up,' he answered.

September 7th, 10:30 p. m., 11:25 p. m.

"Women and girls who frequent what is termed the grill here are
older and of a different class from those found at hotels X80, X82 and
X83 or X85. Most of the men purchase something to eat. I over-
heard the following conversation between a man and a girl. The man
had left the table, but returning stood alongside the girl and said:

" 'Can't get anything here tonight. He said to go to the X84 Hotel
or up to the next corner to X86's Hotel, which place will we go?'

" 'Let's go X250's place, at the X73 apartments.' Saw them refuse
two men who had been drinking too much liquor.

September 6th

"I met Mr. ———— (an investigator), and we strolled along Salina
Clinton and Willow Sts. I asked him to step into the X85 Hotel. We
entered the ladies' room, and found two men and two women. As one
woman, X87, left the room, I followed and learned the following:

" 'You can get a room here if you work it with the bartender. One
time this place was fierce, but a new man took it and it changed. X86
Hotel, at the next corner, is all right.'

"I asked her to take me around and show me the town. She agreed
So I left Mr. ————, and she did the same with her friends. We went
to the X80 Hotel. She told me that she had been out drinking all the
afternoon, and made $7 from a 'guy.' He gave her $2 and she stole $5
He was so drunk, he never knew. They had stayed at the X84 Hotel. At
one time she had lived in a $1 house, on E. Washington St., but the
landlady had forced the girls to go the limit (perversion). She left
and went to house X45, E. Washington St., for three months, then went
away *as child's nurse* for the summer. The X83 Cafe, she said, has
been raided twice. They would not have young girls, but the X80 Hotel

ok anything. Girls would go upstairs there just for a drink. Young
ys go there with only price of room rent. After being at X80 Hotel
r about an hour, I suggested that we leave. At Warren St. she met
man whom she knew.

"At the X84 Hotel we were invited to a curtained booth by the clerk.
fter we were served, the curtains were drawn together. A room was
ter offered to us for one dollar.

"I also visited the X94 Hotel, one of the worst dives I have ever
en in. Colored men and women were in the bar, the women openly and
azenly soliciting."

2. SALOONS

One of the most pernicious sources of immorality is the association of the saloon with prostitution. This evil is rampant in Syracuse. According to the United States Census for 1910, the city has a population of 137,249. There are 383* retail liquor places, or one saloon to every 358 residents. This is an abnormally large relative proportion of saloons to inhabitants, larger than that of New York City, for instance, where there is one saloon to over 500 inhabitants. Des Moines, Ia., has only one saloon to every thousand inhabitants.

The direct result of flooding the community with saloons is that many liquor dealers are forced by over-competition to add immoral conditions to their saloon trade. If they sold liquor in obedience to the law only, they would lose money and become bankrupt. So they open rear room trade where women drop in to drink and meet men. This, in turn, leads to the opening up of bedrooms overhead. One saloon to every 358 persons means that there is a promiscuous secret drinking between the sexes in many sections of the city. It also means many danger spots, where the social evil is supplied with victims and practitioners. *But little headway can be made against the social evil until the number of saloons is so reduced as to bear some reasonable relation to the normal demand for liquor,* and not a demand falsely stimulated by mixing the sexes in secret drinking places.

In many of the saloons in Syracuse the law is not enforced. This is especially true of the late closing and Sunday closing laws. There are curtained booths, open soliciting at the bar, beckoning from the booths and entering the rear room of the bar. These rear rooms are used by unescorted women; and open solicitation is common in them. There are also rooms for prostitution over many of the saloons.

The law now on the statute books is adequate to meet much of this crying evil. The licenses of many of the saloons which are now centers of sexual vice could be withdrawn by a fearless enforcement of the law. Thus the number of saloons, now so greatly in excess of the average in other cities of the United States, would be reduced and the saloon keeper would be freed from the necessity, which many of them now feel, of adding prostitution to the sale of liquor in order to make a living.

The investigators made the following reports of conditions in saloons and cafes:

---

*The number was given in January, 1913, by the Excise Commissioner for Onondaga County. It includes only hotels and saloons within the city limit.

"It is the rule rather than the exception for the saloons to have bed-
~oms connected with wine rooms, and the bedroom can be had by hand-
~g the waiter the price, usually one dollar, and stepping down the hall."

"The X52 cafe is known to all women as a meeting place. On
~ugust 3rd, I was solicited by two prostitutes of a State St. flat. They
~ake the X52 cafe their headquarters."

"Fellows and girls from the dance hall and the streets intermingle
~ the saloons, and go to rooms together. Often a prostitute from one of
~e parlor houses will ask the girls in the saloon to come and see her.
~ this way the girls of the street meet working girls and acquaint them
~ith the atmosphere of the parlor houses.

"A case in point is that of girl X91. She first began to go out with
~ man named X190, who is now running a saloon. Later she went to
~ve with him. In visiting the saloon she became acquainted with most
~ the madames who came there to drink. The madames have used
~very possible means to induce this girl to go into a house. X91 herself
~aid that Madame XI offered to buy her a diamond ring. She told me
~he intended to enter a house, but she met a fellow she liked and went
~ live with him. She will undoubtedly go into a house when he drops
~er."

The investigators found thirty-two saloons where disorderly condi-
~ions exist. With further investigation this number would undoubtedly
~ increased. As with all the figures of this report, this number affords
~ conservative and minimum basis for estimating the extent of the busi-
~ess done in vice. The investigators counted 209 unescorted women in
~he rear rooms of these saloons. Very frequently the saloon girls take
~heir men to the disorderly hotels, such as X80, X82, X84, X94, X95,
~96 and X81. Sometimes they take them to rooms over a saloon, or
~ furnished rooms where they live. The average room run in connec-
~ion with a saloon is one dollar. The girls charge one dollar and two
~ollars. One girl offered herself for fifty cents and another asked five
~ollars.

Typical Instances

"July 24th, 4 p. m.—The X98 saloon has bedrooms on the second
~oor opening off the wine room. No registration is required. One in-
~estigator saw two unescorted women in the rear room. This place is
~ery dirty and the bedding is not changed. Two men and two women
~btained a room co-operatively on July 24th, at 4 p. m., each man paying
~fty cents."

"At the X52 cafe I counted eleven unescorted women, thirty-one
~en and eight couples during my stay on September 4th from 8 to 10:30

p. m. I made the acquaintance of three women who were together. On
of them said, in answer to my inquiry for the real sporting cafes, 'Th
is all right, and these two waiters (referring to the two young men wh
were serving) are all right. They can put you on to some good thing
here. We were arrested yesterday for slumming (I knew they mean
soliciting, but felt timid with me at first), but were let off with a fin
Everything is pretty close, but there is plenty doing.' Men from th
opposite table began sending drinks to our table, so I left. I foun
more men addressing women than women speaking to men."

"I entered the X52 cafe at 12:10 p. m. on September 10th. Ther
were twenty-three unescorted women present, but they were soon sup
plied. The women here seem to be in a more advanced state of prostitu
tion than most of those who frequent the X80 hotel. The place is ver
poorly ventilated, and the smoke is so thick that you can hardly discer
those at the lower end of the hall. Many young men were present, som
very intoxicated. There were also young girls with soldiers and mus
cians in uniform. I followed two couples out. The girls took the me
to the X82 hotel. The men refused to go upstairs, however, and th
girls left them and returned for more."

"I visited the X99 saloon, which has a very bad reputation. Girl
enter the bar just as the men do. As you enter the bar there is a booth
where the street walkers congregate. I joined four girls in that booth
While there I was solicited and invited to go upstairs.

Following is conversation of one of the investigators with three o
the saloon and hotel girls: "On September 5th at 8:30 p. m., I met girl
X66, X67 and X68 and we went into the X83 cafe. I ordered some re
freshments, remarking that I had spent the day flat hunting, and wante
to open a place for the Fair. X66, who appears to be the most talkative
said, 'We've taken a flat today, and there's one vacant on the next floo
We have some stuff: put up $5 and got some more; one dollar down
and one when they get you. We'll keep it till after the fair, and the
beat it.' Upon my saying that I was in a quandry where to take a man
she replied, 'There is the X82 hotel—very nice—the X84 hotel, wel
that's not swell, but you don't marry the man. I will take you to th
X80 Hotel. You can get in for one dollar. Of course if the fellow look
easy, they charge him double now (State Fair Week), but believe me
men are few who pay over two dollars, one for you and one for the room
Do you know there is only one five dollar house in town, the rest are on
dollar, and they go the limit. It's ——— to get along. We were i
Montreal, and heard that you could coin your money here, but we hav
not seen one live one since we came, four months ago. I was in New
York for a while, and lived with a madame on 66th St., near Centra

Park W. She had a dandy flat for fifty dollars a month. Business was good, but men advised her to move down to the Forties, and we starved to death. I beat it to Detroit for the races. Then I got it into my head to travel. I went first to one place, then to another; and finally landed in Montreal. We three had a good time there, but we heard about this place and here we are till after the Fair—then for Detroit, where you can meet live men. This is the only place in town where you can meet with a dollar. At the X80 hotel they treat, but hate to spend.'

"I inquired about the X2 hotel and she said, 'You must have your suitcase and your certificate now, until you can get in right. If you can get a good man (I mean a man well known in town) to take you there, say, you are fixed. It's a cinch then. I believe it was loose at one time, but now they are closing the lid down tight. The fellow who runs it stands pretty high and wants to be safe.'

After we had been in the X83 cafe for about an hour, she suggested that we go to the X80 hotel, saying that the girls are cheap at this place. She and her companions were very chummy with the waiter. She assured me that rooms could be had there."

One of the investigators reports that he was solicited by three women in the rear room of a saloon on July 15 at 11-30 p. m. A police officer entered the room, and the waiter gave him a glass of beer. The officer drank the beer without paying for it, spoke to the women, and went out.

"Perhaps more girls, craving amusement and fun, have traveled to their ruin over the smooth, glistening floors of innocent looking dance halls, than in any other way. Not that the dances in themselves are so bad, but the surroundings are bad. The beautiful, graceful dance is not in vogue there, but the bawdy sham, trying in its limp, lame fashion to mimic society and the good, wholesome, refreshing merrymaking of a refined social evening.

" The dance hall, with the saloon or bar in connection or adjacent, is the curse of the present century."

CLIFFORD G. ROE.

CHAPTER III

Summer Amusement Resorts and the Social Evil

Dance halls at two amusement resorts just outside Syracuse are loosely managed. The sale of liquor is an important source of income at these resorts. In neither place is liquor actually sold in the dance hall, but pass checks are handed out good for long intermissions between the dances, and bars and wine rooms are close at hand. These resorts are mostly patronized by working girls seeking amusement.

An investigator reports of these resorts: "I saw an inmate of one of the houses of prostitution dancing and mingling with the girls. While I actually saw only this one prostitute there, I was told in different houses that the girls were off for the afternoon at one of these resorts. It is customary for the girls to go out with companions during the intermissions. Thus an innocent girl may unwittingly be in a party with one or more prostitutes, and follow their lead. I have seen a prostitute from X106 tenement and her friend at both resorts.

"I danced at one of the resorts with five girls just as they came. Four of them admitted going out and drinking and going to bedrooms afterwards. Two of the girls had men with them. One girl requested a date for another evening. They said that as the other two were together, I would have to get a friend. The fifth would not dance close, and did not leave an opening for this kind of conversation. Close dancing (a follow step, like the 'Turkey Trot' and 'Grizzly Bear') is allowed, and those who dance in this manner are most sought after. Dancing once round the hall in this fashion often results in a mutual understanding which permits of any kind of conversation."

On July 27th, 8 p. m., "there were about 200 present at this resort, of whom about fifty were minors. Working girls were among those dancing. A card prohibiting tough dancing was posted, but nearly everything was in evidence—the Turkey Trot, the Grizzly Bear, etc. Liquor was sold to minors nearby and eight or ten persons were intoxicated. Extra tickets for dance admissions were sold to good looking girls. Men were soliciting the girls to go to the X108 hotel."

"I was with X25 last night. He lives at X108 and works now in X109 store. He is a New York cadet and crook. He brought his girl here from Hartford, Conn., where he 'stuck up a man for a pin, and skipped town.' His girl is afraid to go out on the street, and he would not let her work for a madame. 'I am working fourteen hours a day for twelve dollars a week' he said, 'so I shouldn't starve. Ain't that the limit?' He is going to 'put me wise' to some charity (clandestine prostitution). He said he would help me 'grab a girl,' so that I can 'get a front.' He also told me that he picked up 'a kid' the other night on So. Warren and Fayette Sts. He treated her to ice cream and took her to a nearby resort. There he attempted to assault her and she screamed. He put his hand on her mouth and told her he would let her up if she would stop her hollering. She promised, so he let her up, put her on a car and after riding some distance with her, jumped off. 'They'd hand me eighty years,' he said. 'The kid was only 15 years old.' " The investigator adds that he secured a few more such cases.

September 8th. "I met X25, the cadet, at 1 p. m. and persuaded him to initiate me into the secrets of one of these resorts. We took a car and went there. He showed me several places where he takes his prey every evening. Cadet X25 took me down X110 St. and showed me the spot where he had seduced a girl on another occasion. We then walked on further and he showed me another secluded spot where he brings girls. We then went back to the city, and he made an appointment for 8 p. m., as he had an engagement with a 'couple of kids' to take them to this resort. He also told me that three friends of his from New York were due that day, and asked me to be sure and meet him, as I knew his friends, too.

"I purposely failed to meet him, but followed him to the resort at 8:30. As I expected, I found the men in company with the three girls on the porch of the X111 hotel. Of the three cadets who came from New York I only know one, an Italian, nicknamed ———. He is a thoroughly vicious man. The other two were Jewish fellows. I had seen one of the three girls, but could not place her till she made a bad break about X112 store. I then knew that she had sold me some Syracuse pennants, and after awhile she admitted that she was working there. Not one of these girls was 18 years old. Cadet X25 and two of the other men walked with the girls to a valley right below the hill, while I remained with the fourth fellow. When they returned, I began 'kidding' the X112 store girl about her very recent valley experience (in order to be sure just what happened), and she said to me, 'Go on, you ain't got the nerve to take me down that valley.'

"After a while I 'lost myself' and began to explore that valley. I counted eight couples, the girls all young; the men young, middle aged and elderly, go down the valley below the hill. It is so dark there that you can scarcely see your hand before your face. As you go slowly along you can *see* nothing, but you can hear whisperings all about. I do not think that husbands take their wives, or sons their mothers, or honest lovers their sweethearts there. And besides when you pick up a clandestine girl on the streets of the city, she usually suggests this resort to you."

The investigator's report of another amusement resort is as follows: "On July 28th there were from three to four hundred persons present at the dance here. Many of them working girls, and about one-half were minors. A card prohibiting tough dancing was displayed, but the Grizzly Bear and the Turkey Trot were being performed. Liquor was sold in a place opposite. I counted thirty-five who were intoxicated. Men solicit women to go to nearby resorts for bed house privileges. These nearby resorts derive a considerable income from people from the dance hall here.

"One-half of the men returning to Syracuse on the car July 28th were intoxicated.

"Very frequently girls in couples, after waiting at the entrance of the dance hall or walking about the park on the chance of securing partners, enter in the hope of making men acquaintances. I counted two such couples on the hunt during fifteen minutes on July 31st at about 9 p. m. Girls hover around the spectators in the billiard room in order to make acquaintances. I noticed one girl entering and reentering the billiard room. These girls are mostly young, averaging 16 to 18 years of age.

"A 'wheel' is run at this place. This is a wheel with sixty numbers. Twenty paddles, with three numbers on each, are sold for ten cents per paddle. Thus the proprietor of the wheel collects two dollars. The purchaser of the winning paddle received one dollar and fifty cents if the wheel stops at the number on the top of his paddle, one dollar if it stops on the second number and seventy-five cents if it stops on the third number. The man who runs the game is bound to receive from fifty cents to one dollar or one dollar and quarter each time the wheel spins. They take the money from children as well as from adults.

"A danger spot at this resort is the large unlighted grove near the dance hall.

CHAPTER IV

Tenements, Furnished Rooms and Miscellaneous Places

1. TENEMENTS AND FURNISHED ROOMS

While searching conditions in the parlor houses, disorderly hotels and saloons, the investigators found that many of the fast women about own live in flats and lodging houses where they take men from time to time. Thus girl X191 runs a place, living at No. — State St. X192 lives opposite and is summoned over to girl X191's when a man comes. Beer is sold at twenty-five cents. X192 has a little girl about 12 years old. The two women frequent the X52 cafe. The charge for a room is one dollar, and X192's price is two dollars up.

No. — E. Genesee St., X54 solicited the investigator on July 15th at 7:45 p. m. She lives upstairs and said that the woman rents the rooms to her knowing that she uses them for prostitution.

X55 solicited the investigator to go to her room at No. — Wyoming St.

X57 entertains men friends at the X58 apartments. The elevator boy also sent the investigator to X59, at apartment No. —.

On July 11th, the investigator saw two street solicitors take men to No. — E. Genesee St. X61, a cadet, stated that the flats were rooming places for cadets and their girls.

The women who live at No. — let men visit them without charge. Girls X193 and X194, 21 and 24 years old, bring a boy home occasionally.

At ———— is an apartment conducted by Girls X66, X67 and X68. Girl X66 has a cadet. He appears to be a rough sort. X66 and her cadet rent the flat, stating to the landlady that they desired to rent out rooms.

At the X71 apartments the investigator saw many cards on the door with just the first name. The elevator man said, "The elevator runs all night. It is mostly all girls who are in here—all jolly good fellows." When asked if one's men friends can come in, he said, "They simply get in the elevator—ask no questions."

Girl X72 rooms in this place with a married couple, and meets some of her "friends" here. She said, "There are lots of good people living here, but many real bad girls."

47

Girl X74, living at the X73 apartments, said, "We have three rooms
X186 and I. I take most of my men outside."

X76, living at No. — W. Genesee St., said, "Some nice men, whom
I know very well, I take to my room." There are furnished rooms at
this place, and women of rough appearance were soliciting at the door

At the X77 apartments the elevator man said, with a knowing wink
"You don't have to have a license to breathe." Girl X78 said, "I room
with a friend here, and meet my friends quietly. There are several girls
besides myself living here."

In addition to the parlor houses, disorderly hotels, saloons, tenements
and furnished rooms, there are a number of other places in the city
closely connected with prostitution. Among these are the stores where
the inmates of the parlor houses are exploited by the exorbitantly high
prices paid for purchases, and the places where the cadets and prosti
tutes gather.

Of these places, the investigators report as follows:

X100's store, No. ————. The parlor houses send here for tobacco
candy and other goods. A young girl is messenger to and from the
houses. Cadets and prostitutes frequent this place.

X105's store. "I called here, and while I was talking in the store
three public women from the nearby house came in and made purchases
One girl bought silk hose, ribbon, and silk undervests at $2.50 a gar
ment. A colored woman bought a pink silk wrapper for $12.50. A gir
from X10 house took two wrappers to the house on approval. This stor
appears to cater to this particular class, carrying everything in thei
line."

"I asked a waitress in X101 restaurant if she could tell me where
could buy some 'hop' (opium). She asked a Chinaman and he sent m
to X102 restaurant. The Chinaman had 'hop' but would not sell m
any. His partner had left for New York to lay in a supply. I met X10
here, and he sold me two dollars worth of 'hop.'"

Of this X101 restaurant another investigator reports: "I visited th
place September 7th, 1912, at 12 p. m. to 1:30 p. m. and found
crowded. A small room in front is set apart for unescorted women; bu
this was occupied mostly by men. I counted fifteen women (thre
unescorted) and forty men passing in. I saw here three girls whom
had seen at all my visits to the X80 hotel, two from the X83 cafe, an
two women, who, I understood, were from the X7 house. A prostitut
came in, accompanied by a man and a little girl about 10 years of ag
The conversation and the actions of the woman were vile. The me
were of the working class. The cadets of Syracuse are not of the 'dand

class of other cities. They dress, as do the women, rather plainly. Three white girls act as waitresses here. The place is very rough."

"At X195's, hard cider is sold. Two prostitutes were met here. A room may be obtained here for one dollar, and the girl charges the same amount.

"Among these miscellaneous places may also be included certain waiting rooms, the State Fair Grounds and the Post Office.

"Of one of these waiting rooms the investigators report: This is a meeting place. Girls use the ladies' waiting room as a blind. This room is one of the dirtiest places I ever visited. Decayed fruit, paper and dirt are strewn around. Six girls in groups of three were standing outside and soliciting. They were telling of escapades with men, and seemed of the type that would not ask for money. One girl said to me, 'I hang around here, and pretend I am waiting for a car. I have met many a good fellow that way. A married woman did something to me in the women's waiting room. She comes here often and is known as the muffler. She picks out blonds and girls living at home.' And another girl said, 'You can meet good men here;' and still another, 'You can hang around outside and make believe to wait for a car, and meet some good fellows some times.'

"On September 11th, I counted eight women, who, I am sure, were out for money. Girls, 17 and 18 years old, were standing around flirting, and would meet men without asking money. I have seen many clandestine arrangements made here. It is a rendezvous for married women. Many girls take rides to continue a flirtation which ends at a park or hotel. This place seems to be a rendezvous where girls who live at home stand and flirt. On September 14th, I counted eight who appeared to be thoroughly public women.

"At another waiting room, eleven women and girls were counted soliciting on September 11th and six on September 13th. Of these the investigator reports: They are bolder than any I have seen elsewhere."

"The Post Office corner is a rendezvous for the married women and day girls. They pass around the corner, enter one door and leave at the opposite side." On September 7th, eleven women were counted soliciting here.

State Fair Grounds

"On September 11th, I met here eleven women whom I have met in New York, and several men who stand around 42d St. and Broadway. I noticed more out of town women here than on the streets. They were soliciting around the booths and in the amusement tents. One woman said to me, 'My man has the booth here. We work together. He always follows the fairs, and I travel along, picking up a good many live ones that way.' She was very bold in her soliciting, accosting men as they passed by. She was accompanied by another girl. They are both New York women. 'Business is very good around here,' she said.

"On September 13th, I found X239 and X225, New York girls, soliciting along the roadway in front of a dining tent. One told me, 'I came to town with X239 and two men. Have met many good men. Am here for the convention and intend to stay a few weeks longer to see how business is. I may enter a house.' I found many women soliciting along the walk, four of whom were from New York. X239 had a man friend with her who was playing the races. He had left her in an automobile and she was soliciting men as they passed."

"The life of an unprotected girl who tries to make her living in a great city is full of torturing temptations. She faces the problem of living on an inadequate wage. She quickly learns of the possibilities about her, of the joys of comfort, good food, entertainment, attractive clothes. Poverty becomes a menace and a snare. One who has not beheld the struggle or come in personal contact with the tempted soul of the underpaid girl can never realize what the poverty of the city means to her. One who has never seen her bravely fighting against such fearful odds will never understand. A day's sickness or a week out of work are tragedies in her life. They mean trips to the pawn-brokers, meagre dinners, a weakened will, often a plunge into the abyss from which she so often never escapes."

Report of the Chicago Vice Commission.

CHAPTER V

Street Soliciting and Clandestine Prostitution

1. STREET SOLICITING

One of the most pernicious aspects of the social evil in Syracuse is the prevalence of street soliciting. *There is no city ordinance dealing with this evil.* There was such an ordinance, but it was repealed; and an effort to replace it on the statute books made in 1907 failed. As a result of this condition street solicitation is openly practiced in defiance of the police. Thus the investigators report many cases of solicitation with police officers close at hand. The date, hour and location are given in each case.

Most of the street soliciting was observed in the narrow boundaries of the hotel and crowded business section, at the very center of the city. Instances were observed in front of numerous hotels, up and down Salina St., on Water St., on Warren St., along Fayette St., on Washington St., and opposite City Hall. So. Salina St., from the canal south for half a dozen blocks is a favorite section for street solicitation; also North Salina St., near the canal. Numerous cases of solicitations were witnessed by the investigators on E. Washington St., West Washington St., East Fayette and West Fayette, So. Warren, James, E. Genesee, W. Genesee and So. Clinton Sts. Our investigators saw in all 441 women whom they believed to be prostitutes. They were actually solicited by seventy-eight girls. Twenty-one of the women asked one dollar; twenty asked two dollars; one asked three dollars and one five dollars. Many made such answers as " Leave it to you," "What you think is right," "Don't care." They solicited men to go to the X115, X116, X117, X118, X84, X119, X80, X82, X94 and X95 hotels; X97 and X121's saloons and madame X120's parlor house, and to furnished rooms and apartments. The price of nineteen of the rooms chosen by the girls was one dollar. One room was priced at fifty cents and one dollar.

An investigator reports: "Walking on Salina St. I found eleven women in seven blocks soliciting. I met several girls who appeared to be employed during the day. The public women are more reserved in their manner than the general type I have observed. They are not so bold on the street as in other towns. They do not have the dissipated look and are less vulgar in their conversation. They range from 17 to

35 years of age. I have particularly noticed many who appear to be married women, modestly dressed, soliciting around the hotels, at the main post office, on Salina St., and on Warren St. These women seem more bold than those who appear to be professionals. The general method adopted by the street girls is to stand in the doorway of a store. They are sometimes alone; but usually travel in groups of two or three. They are bolder when in groups, but dress quietly, and use but little paint or powder.

"I find the streets crowded at night with girls from every walk of life—the home girl out for a little flirtation, the working girl out for fun and small change, and the professional prostitute. Many of the latter live exclusively by prostitution; others add thievery to it. The girls are not as mercenary as in other towns, and they seem to have no fear of going to the woods, parks or hotels with strangers. Many of the girls are just starting out on the life of vice. Some of the older ones go to one of the summer resorts. I have seen lots of fellows and girls there, and know what the purpose is. Fellows buy whiskey and cocktails; take the girl to the woods, get her half intoxicated, and then persuade her to her ruin. I have found many married women soliciting during the day on E. Washington St., on Fayette St., and around the doorways of stores generally. This is their method, and more soliciting is carried on in this way than by walking about."

"On September 10th, crowds of people were on both sides of Salina St., girls of 14 years to women of 40, boys of 18 to men of 50. It was hard to discriminate no-money girls from those who ask for money. Policemen No. X—— and No. X—— were standing there. They both seemed to be acquainted with some of the girls who were hustling backward and forward on the two blocks. Young men at the corners addressed these girls, and each girl had a vulgar reply ready. I counted seventeen girls whom I knew were soliciting."

Typical Cases of Street Solicitors

X170 solicited an investigator on S. Warren St. and took him to X82 hotel. She wanted $2 for a little while. She said she has lived in Syracuse for two years. On July 23d, she solicited another investigator and took him to the X82 hotel.

On June 26th girl X171 solicited the investigator at Salina and Washington Sts. She gave her age as 26 years, and her occupation as a nurse. She asked the investigator to go to Hotel X84.

On June 27th, 4:30 p. m., girl X55 gave her age as 24 years. She practices perversion for two dollars. She said that her home was in the west, that she is a stenographer, and lives at No. —. She solicited the investigator on Wyoming St. and took him to X97's saloon and hotel. On July 27th at 2 p. m. she solicited another investigator on So. Clinton St. This time she asked one dollar and gave her address as No. —. She had another girl with her who said she came from Utica, N. Y.

July 6th, 2 a. m., X256 was in the parlor house, X172, where the made is X137. She stated that she had been "in the game" for two years. She gave her age as twenty-eight, and had a certificate of freedom from venereal disease signed by physician X49.

July 22d, 9 p. m., July 27th. Girl X191 solicited the investigator and took him to the X108 hotel. She stated that she lived on the premises, where she had light housekeeping rooms and that three other women have privileges there. She is about 35 years old, and comes from ———, N. Y. She has been married, but left her husband, and has been in the business for over a year.

June 28th. Girl X39, an inmate of Madame X26's house is about 24 years old, and came to the house on August 18th. This is the girl whose account book, showing her earnings for a period of six months, appears in the appendix of this report. Besides giving her accounts in a very haphazard way, and with an altogether original method of bookkeeping, the book serves as a memorandum and address list of her friends of both sexes. The names of eleven other girls are recorded, evidently inmates of Madame X26's house. A number of men "friends" from nearby cities are classified. From the general tone of the book, the girl appears to be a pervert.

On June 1, at 6 p. m., X174 solicited the investigator. She is about 19 years old. She said she came from ———, N. Y., and is now living with her parents. She graduated from a high school, married when 17, and is now divorced. She practices perversion for five dollars.

On July 10, X175, 18 years old, X176, 19 years old and X177 drank much beer at the grill room, later changing to highballs. At the girls' suggestion the party took an automobile to a roadhouse, where the girls asked three dollars. X176 said that three dollars is cheap as they get five dollars "down the line."

2. CLANDESTINE PROSTITUTION

Another baffling feature of the social evil, very closely connected with street soliciting, is the clandestine prostitution which is common in the city. The clandestine prostitutes do not and will not solicit, but they will permit solicitation and "follow you." Here is a typical case, as reported by one of the investigators: "A girl about 19 years old stood on the corner of Salina and Washington Sts., looking in a window. I opened negotiations by passing the time of day. Here is her story: She is employed at X124 store, and earns six dollars a week, which, she said, 'Is simply not enough for a girl who must bring the greater part of it home.' For that reason, 'If I am lucky enough to be picked up by a stranger, I will follow him.'"

This investigator states that anyone can easily "pick up" a dozen girls a night on Salina St. alone. They do not openly solicit, but give a stranger just enough room to approach them. They name no price, but will "follow you" preferably to one of the nearby summer resorts, where nobody sees or knows them. Their only worry is not to be seen. The conditions around the X2 hotel, the investigator declares, are a disgrace to Syracuse. Girls from 15 to 19 years of age gather around there, with chauffeurs, who have their machines in front of the hotel.

Continuing his report, the investigator states, "Of course the girls show encouragement to the prospective customer, you can not possibly go wrong. On one occasion, I spoke to five women (including two girls about 15 years old), and all of them were ready and willing to follow me. The two girls were looking into a jewelry store window, admiring the paste display. I stopped and looked into the next window. They opened the conversation by asking me if I would not buy them 'that' necklace. They said that they would come with me to any room, etc., etc."

The following reports of the investigators will give an idea of this clandestine prostitution:

"While doing some shopping in the X163 store, I got into conversation with two girls about 15 and 16 years of age respectively. The 16-year-old girl very readily consented to meet me when the store closed. I asked her where we could go, and she suggested one of the nearby resorts.

"I had my meals at the X164 restaurant twice during the day, and was able to make an appointment each time with a waitress. *I readily see now why I got so many histories in New York of girls from Syracuse, Rochester, Schenectady and up-state. It seems that the prostitution from*

56

which New York's vice is recruited, begins right here and in this vicinity."

"I made an appointment tonight with a waitress in the X164 restaurant. She works at night, and is getting about eight dollars a week salary, and about five dollars in tips. But that is not enough. She wears lace inserted waists, patent leather shoes, silk hose, and 'must' have her hair dressed, etc. She is satisfied with four or five men a week."

"Being unable to get any breakfast in the city, owing to the tremendous crowds, I went out of my way to the X165 restaurant. A waitress, X166, a very pretty girl about 19 years old, readily 'picked me up' and made a date to go to a near-by resort with me that night. I very bluntly asked how it happens that she goes out with men when she is working. She replied, 'I am getting six dollars a week in this joint, and hardly any tips, and what's the difference, it's in the air.' "

Certain of the fast women work in restaurants. Such is X91, who works in X92 restaurant. Of this woman and her associates, one investigator reports as follows:

"A student named X167 was introduced to me by X91 in a restaurant. He looked healthy on July 23d. I met him on the street on August 3d and did not recognize him till he spoke to me. He has been living with X91. He seems a bright fellow, and gave me much information regarding the houses of prostitution. He is one of the fellows who stands in with the madames because of acquaintances in college. In conversation with him I said, 'You are pretty well known down the line; they must like you.' 'There are several of the fellows who are well known,' he replied.

"He said that 'the madames like to have the girls get acquainted with students who are on the teams or are well known in college. Then they can go up round the stadium, get acquainted with fellows, and drum up business.' Student X168 'stands in' at one of the houses of prostitution. A woman used to loan him twenty-five dollars at a time.

"I do not know that any of these fellows have actually introduced girls into the houses. The only evidence as yet is that they have indiscreetly told the madames of several 'joy' girls, and given addresses. I have not found any direct evidence of white slavery, but I have found that much pressure is brought to bear upon girls who are loose morally to go into the houses of prostitution by the following methods: Fellows who have taken girls out, or have lived with them for a time, talk of them in the houses, and direct the madames where to find them. In some cases they introduce the girls to inmates for drinking parties and the like. Thus many means are employed to get the girls into the houses. In this way waitress X91 has become acquainted with every place in the district."

The breeding-place of all venereal diseases without exception is in the social institution called prostitution, or sexual promiscuity; in the debasement and degradation of what should be the highest and most revered of physical powers, those involved in the act of generation. Bred and cultivated in prostitution, venereal disease spreads thence through the community, attacking the innocent as well as the guilty, the pure as well as the impure, just as typhoid fever is no respecter of persons, no matter how strict their own sanitary standards may be.

The genuine prevention of venereal disease is only made possible by the prevention of prostitution. Prostitution cannot be retained and the diseases fostered in it be eliminated.

LAVINIA L. DOCK, R. N.

CHAPTER VI

The Social Evil and Disease

The spread of venereal diseases is a direct result of prostitution. These diseases are parasitic. Pasteur said that forty per cent of human deaths are caused by parasitic diseases, all of which are preventable; and that if this cause of death were removed the average of human life would be increased fifteen years.

Dr. Prince A. Morrow of New York, President of the Society of Sanitary and Moral Prophylaxis, has written as follows upon the venereal diseases:

"*Prevalence of these Diseases and their Danger to Public Health.* In point of prevalence they vastly overshadow all other infectious diseases, both acute and chronic combined. It is a conservative estimate that fully one-eighth of all human disease and suffering comes from this source. Moreover, the incidence of these diseases falls most heavily upon the young during the most active and productive period of life. Every year in this country 770,000 males reach the age of early maturity, that is, they approach the danger zone of initial debauch. It may be affirmed that under existing conditions at least forty per cent, or over 300,000, of these young men will some time during life become infected with venereal disease. Twenty per cent of these infections will occur before their twenty-second year, fifty per cent before their twenty-fifth year, and more than eighty per cent before they pass their thirtieth year. These 300,000 infections represent the venereal morbidity incident to the male product of a single year. Each succeeding group of males who pass the sixteenth year furnishes its quota of victims, so that the total morbidity from this constantly accumulative growth forms an immense aggregate.

"*Dangers to the Innocent Members of Society.* Of the large proportion of men who contract venereal disease, many of them carry this infection into the family. Unfortunately, these diseases are markedly accentuated in virulence and danger to the wife and mother in fulfilling the functions for which marriage was instituted. There is abundant statistical evidence to show that eighty per cent of the deaths from inflammatory diseases peculiar to women, seventy-five per cent of all special surgical operations performed on women, and over sixty per cent of all work done by specialists in diseases of women, are the result of gonococcus infection. In addition, fifty per cent or more of these infected women are rendered absolutely and irremediably sterile, and many are condemned to life-long invalidism. Every year in this country thousands of pure young women are infected in the relation of marriage, their conceptional capacity destroyed, the aspirations which centre in motherhood and children swept away, or the holy office of maternity desecrated by the bringing forth of tainted, diseased, or dead children, and the women themselves often ruined in health or condemned to mutilation of their maternal organs to save their lives.

Dangers to the Offspring. The effects of these diseases introduced into marriage are not measured alone by the danger to the life and health of the mother, but are still further manifest in their danger to the offspring. Fully eighty per cent of the ophthalmia which blots out the eyes of babies, and twenty to twenty-five per cent of all blindness, is caused by gonococcus infection. Syphilis is the only disease which is transmitted to the offspring in full virulence. Its effect upon the product of conception is simply murderous. Sixty to eighty per cent of all infected children die before being born or come into the world with the mark of death upon them. Those that finally survive—one in four or five—are the subjects of degenerative changes and organic defects which may be transmitted to the third generation.

Such are some of the undeniable and scientifically demonstrated dangers of a class of diseases, aptly designated as the 'Great Black Plague,' whose ravages have always been covered up and concealed from the public. *There are some facts which it is more dangerous to conceal than to expose.*

Economic significance. The fact that these diseases constitute the most potent factor in the causation of blindness, deaf-mutism, idiocy, insanity, paralysis, locomotor ataxia, and other incapacitating and incurable affections, imposes an enormous charge upon the state and community. *Millions of dollars are contributed to the support of defectives, but not a dollar for the dissemination of the saving knowledge which might prevent.*

Relation to Tuberculosis. It should be known that the spread of tuberculosis is not simply a question of seed and environment, but chiefly one of soil suitable for the development of the tubercle bacilli. It is a fact well recognized by the medical profession that syphilis, by lowering the vitality and weakening resistance, produces a condition favorable to the development of tuberculosis. Until the spread of syphilis is effectively checked the fight against tuberculosis will be but partially successful.

Objects and Aims. The more immediate objects of the educational work undertaken are: (1) The prevention of the large number of infections which occur in the young, the immature and the irresponsible through ignorance. (2) The preservation from infection of virtuous wives and innocent children who are powerless to protect themselves. (3) The prevention of the vast mass of disease and misery engendered in the descendants. It will thus be seen that this work, apart from its sanitary and economic importance, has a distinct humanitarian value.

Remedial Measures. While there are other causes which contribute to the spread of these diseases, the basic cause is ignorance. The educational part of the work embraces as its most essential features:

The general dissemination of knowledge among the public, in a proper and discreet manner, of the extent and dangers of these diseases, and their modes of contagion, direct and indirect.

The enlightenment of the public respecting the social dangers of these diseases, especially to the innocent members of society through their introduction into marriage.

The education of young people into a knowledge of their physical selves and of the laws and hygiene of sex.

It is believed by medical men who are competent to judge that the knowledge we seek to convey would be of inestimable benefit in preventing thousands of ignorant and reckless exposures to the dangers inseparable from immoral relations. Whatever may be the value of educational and moral training as a preservative against voluntary exposure to infection, it would certainly constitute a valuable prophylactic measure against the introduction of these infections into marriage. The vast majority of infections in married life are effected through ignorance. The average man is not a criminal; he does not wreck the life and health of his wife and children knowingly and wilfully. In most cases he does it through ignorance of the nature and terrible consequences of his disease, ignorance of the prolonged duration of its contagious activity, and especially ignorance of the fact that it is often infectious after apparent cure.

It is also believed that publicity of these evils, especially the havoc wrought in the home and family, cannot fail to create a public sentiment in favor of this work, which will lead to a sympathetic and active co-operation on the part of all men and women interested in the social welfare."

The Social Diseases in Syracuse

In January, 1911, the Syracuse Society for Prevention of Social Diseases made an investigation to determine the extent to which gonorrhoea and syphilis exist in Syracuse. The statistics were obtained by sending a letter of inquiry to each of the 240 physicians in Syracuse who were general practitioners and to those specialists who might treat these diseases in their practice. One hundred and five physicians replied, of whom ninety reported venereal cases under treatment.

	Gonorrhoea	Syphilis
The 90 physicians reported existing cases...........	524	452
Of these 13 specialists reported existing cases........	253	289
The remaining 77 physicians reported existing cases..	271	163
Average per physician not a specialist, existing cases..	3.52	2.12
At these averages the 115 physicians not reporting had existing cases	405	244

The estimate is conservative, as three specialists did not report, who together, were treating probably a total of at least 125 cases.

A large proportion of gonorrhoea never comes to a physician, but is treated by experienced friends or with advertised medicines. Estimating this proportion at one-third of the cases treated by physicians, the number of such cases is 310.

The total number of existing cases is, therefore:

	Gonorrhoea	Syphilis
Reported by 90 physicians........................	524	452
Estimated as being treated by 115 physicians not reporting	405	244
Estimated as being treated by the patients themselves	310	0
Total	1,239	696
Total of both diseases existing in Syracuse..........	1,935 cases	

Estimate of Total Cases in 1910

Ninety physicians reported total of both diseases treated in 1910 as being 3,338 cases. The ratio of existing cases reported to total cases treated is 1 to 3.42. If we reduce this ratio one-third for cases reported by more than one physician the ratio becomes 1 to 2.28. Using this ratio, the 1,935 total existing cases represent 4,412 separate infections treated during the year 1910, which is 3.21% of the total population of 137,249 persons.

Proportion of the Total Population Infected

Assuming that the danger zone of venereal infection in each human life is of ten years' duration—and this is conservative, as proven by the case of a girl 10 years old infected by a man 66—these 4,412 separate ıfections in 1910 represent 44,120 total infections, present and past, in ıe population of Syracuse in 1910. Reducing the total by more than ıe-quarter to allow for re-infections, recurrent attacks and for the ıaller population in the years prior to 1910, thereby making it 32,000 ›tal infections, and dividing the number between males and females on ıe basis of the 976 existing cases reported, which were 75% among males ıd 25% among females, the 32,000 total cases indicate 24,000 infections ⁚ males and 8,000 infections of females.

In other words, 35% to 40% of the men and boys in Syracuse and)% to 13% of the women and girls in Syracuse are, or have been, in- ›cted with venereal disease.

Infection in Children

Fifty-one cases were reported of infection in children under 16 years ⁚ age, which at 0.57 cases per physician reporting, equals 116 total :isting infections of this class. Of the 51 reported cases, 33, or 64.71%, ere recent infections.

Several of these recent infections were reported for children 2 to 3 ›ars old, though these were believed to be accidental. One case was ported of a girl 10 years old infected by a man of 66; which proves no ⁚riod of life exempt from these diseases.

Large Proportion of Syphilis

A striking feature disclosed by the reported existing cases is the large ⁚oportion of syphilis, a disease which is popularly believed to be rare. ⁚ the 976 existing cases reported, 452, or 46.31%, were syphilis—452 ses equals 3.29 cases per 1,000 inhabitants.

Comparison with Tuberculosis

In 1910, 2,124 persons died in Syracuse, of whom 150, or 7.07%, died ⁚ tuberculosis. Tuberculosis is approximately five years in its course, so ⁚at there are 750 people now in Syracuse who are infected with tuber- ⁚losis which is destined to prove fatal. These 750 tuberculosis infec- ›ns are but 17% or only one-sixth as many as the total 4,412 cases of ⁚nereal disease reported and estimated as existing in 1910.

Conclusions from the Investigation

The investigation found the physicians unanimous in the opinion that ⁚ildren must be taught sex hygiene and the existence, wide prevalence ⁚ dangerous character of venereal diseases. Of other suggestions sub-

mitted by the physicians, the most valuable were that ·these diseases ▮
officially recognized by, and reported to, the Bureau of Public Health aɪ
controlled by that Bureau like other contagious and infectious disease
that street solicitations be abolished; that the advertisement of allege
cures be regulated; that all male children be circumcised; that youɪ
people be protected against alcoholic drink, because most venereal infe
tions occur when the men or women, or both, are under the influence ₄
liquor, and that every man be required to prove himself free from v
nereal disease before being granted a license to marry, by presenting
certificate from an accredited physician of a diagnosis by the Wasse
man or other accepted biological tests.

The fact that physicians report 75% or more of the infections in me
as having originated from occasional prostitutes proves that class ₄
woman much more dangerous than they are usually believed to be.   O
the other hand, if 40% of the male population are, or have been, infecte
with venereal disease, as the investigation indicates, it is a certainty th
the occasional prostitute cannot long avoid venereal infection.

The serious attention given by the physicians to this investigation aɴ
their earnest desire to deal in an enlightened manner with the problem ₄
the social diseases, is well illustrated by the sentiment of a leading. ph
sician of Syracuse, who writes: "It seems to me that there are two thiɴɢ
which this Society ought to further in the very highest degree.   In tʜ
first place, a high and noble conception of the relation of the sexes, anₐ
in the second place, a correct idea of the physiological processes—repɾₑ
duction in nature.   Until young men and young women have a right aɴ
lofty conception of what the sex problem really means, we shall have tʜ
perversions which are common now, and not until young men and youɴ
women know the laws of reproduction, are they properly prepared fₑ
marriage.   And, finally, in the last analysis, the correction of the evi
which we now deplore will depend upon the training at home and ᵢ
schools and in self-control."

"In 1897, and 1898, the writer conducted an examination into the actu
number of girls and women who were at that time inmates of houses
ill-fame in the United States. Correspondence and interviews were h
with mayors, chiefs of police, reformers and ministers in cities of 25,0
inhabitants and over. From the facts thus gathered we estimated the nu
ber of professional prostitutes in this country at that time to be 300,0
which figure we felt to be conservative. . . . Accepting these estimates
approximately correct, we see that at least 60,000 girls and women are
quired every year, or 5,000 every month to provide for the constant dema
of the public houses of shame. No one can doubt that with the enactme
of proper laws and their enforcement, which can and will come throu
the demands of our people as light is given, vice as a public business whi
consumes 60,000 of our girls each year can be suppressed."

B. S. STEADWELL, Pres. American Purity Federation.

"Where shall we look to recruit the ever-failing ranks of these po
creatures as they die yearly by the tens of thousands? Which of the lit
girls of our land shall we designate for this traffic? Which of them sh
we snatch, as they approach maturity, to supply this foul mart?"

DR. HOWARD KELLEY.

CHAPTER VII

Histories of Professional and Clandestine Prostitution in Syracuse

The girls whose cases were studied and their names obtained by the investigators numbered 135. They were of all ages, from 13 to 50. The average estimated age was 24 years, though this figure is, of necessity, a guess. The list includes girls living in parlor houses, in disorderly hotels, frequenting fast cafes, living in flats, in furnished rooms, in homes, working in restaurants, factories, stores, etc. The girls are of every degree of professionalism. There are girls receiving $10 for perversion and $5 for normal intercourse; parlor house girls rendering service at $1 or $2, leading the men from the wine rooms to the near bed-rooms; girls who are too shy to ask for money, but will accept it if offered; and the girls, many in number, who go out with men for an evening of pleasure and drink and intercourse where no money is asked or offered. There are married women who put in a quiet afternoon on the sly in respectable looking places, such as waiting rooms, and certain of the restaurants. There are girls who come in two or three times a week from the surrounding country districts. Saturday and Sunday are favorite days for these girls to visit Syracuse. There are working girls from the department stores, factories and restaurants. The evening brings these girls out in numbers. The number of girls who are working part of the time and carrying on prostitution is large. There are many who live and board with private families and go out at night. These girls take into the saloons the men whom they pick up on the streets, and then go to the bed houses, especially to those where they do not have to register. Often this class of girls go with men entirely for pleasure with no economic pressure responsible for driving them to the life. Thus, one of the girls in X124 department store, who had a job paying $30, but took to evil practices.

As an illustration of the youth of the girls: Four girls were examined by Dr. ———, found in a box car with men. The doctor's certificate gives their ages as 14, 13, 15, 13. The girls had been used four or five times in one night.

September 5. Girl X66 was talked with at the X52 cafe and the X80 hotel. She was born in Pennsylvania about 28 years ago. Four

months ago she came to Syracuse, for the purpose of soliciting. She wa
arrested on September — in the X181 cafe, along with two other girl
but was set free without a fine. She fell more than six years ago and ha
practiced prostitution continuously. It is her only means of suppor
Once she lived in a disorderly flat in New York, and has visited i
Montreal, Detroit, Rochester and Buffalo. She would not tell much.

September 14. Girl X179, 22 years of age, was talked with in th
X52 cafe, the X178 cafe and the X82 hotel. Her birthplace wa
————, N. Y. She came to Syracuse recently to work. A friend cause
her downfall six years ago. She is now employed in X182's store, S
Salina St., and has practiced prostitution continuously the last five year
The highest sum she has earned from prostitution is $35 a week. Fro
other sources, $8. She was seduced at a picnic—tried to keep straigh
afterwards, but could not resist the fellow. He died; she met another an
then decided to take money. She works to keep up appearances at hom

September 12. Girl X218 was talked to at the State Fair Ground
X84 hotel and X183 hotel. She gave her birthplace as ————, an
her age 24 years. Comes to Syracuse two weeks every year to "hustle
Was seduced by her sweetheart, husband now, four years ago, and ha
practiced prostitution continuously. When her husband has work sh
does not go out. She is of a decidedly low type, and is a drug fiend.

September 13. Girl X184 was talked to in the Central R. R. Sta
tion, the X257 hotel and on Franklin St. She was born in Syracus
22 years ago. A stranger caused her downfall four years ago an
she has practiced prostitution for past three years in ————, th
being her only means of support. She lives at home. She not onl
prostitutes herself for the money but also because she likes the societ
of men.

September 6. Mrs. X196 was talked to at the Hotel X84. He
story was that she was born near Syracuse and comes to Syracuse ofte
to do her shopping. A stranger caused her downfall one year ago an
she has practiced prostitution since. She intends to leave her childre
and go to New York City, where she feels she will meet a real man wh
will care for her.

September 14. Girl X197 was talked to at the X85 hotel. She sai
she was 24 years old and was born at ————, Canada. A strang
caused her downfall two months ago, and she prostituted herself for pa
for first time six weeks ago. Since then it has been her only means
support. The highest pay she has received from this practice is $17
week; from other sources, $20 per month. She got tired of living alo
and met a charming fellow who persuaded her to go to New Yor

She expects to take a flat there for her work and that the man will marry her. She does not seem normally bright.

September 11. Girl X198 was talked to at State Fair Grounds, Hotel X84 and the X180 hotel. She was born in ———— and is 23 years old. A friend ruined her five years ago and she has practiced prostitution continuously since, it being her only means of support. The highest sum she has received from this practice is $200 per month. The man who is taking care of her is married, but wife will not divorce him. The girl is very pretty, but thoroughly degenerate.

September 12. Girl X76 was talked to at the X82 hotel. She was born near Syracuse, 21 years ago (looks younger). A stranger caused her downfall two months ago and she has been practicing prostitution since. Highest sum earned $23 per week, lowest $3. She is married, but ran away from home, as she did not want to live among a lot of "dead ones."

September 7. Girl X200, 21 years of age, was talked to at the X80 house and in the X82 hotel. She was born in ————, N. Y., and came to Syracuse three months ago, getting employment during the summer in a small store. A stranger seduced her three years ago and she has practiced prostitution continuously since then. The highest sum received from this practice is $25 per week, lowest $5; highest sum received from other sources, $6. She is married, has one child, but is separated from husband. As soon as the Fair is over she is going to Albany as she understands there is money in houses there. She is very easily led.

September 11. Girl X201 was talked to at the State Fair Grounds and at the X180 hotel. She was born in New York City 26 years ago and has practiced prostitution for seven years. From this practice she has received as high as $150 per week. She has one child. She has been living with a man six years and said, "Well a good pal is worth a whole lot. I have had a hard life. When he has money I have it—when I have it, it is his. We are good partners and I love him. He makes good money, and I can turn good tricks myself. She is rough and thoroughly degenerate.

September 11. Girl X202 was talked to in the X203 cafe. She is 26 years of age, and was born a few miles from Syracuse. In X124's store she earned $5 a week. A stranger ruined her three years ago, and she has practiced prostitution continuously since, receiving as much as $40 and as low as $10 per week for this service. She is married and has children. She is a very plain woman and careful whom she meets.

September 14. Girl X204 was talked to in a moving picture theater on North Salina St. She was born in ————, 24 years ago, and has lived in Syracuse ten years. Her sweetheart caused her downfall six years ago, and she has been practicing prostitution for the past five years. The highest sum she has received weekly for this practice is $40 and the lowest $6 per week. From other sources $5 per week with dinners.

September 12. Girl X205 was talked to in the X84 hotel. She gave her age as 19 years and her birthplace Syracuse. A friend seduced her three years ago and she has now practiced prostitution for one year receiving as the highest sum from this practice $40 a week, and from other sources she has received as high as $10 a week, working in a restaurant. She lives at home, but likes the pleasure of men's company She is very pretty and easily led.

September 7. Girl X74 was talked to in the X71 Apartments. She was born in Syracuse 24 years ago. Said she was employed, and received $12 a week. Would like to go to New York.

September 10. Girl X206 was talked to in the X81 hotel. She was born in ———, 23 years ago. She came to Syracuse three years ago to work. Her brother-in-law seduced her when she was 15 years of age and since then she has practiced prostitution, receiving as high as $30 weekly. The highest amount received from other sources was $6 a week

September 11. Girl X207 was talked to in the Central R. R. station and the X208 hotel. She gave Syracuse as her birthplace and her age 22 years. She was seduced at the age of 14. She has practiced prostitution for the past four months. The highest sum received weekly from this service being $30, the lowest $3. She is not compelled to work as her family is in moderate circumstances, but she likes the society of men and will run away with the first man who offers to take her out of town.

September 9. Girl X209, 22 years of age, was talked to at the X80 house. She said she was born in ———. Her sweetheart caused her downfall, and she has been prostituting herself for the past four months. the highest sum received weekly for this service being $20. She works at X210 store for $7 a week. She wanted change and a good time. Close friends thinks she is a very good girl. She does not solicit on the street.

September 6. Girl X211 was talked with at the X82 hotel. She was born near Syracuse, 24 years ago. Her sweetheart ruined her, and she has been practicing prostitution for the past three years. The highest weekly sum received from this source being $20. She worked as sales girl in X212's store for $9 a week. Expects to go to work after the Fair.

September 13. Mrs. X213 was talked with at the X214 hotel. Her birthplace was given as Syracuse and her age as 24 years. A friend caused her downfall six years ago, since which time she has practiced prostitution, receiving at high as $20 weekly. She worked in the X214 hotel. She earned $5 a week. She is a cigarette fiend and formerly was an inmate of a disorderly house. Her home life is unpleasant and she is sorry she ever stayed in Syracuse. She could be made a very good woman.

September 13. Girl X216, 23 years of age, was talked with in disorderly house X10. She was born in Syracuse. Once she was arrested in New York City for soliciting and sent to the Island for ten days. Her sweetheart seduced her seven years ago, and she had been practicing prostitution continuously since, the highest sum received weekly from this service being $100, the lowest $20. She worked one year for a firm in New York City at a salary of $8 a week. The sweetheart who seduced her is now her "lover," and they live together. She is very fond of him and he saves her money. She is a thorough degenerate.

September 12. Girl X217 was talked with at State Fair grounds, X84 hotel and the X183 hotel. She was born in ——— and is 22 years of age. A stranger caused her downfall three years ago. She came to Syracuse for the fair to "hustle." She is married but has practiced prostitution for the past three years, her highest weekly income being $75, lowest $10. She is a drug fiend, a degenerate and avoided answering questions. She seemed to be under complete control of girl X218.

September 11. Girl X219 was talked with at the X84 hotel. She was born in ——— and is 28 years old. Four years ago she came to Syracuse because the man she married worked here. She has been practicing prostitution for the past two years. She lives with husband at home but is not satisfied with him. She is a degenerate and will mingle with anyone for pleasure and drink.

September 9. Girl X72 was talked with at X220's saloon and the X71 apartments. Her birthplace was ———, N. Y., 26 years ago. She came to Syracuse this summer after a quarrel at home. She is married and has been working in X112's store on S. Salina St. for $6 a week. She has been practicing prostitution for the past two months, receiving as high as $30 a week and as low as $3. She knows several traveling men, and often goes out for company's sake. She is a low type of girl.

September 7. Girl X221 was talked with at X80 hotel, the hotel X84 and the X101 restaurant. She was born in Syracuse and is 26 years of age. When it is too cold to go out soliciting, she work for $8 a week.

She has been practicing prostitution for six years, the highest sum received being $30 a week, the lowest $10. She is known among the girls as a degenerate and one of the roughest types. Men in the X101 restaurant call after her. She would not speak much of herself.

September 10. Girl X222 was talked with at the X80 house. She was born near Syracuse 21 years ago. She was employed at the X22 factory at $8.50 a week. She has been practicing prostitution for the last three years and her highest earnings per week have been $25, lowest $2. She lives at home and pays board.

September 14. Girl X224 was talked with in the X183 hotel lobby and the X2 hotel. She was born in ———, 24 years ago. She came to Syracuse with a show, but was thrown out of work. A friend caused her downfall eight years ago. She has been practicing prostitution for seven years. The highest sum received from this service was $80 per week, from other sources $20 per week. She says she had been disappointed and did not purpose to let anyone get ahead of her. She resorts to all the vile methods.

September 13. Girl X225 said she was born in New York and is 24 years old. She came to Syracuse to "hustle" about two weeks ago. Her step-brother ruined her about ten years ago. She has been a prostitute for past eight years and has been in houses in New York City. The highest sum received from this practice was $150 a week, lowest $10. She has been in houses in Hartford, Conn., and Albany, N. Y., also. She is a very low type of girl, would steal, and use all vile methods.

September 14. Girl X226 was talked with at Hotel X80. She was born in New York City 22 years ago. She came to Syracuse four months ago to live in a house, and has been in houses in New York City, Brooklyn, and Hartford, Conn. She has been a prostitute for four years, her highest weekly earnings being $65. She was ruined by a neighbor in New York, six years ago. He taught her how to make money, and induced her to enter a house. She does not like Syracuse as there is not enough money there, and intends to go to New Haven next week.

September 13. Girl X227 was talked with at the X80 Hotel. She was born in ———, N. Y., and is 20 years of age. She came to Syracuse three years ago because her father was employed here. A friend ruined her four years ago, and she has been practicing prostitution quietly the past two years, her highest income weekly being $25. She "meets some very nice traveling men, but does not mingle with the boys of the town." She goes to Sunday School and Church, and says every girl here goes around on the quiet. She is very pretty and easily led.

September 5. Girl X67 was talked with in the X83 cafe and in the X80 house. She was born in ———, Pa., 26 years ago, and came to Syracuse about four months ago from Montreal, Canada, to solicit. On September — she was arrested in a saloon in company with two other girls. An old sweetheart caused her downfall and she has been practicing prostitution for the past three years. She has been in Detroit and Montreal, also on the street in New York. She would not talk of personal affairs prior to coming to Syracuse.

September 11. Girl X228 was talked with at the X81 hotel. She gave her birthplace as Syracuse and her age as 21 years. A friend caused her downfall three years ago, and she has practiced prostitution for two years. The highest sum received from this source being $25 a week. She also worked as stenographer, the highest sum received from this source being $10 a week. The man who ruined her left her when her condition became noticeable. She goes out only for extra money—not for pleasure.

September 5. Girl X229 was talked with in X258's saloon. She was born in ——— and is 34 years old. She came to Syracuse three years ago "with the old folks." A stranger, with whom she now lives, caused her downfall three years ago. His name is X231. This woman sometimes works at the X232 hotel—is very dissipated looking.

September 14. Girl X230 was talked with at the State Fair grounds. Her birthplace was New York City and her age 24 years. She was seduced by a relative when she was fourteen years old, and has been practicing prostitution for eight years. Her highest weekly earnings from this source being $100, lowest $10. She shares her money with a friend, who, she says, is kind to her. They travel around together and take in the sights. She is very much hardened to the life.

September 5. Girl X68 was talked with at the X80 hotel. She is about 25 years old and came to Syracuse four months ago to solicit, from Montreal, Canada. On September — she was arrested in a saloon with two other girls. She has been practicing prostitution for about two years and makes "enough to live." She looks to be one who would stoop to all practices. Would not talk much.

September 12. Girl X233 was talked with at the X80 hotel. She is 22 years old and was born in Syracuse—has lived here always. A friend ruined her four years ago and she has been practicing prostitution for two years, her highest weekly earnings from this practice being $20. She also works at X122's store for $8 a week and lives at home. Would talk on any subject except this.

September 6. Girl X87 was talked with at the X80 hotel. She was born just outside of Syracuse and is 28 years of age. A friend caused her downfall six years ago, since which time she has practiced prostitution continuously, her highest weekly earnings from this source being $25. She also worked as child's nurse during the summer for $5 a week and board. She has been in ———, Canada, and intends to stay in Syracuse until after the Fair, when she will got to New York. She drinks heavily.

September 10. Girl 234 was talked with at the X84 hotel and the X81 hotel. Her birthplace was ——— and her age 24 years. An old friend of the family, who was visiting her home, ruined her eight years ago, and she has been practicing prostitution for six years, her highest weekly earnings from this source being $28, her lowest $1. She also works in X124's store for a salary of $6. She complains that the poor salaries paid are inadequate to meet expenses, and is very much discouraged with life. She is a respectable looking girl and no doubt would live differently under better conditions.

September 5. Girl X235 was talked with in X258's saloon. She was born in ——— 29 years ago. She came to Syracuse a few years ago to get married, and "stuck to husband until she had nothing to wear." Her first sexual offence was with a friend three months ago, and she has practiced prostitution since then. She intends going to New York "where money is better, and live." She is of a very low type.

September 9. Girl X78 was talked with in the X77 apartments. Her birthplace was Syracuse 24 years ago, where she has lived all her life. A friend whom she expected would marry her, caused her downfall six years ago, and when her condition became noticeable he left her. Her highest weekly earnings from the practice of prostitution has been $25. She also works as saleslady in X212's store, where she receives $7 a week. She spends all her money on clothes. She says there are not enough "sure things" in Syracuse to depend on, and intends going to Buffalo after the last of the month as there is more money there.

September 13. Girl X236 was talked with at X86's hotel. She was born in ——— and is 26 years of age. She came to Syracuse four months ago, having run away from husband who was cruel to her. Her first sexual offense was with a stranger two years ago. She has been practicing prostitution for two years, her highest weekly earnings from this source being $21, lowest $6.

September 7. Girl X237 was talked with in front of the X84 hotel. Her birthplace was near Syracuse and her age 23 years. A friend caused her downfall four years ago and she has been practicing prostitution for he past three years. She comes to Syracuse every week "to see the boys." Her highest weekly earnings from prostitution were $15, lowest $3, from other sources $7. She has one child, father unknown. Just wants company and a good time, and has two fellows whom she is sure of meeting every week. From conversation investigator thinks she is diseased, but is ashamed to go to see a doctor.

September 7. Girl X238 was talked with at the X80 hotel. She was born in ———, N. Y., 24 years ago, and came to Syracuse two years ago to live in a "house." A married man seduced her when she was 15 years old. She has one child by him still living. She has practiced prostitution for past five years, her highest weekly earnings being $40. Her parents quarreled with her so much that she left the child with her mother and came to Syracuse to work in a "house." She prefers to work for herself, however. She admits being a degenerate since child was born, and claims to have adopted perversion through fear of having more children.

September 13. Girl X239 was talked with at the State Fair grounds, and one other place. Her birthplace was New York City, age 21 years. A sweetheart caused her downfall four years ago, and she has traveled with this man, who is a gambler, since. She is a close friend of girl X225, is perfectly happy, and claims she does not give her man money, although the investigator believes she does.

September 12. Girl X240 was talked with at the X85 hotel and the X82 hotel, is 24 years of age and came to Syracuse two years ago to live. A stranger caused her downfall when she was 15 years of age. She has practiced prostitution for seven years, her highest weekly earnings being $50. Has been on the stage as an actress, lived in houses of prostitution and is an all round "sport."

September 13. Girl X241 was talked with at the X2 hotel and the X84 hotel. She is married, lives at home and has children. She comes to Syracuse to shop. Her first sexual offense was with a stranger three years ago. She has practiced prostitution for two years for "some extra money," her highest earnings being $15 a week. She claims that her husband is lazy and has no ambition, and she would like to meet a live, city man. She is easily led.

September 9. Girl X242 was talked with at the X84 hotel and X2 hotel. She was born near Syracuse, and is 26 years of age. She is employed at present in X243's store, at a salary of $9 a week, and comes to Syracuse every day to work. A friend caused her downfall seven years ago. She has practiced prostitution for the past six years, her highest weekly earnings being $40, lowest $10. She says everyone is "dead" in her home town; but she meets some real live business men with money in Syracuse. Has been associating with a girl from a house.

September 14. Girl X244 was talked with at the X81 hotel. She was born in Syracuse 21 years ago and has lived there always. She is employed at X112's store at a salary of $7 a week. A friend caused her downfall three years ago, since which time she has been practicing prostitution, her highest weekly earnings being $30.

September 10. Girl X245 was talked with at the X2 hotel and X86's hotel. She was born in the city of ——— and is 23 years old. A teacher at school ruined her seven years ago. She has been practicing prostitution for five years, her highest earnings being $45 a week. She is going to try to get into X10's disorderly house.

September 14. Girl X246 was talked with at the X180 hotel. Her birthplace was ———, N. Y., and her age 24 years. A friend ruined her eight years ago, and seven years ago she ran away from home and came to Syracuse. She has practiced prostitution since, her highest weekly earnings being $80. At times she has worked as a demonstrator, receiving $12 a week. She would not say much of her private life, is very vain, and could not be drawn into a long conversation, as she was interested in a group of men standing in the lobby.

September 14. Girl X247 was talked with on Salina St. She was born in Syracuse 18 years ago and has lived there all her life. A friend caused her downfall two years ago. She works every day at present, receiving $5 a week salary. She has never received money for prostitution, but likes to go out for a good supper and theatre with men. She is pretty, very foolish and easily led. She lives at home.

September 10. Girl X248 was talked with at the X82 hotel. She was born in Syracuse 24 years ago and has lived there always. Her first sexual offense was with a friend four years ago, since which time she has practiced prostitution continuously, receiving as her highest weekly earnings $30, lowest $10. She is employed at X249's store and receives $8 a week. She lives at home and her family think her respectable. She likes the general excitement connected with the life, and will probably develop into a low type of girl.

SUMMARY OF HISTORY CASES

The following is a summary of data compiled from the History Cases of professional and clandestine prostitutes in Syracuse. For further details see Tables 1 to 8.

Birthplaces. The birthplaces of fifty prostitutes were reported by the investigators. Of this number fourteen gave their birthplaces as Syracuse, the remaining thirty-four came from small places about Syracuse, such as E. Syracuse, Camillus, Wampsville, Baldwinsville, Minoa, Rockwell, and larger places, such as Utica, Binghamton, Troy, New York City, Philadelphia, Pa., Wilkes-Barre, Pa., Providence, R. I., Newark, N. J., New London, Conn., and Bedford, Mass. Three said they were born in Canada, Germany and Ireland respectively.*

Reasons for Coming to Syracuse. The investigator persuaded thirty-nine prostitutes, who came from other cities and now ply their trade in Syracuse, to give her their reasons for coming to this city in the first instances. It must be remembered that in the majority of cases these girls may or may not have been prostitutes when they came to Syracuse. Of the thirty-nine, ten said they came either to solicit on the street or to enter houses of ill-fame as inmates. The rest came for various reasons. Some ran away from home after quarrels with folks or husbands; others live in surrounding towns and come in every day to work or to shop. Three girls came with men, one of these was a traveling salesman. Another girl comes to town every Saturday and Sunday to see the boys.†

Present Age, Age of First Sexual Offense and Age When Girls Entered Life of Prostitution. The investigator secured the ages of twenty-four girls now practicing prostitution in Syracuse. Of this number one is 19, three are 21, four are 22, four are 23, seven are 24, four are 26, and one is 28.

Twenty of these girls gave the ages when they committed their first sexual offense. Of these one was 14, two were 15, four were 16, five were 18, two were 19, two were 20, one was 22, two were 23, and one was 26.

Twenty-three of these girls gave the ages when they entered upon a life of prostitution. Of this number one was 16, one was 17, six were 18, four were 19, two were 20, two were 22, one was 23, and one was 26. Two girls said it was four months after their first sexual offense; two said

---

*See Table No. 1, Appendix II.
†See Table No. 2, Appendix II.

it was two months, and one declared that she began this life six week
after her downfall.*

Wages Received by Girls in Various Occupations. It is interestin
to note that the wages which the girls who are leading irregular lives i
Syracuse receive in various occupations are fair, though some fall belo
what is usually termed a living wage, $8. Of the twenty-five girls wh
gave their occupations, eleven said they either worked or had worked i
department or five and ten cent stores. The average wage given wa
about $8.00 per week.†

Residence of Girls Before Entering Life. Records were secured i
forty-one instances showing their residence previous to entering upon
life of prostitution. Of this number thirty-five said they lived at home
four declared they were living in furnished rooms and two said the
were boarding. Of those who lived at home, eight said they gave al
of their earnings to the family, and six gave only part of their wages
One of the girls who lived in a furnished room said she paid $5 per weel
for the room, and the two who boarded said they paid $4 per week fo
board and room.

*Occupation and Business of Girls Before and After Entering Life o
Prostitution.* Thirty girls told investigator their occupation and busines
before entering upon a life of prostitution. These occupations are quite
varied. Some were salesgirls, cashiers in various places, such as picture
shows and meat markets. Others were employed as stenographers, telephone operators, nurses, maids in hotels, and some were married.

After entering upon a life of prostitution it appears that quite a
number continued at work. This was probably done to maintain a respectable appearance in the community.‡

*Earnings of Prostitutes as Compared with their Earnings in Other
Occupations.* Forty-four prostitutes whom the investigator talked with
in saloons, hotels and on the street in Syracuse gave her the amounts
they had made per week in this business, that is the highest amounts as
well as the lowest in some cases. The fluctuation between these two
points must be considerable; and it would be very difficult to strike an
average from these figures.§

The average weekly earnings of inmates of houses is fairly well
established from various sources. It is not as high in Syracuse as it is
in New York or Chicago. In these places the average in $1 houses is

---

*See Table No. 3, Appendix II.
†See Table No. 5, Appendix II.
‡See Table No. 7, Appendix II.
§See Table No. 8, Appendix II.

about $50 per week. Under the heading "Earnings of Inmates in Houses," it will be seen that the average in Syracuse is about $25 or $30.

Some of the forty-four prostitutes who gave their highest earnings per week from this business said they made as high as $100, $150 and $200 per week. Some said $15 as the highest and $2 as the lowest.

The largest number gave such figures as $20, $25, $30, $35 and $40, as the highest earnings per week and $3, $5, $6 and $10 and $20 as the lowest.

It is interesting to compare the salaries these girls receive in respectable occupations, combined with which they follow prostitution as a side line. For instance the girl who says she makes $200 per week in prostitution receives $15 as an actress. The girl who makes $6 as a salesgirl declares that she earns $25 per week as a prostitute. A maid in a hotel at $5 per week makes as high as $40 from prostitution.*

First Sexual Offense. The partner of the girl in her first sexual offense was secured in forty-six cases. Of this number fourteen were strangers whom the girl met occasionally; eight were lovers, who accomplished the ruin of the girls before marriage; eighteen were designated as friends; five were relatives; one a brother-in-law; one an epileptic uncle; one a cousin; one a brother, and one is mentioned as a relative. A teacher of one of the girls is given.

Prostitutes and their Children. The investigators were only able to learn the facts regarding their children from eleven prostitutes. These women had sixteen children. Of this number four were legitimate, seven illegitimate, and in five cases the investigator could not learn whether or not the mother had been married.

Civil State of Girls. The civil state of girls was secured in forty-seven instances. Of this number three are now living with their husbands, two of these give part of their earnings to these men; ten are separated from their husbands, leaving them for different reasons, such as cruelty, failure to support, on account of drink, etc.; and thirty-four are designated as single.

Reasons Given by Girls for Entering Life of Prostitution. Forty girls gave investigator certain reasons for entering a life of professional or clandestine prostitution. These girls were seen on the street, in saloons and hotels in Syracuse. They belong for the most part to the clandestine type. They work at various occupations. One girl declares that she goes out only with traveling men, and nobody knows it. She goes to church and Sunday School and says that many girls like her go

---

*See Table No. 8, Appendix II.

out on the quiet. Without doubt there is a large number of girls of this type in Syracuse. Of the forty girls who would talk of their personal histories, seven referred to conditions in their family lives, which influenced them in taking up their present life; nine blamed their husbands; nineteen had personal reasons for taking this step, and five declared that insufficient money for food or clothes drove them into immoral living.

Drug Victims. Four of the fifty-one prostitutes interviewed admitted they were drug fiends, victims of cocaine and morphine; several were heavy cigarette smokers and a number were evidently far gone from drink.

Abortions. Two of the fifty-one prostitutes admitted that they had had abortion operations performed. One women was very weak from three such operations. Another woman said she now resorted to unnatural practices to escape danger of having children.

CHAPTER VIII

The Economic and Social Aspects of Commercialized Vice

"There is one great basic fact which underlies all public questions at the present moment. That singular fact is that nothing is done in this country as it was done twenty years ago."

Prior to 1880 the commercialized social evil existed only in a few large seaport cities, because we were an agricultural nation of small cities and rural communities. Our population was mostly native English or North European stock, whose life centered in the home and whose social interests were chiefly those provided by the church.

Hours of labor were long, often from sun to sun, and machinery and industrial equipment crude and exhausting to the worker.

Marriage at twenty to twenty-five was the rule and its strict code of morality was that of our Anglo-Saxon and Germanic ancestors.

The main business of life was living.

The development of industry, and the commercialization of practically every human interest in the past thirty years has completely transformed daily life. Power, transportation and lighting by electricity, automatic machinery, the gas engine, the typewriter, the telephone, the moving picture show, vaudeville and the modern drama, these and scores of other developments of applied science, have shortened labor to nine or ten hours per day. They have relieved many laborers from exhausting toil; made night a continuation of day, and have commercialized much of the social and moral influences formerly left to the home and the church.

The main business of life now is pleasure.

This transformation has brought into industry thousands of women to whom marriage is long deferred, or denied, and whose rate of wages is that established years ago when woman's employment in industry was merely a temporary incident prior to her marriage. This economic and social revolution has accentuated the problem of the social evil by making it easy and profitable to exploit women in vice. If such exploitation be unrestrained it can only result in a hideous political corruption and personal demoralization such as that disclosed in New York by the Rosenthal murder, and the testimony of Mrs. Goode.

As Magistrate Joseph E. Corrigan of New York has said, "Gambling and prostitution have offered for twenty years, and still offer, opportunity for continuous and vastly profitable careers, through which active men starting at the bottom work up to the top, as in any other business." Under our American policy of "Freedom of the Individual," together with a system of antiquated court procedure, criminal law encumbered by trivial technicalities, and courts hampered by the failure of the better type of citizens to do jury duty, it has become exceedingly difficult to obtain convictions of these commercial criminals.

Hence they continue their unobstructed course to murder, or some other culminating crisis. For, as Magistrate Corrigan again says, "Early in 1912 it was very clear to any in a position to see that the criminal population of New York was rapidly rising to a boiling point; and that an explosion of some kind was inevitable."

A like fate awaits every American city, unless the citizens unite to suppress commercialized vice.

Insanity is another phase of the social evil which grows with the rapidity of a cancer. The cost for the care of the insane in New York state for 1909 was $5,600,000. In 1912 it had risen to $8,400,000, an increase of $2,800,000, or fifty per cent in three years. The official estimate for the state for 1913 is $11,792,704, an increase since 1909 of $6,192,704, or one hundred and ten per cent in four years.

Approximately twenty per cent of the insanity among men, and ten per cent among women is incurable paresis, caused usually by syphilis. An additional thirty per cent of the insanity among men and ten per cent among women arises from conditions due directly or indirectly to alcohol. Thus the heavy and rapidly increasing cost of insanity is due, in great part, to the social evil.

The situation is serious, but not hopeless unless we continue to ignore it. We must realize that human nature remains unchanged, and that the normal, healthy young human being who works but ten hours a day at a light task, and who has five hours of leisure each evening, will continue an easy prey to the crafty exploiters of vice for profit, unless we devise powerful measures to thwart these commercial criminals.

Certain of these measures anyone can apply now. We can all do our part in teaching the youth of both sexes the simple truths of life, and the physical and moral dangers which confront them.

We can protect our daughters and sisters by compelling the men who wish to marry them to present a certificate from *an accredited physician of diagnosis by an accepted biological test* showing that they are free from venereal or other contagious diseases. We can uphold the clergy in their efforts to make this requirement general. By so doing we shall exert a powerful restraint upon many young men before marriage.

We can direct the energy of the young people into moral channels by using the school houses, churches, and public buildings as centres of wholesome amusement and social activity.

Every good citizen can help justice greatly by serving on the jury whenever called. Without such men it is difficult to obtain convictions in cases arising from the social evil and violations of the excise laws.

We can accomplish much by persistent demands for the enforcement of existing laws relating to prostitution and the sale of liquor. We can urge the enactment in New York state of laws similar to the thoroughly effective Iowa laws for the suppression of prostitution, referred to in another chapter in this report. And we can insist that the Bureau of Health exercise the same control over the social diseases that it does other contagious and infectious diseases.

We should help maintain the work of making a moral survey of the city from time to time by such non-political agencies as the American Vigilance Association, or the New York Bureau of Municipal Research. Such surveys constitute an audit of the police and other departments of the city government, and are as necessary to an efficient administration of the city as regular examination of banks is necessary to banking efficiency.

Lastly, we must no longer depend wholly upon volunteer committees of citizens for the study and solution of modern city problems. These twentieth century civic evils must be handled by twentieth century methods if we expect to prevent their overwhelming us. They require steady work day by day, and year after year by educated, experienced and paid social workers.

Much of the routine work of this moral survey was done by the Syracuse Associated Charities, it being recognized by the committee as the logical agent for such work.

The bringing of moral defectives under control, in order to prevent the spread of disease and the propogation of more defectives, is an important factor in reducing the social evil to its minimum. That the Associated Charities, whose social workers cover the city, has most efficient means for accomplishing such preventive hygiene is shown by the following cases, taken from many similar ones on file:

Associated Charities Record. Katherine,* aged 32 years, came into the office of the Associated Charities, July, 1912, looking for a place to board her two children, saying she would be willing to pay $2.50 a

*All names given are fictitious.

week for their care. She said she was working in a restaurant, earning $5 a week, but would have to give up her position if she could not find a place for her children. A plan was worked out by the Associated Charities immediately, but it failed because the woman could not be found.

In November the woman was admitted to a local hospital and shortly after gave birth to a child. Investigation proved that the woman had never been married and that this was the fifth child. An orphan asylum in a nearby city is caring for four of the children, and the fifth had been placed with a family in the city. The woman, when admitted to the hospital, came from a house of prostitution, and returned to one. Through the efforts of the Associated Charities she was sent to her home city. The authorities there agreed to send her to a corrective institution.

Associated Charities Record. Jennie,* aged 21 years. Jennie's fifth child was born in October, 1912. The woman's expenses were paid by the Department of Charities. Upon investigation the Associated Charities found that she and John were married under compulsion upon the birth of the second child. He deserted immediately. Since then she has given birth to three children, the Department of Charities paying the expenses of the confinement each time. The Associated Charities Visitor interviewed Jennie's mother and found her caring for the children. Her income was insufficient for their proper care and upon the Visitor's suggestion, the Department of Charities are giving her $2.50 a week instead of forcing her to place the children in an institution. With her consent the last baby has been adopted out. The Associated Charities Visitor swore out a warrant against Jennie, who now has syphilis, and she was committed to Albion, where she will no longer be a menace to society.

Associated Charities Record. Margaret,* 18 years of age, was reported from two sources as being syphilitic. The Associated Charities was asked to make some disposition of the case. The girl was located at one of the hospitals, where she was working. Her parents were living in town and were greatly distressed to know what to do with her. Doctors were consulted as to her condition, and it was found that she needed careful treatment. She was sent to Albion Reformatory. The superintendent of that institution wrote that the girl was in such bad condition, due to syphilis and gonorrhœa, that she had to be put in quarantine. Later reports received from the institution show that Margaret is behaving well, and is much better physically.

Without such preventive work as this, persistently maintained and backed by ample public support, Syracuse and our American cities are

---

*All names given are fictitious.

in danger of being swamped by the swiftly rising tide of dependants, defectives and delinquents now numbering about 10,000 in Syracuse, or seven per cent of the population. They supply a large quota of the prostitutes of both sexes; spread disease broadcast, and crowd our hospitals and asylums. If unrestrained they will produce a numerous brood of their kind to increase the burden society must carry in the immediate future.

CHAPTER IX

Conclusions and Recommendations

This investigation shows that through the tacit permission of the authorities and the indifference of its citizens there has existed for generations in Syracuse what is to all intents and purposes a segregated district where the business of prostitution is openly encouraged and practiced in flagrant violation of the law. The community has thus become a partner in this abhorrent crime. The experience of every city where segregation has been tried has demonstrated its utter failure; and all students of the social evil agree that segregation, so far from repressing prostitution or confining it to any one district, actually tends to its increase and spread throughout the community. The preceding report of conditions in Syracuse amply bears out this contention.

The segregation of prostitution and its permission (tacit or otherwise) in any one section encourages every kind of vicious practice, and gives rise to unnatural vice. Thus the investigators found perversion fearfully common in the houses of prostitution in the city.

If we are to make any headway against the social evil, it must be understood once for all that segregation does not segregate. This is the universal experience. Only with this understanding clearly in mind can the problem be dealt with adequately.

Segregation does not even segregate the venereal diseases. On the contrary it assures their spreading. Even granted that the inmates are periodically examined, and that the examination is adequate (which it very rarely is or can be) this assertion still remains true. An inmate may be examined one day, and be declared free from venereal disease. That same night she may entertain a diseased man, and become infected. All the men who have intercourse with her before her next examination are in danger of contamination. The medical certificate thus gives a false sense of security to the patrons of a segregated district which too often leads to their physical ruin. And besides this, in accordance with our one-sided treatment of this problem, the physical examination extends only to the woman. Men carry the infection as well as women; and vicious men frequently carry it into innocent homes. Vicious women very seldom do so.

This report amply demonstrates that the vice fostered in the segre-

gated district spreads its baneful influence to every part of the community, even invading not only the colleges but the high schools.
Too much emphasis cannot be laid upon this phase of the problem. As
a matter of fact there is actually more of the business of commercialized
prostitution carried on outside the segregated district than within. But
the segregated district is the center where it breeds, and whence it
spreads. Prostitution is there openly flaunted in defiance of law and
decency; it is advertised as other businesses are advertised; and all possible means are employed to encourage every form of unspeakable vice.
If any advance is to be made in the fight against the social evil in this
city *the segregated district must be abolished.*

The investigation also shows unmistakably the pernicious influence
of the association of prostitution with the saloon and the disorderly
hotels, which is common in Syracuse. As has already been stated, the
abnormal number of saloons practically forces many proprietors to associate prostitution with their liquor business in order to make a living.
This type of the liquor business is the means of luring young men and
women into vice. This is its purpose. The business must be made to
pay, and this is the means. The more drink, the more prostitution; the
more prostitution the more drink. Thus is the vicious circle completed.
The young people's self-control is broken down by the first few drinks.
The means of vice are close at hand, and every encouragement for its
indulgence is employed. Seduction or prostitution is the next easy step.

It is safe to say that without this stimulus of liquor the extensive
business of prostitution would materially shrink at once. And the evil
influence is brought to bear upon those who have not yet fallen into
vice, but who, under the influence of the liquor, are made ripe for the
fall.

Thus the investigation shows conclusively that the disorderly hotels
and cafes, together with the saloons run in connection with prostitution,
are a most pernicious source of the debauchery of youth.

The investigation also reveals the prevalence of street soliciting in
open defiance of the police. The professional or semi-professional prostitute carries on her nefarious trade openly throughout the business
centre of the city. As already pointed out elsewhere in this report,
there is no city ordinance prohibiting street solicitation. *Such an
ordinance should be at once enacted and rigidly enforced.*

The evidence of the prevalence of clandestine prostitution, very
largely on the part of young people, is another pitiful outcome of the
investigation. This suggests an ignorance on the part of the youth of
the city regarding the dangers attending sexual vice, and a lax moral

sense. Something must be done to educate our boys and girls in this matter, and to strengthen their moral fibre. We submit this chapter of the report to the earnest consideration of parents, teachers, ministers, and all who have to do with the training of youth.

In this connection we wish to call special attention to the report relative to summer amusement resorts in the vicinity of the city. The committee feels that they cannot too strongly emphasize the evils attending the lax supervision of these resorts.

Information in the hands of the committee also points to the fact that many of the city parks, not alone those on the outskirts, but those in the populous parts of the city, are inadequately policed and lighted, and that this results in vicious practices in the summer time.

The chapter on Prostitution and Disease should also receive the earnest consideration of all citizens. These diseases, so frightful in their consequences, not only to the guilty, but to innocent wives and children yet unborn, are distressingly prevalent in Syracuse.

One very significant fact disclosed by the investigation is that the vice of Syracuse is constantly recruited by girls from the neighboring towns, who, having fallen into prostitution here, pass on to the houses of prostitution in the City of New York. Thus Syracuse and the other cities of central New York become supply stations for the vice of the larger city.

The affidavit of the investigator who visited the city at the time of the Conference of Older Boys reveals in a striking way the pernicious influence for the corruption of youth of a well known segregated vice district in any community. This alone should make the further tolerance of segregated vice in Syracuse an absolute impossibility.

In the appendix following will be found detailed the experiences of certain cities that have faced the problem of vice with the determination that it be reduced to a minimum. This chapter is commended to the thoughtful perusal of the city authorities, police department and citizens generally. *What other cities have done, Syracuse can do.*

In view of these conclusions, and its careful study of the social evil in Syracuse and other cities, the committee presents the following recommendations to state and city authorities, public officials, and various organizations:

Recommendations to the State Authorities

1. That a state law similar to the Iowa Injunction and Abatement Law (See Appendix No. IV) be enacted and enforced whereby houses of prostitution and assignation are declared to be a nuisance, citizens are given the right to institute summary proceedings in equity for the abate-

ment of the nuisance, and the penalty for prostitution is placed upon the owner or owners of the building or property where prostitution occurs.

2.   That the law prohibiting the sale of alcoholic liquors in connection with prostitution be enforced; that violation of this prohibition be punished by permanent revocation of all liquor licenses held by any parties engaged in the violation, and that the revocation of licenses apply not only to the holders of the license but also for a term of not less than one year to the premises where the illegal sale of liquor occurred.

3.   That violations of the liquor laws be punished by the permanent revocation of all licenses held by the violators, and that the revocation apply also for a term of not less than one year to the premises where the violation occurred.

4.   That in dealing with prostitution in the courts, fine be abolished and imprisonment or an adult probation system be substituted.

5.   That the number of saloons in Syracuse be immediately reduced through a rigid enforcement of the excise laws so that it shall bear a normal relationship to the population of the city.

6.   That a course in Sex Hygiene be introduced into the Normal Schools of the state, so that teachers may be prepared to instruct their pupils.

Recommendations to the City Authorities

1.   That a city ordinance be enacted and enforced similar to the so-called "Tin Plate Ordinance" of Portland, Ore. (See Appendix No. IV), whereby the owner of any building used wholly or in part as a hotel, rooming house, lodging house, etc., shall maintain at the principal street entrance a plate bearing the name and address of the owner or owners of the building and the land on which it stands.

2.   That city ordinances be enacted and enforced that shall deal adequately with street solicitation.

3.   That the tacit permission of the segregated district where prostitution is exploited for profit cease, and that the district be abolished by vigorous enforcement of the laws relative to prostitution; and that this abolition of the segregated district be followed by continued and persistent efforts to reduce prostitution in all parts of the city.

4.   That in cases of arrest in disorderly houses or resorts, the men as well as the women be held for trial.

5.   That prostitutes who desire to avail themselves of the opportunity, or who are arrested and convicted, be sent to an industrial home with hospital accommodations.

6. That semi-delinquent girls be separated from delinquents, and enlightened methods of care and education given them.

7. That enlarged and adequate provision be made, in connection with the Juvenile Court, for the care of delinquent young girls held in temporary detention.

8. That all association of saloons and prostitution be absolutely abolished; and that all connections between the bar and other rooms be immediately and permanently closed.

9. That the hotels and cafes of the city be adequately supervised; that bona fide registration of guests occupying rooms be required in all hotels; that all connections between wine room and bed rooms be abolished; and that no screens or curtains be allowed in wine rooms.

10. That dance halls be placed under control of accredited matrons; and that no association of the dance halls with saloons or the sale of liquor be permitted.

11. That the city's system of parks and playgrounds be extended to provide ample recreation centres for children and adults; that the parks be given ample supervision and lighting, and that the playgrounds be supervised by matrons.

12. That women be added to the police force.

13. That public comfort stations be established in appropriate sections of the city.

Recommendations to the Bureau of Health

1. That the Bureau of Health recognize the social diseases as contagious diseases, and subject them to a degree of control equal to or greater than that maintained in relation to other diseases; that the Bureau of Health adopt the methods now employed by the Department of Health in New York City for the control of social diseases, and that the Bureau compile annually the statistics of these diseases in order to ascertain the efficiency of control.

Recommendations to the Board of Education

1. That the Board of Education investigate thoroughly the advisability and methods of teaching sex hygiene to the older pupils of the public schools.

2. That the school houses be used as social centers to as great an extent as practicable for children, young people and adults.

Recommendations to Parents

That parents change their attitude of assumed ignorance regarding sex to one of initial or primary instruction; that they instruct their children in the simple facts of sex life, sex hygiene, and the physical and moral dangers associated with vice, or arrange with some suitable person for the proper instruction of their children in these matters.

Recommendations to the Authorities Where the Summer Amusement Resorts are Located

That such authorities provide adequate supervision of the summer amusement resorts, and that the dark places in the grounds be lighted.

Recommendations to Various Organizations

1.   That the Churches, Clubs, The Chamber of Commerce, Women's Organizations, Labor Assemblies and Labor Unions throughout the city enter upon a vigorous campaign of education regarding the social evil, to the end that the public conscience be awakened to the point of insisting upon its suppression.

2.   That the business men of Syracuse, through the Chamber of Commerce and other business organizations, be informed of the cost of vice and its diseases in reduced efficiency of workers, the cost of sickness and hospital treatment, and premature death.

And Finally to the Men of Syracuse

That they recognize one standard of morality for men and women alike, govern their lives accordingly, and set their faces sternly against every form of sexual vice.   The social evil is fundamentally a man's problem.   It is fostered by men for financial profit, and for the gratification of their passions.   Thousands of unwilling girl recruits are annually forced or lured into its toils by that monstrous product of our civilization, the male procurer, whose business is seduction.

APPENDICES

APPENDIX I

Accounts of an Inmate of a Dollar House of Prostitution from January 1st, 1912, to June 30th, 1912

JANUARY 1st, 1912

	Total Earnings	Her Share	Balance in Debt to Madam	Expenses	Remarks
			$96.00		Began year with this debt
Mon..... 1	$17.00	$8.50	87.50		
ues..... 2	10.00	5.00	82.50		
			109.50	$27.00	Ring
Wed..... 3	9.00	4.50	105.00		
Thurs.... 4	11.00	5.50	99.50		
Fri....... 5	4.00	2.00	97.50		
			120.50	23.00	
Sat...... 6	10.00	5.00	115.50		
			116.00	.50	Show
			126.18	10.18	Waist $4.98, home $5.00, 20c (?)
Sun...... 7	7.00	4.50	121.68		
Mon..... 8	8.00	3.50	118.18		
ues..... 9	6.00	6.50	111.68		
Wed.....10	14.00	7.00	104.68		
Thur.....11	7.00	3.50	101.18		
Fri......12	13.00	6.50	94.68		
			113.68	19.00	Dress $15.00, switch $4.00
Sat......13	11.00	5.50	108.18		
			135.18	27.00	Wash $2.00, ring $25.00
Sun......14	10.00	*2.00	133.18		
Mon.....15	6.00	2.50	130.68		
ues.....16	9.00	4.50	126.18		
Wed.....17	8.00	4.00	122.18		
			123.18	1.00	Show
Thurs....18	5.00	2.50	120.68		
Fri......19	12.00	6.00	114.68		
Sat......20	10.00	5.00	109.68		
			114.68	5.00	(?)
Sun......21	10.00	*2.00	112.68		
			115.68	3.00	Wash and Doctor
Mon.....22	16.00	8.00	107.68		
ues.....23	3.00	1.50	106.18		
Wed.....24	13.00	6.50	99.68		
			103.86	4.18	Com. $1.25, dress $2.50, 15c and 28c (?)
Thurs...25	14.00	7.00	96.86		
Fri......26	12.00	6.00	90.86		
Sat......27	21.00	10.50	80.36		
			84.51	4.15	15c, $3.00, $1.00 (?)
Sun......28	19.00	*6.50	78.01		
			103.01	25.00	Ring
Mon.....29	11.00	5.50	97.51		
			107.51	10.00	Home
ues.....30	10.00	†4.00	103.51		
Wed.....31	10.00	5.00	98.51		
Totals	$326.00	$156.50		$159.01	
				6.00	Board
				$165.01	

Board of inmate, $3.00, taken out of her share of earnings each Sunday.
Inmate's share of earnings not an even half of her total receipts for the day.

APPENDIX I—*Continued*

FEBRUARY 1st, 1912

	Total Earnings	Her Share	Balance in Debt to Madam	Expenses	Remarks
			$98.51		
Thurs.... 1	$9.00	$4.50	94.01		
			96.51	$2.50	Show 50c, shoes $2.00
Fri...... 2	10.00	5.00	91.51		
Sat...... 3	19.00	9.50	82.01		
			84.01	2.00	Washing
Sun...... 4	13.00	*3.50	80.51		
Mon..... 5	12.00	6.00	74.51		
			77.81	3.30	Show (Grand) 30c, dress dyed $3.0
Tue..... 6	8.00	4.00	73.81		
			78.81	5.00	Hat
Wed..... 7	5.00	2.50	76.31		
Thurs.... 8		out al			
Fri...... 9		out al			
Sat......10	18.00	9.00	67.31		
			68.31	1.00	Chss.
Sun......11	21.00	*7.50	60.81		
			63.81	3.00	Doctor $1.00, washing $2.00
Mon.....12	13.00	6.50	57.31		
			58.81	1.50	Lysol 25c, record $1.00, chop sue 25c
Tues.....13	13.00	6.50	52.31		
Wed.....14	4.00	2.00	50.31		
Thurs....15	9.00	4.50	45.81		
			51.56	5.75	Home $5.00, show 75c
Fri......16	10.00	5.00	46.56		
Sat......17	14.00	7.00	39.56		
			41.81	2.25	Washing $2.00, waist 25c
Sun......18	18.00	*6.00	35.81		
Mon.....19	13.00	6.50	29.31		
Tues.....20	9.00	4.50	24.81		
			25.16	.35	Cream (Cold)
Wed.....21	6.00	3.00	22.16		
			22.66	.50	Show
Thurs...22	11.00	5.50	17.16		
Fri......23	9.00	4.50	12.66		
Sat......24	23.00	11.50	1.16		
			30.16	29.00	Washing $3.00, Doctor $1.00, rir $25.00
Sun......25	12.00	*3.00	27.16		
Mon.....26	9.00	4.50	22.66		
Tues.....27	9.00	4.50	18.16		
Wed.....28	10.00	5.00	13.16		
			16.76	3.60	Furs, sandwich, go out $2.60, o lady $1.00
Thurs....29	2.00	1.00	15.76		
			19.76	4.00	Doctor $1.00, washing $2.00, ($1.00
Totals	$309.00	$142.50		$63.75	
				12.00	Board
				$75.75	

*Board $3.00, taken out each Sunday.

APPENDIX I—*Continued*

MARCH 1st, 1912

	Total Earnings	Her Share	Balance in Debt to Madam	Expenses	Remarks
			$19.76		
ri..... 1	$11.00	$5.50	14.26		
at...... 2	20.00	10.00	4.26		
			7.26	$3.00	Doctor $1.00, washing $2.00
un...... 3	11.00	*2.50	4.76		
			14.76	10.00	Clothes
Ion..... 4	7.00	3.50	11.26		
ues..... 5	13.00	6.50	4.76		
			8.26	3.50	Dress $2.50, bank $1.00
Ved..... 6	11.00	5.50	2.76		
hurs.... 7	17.00	*5.50	†2.74		
			8.26	11.00	Dress $8.00, washing and Doctor $3.00
ri...... 8	17.00	8.50	† .24		
at...... 9	16.00	8.00	†8.24		
un......10	14.00	4.00	12.24		
			12.76	25.00	(?)
Ion.....11	10.00	5.00	7.76		
			17.76	10.00	Suit
ues.....12	14.00	7.00	10.76		
Ved.....13	16.00	8.00	2.76		
hurs....14	9.00	4.50	†1.74		
			†.99	.75	Corset
ri......15	19.50	9.75	†10.74		
at......16	30.00	15.00	†25.74		
			†22.74	3.00	Doctor and washing
un......17	9.00	*1.50	†24.24		
Ion.....18	7.00	3.50	†27.74		
			†15.74	12.00	Hat
ues.....19	12.00	6.00	†21.74		
			15.76	37.50	Suit
Ved.....20	8.00	4.00	11.76		
			15.76	4.00	Shoes
hurs....21	11.00	5.50	10.26		
			14.76	4.50	Shirtwaist
ri......22	15.00	7.50	7.26		
at......23	17.00	8.50	†1.24		
			2.41	3.65	Doctor and washing (Jew)
un......24	11.00	*2.50	†.09		
			33.89	33.98	(?) $3.00, skirt $2.98, ring and presents $18.00, go home $10.00
Ion.....25	11.00	5.50	28.39		
ues.....26	Home				
Ved.....27	Home				
hurs...28	Home				
ri......29	Home				
at......30	14.00	7.00	21.39		
			32.39	11.00	Washing and Doctor $3.00
un......31	13.00	*3.50	28.89		
Totals	$363.50	$163.75		$172.88	
				18.00	Board
				$190.88	

Board $3.00 taken out each Sunday.
Balance ahead. Madam owes inmate.

APPENDIX I—*Continued*

APRIL 1st, 1912

	Total Earnings	Her Share	Balance in Debt to Madam	Expenses	Remarks
			$28.89		
Mon..... 1	$7.00	$3.50	25.39		
			27.39	$2.00	"Comond"
Tues..... 2	3.00	1.50	25.89		
			26.89	1.00	Show
Wed..... 3	6.00	3.00	23.89		
			24.89	1.00	Bank
Thurs.... 4	6.00	3.00	21.89		
Fri.......5	10.00	5.00	16.89		
			26.89	10.00	Bank X B
Sat...... 6	16.00	8.00	18.89		
Sun...... 7	21.00	*7.50	11.39		
			14.39	3.00	Doctor and washing
Mon..... 8	15.00	7.50	6.89		
			32.64	25.75	(?) 75c, ring, fish $25.00
Tues..... 9	10.00	5.00	27.64		
			29.14	1.50	Doctor $1.00, lysol 25c, powder 2.
Wed.....10	3.00	1.50	27.64		
			65.89	38.25	Dresses $15.00, coat $6.00, powd
Thurs....11					25c, wash $3.00, Doctor $1.0
Fri......12					combination $7.50, Doctor $1.0
Sat......13					combination $4.50
Sun......14					
Mon.....15					
Tues.....16					
Wed.....17					
Thurs....18	13.00	6.50	59.39		
Fri......19	10.00	5.00	54.39		
			54.64	.25	(?)
Sat......20	12.00	6.00	48.64		
			51.64	3.00	Doctor and washing
Sun......21	16.00	*5.00	46.64		
Mon.....22	10.00	5.00	41.64		
			86.64	45.00	Ring $30.00, coat Mr. F. $15.00
Tues.....23	8.00	4.00	82.64		
Wed.....24	11.00	5.50	77.14		
			92.64	15.50	Dress
Thurs....25	10.00	5.00	87.64		
Fri......26	12.00	6.00	81.64		
Sat......27	19.00	9.50	72.14		
			75.14	3.00	Doctor and washing
Sun......28	14.00	*4.00	71.14		
			75.64	4.50	(?) $2.50, "Borred" $1.50, (?) 5
Mon.....29					
Tues.....30	8.00	4.00	71.64		
Totals	$240.00	$111.00		$153.75	
				9.00	Board
				$162.75	

*Board $3.00, taken out each Sunday.

APPENDIX I—*Continued*

MAY 1st, 1912

	Total Earnings	Her Share	Balance in Debt to Madam	Expenses	Remarks
			$71.64		
Wed..... 1	$8.00	$4.00	67.64		
Thurs.... 2	12.00	6.00	61.64		
			63.14	$1.50	(?)
Fri...... 3	10.00	5.00	58.14		
Sat...... 4	21.00	10.50	47.64		
			93.89	46.25	Doctor and washing $3.50, ring $25.00, curtains $17.75
Sun...... 5	15.00	*4.50	89.39		
Mon..... 6	10.00	5.00	84.39		
Tues..... 7	10.00	5.00	79.39		
			95.99	16.60	"Comond" $16.00, borrowed 60c
Wed..... 8	7.00	3.50	92.49		
Thurs.... 9	3.00	1.50	90.99		
			107.99	17.00	Hat
Fri......10	8.00	4.00	103.99		
Sat......11	18.00	9.00	94.99		
			95.99	1.00	Express
Sun......12	14.00	*4.00	91.99		
			93.99	2.00	Laundry
Mon.....13	9.00	4.50	89.49		
Tues.....14	14.00	7.00	82.49		
			83.69	1.20	Towels
Wed.....15	7.00	3.50	80.19		
Thurs....16	7.00	3.50	76.69		
			77.44	.75	Show
Fri......17	8.00	4.00	73.44		
			76.54	3.10	Doctor and washing $3.00, (?) 10c
Sat......18	20.00	10.00	66.54		
Sun......19	16.00	*5.00	61.54		
			91.54	30.00	Home
Mon.....20	8.00	4.00	87.54		
Tues.....21	11.00	5.50	82.04		
Wed.....22	12.00	6.00	76.04		
			78.54	2.50	(?)
Thurs....23	2.00	1.00	77.54		
Fri......24	16.00	8.00	69.54		
Sat......25	22.00	11.00	58.54		
			61.84	3.30	Doctor and washing, $3.00, (?) 30c
Sun......26	16.00	*5.00	56.84		
Mon.....27	9.00	4.50	52.34		
			53.34	1.00	Dress
Tues.....28	8.00	4.00	49.34		
Wed.....29	16.00	8.00	41.34		
Thurs....30	21.00	10.50	30.84		
Fri......31	10.00	5.00	25.84		
Totals	$368.00	$172.00		$126.20	
				12.00	Board
				$138.20	

*Board $3.00, taken out each Sunday.

APPENDIX I—*Continued*

JUNE 1st, 1912

	Total Earnings	Her Share	Balance in Debt to Madam	Expenses	Remarks
			$25.84		
Sat...... 1	$16.00	$8.00	17.84 / 19.84	$2.00	Washing
Sun...... 2	13.00	*3.50	16.34 / 18.84	2.50	(?)
Mon..... 3	8.00	4.00	14.84		
Tues..... 4	19.00	9.50	5.34 / 28.34	23.00	(?)
Wed..... 5	Home				
Thurs.... 6	Home				
Fri...... 7	11.00	5.50	22.84		
Sat...... 8	19.00	9.50	13.34 / 15.34	2.00	Washing
Sun...... 9	13.00	*3.50	11.84 / 17.84	6.00	Gloves $1.00, shoes $5.00
Mon.....10	8.00	4.00	13.84		
Tues.....11	8.00	4.00	9.84		
Wed.....12	11.00	5.50	4.34 / 20.34	16.00	Coat $13.15, (?) $2.50, 35c
Thurs....13	5.00	2.50	17.84		
Fri......14	7.00	3.50	14.34		
Sat......15	17.00	8.50	5.84 / 10.84	5.00	Washing $2.00, Doctor $1.00, Miss — $2.00
Sun......16	20.00	*7.00	3.84 / 31.34	27.50	Dress
Mon.....17	10.00	5.00	26.34		
Tues.....18	10.00	5.00	21.34		
Wed.....19	22.00	11.00	10.34 / 14.49	4.15	Waist $4.00, (?) 15c
Thurs....20	16.00	8.00	6.49		
Fri......21	7.00	3.50	2.99 / 6.99	4.00	Doctor and washing
Sat......22	17.00	8.50	†1.51 / 2.99	4.50	Dress $4.00, (?) 50c
Sun......23	9.00	*1.50	1.49 / 26.49	25.00	Ring $20.00, locket $5.00, (following original entry torn out)
Mon.....24	7.00	3.50	22.99 / 40.49	17.50	(?)
Tues.....25	13.00	6.50	33.99 / 35.49	1.50	(?) $1.00, (?) 50c
Wed.....26	10.00	5.00	30.49		
Thurs....27	14.00	7.00	23.49 / 44.49	21.00	(?)
Fri......28	16.00	8.00	36.49 / 43.49	7.00	(?) $1.00, (?) $6.00
Sat......29	18.00	9.00	34.49		
Sun......30	12.00	*3.00	31.49		
Totals	$356.00	$163.00		$168.65 / 15.00	Board
				$183.65	

*Board $3.00, taken out each Sunday.

†Balance ahead. Madam owes inmate.

APPENDIX I—*Continued*

TOTAL EARNINGS, HER SHARE OF EARNINGS, EXPENSES, AND BALANCE OF DEBT TO MADAM, JANUARY 1ST TO JUNE 30TH, 1912, ACCOUNTS OF X39, INMATE OF ONE DOLLAR HOUSE OF PROSTITUTION.

	Total Earnings	Her Share (deducting board)	Expenses, (excluding board)	Deficit	Surplus
Jan.............	$326.00	$156.50	$159.01	$2.51	
Feb.............	309.00	142.50	63.75	......	$78.75
March..........	363.50	163.75	172.88	9.13	
April...........	240.00	111.00	153.75	42.75	
May............	368.00	172.00	126.20	......	45.80
June...........	356.00	163.00	168.65	5.65	
Total..........	$1962.50	$908.75	$844.24	$60.04	$124.55
Average per week..	$75.48	$34.95			

Balance debt to Madam January 1st, 1912.........................	$96.00			$96.00
Expenses, January 1st to June 30th, 1912........................	844.24	Deficit	60.04
	$940.24		$156.04
Earnings, January 1st to June 30th, 1912........................	908.75	Surplus	124.55
Balance debt to Madam June 30th, 1912.........................	$31.49		$31.49

TOTAL EARNINGS AND AVERAGE EARNINGS PER DAY BASED UPON THE ACTUAL NUMBER OF DAYS WORKED FROM JANUARY 1ST TO JUNE 30TH, 1912. ACCOUNTS OF X39, INMATE OF ONE DOLLAR HOUSE OF PROSTITUTION.

	Total Earnings	No. Days Worked	Average Working Day	Every Day	Highest	Lowest
Jan.......	$326.00	31	$10.50	$10.50	Jan. 27, Sat. $21.00	Jan. 23, Tues. $3.00
Feb.......	309.00	27	11.45	10.65	Feb. 24, Sat. 23.00	Feb, 29, Thurs. 2.00
Mar.......	363.50	27	13.46	11.73	Mar. 16, Sat. 30.00	Mar. 4 & 18, Mon. 7.00
April......	240.00	21	11.43	8.00	April 7, Sun. 21.00	April 3, Tues. 3.00
May......	368.00	31	11.87	11.87	May 25, Sat. 22.00	May 23, Thurs. 2.00
June......	356.00	28	12.71	11.87	June 19, Wed. 22.00	June 13, Thurs. 5.00
	$1962.50	165				

Average per working day, $11.90.
Average per working week, $83.30.
Average per working year, $4,331.60.

CLASSIFIED EXPENSES OF X39, INMATE OF A DOLLAR HOUSE OF PROSTITUTION, JANUARY 1ST TO JUNE 30TH, 1912

	Jan.	Feb.	Mar.	April	May	June	Total	Per Cent
Dress.................	$28.16	$10.25	$82.23	$70.00	$34.00	$73.65	$298.29	32.50
Jewelry..............	77.00	25.00	18.00	55.00	25.00	25.00	225.00	24.60
Home................	15.00	5.00	20.00	.....	30.00	.....	70.00	7.60
Doctor amd Washing....	2.00	14.00	15.65	15.00	9.50	11.00	67.15	7.50
Shows...............	1.50	2.05	.....	1.00	.75	1.00	6.30	.70
Miscellaneous.........	35.35	7.45	37.00	12.75	26.95	58.00	177.50	19.20
Total................	$159.01	$63.75	$172.88	$153.75	$126.20	$168.65	$844.24	92.10
Board...............	6.00	12.00	18.00	9.00	12.00	15.00	72.00	7.90
Total................	$165.01	$75.75	$190.88	$162.75	$138.20	$183.65	$916.24	100.00

APPENDIX II

Table No. 1

TABLE SHOWING BIRTHPLACE, NATIVITY

Record of fifty cases showing birthplaces of prostitutes as stated by them to investigators

Birthplace	Foreign	Native	White	Colored
Syracuse..................14	3	48	51	0
E. Syracuse................ 2				
Camillus, N. Y............. 1				
Wampsville, N. Y........... 2				
Baldwinsville, N. Y......... 3				
Minoa, N. Y................ 1				
Rockwell Springs, N. Y...... 1				
Utica, N. Y................ 1				
Oneida, N. Y............... 2				
Binghamton, N. Y........... 1				
Troy, N. Y................. 1				
Rochester, N. Y............ 2				
New York, N. Y............. 9				
Philadelphia, Pa............ 1				
Pennsylvania............... 1				
Wilkes-Barre, Pa............ 1				
Newark, N. J............... 1				
New London, Conn........... 1				
Bedford, Mass.............. 1				
Providence, R. I............ 1				
Canada.................... 1				
Germany................... 1				
Ireland.................... 1				
Total..................50				
1 not learned				

Table No. 2

TABLE OF 39 CASES GIVING REASONS WHY PROSTITUTES CAME TO SYRACUSE

	Total
To work................................12
To shop............................... 3
To solicit.............................. 7
To enter house......................... 3
With man.............................. 3
To live................................ 2
To marry.............................. 2
Ran away—quarrel at home.............. 3
Came with show........................ 1
To be with father—employed............. 1
From Ireland—to be with folks........... 1
To see the boys every Saturday and Sunday... 1
	39

APPENDIX II—*Continued*

Table No. 3

TABLE SHOWING PRESENT AGE OF GIRL, HER AGE WHEN THE FIRST
SEXUAL OFFENSE WAS COMMITTED, AND AGE WHEN SHE ENTERED
LIFE OF PROSTITUTION. TWENTY-FOUR CASES CONSIDERED.

Present Age of Girl	Age of First Sexual Offense	Age of Entering Life of Prostitution
24	20	20
22	18	19
23	22	22
24	23–10 months	6 weeks after
23	18	18
21	20–10 months	2 months after
21	18	18
26	. .	19
26	23	23
24	18	19
19	16	18
24	. .	. .
23	15	20
22	14	4 months after
22	. .	4 months after
24	19	22
24	18	18
23	16	16
22	19	19
28	26	26
26	. .	2 months after
26	16	18
21	15	18
24	16	17
—	—	—
Average 24	Average 20	Average 23

Table No. 4

FIRST SEXUAL OFFENSE

Record of Forty-six cases showing partner of first sexual offense,
as stated to Investigator.

Stranger	Lover	Friend	Relative	Teacher	Total
14	8	18	5	1	46

APPENDIX II—*Continued*

Table No. 5

TABLE SHOWING WAGES RECEIVED BY 25 PROSTITUTES IN VARIOUS OC-
CUPATIONS IN SYRACUSE ENGAGED IN BEFORE AND AFTER BECOMING
PROSTITUTES.

Occupation	Salary Per Week	Domestic Servant	Salary
Cloak model............	$15.00 and expenses	Cook	$20.00 per month
Candy stand............	6.00		
Cashier.................	5.00 and dinner	Extra servant at hotel	5.00 per week
Waitress in Restaurant....	10.00		
Cashier.................	12.00		
Meat market...........	6.00	Maid in hotel	5.00 per week
Store..................	8.00		
Store..................	8.50	Maid in hotel	6.00 per week
Actress................	20.00		
Telephone operator......	8.00		
Stenographer...........	10.00		
Nurse.................	5.00 and board		
Demonstrator...........	12.00		
Laundry...............	5.00		
Sales girl..............	7.00		
Sales girl..............	6.00		
Sales girl..............	7.00		
Sales girl..............	8.00		
Sales girl..............	6.00		
Sales girl..............	8.00		
Sales girl..............	7.00		
Sales girl..............	7.00		
Sales girl..............	9.00		
Sales girl..............	8.00		
Sales girl..............	9.00		

Table No. 6

CIVIL STATE OF GIRLS

Record of Forty-seven cases showing the Civil State of Prostitutes.

Living with Husband	Separated from Husband	Single	Total
3	10	34	47

APPENDIX II—*Continued*

Table No. 7

TABLE SHOWING OCCUPATION AND BUSINESS OF GIRLS BEFORE AND AFTER BECOMING PROSTITUTES

Trade or Business Before Becoming a Prostitute	Domestic Service	Trade or Business Combined with Prostitution	Domestic Service
Married	Maid	Sales girl	Maid
Married	Maid	Cashier	Maid
Cloak model	Maid	Waitress	
Married		Cashier	
Married		Sales girl	
Cashier		Married	
Waitress		Married	
Cashier		Actress	
Sales girl		Telephone operator	
Married		Stenographer	
Sales girl		Sales girl	
Actress		Nurse	
Cashier		Sales girl	
Telephone operator		Married	
Manufacturing		Sales girl	
Sales girl		Sales girl	
Nurse		Married	
Sales girl		Sales girl	
Sales girl		Demonstrator	
Married		Laundry	
Sales girl		Sales girl	
Married		Sales girl	
Sales girl			
Demonstrator			
Laundry			
Sales girl			
Sales girl			

APPENDIX II—*Continued*

Table No. 8

TABLE SHOWING EARNINGS OF PROSTITUTES AS COMPARED WITH EARNINGS IN OTHER OCCUPATIONS

Earnings from Prostitution Weekly		Earnings Combined With Prostitution	Earnings from Prostitution Combined with Domestic Service	Disposition of Earnings
Highest	Lowest			
$40.00				
10.00				Husband
100.00	....	....	$20.00 per month, maid	Friend
17.00	....	....		
200.00	....	$15.00 per week, actress		
23.00	$3.00			
25.00	5.00	6.00 sales girl		
150.00			5.00 maid	
40.00	10.00	....		
40.00	6.00	5.00 cashier		
40.00	....	10.00 waitress		
....	....	12.00 cashier		
30.00	5.00			Lives home
30.00	3.00	7.00 sales girl		
20.00	....	9.00 sales girl		
20.00	....	....	5.00 maid	
20.00				Friend when he is not working
100.00	20.00	....		
75.00	10.00			
15.00				
30.00	3.00			
30.00	10.00			
25.00	2.00			
80.00	....	20.00 actress		Friend
150.00	10.00	....		
65.00				
25.00	....	8.00 telephone operator		
25.00	....	10.00 stenographer		
100.00	10.00			
20.00		8.00 sales girl		
25.00	....	5.00 and board-nurse		Lives home, pays all
28.00	1.00	6.00 sales girl		
25.00	....	7.00 sales girl		
21.00	6.00			
15.00	....	7.00 sales girl		
40.00				
70.00				
50.00				
15.00				
40.00	10.00	9.00 sales girl		Lives home, pays all
30.00	....	7.00 sales girl		
45.00	5.00			
80.00	....	12.00 demonstrator		
....	....	5.00 laundry		Lives home, pays $5.00
30.00	10.00	8.00 sales girl		
35.00	....	8.00 sales girl		
Average $44.00				

Results Following the Abolition of the "Red Light District" in Seattle, Wash.

LETTER FROM THE MAYOR OF SEATTLE

"Honorable F. A. Hartenstein,   "July 9, 1912.
   "Mayor of Youngstown, Ohio.

"My Dear Mayor:—

"In reply to your inquiries in your letter of the 2nd inst., I would answer One and Two:

"We have no 'Red Light District' in Seattle. It was abolished as a result of agitation leading up to an injunction proceeding against owners, city officials, etc., in October, 1910.

"Third: Since October, 1910, there have been no recognized, tolerated houses of prostitution, and it is and has been for eighteen months the policy of this and the last administration to suppress and so far as possible eliminate this evil.

"Fourth: The result of the above action and policy has clearly been to decrease in a very marked degree the number of persons engaged in or in any way suspected in connection with this line of vice. It has been established, I believe I may say, without question, by experience here, that the so-called 'Restricted' or 'Red Light District' acts as a nucleus well advertised breeding center for the social evil, from which it radiates and permeates throughout the entire city.

"The idea that 'segregation' accomplishes the result which the name indicates, and produces better conditions outside of the 'Restricted District' has been abundantly disproven here.

"Fifth: Our control of the social evil consists in constant watchfulness of houses suspected of harboring or inviting traffic of this sort, arrests when necessary, and a constant, persistent effort to reduce it to a minimum. Any form of public solicitation is promptly dealt with and I believe there is little of that sort of thing in our city.

"While we do not claim in any sense to have absolutely eradicated the social evil, we do believe that Seattle, a cosmopolitan seaport city of nearly 300,000 population, has made a great stride forward toward municipal cleanliness in this respect. The absolute refusal of any form of official recognition or toleration, the discontinuance of any form of fining policy for any purpose of raising revenue, the attitude of constant watchfulness and prosecution, particularly of the owners of premises said to be used for prostitution purposes; these things, backed up by the attitude of the community expressed in the last two city elections (especially since women's suffrage was adopted in our state constitution in November, 1910) have altogether combined to give us a greater degree of accomplishment towards the solution of this old and terrible social problem.

                                        "Very truly yours,
                              "(Signed) GEO. F. COTTERILL, Mayor."

108

APPENDIX III

The Reduction of Vice in Certain Western Cities Through Law-Enforcement

By Wirt W. Hallam, Chicago

(Reprinted from "Social Diseases," April, 1912)

In speaking upon the subject assigned to me, I will begin with a few general comments.

First. The recent improvements in the administrative control of vice in several large cities have shown that it is an easy matter to enforce the law when public opinion and public officials wish it enforced.

Second. That it is an extremely difficult matter to enforce the law when public opinion is not especially interested, or when public officials, for any reason, do not want it enforced.

Third. The influences which make public officials disregard their oath of office and neglect their sworn duty are: First, political influence; second, failure of the general public to support the work of law-enforcing officials. I mean by this that a law-enforcing official makes enemies of criminals and receives neglect instead of friendship and support from the law-abiding. Third, the secret financial contributions available for any official who will neglect to prosecute criminals. The latter condition would not be possible were it not for the existence of the two former. In Chicago, in Des Moines, and in Seattle the promoters of vice left the city in large numbers as soon as they found that the illegal protection which had been extended to them was being withdrawn, and they left without waiting to be prosecuted. These people know only too well how easy it is for officials to prosecute them, and they either pay heavily for protection or disappear at the first sign of real danger.

Considering these facts, you will easily appreciate the statement that while administrative reform is valuable, it is only one of several reforms which are needed.

When I first became interested in the problem of vice, I was far from appreciating its many-sidedness. There are many good and thoughtful people who are daily making similar mistakes, and underestimating the number of influences which work to make victims for that arch enemy of humanity, the vice of prostitution, which numbers its diseased victims by the thousands every year; with its moral and physical wreckage drawn from the daughters of the poor and the sons of the wealthy.

Some people may, in fact, tell us that prostitution is purely an economic problem. If that were correct, the wealthy and the well-to-do would all be moral. But we find that while many of these are moral, many others are

109

not; on the other hand, many of the poor are of good moral character, even under the most adverse circumstances.

Other persons expect great results from education, which has indeed proven to be of great value—perhaps the greatest of all the influences exerted during the past ten years. But as knowledge is not wisdom, so education is not moral character, although it is of infinite help to moral character.

There have been, and still are, others who expect great benefit from sanitary measures; but these, without educational and moral influences, have shown most disappointing results. In England, investigations have proved that the Contagious Diseases Act increased the volume of vice and that the number of girls wrecked for the profit of the business of vice was greater than before they went into effect. The sanitary supervision of prostitution does not decrease the total of disease or of social disaster which is inseparable from the existence of vice in any community.

CHICAGO

The work recently accomplished in Chicago for the improvement of vice conditions is important because it proves how much can be done in large cities when public officials really make the effort and have substantial public opinion to back them up. We must not blame public officials entirely for the evils which exist. They must have a strong public opinion behind them if any public good is to be accomplished.

Chicago has been studying and discussing the consequences of vice for about five years. First, the Chicago Society for Social Hygiene was organized through the influence of the American Society of Sanitary and Moral Prophylaxis; second, the Illinois Vigilance Association made a protest, handling the subject from the ministerial point of view, attacking more especially the white slave traffic and the general institution of prostitution; third, the Social Hygiene Committee of the Chicago Woman's Club, which sent lecturers to women's clubs in Chicago and many neighboring cities, and introduced into the National Federation of Women's Clubs a discussion of Social Hygiene and the protection of the family; fourth, the outcome of the three above mentioned movements was the Chicago Vice Commission. This was not a prosecuting body, but its investigations were made with a view of encouraging prosecutions eventually and of developing a better method of administrative or governmental control of the vicious element.

The Vice Commission made its investigation and report. A new administration came into office, and while these officials did not follow the Commission's recommendations, they did make some very remarkable clean-ups in vice conditions, and put a number of police officials out of office because they had permitted the existing conditions.

After the present mayor was installed in office late in the spring of 1910, vice conditions, which had been bad, immediately grew very much worse. The impression had gotten out that it was to be a wide-open town. The public made complaint and things improved slightly; the Mayor promised several additional improvements, but they developed very slowly. He then ordered the City Civil Service Commission to investigate charges against police officials, namely, that they were incompetent or were in partnership with gambling and with prostitution.

The Commission summoned the police officials before it and asked if they knew of the existence of certain laws and regulations, and whether these were being enforced. Most of the officials knew of the laws and regulations and assured the Commission that the same were being enforced, either as specified or very nearly so.

The next step was to start an investigation to learn if conditions were as good as the police reported; the results showed that they were not. Consequently, there was but one conclusion to be drawn, either that the police officials were incompetent or that there was collusion with the law-breakers; in either case, there was sufficient cause for discharge from office. Since the trial began, three inspectors, one captain, and five or six lieutenants have been discharged. One captain resigned and went to Europe; another held his place only by establishing his claim that he had endeavored to enforce the law but found his efforts blocked by the inspector who was his superior officer. The lieutenant at this latter station held his position on the plea that he had obeyed orders.

The police inspector, captain and two lieutenants on the West Side were the first to be tried. Some of the worst saloons were promptly closed. One of the large furniture dealers of the West Side took back $46,000 worth of furniture which he had sold on the installment plan. The streets that had been filled with a rough element were now quiet. A group of twenty so-called "business men" waited on the Mayor to make complaint that business was dead on the West Side, and to ask him to ease up on his law enforcement. The Mayor told them "what he thought of them," and they went home, refusing to give their names to the newspaper people who wanted to write up the interview.

When the trial of the police officials began on the North Side, an immediate reduction in vice developed there also. There was hardly a streetwalker to be seen anywhere. The back rooms in saloons had practically no customers; in one of the most notorious of these the investigator found only a boy, who, upon being questioned, said there was "nothing doing for the present. The police said we had to close this thing up for a month."

In the preliminary report of the Civil Service Commission, the medical inspection of prostitutes is commented upon priefly, as follows:

"The system of medical examination of prostitutes and the issuance of certificates of alleged freedom from venereal diseases is a species of graft that should be eliminated. Investigation on this line is just starting, but the Commission expects to show the following:

"That certain physicians catering to this class of patients make such examination and issue certificates, many of which they know to be false, and divide the proceeds with the dive-keepers. That in many cases the certificates are issued weekly, without examination, and that the police in certain districts are in collusion therewith."

As for White Slavery, the girls who are forced into this or into immorality through the physical violence or intimidation of the vice promoter, are not the only ones who need our sympathy and our help. The girls who are enticed into vice by any means are often as much helpless victims as though they were taken into its nets by force. Both classes soon become hopeless human wrecks. They are somebody's daughters and, sensational as it may

sound, somebody is slowly killing them for profit. Clifford G. Roe says:
"My experience in handling several hundred White Slave cases is that
severe punishment is likely to follow a woman who gives evidence in court
against a procurer. In most cases the victim is slashed with a knife."

Our failure to protect the witness and the victim is too unjust for words.
In White Slave cases, as well as in cases of crime against little girls or
women, the effort to prosecute the criminal is filled with dangers and injus-
tices which should not be allowed to exist.

As for street-walking, this vice condition, which exists in New York in a
form equal to the worst we have ever had in Chicago, has been greatly
reduced in the latter place by the prosecution of high police officials in
whose district it existed and with but little or no change in the way the
courts treat the girls.

In Chicago, as already mentioned, street soliciting stopped immediately
when the city began prosecuting officials for neglect of duty. In Seattle, the
majority—1,000 women and 2,000 men—left the city without prosecution,
though some others tried to continue, notwithstanding the new officials. In
Iowa, cities where the law made it seemingly impossible for politics or graft
to give illegal protection, dive-keepers left without waiting to be prosecuted.
Other cities and States can do the same and thereby save lives and money,—
and save large percentages of both.

IOWA

The experience of Iowa is unusual and extremely valuable. Since her
earliest history, her towns have had red light districts. For years they have
passed laws and attempted prosecutions, but with little success. Many people regarded the institution as necessary and inevitable; grand juries would
not indict; petit juries would not convict. When the commission form of
government was established at Des Moines, John L. Hamery was made Superintendent of Public Safety. He endeavored to enforce the law, but finally
declared that prosecutions of this nature invariably found their grave at the
County Court House. It was sometimes found that one man on the jury—
from prejudice, corruption or a misunderstanding of the nature of his duties
—would defeat the laws of the State and the judgment of the other eleven
men on the jury.

In commenting on this state of affairs, Mr. John B. Hammond—also of
Des Moines, and a most valuable and active worker for improved conditions
in Iowa—says that the people of Iowa, seeking some avenue for escape and
finding no precedent that would meet their needs, set about to establish one.

As a consequence of their efforts, the Iowa Injunction and Abatement
Law was drawn up and passed through the Legislature. There has been for
years an Injunction and Abatement Law in regard to liquor selling in prohibition districts, and there was also another law—an "ouster law"—by which
officials who failed to enforce the law could be promptly put out of office;
this had been used to help the liquor prohibition legislation of the State.
These two laws regarding liquor, about which no constitutional question
could be raised, were united and made applicable to the social evil. The
result was that the day after the laws in regard to the social evil went into
effect cities which had had open houses of prostitution for fifty years found

them closed; and shortly afterward it was claimed that there was not an open house of prostitution in the State of Iowa.

The new law which produced this remarkable effect is known as the Carson Law, or the Iowa **Red Light** Injunction and Abatement Law, and it provides the following:

1. **An injunction against the keeper of the house of prostitution;** also against the **owner of the property,** since it was usually found that the owner of the house and the keeper of it were different individuals.

2. A temporary and, upon conviction, a permanent **abatement of the nuisance,** and the admission of general reputation as evidence upon which to establish the existence of a nuisance.

3. **A fine for the keeper** of the house, amounting to not less than $200 or more than $1,000, or imprisonment for not less than three months or more than six, or both fine and imprisonment.

4. **A fine of $300 against the property,** which fine is a tax lien and comes ahead of a mortgage, and acts as a cloud upon the title until paid.

5. **The property is enjoined forever from use for immoral purposes, and for one year from use for any purpose whatever**—the only exception being that the owner, by giving bond to the amount of the full value of the property and convincing the court of his good intentions, will be permitted, after all fines are paid, to open the building for legitimate business or residential purposes.

In addition, the "ouster" law regarding liquor was made applicable to vice cases also, and the law-breakers of Iowa thus found themselves without any means of **illegal** protection.

The advantage of the Iowa law is that any citizen or official who finds that the law is being broken can bring prosecution; and it is useless for the criminal to try to stop one complainant, whether office-holder or citizen, because another complainant can bring a similar prosecution the following day, if the offense is continued.

The danger of fine and imprisonment, the danger of loss of personal property or loss of a year's rent on the building are sufficient to make it unprofitable and undesirable for anyone to take the risk of permitting his property to be used for immoral purposes; and persons now owning property in Iowa make it their business to know what kind of tenants desire to rent it, and look with suspicion upon people who offer to pay two or three times the normal rent.

In one city the people went to the Mayor and asked about the new law which was going into effect the next day; they wanted to know if it would make any difference. He replied that he didn't know, but would look it up. In a few hours he told them that the new law was going to make a very great difference, and that they would have to move at once. They began work at six o'clock that night, and by daylight next morning most of the houses were empty. In the cities along the Mississippi River the dive-keepers moved across to the cities on the Illinois side.

Let us now consider the effect of the enforcement of the new law—the law which really worked.

A great many people thought that if the red light districts were wiped out vice would be scattered throughout the cities. The chief of police in one city said publicly that he hoped the good people of the town would get enough of this scattering business once and for all. He hoped a house of prostitution would be set up by the side of every minister's house in town until they were sick of it. He was sure that women and children would not be safe in the street. Many good people feared the same thing, and doubted the wisdom of such vigorous efforts to eradicate the evil.

After the law went into effect—to the surprise of both its friends and its enemies (for even its friends were sometimes fearful of evil effects from it) —the change in every direction was prompt and for the better. Many of the immoral women left town, while others gave up the business entirely and sought respectable work. When the women left town the hangers-on in the vice district accompanied them. The petty criminals, such as pickpockets, hold-up men, thugs, etc., disappeared almost entirely, as well as almost simultaneously with the women.

Dubuque, Davenport, Sioux City, Burlington, Keokuk, Ottumwa, and other cities had their red light districts—Davenport probably being the only one which provided a medical inspector as a means of increasing patronage.

Mayor A. J. Mathis of Des Moines says:

"There is no question but that the so-called 'red light' has been driven out of the city. There is no such district here. This plan brings much better results than segregation. The credit is due to Mr. John L. Hamery, who took the advanced ground that the red-light district was unnecessary."

Mr. Hamery, in a speech before the National Purity Congress (October, 1909), at Burlington, Iowa, said, among other things:

"Cheap lawyers, bondsmen, and money sharks, all of whom hung like blood-suckers on the segregated districts, have been forced to relinquish their prey. Crime has been reduced to a minimum. The decrease has been so marked within the past thirteen months that the city passed through the recent State Fair and the U. S. Military Tournament with an average daily attendance of 30,000 people, extending over a period of two weeks, without a single case of professional hold-up, burglary, robbery, or other crime more serious than intoxication being reported to the police.

"Preceding the present administration, the records show that the police department was called upon almost daily to investigate robberies. Those same records will now show that we oftentimes pass through a period of two weeks without a single case of even petty larceny."

The Attorney-General of Iowa says:

"The bill has had a marked effect all over the State because property owners having small buildings leased at exorbitant rental to vice have been afraid to continue the leases. I believe that every State in the Union should have a similar law, and also the removal bill providing for the summary removal of all law-enforcing officials without the intervention of a jury."

Mayor Hanna, in a letter dated Feb. 6, 1911, says:

"It is claimed by those favoring segregation that the prostitutes scatter through the residence districts; but this is not true in this city. Des Moines is in a great deal better condition morally to-day than in the days of segregation."

In the "Register and Leader" of Des Moines, the Assistant Chief of Police—an officer of high character—makes the following statement:

"It is not generally known to persons outside of the police department that in the days of the 'Red Light' district, when it was commonly believed that lewd women were segregated, not more than 15 per cent. of the traffic was really carried on in the district. Everywhere in the city were disorderly houses. It was impossible to control them. The best evidence of the decrease in business is the fact that complaints from the residence districts have decreased at least 75 per cent."

In the Biennial Report of former Attorney-General H. W. Byers, dated January 1, 1911, he says:

"We cannot resist the temptation at this point to state what will be fully shown by the record as we unfold it, and that is that these laws have placed Iowa in the very front in the matter of civic righteousness and moral cleanliness. The good that has flown from them in cleaner towns and cities, in money saved to the needy, in boys and girls turned from the haunts of vice into paths of virtue, in making sober and industrious husbands and fathers, in making homes happy and inspiring respect for law and order, is so immeasurably great that no matter what may come to us in the future we will never cease being grateful for the opportunity we had to take even a small part in this great work."

There was one other significant feature in connection with Iowa's experience.

Prior to the existence of the Abatement Law, Mr. Hamery attempted to improve conditions in the vice district by stopping the sale of liquor in the houses of prostitution. After this order went into effect houses which had rented for $150 per month had to be reduced to $100 and later to $75.00 per month, because the keepers could not pay the higher rent. Some of the keepers went out of business altogether.

It is interesting to note that in Chicago, after the issuance of a similar order, one dive-keeper who had been paying $500 a month rent was obliged to have her rent reduced just half, and even then told the investigator that she would gladly pay $500 again if they would let her sell liquors. Such statements indicate more clearly than almost anything else that city authorities can reduce vice; that vice and drunkenness work together each for the profit of the other—and how thoroughly they both work for the destruction of their devotees is shown by the hospital records of any city.

SEATTLE

The improvement in the civic control of vice conditions in Seattle is interesting for several reasons: First, because the city could not get improvement until it put the mayor and chief of police out of office and elected other men in their places. This is a striking proof that the trouble was not so much a question of law or a question of controlling the prostitutes and their associates, as it was the finding of some way to get rid of the politicians and the dive-keepers, who were dividing the money profits of vice. Second, that the women took an active part in the campaign, exercising for the first time their right to vote. Third, that conditions promptly improved; and while Seattle is by no means free from vice, the great improvement was brought about simply by having in office good, honest men who wanted to enforce the law.

To go a little into detail, let me quote from an article written by Mr. Harry E. Moore, president of the Public Welfare League of Seattle, who has given in "The Light," of La Crosse, Wis., a history of the movement.

"With the discovery of gold in Alaska, in 1897, Seattle began to grow rapidly. Up to 1910 most of the mayors had believed in an open town, although most of them had controlled the vice element fairly well. The segregated district was near the depot, and every effort to move it brought a vigorous storm of protest from the locality to which it was proposed to move the district. The mayor at one time ordered the district closed. Several hundred prostitutes gathered and marched out in a body; many left town, some drifted back; others established themselves in hotels, rooming-houses, flats and residences. No very strong effort was made to prevent this.

At last Hiram C. Gill, who had posed as "the poor man's friend," was elected mayor. Immediately undesirables began flocking to Seattle. The old district was enlarged three or four times, exploited and capitalized by Gill supporters. New buildings were erected, not less than a dozen crib-houses were in operation, and in these the sanitary as well as moral conditions baffled description. People had seemingly accepted the idea that a segregated district must be tolerated somewhere, but each wanted it in some place remote from himself.

On April 16, 1910, a general mass meeting was called. A clean city movement was organized and on June 16, 1910, was incorporated as "The Public Welfare League." This League secured attorneys of ability and character who were thoroughly in sympathy with the work, and through their continued efforts a sweeping injunction was granted. When, after some time this was violated, application was made to the court, on the ground of contempt of Court for some four hundred warrants, involving city officers, owners, managers, and others in the district. The Judge of the Criminal Court, while not issuing the warrants at once, did bring officials into court, telling them that if the nuisance was abated at the end of a week the court and the law would be satisfied. He also reprimanded the mayor, the chief of police and the prosecuting attorney, reminding them that prostitution could not exist fifteen minutes without their knowledge, and that they must perform their duty.

While the Public Welfare League was working for substantial improvements a conference was held in Seattle, members of which addressed a number of meetings in the city. About this time a petition for the recall of the mayor was circulated, a few new laws were passed in the Legislature in order to make the recall feature of the law effective, and a committee from the League began securing signatures to the petition. It is interesting to note the vigorous language of the recall. It stated that the mayor had shown himself incompetent and unfit; had abused his appointive power for personal reasons, and had put unfit men in office; had wholly failed, refused and neglected to enforce criminal law; had permitted the city to become the home and refuge of criminal classes; had failed to enforce law impartially, and that his continuance in office was a menace to business and the moral welfare of the city. This petition had to be signed by 25 per cent. of the entire vote cast for all candidates at the last preceding general election. They secured 10,701 names, of which about 16 per cent. were thrown out on technicalities. This, however, left enough to make the recall effective without using the names of women who had signed through their recently acquired right. Many meetings were held all over the city. The subjects assigned included "Vice and Business," "Vice and the Law," "Vice and Disease," "Vice and the Home," "Vice and Education," "Vice and the Remedy," etc., etc.

The women were aroused,—they wanted to know the truth. Many spent hours at the telephones, inviting their friends to the meetings. As yet the women had no vote, but the suffrage amendment carried in November and the proclamation issued by the Governor, November 28th, made the women legal voters. They registered to a number equaling perhaps 50 per cent. of the male vote. One leading feature of the campaign which did much to shatter the hope of the Gill forces was a women's mass meeting for Dilling, the new candidate. This meeting filled the Grand Opera House to the limit, packed the Seattle Theatre with the overflow, and still turned away hundreds. The election hinged squarely upon the issue of civic decency or civic indecency. Nearly eighty per cent. of the registration voted. When the votes were counted civic decency won with a majority of about 30 per cent. over the vote cast for the man who held office. Gill attributes his defeat to the women.

The election of the new mayor and the appointment of a new chief of police was followed by a change in the City Council; the number was reduced from eighteen to nine, and good men were elected. Reforms were instituted, and it is interesting to note that these reforms included efficiency in public office, improvement in public service and a reduction in the waste of the city's money,—as well as a reduction of vice conditions.

One thousand women and two thousand men have been driven out of the city. Note that 2,000 men went with the 1,000 women; most of them were petty criminals, and it is estimated that 500 of them were living upon the earnings of immoral women.

The restricted district has been closed and white slave traffic made much more difficult,—perhaps practically impossible; prostitution was very largely driven out of hotels and lodging houses; immoral women were not allowed in cafes; disorderly houses were prosecuted; 90 per cent. of the men on the police force were clean, honest men; the 'ire department and public service of all kinds were improved.

There is one difference between the clean-up in Seattle and the clean-up in Chicago. In the former place the police department and police courts greatly increased their work in prosecuting the criminals themselves, even after the 3,000 had left the city. In Chicago there was only a slight change in the prosecution of criminals, but a large amount of vice was discontinued as soon as the prosecution of high police officials began.

Regarding the cost of the clean-up in Seattle, Mr. Moore, president of the Public Welfare League, makes this statement:

"The total expense incurred by the Public Welfare League and its individual members,—including all legal expenses, recall petition, etc.,—did not exceed $8,000, while the expense of the Dilling Campaign Committee in the election of Mayor Dilling, the new Mayor, was very close to this amount.

"When a city the size of Seattle can get rid of notoriously bad officials, rid itself of 3,000 law-breakers and easily control the remaining ones at a total cost of $16,000, including the expense of putting good men in office, it is certainly worth while. Again, this shows that the immoral or vice element is far from being hard to control, and that the difficulties which stand in the way of proper conditions are mostly public indifference and the aggressive talk of those who are profiting by vice. The criminals themselves leave quickly when corrupt officials are no longer in power to protect them.

"Never again will Seattle be allowed to sink to the level of a year ago. One by one we have added safeguards; the direct primary, the recall, the initiative and referendum and the enfranchisement of the women make it more difficult for the liquor interests, the political demagogue, and the ward boss to thwart the will of the people, and eliminating these elements it becomes a matter of education."

LOS ANGELES AND MINNEAPOLIS

Several years ago Los Angeles abolished her villainous crib system, recalled a corrupt mayor and elected a good one. It has since steadily kept conditions in far better shape. It had a segregated district with crib houses for the women. Two ministers, Kendall and Phillips, were passing some place near when they heard a girl in one of the upper rooms of the crib house cry out: "My God, if I could only get out of here!" The ministers investigated; they told the people of Los Angeles the facts, and did not stop telling these and working until the whole city was aroused, the mayor put out of office and a new city government installed.

Minneapolis has abolished the Red Light District and has made an excellent report of the improved conditions. Both of these cities deserve more attention than space permits me to give here.

I am firmly of the opinion that if any city will take the profit out of vice it will immediately reduce the volume of vice at least 50 per cent. If, in addition to this measure, it will make vice dangerous to men as well as to women; to patrons, property owners and business men, as well as to dive-keepers and women street-walkers, that city will quickly reduce vice a total of 75 per cent. or more and will accomplish the reduction of wreckage of health and morals in much the same proportion.

Those who are promoting vice are getting a money profit every day that we let them alone. We can stop it if we will. It should be done, and done soon.

APPENDIX IV

The Iowa Injunction and Abatement Law

SUMMARY OF THE LAW

First. The law declares houses of lewdness, prostitution and assignation to be nuisances.

Second. It gives to citizens of the county, and the county attorney, the right to instigate proceedings against such places.

Third. These proceedings are brought in a court of equity, where the hearing is conducted before a judge, or court of judges, and not before a jury; and the enjoinment and abatement of the nuisance may be had.

Fourth. A temporary injunction issues in case the court finds that the petition of the plaintiff is well founded, restraining the defendants from conducting the nuisance during the trial.

Fifth. At the trial the general reputation of the place is admissible to establish the nuisance.

Sixth. If any injunction is granted and the defendant violates it, he may be arrested and summarily tried for contempt. If found guilty, he may be fined or imprisoned.

Seventh. As a part of the final decree of the court an order of abatement is entered by which the movable property of the building is seized and sold as chattels under execution; and the building is closed for one year unless sooner released by the court.

Exception. If the owner of the property appears before the court and pays all costs and files a bond to the full value of the property, stating that he will abate the nuisance, the court may withhold the sale of the property.

The first five sections of the law are as follows:

"Section 1. Whoever shall erect, establish, continue, maintain, use, own or lease any building, erection or place used for the purpose of lewdness, assignation or prostitution is guilty of a nuisance, and the building, erection or place, or the ground itself, in or upon which such lewdness, assignation or prostitution is conducted, permitted or carried on, continued or exists, and the furniture, fixtures, musical instruments, and contents are also declared a nuisance, and shall be enjoined and abated as hereinafter provided."

"Section 2. Whenever a nuisance is kept, maintained or exists, as defined in this act, the county attorney or any citizen of the county may maintain an action in equity in the name of the State of Iowa upon the relation of such county attorney or citizen, to perpetually enjoin said nuisance, the person or persons conducting or maintaining the same, and the owner or agent of the building or ground upon which said nuisance exists. In such action the court, or a judge in vacation, shall, upon the presentation of a petition therefor alleging that the nuisance complained of exists, allow a temporary writ of injunction without bond, if it shall be made to appear to the satisfaction of the court or judge by evidence in the form of affidavits, depositions, oral testimony or otherwise, as the complainant may elect, unless the court or judge, by previous order, shall have directed the form and manner in which it shall be presented. Three days' notice in writing shall be given the defendant of the hearing of the application, and if then continued at his instance, the writ as prayed shall be granted as a matter of course. When an injunction has been granted, it shall be binding on the defendant throughout the judicial district in which it was issued, and any violation of the provisions of the injunctions herein provided shall be a contempt as hereinafter provided."

"Section 3. The action when brought shall be triable at the first term of court after due and timely service of the notice has been given, and in such action evidence of the general reputation of the place shall be admissible for the purpose of proving the existence of said nuisance. If the complaint is filed by a citizen, it shall not be dismissed except upon the sworn statement made by the complainant and his attorney setting forth the reason why the action should be dismissed, and the dismissal approved by the county attorney in writing or in open court. If the court is of the opinion that the action ought not to be dismissed, he may direct the county attorney to prosecute the said action to judgment, and if the action is continued more than one term of court, any citizen of the county or the county attorney may be substituted for the complaining party and prosecute said action to judgment. If the action is brought by a citizen and the court finds there was no reasonable ground or cause for said action, the costs may be taxed to such citizen."

"Section 4. In case of the violation of any injunction granted under the provisions of this act, the court, or in vacation, a judge thereof, may summarily try and punish the offender. The proceedings shall be commenced by filing with the clerk of the court an information under oath, setting out the alleged facts constituting such violation, upon which the court or judge shall cause a warrant to issue, under which the defendant shall be arrested. The trial may be had upon affidavits, or either party may demand the production and oral examination of the witnesses. A party found guilty of contempt under the provisions of this section, shall be punished by a fine of not less than two hundred nor more than one thousand dollars, or by imprisonment in the county jail not less than three nor more than six months, or by both fine and imprisonment."

"Section 5. If the existence of the nuisance be established in an action as provided in this act, an order of abatement shall be entered as a part of the judgment in the case, which order shall direct the removal from the building or place of all fixtures, furniture, musical instruments or movable property used in conducting the nuisance, and shall direct the sale thereof in the manner provided for the sale of chattels under execution, and the effectual closing of the building or place against its use for any purpose, and so keeping it closed for a period of one year, unless sooner released. If any person shall break and enter or use a building, erection or place so directed to be closed, he shall be punished as for contempt as provided in the preceding section. For removing and selling the movable property, the officer shall be entitled to charge and receive the same fees as he would for levying upon and selling like property on execution, and for closing the premises and keeping them closed, a reasonable sum shall be allowed by the court."

"Section 6. The proceeds of the sale of the personal property, as provided in the preceding section, shall be applied in payment of the costs of the action and abatement, and the balance, if any, shall be paid to the defendant."

"Section 7. If the owner appears and pays all costs of the proceeding, and files a bond with sureties to be approved by the clerk in the full value of the property, to be ascertained by the court, or in vacation, by the clerk, auditor and treasurer of the county, conditioned that he will immediately abate said nuisance and prevent the same from being established or kept therein within a period of one year thereafter, the court, or in said vacation, the judge, may, if satisfied of his good faith, order the premises closed under the order of abatement to be delivered to said owner, and said order of abatement cancelled so far as the same may relate to said property; and if the proceeding be an action in equity and said bond be given and costs therein paid before judgment and order of abatement, the action shall be thereby abated as to said building only. The release of the property under the provision of this section shall not release it from any judgment, lien, penalty or liability to which it may be subject by law."

"Section 8. Whenever a permanent injunction issues against any person for maintaining a nuisance as herein defined, or against any power or agent of the building kept or used for the purposes prohibited by this act, there shall be assessed against said building and the grounds upon which the same is located and against the person or persons maintaining said nuisance, and the owner or agent of said premises, a tax of $300.00. The assessment of said tax shall be made by the assessor of the city, town or township in which the nuisance exists and shall be made within three months from the date of the granting of the permanent injunction. In case the assessor fails or neglects to make said assessment the same shall be made by the sheriff of the county, and a return of said assessment shall be made to the county treasurer. Said tax shall be a perpetual lien upon all property, both personal and real, used for the purpose of maintaining said nuisance, and the payment of said tax shall not relieve the person or building from any other penalties provided by law. The provision of the law relating to the collection and distribution of the mulct liquor tax shall govern in the collection and distribution of the tax herein prescribed in so far as the same are applicable, and not in conflict with the provisions of this act."

APPENDIX V

The "Tin Plate" Ordinance

The City of Portland, Ore., passed a law which is commonly characterized as the "Tin-Plate Ordinance." A law, resembling in many respects the Portland ordinance, but which is much broader in its scope, has been introduced in the Council of the City of New York.

The Portland ordinance provides:

"Section 1. Any person, firm, co-partnership, association or corporation owning any real property within the corporate limits of the city of Portland upon which is erected any building used either in whole or in part as a hotel, rooming house, lodging house, boarding house, tenement house, or saloon, shall place and maintain at the front of every such building at the principal street entrance thereof a conspicuous plate or sign bearing the name and address of the owner or owners of such building. The letters or characters on such sign or plate shall be of such size and distinctness and the sign or plate shall be so placed that the name and address can be easily read by persons passing along the street before such entrance."

"Section 2. When any building of the kind and character mentioned in Section 1 of this ordinance is owned by any person or persons other than the owner or owners of the land upon which such building stands the provisions of this ordinance shall apply to the owner or owners of both the building and the land."

"Section 3. Whenever the title to any property contemplated in this ordinance shall be held in a representative capacity, the name of the person, persons, co-partnership, corporation, estate, or association sustaining the representative relation to such property shall be displayed upon the plate or sign required by this ordinance."

"Section 4. Any person violating any of the provisions of this ordinance shall, upon conviction thereof in Municipal Court, be punished by a fine of not more than $100."

"Section 5. Each day during which the sign or plate mentioned in Section 1 is not maintained as required by this ordinance, shall be and constitute a separate offense."

We, the Undersigned, Do Hereby Approve the Publication of the Report on the Social Evil in Syracuse Made by the Committee of Eighteen and Endorse the Recommendations Contained Therein.

Rev. Charles E. Hamilton

John L. Heffron, M. D., Dean of the Medical College, Syracuse University

Mrs. John L. Heffron

A. S. Hotaling, M. D.

Percy M. Hughes, Superintendent of Public Schools

H. B. Husted

Nathan Jacobson, M. D.

Marie R. Jenney

J. Roberts Johnson, M. D.

Chester H. King

Martin H. Knapp

Louis Krumbhaar

Albert E. Larkin, President of the Board of Education

I. Harris Levy, M. D.

T. Aaron Levy

E. H. Lewis

K. A. Luther

Professor William H. Mace

A. Clifford Mercer, M. D.

Mrs. A. B. Miller

Frank J. McMorrow, M. D.

N. L. Mulvey, M. D.

Ezekiel W. Mundy, Public Librarian

D. H. Murray, M. D.

Mrs. William Nottingham

Mrs. James Pass

Professor Phillip A. Parsons

John D. Pennock

Mrs. John D. Pennock

Henry Phillips

Mrs. W. W. Porter

Rev. B. Van Vliet Putnam

Mrs. Percy E. Roche

Professor Frederick A. Saunders

Mrs. Frederick A. Saunders

Mary Scott, M. D.

F. W. Sears, M. D.

B. W. Sherwood, M. D.

Elizabeth L. Shrimpton, M. D.

F. H. STEPHENSON, M. D.
MRS. F. H. STEPHENSON
GILES H. STILWELL
MRS. BENJAMIN STOLZ
MRS. C. L. STONE
JACOB R. STREET, Dean of the Teachers' College, Syracuse University
MRS. MAX THALHEIMER
MRS. W. G. TRACY
EDWARD N. TRUMP
MRS. EDWARD N. TRUMP
E. D. WINKWORTH
MRS. E. C. WITHERBY
EDWARD J. WYNKOOP, M. D.
FREDERICK K. ZERBE

Resolved, That the Academy of Medicine believes that the agitation or the improvement of social vice conditions existing in Syracuse is imely, and endorses the movement undertaken by the Moral Survey Committee.

Syracuse, N. Y., February 18, 1913.

REPORT

OF THE

COMMISSION FOR THE INVESTIGATION

OF THE

WHITE SLAVE TRAFFIC, SO CALLED.

FEBRUARY, 1914.

BOSTON:
WRIGHT & POTTER PRINTING CO., STATE PRINTERS,
32 DERNE STREET.
1914.

CONTENTS.

The Commonwealth of Massachusetts.

BOSTON, Feb. 7, 1914.

To the Honorable Senate and House of Representatives.

The undersigned, members of the commission created by the following resolve: —

CHAPTER 64, RESOLVES OF 1913.

RESOLVE TO PROVIDE FOR AN INVESTIGATION OF THE WHITE SLAVE TRAFFIC, SO-CALLED.

Resolved, That the governor, with the advice and consent of the council, shall appoint a commission of five persons, one of whom shall be designated as chairman, and not more than two of whom shall be residents of any one county, to investigate the white slave traffic, so-called, and to determine, so far as is possible, by what means and to what extent women and girls are induced or compelled by others to lead an immoral life, or are brought into this commonwealth or from place to place for that purpose. The commission shall endeavor to devise plans for preventing such evils as it finds to exist, and shall report to the general court not later than the tenth day of January, in the year nineteen hundred and fourteen, with such drafts of bills as may be necessary to carry its recommendations into effect. The commission may give public hearings, if it deems them necessary, and shall have authority to administer oaths, and to require the attendance of witnesses and the production of books and documents. The commission shall serve without compensation, but shall be allowed from the treasury of the commonwealth such sums for its necessary expenses as may be approved by the governor and council not exceeding ten thousand dollars. *Approved April 21, 1913.*

herewith present this report.

WALTER E. FERNALD.
CHARLES W. BIRTWELL.
LUCIA L. JAQUITH.
EDWIN MULREADY.

Report of the Commission for the Investigation of the White Slave Traffic, so called.

The first duty placed upon the commission was to investigate the " white slave traffic, so called," and to determine, so far as possible, by what means and to what extent women and girls are induced or compelled by others to lead immoral lives.

Such an investigation would necessarily lead to a study of all forms of commercialized prostitution, for any man or woman who traffics in the sexual life of any woman or girl for financial reward or gain is a trafficker in women, and therefore is a " white slaver."

In the more restricted meaning the " white slaver " is a man who by means of coercion or bodily punishment compels a woman or girl against her will to sell herself to some other man for money which he, the " white slaver," takes from her for his own benefit.

The commission has used the broader as being the more correct interpretation, — the interpretation embodied in the federal law in the so-called Mann White Slave Act, and in our State law in chapter 424 of the Acts of 1910, the so-called Massachusetts White Slave Act.

The commission has endeavored to obtain the fullest information possible upon the subject outlined in the resolve creating it. Many meetings have been held. Conferences in various cities and towns have been held with police officials, judges, probation officers, district attorneys, physicians, charity workers and other citizens. Stories and rumors that have excited the public mind have been investigated. The members of the commission have personally investigated street conditions, cafés, hotels, etc., in different communities.

Field investigations of actual conditions throughout the State have constituted the most important part of the inquiry.

A force of expert male and female investigators, with wide experience in conducting similar inquiries in other cities and States, made a searching investigation of commercialized prostitution in the various cities and towns of the State. The experience and knowledge of these carefully selected investigators enabled them to mingle freely with the prostitutes and their customers, and the various classes of people who profit financially by the traffic in women, to talk freely with them, to obtain their confidence, and to secure a reliable measure of the extent and conditions of sexual vice in the different localities.

Groups of prostitutes under arrest in the House of Detention in Boston, or serving sentences in various penal institutions and reformatories, have been carefully questioned and studied by a corps of agents, with a view to ascertaining their antecedents, personal history, mentality, assigned causes of their immorality, etc.

An experienced lawyer has gathered for the commission the facts as to the administration and enforcement of the laws relating to sexual offences for the past year in practically all of the courts of the State.

THE BUSINESS OF PROSTITUTION.

The methods of conducting the business of commercialized prostitution in Massachusetts at the present time, and the extent of the traffic in women, are indicated in the following part of the report.

The inquiry was limited, of course, by the time and money available. The prostitutes of the State have not been counted, nor any attempt made to estimate their total number. Manifestly, not every community in the Commonwealth could be individually studied. In all, 79 cities and towns were investigated, including all of the large cities and the more important towns. Certain cities and towns where the conditions were found to be unusually flagrant received especial attention. The strikingly cumulative nature of the evidence from city after city and town after town appears

to the commission to justify its belief that the facts in its
possession reveal the actual conditions as to commercialized
vice in this State.

The information obtained by the investigators was daily
submitted in writing to the director for study and analysis,
and for the use of the commission. The daily reports were
verified by other agents of the commission, observing individually, and by conferences of the members of the commission with local police and court officials, social workers and
other citizens. The reports of the investigators give most
explicit data as to the location of immoral establishments,
including houses, apartments, cafés, hotels, lodging houses,
road houses, street conditions, etc.; names of owners and
proprietors; number of inmates and names of inmates; manner of conducting the business, of securing customers, prices
charged, etc. It is not necessary to publish these unpleasant
details in this report, or to publish names of individuals and
localities, but it should be understood that the findings and
generalizations are based upon exact information in the possession of the commission.

Parlor Houses of Prostitution.

The old-time habitat of commercialized prostitution in
this State was the so-called parlor house of prostitution, or
the house of ill fame. A parlor house of prostitution is a
dwelling exclusively used for the business of prostitution.
In some cases only the upper floors of buildings are used for
this purpose, and the ground floors are used for business
purposes.

At the present time the relative number of parlor houses
varies greatly in different cities and towns in the State. In
some of the larger cities no parlor houses were found; in
others there were only one or two such houses. In one city
of about 25,000 inhabitants there were 21 houses; in one
of about 100,000 inhabitants there were 13; and in another
of similar size there were 16.

The commission has definite reports regarding 108 parlor
houses of the old type which were in active operation in vari-

ous cities and towns in Massachusetts on the days when the investigation was made.

While the officials in no city in the State have openly adopted the policy of segregation and toleration, yet it is a fact that in certain cities there are streets where there are many houses of this class. For instance, in one city there were 11 houses on one street, 4 on another, 3 on another and 9 on still other streets. In another city there were 12 parlor houses on different streets in the same section of the city. The houses in both cities are open and any one may enter. The inmates openly solicit customers from the doors and windows. In these cities the business is conducted in much the same way as in cities in other States where segregation and toleration is the accepted official policy.

One well-known parlor house occupies two buildings, connected by a covered corridor or gallery. One is located just across the State line in Massachusetts, and the other just across the line in a neighboring State. When the Massachusetts authorities interfere, the women are moved to the house across the State line, and nothing can be done. If the authorities of the other State interfere, the inmates move back to the house in Massachusetts. This house has been run in this manner for years, and apparently is seldom molested by the officials of either State. This scheme of evasion clearly involves a violation of the federal law known as the Mann White Slave Act.

Each parlor house is usually managed by a woman employed for that purpose, although the real proprietor is frequently a man. These women are often arrested as keepers of houses of ill fame, while the proprietors escape. Men proprietors are seldom arrested.

These proprietors and women managers speak of their business in a matter-of-fact way, as they would of any legitimate occupation. One man who has been in business in one city for over twenty years showed our investigator over his establishment with great pride, and discussed in detail the manner of conducting the business, expenses, profits, etc. In another city, the man proprietor, who has conducted the house for many years, has his name on a large sign on the

front of the house. Another man proprietor sits in an arm-
chair and collects the proceeds of his business, as would a
cashier in any commercial establishment.

The character and business of these parlor houses are generally well understood by the neighbors, — indeed, by the
whole community in the smaller cities and towns. Information concerning their location is freely given by cabmen,
street-car conductors and others.

Typical parlor houses of prostitution were found some distance from the centers of population in small country towns.
The commission secured photographs of several such houses.
Barns and sheds surround them, trees are growing in the
yards and dogs are playing about the steps. These rural
houses of ill fame usually have from three to six inmates.
The proprietors of these isolated houses are usually men, who
secure inmates, sell liquor and drum up trade in the surrounding towns. These houses are conducted in the same
manner as those in large cities. In some instances the same
men have conducted the house for years. In two instances
one man owns and operates a chain of three parlor houses
of prostitution of this rural type, each located in a separate
country town. The owner solicits customers for these
houses in the neighboring towns and cities, often bringing an
automobile load of patrons at a time. In one instance the
driver of the mail stage at the nearest railroad station glow-
ingly described the house and its inmates, and urged the
investigator to ride with him to the house, saying that he
carried many men to it.

In the country, as well as in the cities, commercialized
prostitution is often carried on in a tenement or an isolated
house by one woman, or, as has been observed in several
instances, by a woman and her own daughter. This type
of prostitute generally caters to regular customers only, and
is usually free from arrest or interference.

Houses of Prostitution in Apartment Buildings.

A house of prostitution in an apartment building means
that one of several apartments in a building is used for
the purpose of prostitution. Under present conditions in the

larger cities the apartment house has largely superseded the old type of parlor house. A large part of the entire business of prostitution in these cities is carried on in such apartments. Many of these small apartment houses contain from six to twelve or even eighty or more suites of the two or three room kitchenette type, and are occupied chiefly by women. There are also usually many respectable residents in these same apartment buildings. There are generally two women to a suite. Some of them have a legitimate occupation in the daytime, — working in stores, offices, factories, cafés, restaurants, etc. Many of them have a list of regular customers. Several lists of this sort, containing the names and addresses of many customers, came into the possession of the commission.

The landlords of many apartment houses, even in the questionable districts, do not knowingly permit this immoral use of the premises; others are not so particular, and often charge an exorbitant rent for the apartments so used.

There are certain apartment buildings built especially to be used for these immoral purposes. Persons renting these premises are not asked for character references. They are tenants at will, paying a high rent in advance, and, unless they become too noisy, are not questioned as to their mode of life. The profit from the rental of these apartments for immoral purposes is large.

As a rule, great secrecy is observed in the operation of this type of house, and it is difficult to obtain legal evidence of actual prostitution in the apartments. Usually liquor is not sold. It is practically impossible for prospective patrons to enter unless they come properly introduced and vouched for by friends, or by the runner, chauffeur or cabman who brings them to the door. These solicitors for prostitutes do a large business, and often receive a commission on the money spent by the patrons.

The commission has definite reports concerning 107 different houses of prostitution in apartment houses in different cities. This list includes many buildings where the management is known to be vigilant in keeping out undesirable patrons.

Disorderly Lodging Houses or Furnished-room Houses.

A disorderly lodging house is a dwelling where the occupant of a single room uses that room for immoral purposes. This is another frequent form of expression of commercialized prostitution in this State.

These immoral lodging houses are used for the most part by the prostitutes who secure their customers in the cafés, saloons, restaurants and other public places, and on the streets. The women rent the rooms by the week or visit, in many cases paying the landlady a certain sum in excess of the regular rental for the privilege of bringing in their customers for immoral purposes. The character of many of these immoral lodging houses is well known to the police, and they are sometimes raided, but it is obviously difficult to secure positive evidence.

There is no legal supervision or control of lodging houses. No license is required. Any one may open and run one. No record or register of lodgers is kept. In many houses no questions are asked or references required. Men and women occupy rooms on the same floor, — perhaps adjoining rooms. The same bath and toilet rooms are often used by both sexes.

As a rule, these houses have no parlors or reception rooms. Both men and women roomers receive their callers of the opposite sex in their bedrooms.

The majority of boarding and lodging houses are run by honest persons in a respectable and proper manner, but these honest persons often find it difficult to make a living. The necessity of letting as many rooms as possible almost inevitably leads to the easy-going habit of not knowing much about the lodgers or their morals or habits. Unscrupulous landladies know that a high price can be charged for rooms rented for immoral purposes.

The inexperienced young man or woman who comes to the city for the first time to work or study finds it difficult to secure desirable rooms with respectable surroundings, and is about as likely to find lodging in a disreputable house as in a safe and decent place.

The conditions in many of these houses not only facilitate immoral conduct, but are also well calculated to suggest and encourage such conduct in those who have previously led virtuous lives.

The lodging-house question is especially pertinent in Massachusetts, as a large part of the population of the State live in manufacturing or commercial cities and towns. Modern industrial conditions calling men and women away from their homes to the locality of their employment make some form of lodging house an economic necessity. Many young men and women must live in lodging houses. The lodging house is one of the great social and moral problems of our modern city life.

The commission has reports of 190 addresses of furnished-room houses which are used for purposes of prostitution.

" Call" or " Telephone" Houses.

The " call house " is another type of house of prostitution evolved by recent conditions. The " call house " is usually an apartment or room where a man or woman arranges over the telephone for the meeting of the prostitute and her patron, usually in some other house or apartment. This is a common method of conducting the business of prostitution in the larger cities at the present time. A memorandum book containing the names, addresses and telephone numbers of 49 different prostitutes was found in one " call house." Several of the addresses given were in the suburbs or near-by towns. Nearly all were in apartment houses in the city itself.

Immoral Cafés, Saloons and Restaurants.

A disorderly café, saloon or restaurant is a place which known prostitutes habitually frequent for the purpose of attracting the attention of prospective customers, or actually soliciting for immoral purposes.

The Massachusetts excise law is quite explicit regarding solicitation by immoral women in rooms where liquor is sold, but the proprietors of such places find no difficulty in permitting known prostitutes to make them the market places where they openly attract and secure customers.

Indeed, in the larger cities of Massachusetts the most flagrant and open expression of the commercialized aspect of prostitution is in connection with certain cafés and saloons. In some of these places from 25 to 50 known prostitutes, of unmistakable appearance and characteristics, may be seen sitting at tables, either in the center of the room or along the walls, where they wait from early afternoon to the closing hour, day after day, for some man to make a sign that he desires their company.

While the letter of the excise law forbidding communication with men at other tables is skillfully observed, the solicitation and bargaining by the women is most brazen and unmistakable. The women buy drink after drink, and each time they pay they tip the waiter. The more liberal they are with tips, the more secure their seat while looking for trade.

The cuisine is excellent in the most notorious places, and the price of food is very reasonable, — added inducements for attracting the presence of men to drink and trade with the women. Men flock to these places at the dinner hour or late at night to appraise the women and decide which one they will select. After the bargain is made, the couples go to a room in some apartment, lodging house or hotel.

The commission has the addresses of 110 different cafés and saloons in the State habitually frequented by prostitutes for the purpose of securing customers. The investigators have actually counted 6,649 escorted or unescorted women in these places, who, by the frequency of their presence, their actions, conversation and dress, were believed to be prostitutes. In fact, the investigators have been either openly or secretly solicited in these places by 171 different prostitutes to go with them to various hotels, apartments or furnished rooms, etc., for immoral purposes.

These immoral cafés and saloons are also the favorite resorts of pimps and procurers, well-known thieves, pickpockets and ex-criminals.

Many of these immoral cafés and saloons are located in densely populated tenement-house districts, subjecting the honest poor to the most evil influences.

These places are known to be very profitable from a commercial point of view. The reason for their existence is the profit from the sale of alcoholic liquor to the prospective customers of the prostitutes. A careful study of the disorderly cafés and saloons will show that the chief business in these resorts is done with known prostitutes and their prospective customers. The presence of these women stimulates the business, and the proprietors know it and encourage them to enter and remain. There is keen competition in securing attractive prostitutes to frequent their places. The music, the novel and alluring decorations, the excitement, the crowd of gaudy prostitutes, are the attractions employed to drum up trade.

The so-called respectable men in the community who conduct hotels, cafés and saloons where well-known prostitutes resort for business purposes would protest if they were branded as traffickers in women, yet these individuals actually come under this heading, with the pimps and procurers and the managers of houses of prostitution. The police take the position that they have no right to interfere if the letter of the law is observed, but it is difficult to understand why these immoral cafés and saloons are tolerated, as the licensing authorities have full power to cancel the licenses.

Some of the restaurants conducted by Chinamen in various cities in Massachusetts are favorite resorts of professional prostitutes and their pimps and customers. Certain white prostitutes solicit exclusively in Chinese restaurants, and cater only to Chinese patrons. Many of these are quite young women. A certificate of marriage with a Chinaman is a frequent excuse for the presence of the woman in the place. It is known that these marriage certificates are sometimes used by women as evidence of their marriage to different Chinamen. The same woman may be seen in Chinese resorts in different cities at different times.

These restaurants are also the meeting places of young white men and immoral young girls who have not yet become commercial prostitutes.

Private booths in these restaurants are curtained, and couples may enter and draw the curtains together, with the understanding that the waiter is not to open the curtains until he is told to do so by the occupants. Young girls often become intoxicated in these places. Some Chinese restaurants have rooms upstairs which they rent to couples for immoral purposes.

Disorderly Hotels.

A disorderly hotel is one to which prostitutes habitually bring their customers for immoral purposes from the streets, cafés, saloons and other public places. One of the most frequent and conspicuous expressions of prostitution in Massachusetts is the use made of the disorderly hotel by prostitutes. Certain hotels were evidently planned and built and are run for this special purpose. The prostitutes and their male customers, who usually pretend to be man and wife, are the principal patrons of many of these hotels. In many, no register is kept. Those who register usually do so under fictitious names. Few of the couples have any baggage. The women often take a room at the same hotel with different men several times in one week, or even several times in a single evening. These women are known and habitual prostitutes. Absolutely no questions are asked. Young girls are often assigned to rooms with men much older than themselves. This is especially true of some of the smaller cities of the State. These hotels are often the place of seduction of young girls. Many young girls not yet professional prostitutes have admitted to the investigators that they often have occupied rooms with men in certain specified hotels.

Women who come to the desk in these hotels to register are often connected with the hotel, — that is, they solicit in the saloon attached to the hotel, and are on intimate terms with the waiters and other employees, who aid them in securing customers. Some disorderly hotels, especially in the smaller cities, keep immoral women in the house, ostensibly as waitresses or chambermaids, or prostitutes from the town. Most business is done in these hotels on Saturday and Sunday. The same room is often assigned to many different couples in one day.

It would be impossible to describe here the disgraceful scenes observed in some of these hotels.

The character of the principal business of this class of hotels is perfectly obvious to any intelligent person who cares to observe the process of securing prospective guests and assigning them to rooms.

The use of these hotels by so many persons for immoral purposes at relatively high prices, and the profit from the incidental sale of liquor to these same guests, give these hotels an earning value far in excess of that to be obtained if used for any legitimate purpose. In many localities the number of hotels and the number of rooms in these hotels are greatly in excess of any possible legitimate demand for hotel accommodations in that locality. The only way they can be made profitable is to allow them to be used for purposes of prostitution or assignation.

In some cities even hotels of good general reputation are used by prostitutes for immoral purposes.

The commission has definite reports on 126 hotels in the State habitually used by prostitutes for immoral purposes.

It is true that a person holding an innholder's license must not discriminate, and must furnish food and shelter to all legitimate travelers. Even the most carefully conducted hotel cannot question its guests and determine their legal relations to each other, but the many properly conducted hotels prove that it is entirely possible and feasible to exclude practically all of this illicit business if the managers really desire to do so. It is inconceivable that the state of affairs described above, which may be verified by any observer, cannot be remedied by proper legislation, or by modifications of existing licensing conditions.

The Liquor Traffic and Commercialized Prostitution.

There is an intimate connection between certain phases of the liquor traffic and prostitution. In practically all of the open houses of prostitution, and in some of the apartments used for that purpose, both in cities where the evil is openly tolerated and in closed and secret places, liquor is sold at an exorbitant price for the purpose of stimulating trade, as well as for the direct profit involved.

It has been shown that in the immoral cafés, saloons and hotels the profit from the liquor sold to prostitutes and their prospective customers is the financial inducement for cultivating and encouraging the business.

It is probable that the men engaged in the legitimate liquor business would co-operate in efforts to destroy this alliance in Massachusetts.

Dance Halls.

The investigators visited many public dance halls, where any one is admitted for a small admission fee, as well as dances held in private halls by various organizations. Some of these dances are decorously and properly conducted, are attended only by respectable men and women, and are wholesome and proper places of recreation. Others are managed by disreputable persons, and are attended by immoral people, including well-known prostitutes.

Certain public dances are arranged mainly for the purpose of attracting men who may be secured as customers by these professional prostitutes. Students and others are induced to attend by enticing invitations. Many respectable young girls innocently attend these dances to satisfy their natural need for social life and recreation. There is often no pretence of supervision. Suggestive dancing and behavior are allowed. The pimps and procurers find this type of dance a fertile field of opportunity for meeting and inveigling young girls. The male solicitors for immoral purposes often referred the investigators to these public dances, as the places where they would secure girls and women for purposes of prostitution.

Recreation Parks.

The dance halls of many recreation parks in the suburbs of the cities as well as in the country — with no effective supervision, with the near-by fields and woods and the darkness — are freely used for purposes of prostitution. Not only do well-known professional prostitutes ply their trade in these dance halls at parks and recreation resorts, but here also pimps and procurers and other immoral men resort to take advantage of innocent, pleasure-seeking young girls. The evidence is indubitable that the seduction of many young girls occurs in recreation parks as at present conducted. The investigators actually witnessed the most gross and open immorality at several parks and seashore resorts.

Street Solicitation by Women.

In the smaller cities and towns investigated by the commission very little open street solicitation by professional prostitutes has been observed. In these cities and towns the police seem to have inspired the prostitutes with fear of arrest; therefore these women are very adroit in their solicitations. A man who is not looking for solicitation will seldom be subject to it. Even then the solicitation is usually not openly done, but the women give a more definite invitation to be approached or followed. If the man shows the slightest interest the woman is quick to see, and he is encouraged to approach or to follow her to a side street, away from the regular beat of the police officer. It is not easy for the police to secure evidence of streetwalking or soliciting that will be accepted by the courts.

In all the cities of the State a large number of girls from twelve to eighteen years of age roam the streets at night, or frequent the parks far from their homes, rapidly learning the lessons of prostitution. This practice is believed to have increased greatly in the past few years.

Pimps and Procurers.

The commission has definite information, including names and addresses, of many men who are procurers of women and girls for the business of commercialized prostitution.

The pimps constitute a well-recognized class of exploiters of women. These idle, flashily dressed, smooth-talking men, often with no visible means of support, may be found in every city of any size. They usually spend their time in low drinking places, amusing themselves by gambling, playing pool, etc. There are certain cafés much frequented by this class.

They are keenly on the lookout for young girls who have just begun a life of immorality. They openly boast of the girls they have seduced, and tell of their carefully planned schemes for the seduction of other innocent girls who have attracted their notice.

These pimps and procurers frequent public dance halls, cheap theatres, moving-picture shows, entrances to stores and factories, seashore and other popular summer resorts, — in fact, are found wherever young girls congregate for work or pleasure. They endeavor to strike up acquaintance with girls looking for adventure, and are skilled in the selection of those likely to be pliant to their will. They understand a certain type of women and girls very thoroughly. By adroit flattering attentions and plausible love-making they win the affections and effect the seduction of the girl, under promise of marriage or by other inducements, and eventually persuade or force her to engage in commercial prostitution for their benefit. They act as agents to secure trade for these women. The women so enslaved turn over a large part of their earnings to their professional lovers and pimps. Two or more women often work for the benefit of one pimp. These men live in idleness and perhaps in luxury, while their women ply their trade in houses of ill fame, in cafés and saloons, or on the streets of the city itself or in neighboring towns.

The commission has found very little evidence of coercion or threats of bodily punishment on the part of these pimps or procurers, compelling these women to do their bidding. As a rule, these men are now safe from prosecution, as the women will not testify against them.

During the period of this investigation pimps and their women from other States were known to be plying their trade in Massachusetts.

" White Slavery."

A large number of stories have been furnished the commission which would indicate that attempts have been made and are now being made to force women and girls in Massachusetts into an immoral life, or to compel them to remain in it under physical coercion or restraint. The persistence of these detailed stories will warrant the relation of a few.

The most frequent accounts refer to a young girl customer in a department store who was asked by a well-dressed lady to assist her to her carriage, as she was ill and faint. At the carriage door the girl was asked to accompany the woman to her home, but at that moment a policeman warned the young girl that the woman was a notorious procuress, and that she was being abducted for immoral purposes.

A variation of this story took the girl to the woman's richly appointed Back Bay home, where she was held a prisoner until rescued.

In another story a girl at a soda fountain observed a man dropping a powder into her glass. After drinking the soda she became dizzy and semiconscious, and the man took her by the arm, saying to the attendant, " This is my sister. She often has these fainting attacks. I will take her home in a carriage." The girl was sufficiently conscious to object, was rescued by a bystander and the procurer escaped.

Another account alleges the administration of a narcotic drug by the use of a hypodermic needle by a procurer, who plies the needle on his victim as he passes her on the street, or as he sits beside her in the street car or in the theatre.

Every story of this kind has been thoroughly investigated, and either found to be a vague rumor, where one person has told another that some friend of the former (who invariably in turn referred the story farther back) heard that the thing happened, or, in a few instances, imaginary occurrences explained by hysteria or actual malingering. Several of the stories were easily recognized versions of incidents in certain books or plays.

It has been shown that pimps and procurers in many localities in the State systematically persuade and induce girls and women to enter the business of commercialized prostitution.

It is also true that in the resorts which they frequent these pimps and procurers bargain for girls, whom they control and whose transfer from city to city they arrange. The prostitutes themselves profess not to know of any market place for prostitutes except the well-known immoral cafés and hotels, where they make their own arrangements for entering houses of ill fame in the same or other cities.

The evidence indicates that " procuring for prostitution " or " enticing to prostitution " in this State is done as a private venture, and not as part of an organized plan.

In this investigation it has also been shown that pimps and procurers do bring women from other States to practice prostitution in this State. This fact is also proved by the cited convictions under the Mann Act.

The commission has received no evidence which would show that any organization exists in this State for the buying or selling of women for immoral purposes.

Solicitation by Men for Prostitution.

In every city and large town investigated in Massachusetts men have been found who were anxious to give the investigators the names and addresses of places where prostitutes could be found or where they were engaged in business. The significant fact is that many of these men made this practice a part of their business, and demanded money for the information. In other words, they were acting as the agent of the prostitute, stimulating business for her, and receiving commissions from her as well as from her customers.

In the larger cities some of the cabmen and chauffeurs do a profitable business as agents or runners for vice resorts. These men have lists of resorts, and a business understanding with the proprietors as to the commission to be paid for each customer. In one large city a chauffeur said he was constantly on the lookout for new places to add to his list, as the more he had the more money he made.

In some cities the bell boys and elevator men in the hotels eagerly supply addresses to prospective customers, and even accompany the visitor to the house or apartment and introduce him.

The investigators have found many men in various cities who for a certain price offer to introduce young girls who have not yet become professional prostitutes, with the statement that they are available without the payment of money to the girl herself. The solicitors offer to find these girls on the street, or at moving-picture shows, at cheap dances, public parks, etc.

During the investigation the commission secured the occupations of many men and boys who were acting as agents for prostitutes. They are as follows: doctors, barbers, bartenders in hotels, cafés and saloons, hotel bell boys, bootblacks, business men, check-room men in hotels, cabmen, chauffeurs, clerks in various places, elevator boys in hotels, landlords, messenger boys, newsboys, etc. Many of these persons are likely to develop into pimps and procurers. Many of them already have girls who share their earnings with them. Invariably they are looking for girls, whom they approach and seek to attract.

Customers of Prostitutes.

The investigators were instructed to note carefully the apparent social status and occupations of the customers in vice resorts. It can be said that the men who are frequent customers in these resorts come from many walks and occupations, from the loafer on the corner with no visible means of support to prosperous looking clerks, mechanics, business and professional men.

The investigators of the commission had access to two address books containing the names and addresses of 201 men who were customers of two apartment houses of prostitution in one city.

A constructive plan for favorably modifying the conditions of prostitution demands definite knowledge of the class of men who patronize the prostitute. Too little attention has been paid to the male customers of these women. A study of their antecedents, heredity, mental status, family life, etc., would prove a fertile field for research. It is obviously not true that all men belong to this class. From the stories of the women themselves, and the confessions of their customers to our investigators, it is probable that a certain relatively small group of men in each community are the regular and principal customers of the different prostitutes in that town. The profitable continuance of the business depends upon frequent attraction of new patrons, who are more than likely to become regular customers. By every means in their power these women, their pimps and their business agents of the many types described seek to add new customers to their clientele. In city after city our men investigators were urged to patronize these women for immoral purposes.

It is a much mooted question whether the supply of prostitutes creates the demand for their services, or whether the demands of licentious men induce indolent and weak-minded or discouraged women to begin and continue the life. It would be difficult to convince the parents of young men that the presence of open houses of prostitution, or attractive young prostitutes soliciting on the street or in gaudy cafés and saloons, does not often tempt these young men to accompany these women to immoral hotels and lodging houses, who would not be so tempted if it were not for the wanton public exploitation and advertisement of these prostitutes and their resorts. The conditions of temptation and opportunity have much to do with the volume of the business of prostitution.

Owners of Property.

The commission has the names of the owners of houses of prostitution, apartment houses of prostitution, immoral lodging houses and cafés and hotels used for the purposes of prostitution. The general reputation and standing of some of these owners would indicate that they are not aware of the uses to which the property is subjected.

The detailed reports of the investigators show that prostitution in all its ramifications constitutes a vast business extending all over the State. Millions of dollars are invested in the parlor houses, call houses, road houses, apartments, lodging houses, cafés, saloons, hotels, etc., utilized in this business. The large amount of money required to produce the income for this investment is derived from the proceeds of the prostitution of the inmates and the incidental sale of intoxicating drinks. A large number of persons are employed directly or indirectly in this trade, and share in its proceeds; the prostitutes, the owners of property used for immoral purposes, proprietors and housekeepers, pimps, procurers, runners, cooks, maids, waiters, bartenders, lawyers, physicians, etc., — all receive money from this traffic in women. The individual prostitute ultimately receives only a small portion of the proceeds of the traffic in her person. The financial profit of the business of prostitution is the principal reason for its existence and continuance.

The Prostitute Herself.

The commission obtained as many histories as possible of professional prostitutes actually engaged in the business in Massachusetts at the time of the investigation.

The women examined were in three groups: young girls under sentence in the State Industrial Schools for Girls, the House of Refuge and the Welcome House; those just arrested and awaiting trial in the Suffolk House of Detention in Boston; women serving sentence in the State Reformatory for Women, the Suffolk County Jail and the Suffolk House of Correction.

These three groups represent the young girls who have just begun prostitution, the women plying their trade on the streets at the present time and the women who are old offenders. The houses of prostitution, lodging houses, hotels and cafés named by these women as the places where they plied their trade are the same as those noted by the field investigators employed by the commission.

Although it was obviously impossible to examine many inmates of the relatively few exclusive and expensive houses of prostitution, it is believed that the women examined fairly represent the class of public prostitutes to be found in this State at this time.

No prisoner was questioned who had not been arrested or sentenced for prostitution, or who did not admit commercialized prostitution. In each group 100 women or girls were examined, without selection, except that all had a history of promiscuous sex intercourse for pecuniary gain. The reading of the statistical tables is simplified by the fact that the

number and *per cent.* are the same in any one of the three
groups, as in each case exactly 100 were examined.

Under the immediate direction of the commission, the examination of these prisoners was conducted by a staff of
four women, two of whom were physicians familiar with the
diagnosis of feeble-mindedness and mental disease; one a
psychologist of wide experience with the Binet and other
laboratory tests for mental capacity; and one an experienced
field worker in eugenics and general social investigations.
All were genial, cultivated women who had no difficulty in
securing the confidence of the persons examined.

The apparent willingness, even eagerness, of most of the
women to tell their family history, the story of their childhood, school life, occupations, experiences, — even the most
intimate and personal details of their sex history and life of
prostitution, — was most surprising and illuminating.   In
nearly every case there were detailed court, probation or institution records, often including the reports of social workers
who had thoroughly investigated the personal and family
history of the women.   There was a remarkable agreement
between the stories told by the women and the official records.

The history of many of the prostitutes met with in the
general field investigation was also obtained.   The investigator selected for this work was a woman who had had
several years' experience in studying women of this type.
This woman understands in a remarkable manner women
and girls of this class.   She knows their language, their
habits and dress, and is able to enter into their lives, and
for the moment meet them on their own ground.

The very wide range of information obtained by this investigator, and by the other field investigators, who met and
talked with several thousand prostitutes in Massachusetts
during the investigation, much of which, though reported in
great detail, is not susceptible of statistical statement, strikingly verifies and corroborates the results of the intensive examination of the 300 prostitutes in custody.   The women
interviewed by the field investigators were actually plying
their trade on the street, in houses of prostitution, in cafés
and hotels.   These women constitute the main body of public

prostitutes, and apparently differ in no way from those examined under arrest or sentence, especially as to their ages, mental capacity, general intelligence, indolence, lack of remorse, and the apparent absence of any desire to leave the life of prostitution.

The Mentality of the Prostitute.

The study of the mental condition of each prostitute involved the following inquiries: a physical examination of the woman; a study of the family and personal history, including moral and social reactions and standards, industrial efficiency, etc., as revealed by probation, court or institution records, or as described by the woman herself; the school opportunities enjoyed and the school grade reached; an informal examination to show ability to read and write, to add, multiply and divide simple numbers, and to make simple arithmetical computations; simple questions to test practical knowledge and general information; inquiries as to associates, recreations, interests, etc. The inquiry generally was intended to demonstrate the woman's power of attention, judgment, common sense and native mental capacity, without regard to her school advantages or education.

The woman of good natural ability, who was merely ignorant from lack of educational opportunity, was easily differentiated from those who were mentally deficient.

The Binet tests were applied to 289 of the 300 women examined, and other psychological tests were used in doubtful cases.

TABLE No. 1. — *The Mentality of the Prostitute.*

| | Examined at — | | | Totals. | Per Cent. |
	Prisons.	Detention House, awaiting Trial.	Industrial Schools.		
Feeble-minded, ...	54	46	54	154	51+
Insane, ...	4	–	7	11	3+
Normal, ...	42	54	39	135	45
Total, ...	100	100	100	300	–

The above table shows that of the 300 prostitutes, 154, or 51 per cent., were feeble-minded. All doubtful cases were recorded as normal. The mental defect of these 154 women was so pronounced and evident as to warrant the legal commitment of each one as a feeble-minded person or as a defective delinquent.

At the Massachusetts School for the Feeble-minded there are an equal number of women and girl inmates, medically and legally certified as feeble-minded, who are of equal or superior mental capacity.

The women in this group as a class came from shiftless, immoral and degenerate families; they were industrially inefficient, as shown by the low wages received, and by their inability to retain a position, even in unskilled callings; they were very deficient in judgment and good sense; they lacked ordinary general knowledge and practical information, as well as ability to perform simple computations, or to read or write except in the most elementary way.

The general moral insensibility, the boldness, egotism and vanity, the love of notoriety, the lack of shame or remorse, the absence of even a pretence of affection or sympathy for their own children or for their parents, the desire for immediate pleasure without regard for consequences, the lack of forethought or anxiety about the future, — all cardinal symptoms of feeble-mindedness, — were strikingly evident in every one of the 154 women.

The mental inferiority of many of these women was masked by the glibness of tongue, the bold and confident manner and the attractive physical appearance which are so often found in such cases. The general appearance and bearing of many would not suggest feeble-mindedness to an inexperienced observer.

The mental age of these 154 women and girls, as measured by the Binet scale, was as follows: —

None had the mentality of a 12-year-old child.
10 had the mentality of an 11-year-old child.
67 had the mentality of a 10-year-old child.
50 had the mentality of a 9-year-old child.
19 had the mentality of an 8-year-old child.
8 had the mentality of a 7-year-old child.

The 135 women designated as normal as a class were of distinctly inferior intelligence. More time for study of these women, more complete histories of their life in the community and opportunity for more elaborate psychological tests might verify the belief of the examiners that many of them also were feeble-minded or insane.

The mental age of the 135 women rated as normal, as measured by the Binet scale, was as follows: —

> 17 had the mentality of a 12-year-old child.
> 71 had the mentality of an 11-year-old child.
> 32 had the mentality of a 10-year-old child.
> 4 had the mentality of a 9-year-old child.
> 11 were not tested.

Some of the women seen at the Detention House were so under the influence of drugs or alcohol as to make it impossible to study their mental condition. Others at the Detention House and in the prisons had used alcohol to excess for years, and in the time available it was impossible to differentiate between alcoholic deterioration and mental defect. These drunken, alcoholic and drug-stupefied women were all recorded as normal.

Of the 135 women rated as normal, only a few ever read a newspaper or book, or had any real knowledge of current events, or could converse intelligently upon any but the most trivial subjects. Not more than 6 of the entire number seemed to have really good minds.

TABLE No. 2. — *The Age of the Prostitute examined.*

	YEARS.																								
	12	14	15	16	17	18	19	20	21	22	23	24	25	26	27	28	29	30	31	32	33	34	35	36 and Over.	Totals.
Prisons, ...	-	-	-	1	3	6	7	8	12	10	6	7	4	5	2	-	3	4	5	-	2	2	1	12	100
Detention House, awaiting trial,	-	-	-	-	2	8	2	6	5	9	5	5	4	7	1	5	7	3	1	3	1	1	5	20	100
Industrial schools, . .	2	8	10	15	26	20	5	11	2	-	-	-	-	1	-	-	-	-	-	-	-	-	-	-	100
Totals, . .	2	8	10	16	31	34	14	25	19	19	11	12	8	13	3	5	10	7	6	3	3	3	6	32	300

Mental Condition.

	12	14	15	16	17	18	19	20	21	22	23	24	25	26	27	28	29	30	31	32	33	34	35	36 and Over.	Totals.
Normal, ...	2	2	4	5	13	9	9	13	5	12	4	4	4	6	1	1	7	5	4	1	-	2	3	19	135
Insane, . . .	-	-	-	3	1	4	-	-	1	-	-	-	-	-	-	-	-	-	-	-	1	-	-	2	11
Feeble-minded, . .	-	6	6	8	17	21	5	12	13	7	7	8	4	7	2	4	3	2	2	2	3	1	3	11	154

Table No. 2 shows the age of the 300 prostitutes examined
The girls in the industrial schools are of course muc
younger than those in the other groups. The striking fac
in the table is that 140, or nearly one-half, are under twenty
one years of age; 158 were between the ages of sixteen an
twenty-two, and 32 were thirty-six or over; 34 were eighteen
years old, the largest number at any one age.

TABLE No. 3. — Age at First Sex Offense.

							YEARS.																			30 and Over.	Not stated.	Totals.
	5	6	8	9	10	11	12	13	14	15	16	17	18	19	20	21	22	23	24	25	26	27	28			
Prisons,	-	-	-	-	3	1	1	5	12	6	13	15	8	5	4	3	3	1	1	-	1	2	2	3	11	100
Detention House, awaiting trial,	-	-	-	-	1	-	1	3	4	4	6	3	9	4	5	3	3	1	-	1	3	1	2	5	41	100
Industrial schools,	2	1	1	5	2	7	7	12	23	13	14	6	-	-	-	-	-	-	-	-	-	-	-	-	7	100
Totals,	2	1	1	5	6	8	9	20	39	23	33	24	17	9	9	6	6	2	1	1	4	3	4	8	59	300

Mental Condition.

	5	6	8	9	10	11	12	13	14	15	16	17	18	19	20	21	22	23	24	25	26	27	28	30 and Over.	Not stated.	Totals.
Normal,	-	-	-	2	1	2	5	11	15	9	13	8	7	4	4	5	4	1	-	1	4	2	3	5	29	135
Insane,	-	-	-	-	-	1	1	-	3	2	1	1	-	-	-	-	-	-	-	-	-	-	-	1	1	11
Feeble-minded,	2	1	1	3	5	5	3	9	21	12	19	15	10	5	5	1	2	1	1	-	1	1	2	-	29	154

Table No. 3 shows the age at the time of the first sex offense in 300 cases as told by the women themselves. Two began sex intercourse at five years, 1 at six, 1 at eight, 5 at nine, 6 at ten, 8 at eleven, 9 at twelve, 20 at thirteen, 39 at fourteen, 23 at fifteen and 33 at sixteen.

> 147, or 49 per cent., began before 17.
> 65, or 21+ per cent., began between 17 and 21.
> 29, or 9+ per cent., began after 21.

The age of fourteen was the period of first sex offense for 39, the largest number beginning at any age. The age at first sex offense is not stated in 59 cases.

Of the 154 feeble-minded, 81 admitted sex offense before they were seventeen years of age, and 116 before they were twenty-one. Of the 32 admitting sex offense under thirteen years of age, 20 were feeble-minded. Twenty-nine did not state or " could not remember " at what age the first sex offense occurred.

Of the 135 rated as normal mentally, 10 began sex offense before they were thirteen years old, 58 before they were seventeen and 81 before they were twenty-one; 29 did not state the age at first sex offense.

TABLE No. 4. — *Age at beginning Prostitution for Money.*

	YEARS																					Totals.
	9	11	12	13	14	15	16	17	18	19	20	21	22	23	24	25	26	27	28	30 and Over.	Not stated.	
Prisons,	–	–	–	–	3	4	10	9	11	13	3	7	4	1	1	–	1	1	1	5	26	100
Detention House, awaiting trial,	–	–	1	–	1	1	2	2	5	1	7	2	5	3	1	1	3	1	2	7	55	100
Industrial schools,	2	2	2	3	12	8	16	2	2	1	1	–	–	–	–	–	–	–	–	–	49	100
Totals,	2	2	3	3	16	13	28	13	18	15	11	9	9	4	2	1	4	2	3	12	130	300

Mental Condition.

	9	11	12	13	14	15	16	17	18	19	20	21	22	23	24	25	26	27	28	30 and Over.	Not stated.	Totals.
Normal,	1	–	1	–	7	5	11	4	9	8	4	5	7	3	1	1	3	1	2	9	53	135
Insane,	–	1	1	–	–	1	3	1	–	–	–	–	–	–	–	–	–	–	–	–	4	11
Feeble-minded,	1	1	1	3	9	7	14	8	9	7	7	4	2	1	1	–	1	1	1	3	73	154

Table No. 4 shows the age at the time the girl or woman began to practice prostitution for money, as told by the women themselves.

Of these, 2 began commercialized prostitution at nine years of age, 2 at eleven, 3 at twelve, 3 at thirteen, 16 at fourteen, 13 at fifteen and 28 at sixteen.

> 67, or 22+ per cent., began before 17.
> 66, or 22   per cent., began between 17 and 21.
> 37, or 12+ per cent., began after 21.
> 130, or 43+ per cent., did not state the age.

The age of sixteen was the period of first commercialized offense for 28, the largest number beginning at any age.

Of the 154 feeble-minded, 1 began at nine years of age, 1 at eleven, 1 at twelve and 3 at thirteen. Of these, 67 began before they were twenty-one, and 73 did not or could not state the age.

Of the 135 rated as normal, 1 began commercialized prostitution at nine years, 1 at twelve, 50 before they were twenty-one and 53 did not state the age.

TABLE No. 5. — *The Birthplace of the Prostitute.*

		EXAMINED AT —			
	Prisons.	Detention House, awaiting Trial.	Industrial Schools.	Totals.	Per Cent.
Native born: —					
Massachusetts, .	47	36	75	158	52+
Other New England States, . .	13	10	11	34	11+
Other States, ...	12	12	3	27	9
Total native born, ...	–	–	–	219	73
Foreign born: —					
Canada, ...	21	20	8	49	16+
Ireland, ...	5	6	–	11	3+
England, ...	2	6	–	8	2+
Russia, ...	–	2	3	5	1+
Other countries, ...	–	6	–	6	2
Total foreign born, . . .	–	–	–	79	26+
Not stated, ...	–	2	–	2	–
Totals, ...	100	100	100	300	–

Table No. 5 shows the birthplace of 300 prostitutes. Of these, 219, or 73 per cent., were native born; 79, or 26 per cent., were foreign born; the birthplace of 2 was not stated.

Of the 219 native born, 158 were born in Massachusetts, 34 in other New England States and 27 in States outside of New England.

Of the 79 foreign born, 49 were born in Canada, 11 in Ireland, 8 in England, 5 in Russia and 6 in other countries.

TABLE No. 6. — *The Birthplace of the Father of the Prostitute.*

| | EXAMINED AT — | | | Totals. | Per Cent. |
	Prisons.	Detention House, awaiting Trial.	Industrial Schools.		
Native born: —					
Massachusetts, ...	17	10	26	53	–
Other States, ...	18	14	17	49	–
Total native born, ...	–	–	–	102	34
Foreign born: —					
Canada, ...	32	25	28	85	–
Ireland, ...	18	23	8	49	–
England, ...	4	7	5	16	–
Other countries, ...	6	15	11	32	–
Total foreign born, . . .	–	–	–	182	60+
Not stated, ...	5	6	5	16	5+
Totals, ...	100	100	100	300	–

Table No. 6 shows the father's birthplace in 300 cases. Of this number, 102 fathers were born in the United States; of these, 53 were born in Massachusetts and 49 in other States.

There were 182 fathers born in foreign countries; of these, 85 were born in Canada, 49 in Ireland, 16 in England and 32 in other countries. The birthplace of the father was not stated in 16 cases.

TABLE NO. 7. — *The Birthplace of the Mother of the Prostitute.*

	Examined at —			Totals.	Per Cent.
	Prisons.	Detention House, awaiting Trial.	Industrial Schools.		
Native born: —					
Massachusetts, ...	18	13	13	44	–
Other States, ...	17	15	26	58	–
Total native born, ...	–	–	–	102	34
Foreign born: —					
Canada, ...	35	23	29	87	–
Ireland, ...	20	22	9	51	–
England, ...	1	7	9	17	–
Other countries, ...	6	13	9	28	–
Total foreign born, ...	–	–	–	183	61
Not stated, ...	3	7	5	15	5
Totals, ...	100	100	100	300	–

Table No. 7 shows the mother's birthplace in 300 cases. Of this number, 102 mothers were born in the United States, and 44 of these were born in Massachusetts and 58 in other States.

There were 183 mothers born in foreign countries; of these, 87 were born in Canada, 51 in Ireland, 17 in England and 28 in other countries. In 15 cases the birthplace of the mother was not stated.

TABLE NO. 8. — *Civil State of the Prostitutes.*

	Examined at —			Totals.	Per Cent.
	Prisons.	Detention House, awaiting Trial.	Industrial Schools.		
Single women, ...	43	43	97	183	61
Married women, ...	47	46	3	96	32
Widows, ...	7	8	–	15	5
Separated or divorced, . . .	3	3	–	6 — 117	2
Totals, ...	100	100	100	300	–

Table No. 8 shows the civil state of 300 prostitutes. Of this number, 183 were single, 96 were married, 15 were widows, and 6 were divorced or separated from husbands.

TABLE No. 9. — *Prostitutes with Children.*

	EXAMINED AT —			Totals.	Per Cent.
	Prisons.	Deten-tion House, awaiting Trial.	Indus-trial Schools.		
Single women with children, . .	13	10	10	33	30
Married women with children, . .	25	32	–	57	–
Married women with illegitimate children.	2	–	–	2	–
Widows with children, . . .	5	6	–	11	–
Divorced women with children, .	4	2	–	6 — 76	69
Totals, ...	49	50	10	109	–

Table No. 9 shows that in 300 cases 109 women had children. Of these 109 women, 33 single women had 39 children, and 76 married women had 174 children. In all, 109 women had 213 children.

Of the 76 married prostitutes with children, 38, or 50 per cent., were feeble-minded and 3 were insane.

Of the 33 single women with children, 22, or 66 per cent., were feeble-minded and 1 was insane. The mental age of the 22 feeble-minded single prostitutes with children was as follows: —

1 had the mental age of a 7-year-old child.
2 had the mental age of an 8-year-old child.
7 had the mental age of a 9-year-old child.
11 had the mental age of a 10-year-old child.
1 had the mental age of an 11-year-old child.

TABLE No. 10. — *Previous Court Records.*

	Examined at —			Totals.	Per Cent.
	Prisons.	Detention House, awaiting Trial.	Industrial Schools.		
No other records, ...	31	41	61	133	44+
1 other record, ...	32	20	34	86	28+
2 other records, ...	15	8	4	27	9
3 other records, ...	8	5	1	14	4+
4 other records, ...	3	3	–	6	–
5 other records, ...	4	2	–	6	–
6 other records, ...	–	2	–	2	–
7 other records, ...	1	5	–	6	–
8 other records, ...	2	1	–	3	–
9 other records, ...	1	1	–	2	–
10 other records, ...	2	3	–	5	–
12 other records, ...	–	4	–	4	–
13 other records, ...	–	1	–	1	–
14 other records, ...	–	2	–	2	–
15 other records, ...	–	1	–	1	–
16 other records, ...	1	–	–	1 — 39	13
40 other records, ...	–	1	–	1	–
Totals, ...	100	100	100	300	–

Table No. 10 shows the number of known previous court records of 300 women. Of these 300, 133, or 44+ per cent., had had no other court record; 86, or 28+ per cent., had had one other record; 27, or 9 per cent., had two other records; 14, or 4+ per cent., had three other records; 39, or 13 per cent., had from 4 to 16 other records; while 1 woman had 40 other records.

TABLE No. 11. — *Where Prostitution was practiced.*

	Examined at —			Totals.	Per Cent.
	Prisons.	Detention House, awaiting Trial.	Industrial Schools.		
Houses of ill fame,	28	11	27	66	22
Hotels only,	23	8	13	44	14+
Lodging houses only, .	9	21	14	44	14+
Hotels and lodging houses,	16	39	9	64	21+
Total in hotels and lodging houses, .	–	–	–	152	50+
Outdoors, .	–	–	14	14	4+
Men's and boys' homes,	1	1	5	7	2+
Not stated, .	23	20	18	61	20+
Totals, .	100	100	100	300	–

Table No. 11 verifies the statement made in the chapter devoted to the business of prostitution as to the habitat of commercialized prostitution in this State. Of the 300 prostitutes examined, only 66, or 22 per cent., plied their trade in houses of ill fame; 44, or 14+ per cent., took their customers to hotels; 44, or 14+ per cent., to lodging houses; and 64, or 21+ per cent., to hotels and lodging houses; altogether, 152, or 50+ per cent., patronized either hotels or lodging houses; 21 used various places and 61 made no statement as to the place.

It will be noted that none of the women named apartment houses and "call houses" as the place of prostitution, verifying the statement as to the difficulty of securing evidence against these places.

Of the 100 young girls in the industrial schools, nearly all under seventeen years of age, 13 practiced prostitution in hotels, 14 in lodging houses, and 9 in either hotels or lodging houses, showing the willingness of the proprietors of these places to allow young girls to use them for purposes of prostitution.

Some of the prostitutes expressed as their highest ambition the wish that they might be able to have stylish and becoming clothing, so that they might be allowed to solicit customers in various well-known cafés, where certain standards of dress seem to be the only required qualifications for admission.

Certain facts recur so often in the stories and records of the 300 prostitutes that they must be significant. Nearly all come from families in adverse circumstances. Immorality, drunkenness and crime are usually a part of the early history. In 29 per cent. of the families the mother was obliged to work out of the home during the upbringing of the child. In 30 per cent. of the families, either one or both parents had died or the family had been broken up by separation or divorce before the child was twelve years old. Only a few even pretended to come from normal, well-conducted homes, with a good father and mother who were able and willing properly to protect and bring up their children.

The examination of the 300 prostitutes in custody shows that the first sex offense was often committed at an early age. The commission has evidence of the very widespread prevalence of the exposure of little girls to various sex indignities in many communities throughout the State. These experiences are often not even suspected by the mothers and others responsible for the care of the children. There is no question but that these exposures are conducive to precocious sex activity and temptation.

The study of the histories of individual prostitutes, both in the field investigation and in the examination of the 300 women in custody, revealed that a period of private immorality almost invariably preceded commercialized prostitution. The descent to prostitution as a rule was gradual. Only a few began prostitution immediately after beginning sex immorality, or deliberately and understandingly entered the life.

The few women found of good mind and of normal family life point to the fact that a massing of contributory causes is necessary before a woman of this type can be so debased.

Of the 300 prostitutes examined, 154, or 51 per cent., were actually feeble-minded. The well-known immoral tendencies and the suggestibility and social incapacity of the feeble-minded cause them to drift naturally into prostitution, and make them easy and willing victims of the pimp and the procurer. The feeble-minded need only opportunity to express their unmoral tendencies.

Prostitution may be defined as " promiscuous sexual intercourse for hire." The early reports from the field investigators in the different cities and towns revealed the existence of large numbers of young girls who habitually have immoral relations with boys and men without expecting or accepting financial reward or gain. But for the absence of the element of hire, these relations of young girls with boys and men are not to be distinguished from those of professional prostitutes. These reports show an amazing state of affairs among the type of girls to be found in cities and towns of all sizes who are permitted to loiter about the streets at night and visit places of amusement unaccompanied.

The information concerning this group was obtained by the men and women investigators, and was verified by the statements of the police, teachers, clergy, social workers, etc. The immoral youth of the town know these girls well, and freely talk of their easy virtue. The " men solicitors of vice," previously referred to, offer to obtain the immoral services of these girls for total strangers.

In practically all cities and large towns many young girls of this class may be seen. These girls, from thirteen to eighteen years of age or older, are seen alone or in pairs, on the street, at the railroad stations, public parks, etc., until a late hour, night after night. Their parents can have no idea of where they go or with whom they associate.

They talk freely with men and boys of the town, or with strangers, and urge that they be taken to theatres, moving pictures, recreation parks, automobile rides, etc. Many have been observed ·with men entering immoral cafés, hotels and lodging houses in their own or neighboring cities. The interurban trolley lines quickly and cheaply transport them to a community where they are not known. To total strangers they talk willingly about themselves, their desire to " see life," to " get out of this dead hole," to go to Boston or to New York, to go on the stage, etc. They profess utter lack of respect for their parents and contempt for their home life. Many are vulgar, profane and obscene.

Many of these girls freely relate their immoral experiences to total strangers. Most of them would resent a suggestion of direct pecuniary reward for their immorality, but they expect to be given a good time, to be taken to supper or to the theatre, etc. Some of them already are willing and anxious to begin a life of professional immorality.

The immoral young girls and their male associates in the various cities and towns investigated informed the investigators that certain physicians would perform criminal abortion for a specified sum. Many of the men and women claimed that they had already employed these physicians for this purpose. The evidence in the possession of the commission leaves no doubt as to the truth of these statements in many cases. The commission has the names and addresses of a number of physicians in various cities and towns who to all appearances are engaged in this criminal practice. The fact that both the girls and their partners are so confident of being able to free themselves of the consequences of their immoral relations has a direct bearing upon the future conduct of these young people, especially the girls.

The commission has information of many of these immoral young girls in different cities and towns. Their employments are varied, — in factories, mills, stores, domestic service, offices, trades and many miscellaneous occupations. Most of them lived at home; some attended school. Some were the daughters of foreign-born parents who do not know the language and customs of this country. The majority were coarse and ignorant. The lack of parental care was strikingly evident in all. They knew nothing of things which they ought to know about themselves. They had wide knowledge of evil, but there was utter lack of valuation of their virtue or the part they were to play in the future as mothers.

It is the belief of the commission that the prostitutes of our community, both the normal and the degenerate, are largely drawn from this class, and should be discovered, studied and treated while still in this class.

PROSTITUTION, AND SYPHILIS AND GONORRHEA.

There are no diseases affecting the human race so widespread and so disastrous and terrible in their immediate and remote consequences as the so-called venereal diseases, syphilis and gonorrhea.

The highest medical authorities are unanimous in agreeing that prostitution is the source and the most common means of spreading these diseases.

The vast majority of professional prostitutes, of clandestine prostitutes, and of girls and women who are promiscuously immoral are affected with these diseases sooner or later. The man who patronizes them risks his health and life at every exposure. The habitual patron of the prostitute is almost certain to contract one or both of these diseases.

Some of the houses of prostitution which were investigated in the State claim to have regular medical inspection of the inmates, and guarantee immunity from infection to the patrons. A prostitute in one of these houses, showed the investigator her weekly medical certificates of freedom from disease, dated and signed for six weeks ahead, as the physician was away on vacation.

The theory that medical inspection of prostitutes, even if carefully conducted, can guarantee the certainty of freedom from infection is no longer held, even in European cities where it has long been practiced. The possibility of infection may exist long after the local signs of the disease disappear. Should the woman herself be free from disease, any one patron may be infected from the last customer who patronized the woman.

A careful examination of 466 young prostitutes, inmates of the Bedford Woman's Reformatory in New York, showed that only 50, or 10+ per cent., were free from infection at the time of the examination. In other words, 90 per cent. were infected with either syphilis or gonorrhea.

Of the 100 prostitutes examined for the commission at the Suffolk County House of Correction, the Charles Street Jail and the Woman's Reformatory, 11 had syphilis, 32 had gonorrhea and 27 had both syphilis and gonorrhea. In 20 of these women the presence or absence of these diseases was not ascertained. Of 80 women, therefore, 70, or 87½ per cent., had one or both of these diseases.

Of the 100 young girls just entering prostitution examined at the industrial schools, 21 had syphilis, 31 had gonorrhea and 4 had both syphilis and gonorrhea. In 10 of these girls the presence or absence of these diseases was not ascertained. Of 90 girls, therefore, 56, or 62+ per cent., had one or both of these diseases.

In a recent inquiry concerning 8,000 male patients over eighteen years of age, admitted to a Boston hospital for all sorts of other medical and surgical diseases, the following result was obtained after careful questioning of all the patients: 35 per cent. admitted a history of gonorrhea and 11 per cent. of syphilis at some period of their lives.

The acute stages of syphilis and gonorrhea involve great suffering and danger, and the remote consequences often result in permanent disability and invalidism, if not progressive fatal disease.

The fact that these diseases constitute potent factors in the causation of blindness, certain forms of insanity, locomotor ataxia and other incapacitating conditions leading to pauperism imposes an enormous direct charge upon the State. The cost of the support of all the inmates of the State institutions whose pauperism is caused by the consequences of these two diseases would total a large sum. The economic loss in the wages to the families of these persons and to the community would make a larger sum.

The consequences of these diseases are not confined to the individuals who acquire them directly from prostitutes, but are shared by innocent men, women and children. The infection is carried into the family. Inflammatory diseases and surgical operations peculiar to women are often the result of venereal infection, innocently acquired. Many women are thus rendered sterile or condemned to lifelong invalidism. Many pure young wives are infected and the hopes of parenthood denied, or fulfilled only in the birth of diseased or dead children. The hereditary results of syphilis reach to the third and fourth generation.

Innocent infection with these diseases is not confined to the marital partners of infected persons. Physicians, nurses and other persons are often so infected. Many children are infected, with no suspicion of immoral sex exposure.

The last report of the State Board of Insanity showed that of the 2,660 first admissions to all the insane hospitals of the State for the year ending Nov. 30, 1912, in 230 cases, or 8.65 per cent., the form of disease was general paralysis, a rapidly fatal form of insanity caused by syphilis. This percentage refers to this one form of insanity only, and does not include other forms of mental disease undoubtedly caused by syphilis, such as a certain proportion of coarse brain lesions of epileptic insanities and of imbecilities.

During the past year at the Boston Psychopathic Hospital, out of a total of 1,671 persons presenting themselves for diagnosis and treatment for some form of mental disease, 246 responded positively to the Wassermann test for syphilis.

At the Danvers State Hospital for the Insane, for the year ending Sept. 30, 1913, 664 patients were admitted. Careful Wassermann blood tests were done on 623. In 15 cases the reaction was doubtful, and of the 608 with definite positive or negative reactions, 123, or 20+ per cent., were positive. In other words, one in five of these patients had presumably at some time suffered from syphilis. Eleven cases, admitted during the year from one city where the commission found much commercialized prostitution, showed a positive reaction in 6 cases, or 54+ per cent. More than one-half of the patients admitted from this city had suffered from syphilis. Of the 53 imbeciles admitted, 9 per cent. gave a positive reaction for syphilis.

At the State Hospital for Epileptics at Monson, 47 patients were admitted from June 1, 1913, to Sept. 1, 1913, and the Wassermann test for syphilis gave positive reactions in 7 cases, or 10.63 per cent.

The Massachusetts Commission for the Blind informed the commission that the investigations of that body showed that of 301 cases of practical blindness treated at three Boston hospitals the past year at least 10 per cent. were directly due to syphilis or gonorrhea. The application of this percentage to the 4,000 odd blind in Massachusetts means that over 400 persons are practically blind as a result of these two diseases.

Practically nothing is being done to control these diseases. The other infectious diseases — some far less dangerous to the individual or to the community — must be reported and quarantined under severe penalties, and are properly treated at public expense. State laws, thoroughly enforced, compel these precautions. There is no law reaching or controlling the men or women suffering from the communicable stage of venereal disease. They may with legal impunity infect other persons. No restriction is placed upon their use of towels, bedding, toilet and other articles which may be used by other persons. They may, and often do, serve as barbers, waiters, bartenders, cooks, waitresses, nurse girls, and in other occupations involving personal contact with other persons.

It is inconceivable that an understanding public would tolerate for a day the liberty freely allowed persons suffering from these diseases, and it is obviously unfair that the few who know should permit this wanton exposure of the many who do not.

The well-to-do victims of these diseases are able to receive and pay for medical treatment, and probably are instructed to observe proper precautions to prevent infection of other persons; but the great majority of persons with these diseases have neither the money nor the inclination to receive adequate medical care, and as a matter of fact are not treated and do not observe precautions.

Patients helplessly ill from syphilis and gonorrhea are unwillingly admitted to almshouses in the large cities. The State Infirmary at Tewksbury receives cases with no local town or city settlement. Otherwise, practically the only opportunity for the free treatment of these diseases is at out-patient clinics of general hospitals and dispensaries in the larger cities.

The commission has interrogated 84 hospitals in Massachusetts for information regarding the treatment of venereal disease. Of the 61 hospitals that replied, only 9 treat cases of syphilis as out-patients, and only 3 treat them as bed patients; 10 hospitals treat cases of gonorrhea as out-patients, and 4 treat them as bed patients. In all but 5 of these, the number of cases was so small as to be negligible.

Law and Law Enforcement.

The study of the actual working of the present laws relating to the various phases of prostitution and the allied forms of sexual vice involved many conferences with city and town officials, and elicited much valuable testimony and information from judges and district attorneys, federal officials, commissioners and chiefs of police, police officers, probation officers, court officials, officers of penal and reformatory institutions, managers of rescue homes, social workers, etc.

The number and disposition of cases of persons arrested, tried and sentenced for all sex offenses for a period of one year in the eight most populous counties of the State were thoroughly examined and analyzed by an experienced lawyer, under the direction of the commission.

These inquiries yielded full and definite information as to the attitude and policy of public officials and the police towards sexual vice, the relative number of arrests for such offenses in various localities, the manner of obtaining evidence, the kind and amount of evidence necessary for a court conviction in different courts, and the final disposition of the cases as to acquittal, fines, imprisonment, probation, etc., in the lower and superior courts.

As a general rule, the investigators have found the public officials of the majority of the cities active in demanding of the police an enforcement of the laws against the various forms of commercialized prostitution. In certain cities, however, houses of prostitution are conducted openly, and women solicit from doorways, windows and on the street. In these cities the proprietors of houses of prostitution explicitly state that houses can be run only by arrangement with certain politicians. One of these politicians spent some time with one of the investigators employed by the commission, assuring her that he could find her a house for carrying on prostitution, and arrange privileges and protection from prosecution. There were other opportunities actually to pay money to certain officials for the privilege to open and operate houses of prostitution in these cities.

At the present time in most of the cities and towns of

Massachusetts the police also are apparently active in the suppression of the more obvious and well-known forms of commercialized prostitution, such as streetwalking and the conventional parlor houses of prostitution. This police activity is evident in Boston and nearly all of the other large cities. The commission has no knowledge of any irregular connection of the police with the business of prostitution in most of the larger cities of the State. The absence of any suspicion of protection and toleration of commercialized prostitution by the police of nearly all the cities investigated is in marked contrast with the conditions revealed in recent vice investigations in other States.

As stated elsewhere, in some cities and country towns certain parlor houses have been in apparently undisturbed operation for many years, and have become a part of the life of those communities. The police know these houses and tolerate them, provided the business is conducted quietly, under certain rules which the police have tacitly formulated. One significant fact is that no " outsiders " are permitted to open new houses in these cities.

The enforcement of the laws against prostitution and allied sex offenses presents many difficulties. From the nature of these offenses, usually committed under conditions of secrecy and concealment, it is difficult to secure evidence which is conclusive or even admissible in a court. Circumstances which seem absolutely convincing to an ordinary citizen, if described as evidence in court, do not prove the guilt of the person " beyond a reasonable doubt." The rules of evidence and the methods of court procedure, which have been carefully formulated to protect the innocent, require certain specific facts and circumstances to prove a crime against a person. The unsupported testimony of one police officer is rarely accepted. The parties concerned, the only other witnesses, will not testify against themselves. The average individual is unwilling to be dragged into these cases, even as a witness. Indeed, the average citizen in good standing believes that participation in the prosecution of any phase of prostitution or any form of sex vice is apt to be regarded as rather discreditable or in bad form. It is only too true that such activity often results in ridicule and in personal, business or political detriment to the individual. A complaining witness in such a case, especially if a woman, is often subjected to humiliating insinuations and questions on the witness stand which would not be tolerated in any other kind of case.

This feeling that interference with prostitution or sex vice is of itself discreditable is confidently relied upon as one of the chief bulwarks of protection of the business of prostitution, and is carefully fostered and cultivated by the many elements which directly or indirectly profit financially from the proceeds of commercialized prostitution.

The long-continued existence of houses of prostitution in so many country towns is largely due to the unwillingness of the good citizens of these towns to take the consequences of initiating prosecution.

Circumstantial evidence of a nature and amount which would undoubtedly have much weight with the court in a case of simple assault, or an offense against property, usually either is not admitted or is disregarded.

In the lower courts the case for the government is usually conducted by police officers. The accused is defended by an adroit and resourceful lawyer.

Whatever may be the intent of the law, the final disposition of these offenses in both the lower and superior courts, and the variation in the sentences given in the different courts, indicate that this whole class of crimes is treated as though they were much less serious offenses than other crimes.

Prosecution of Keepers of Houses of Ill Fame.

It is difficult to prosecute successfully keepers of houses of ill fame. Under the present laws a specific offense must be charged and proved by exact and abundant evidence in the judicial atmosphere of a court, with a skillful attorney employed by the defendant to overthrow the case. The indignant citizen who demands that the police close a house forgets that every person is held to be innocent until his guilt has been proved to the satisfaction of the court or jury.

He does not realize that perhaps the facts or information which convinced him are not even admissible as legal evidence.

The only practicable way in which the police can legally enter a house of ill fame is by means of a search warrant for liquor, obtained in advance from a court. In applying for a search warrant of this sort in Boston, a police officer must stand in line in a courtroom, with perhaps twenty or more men within hearing, and present his reasons for asking for the warrant. The record of this application is open to public inspection. It is believed that these bystanders sometimes notify the suspected persons of the impending raid.

If the house is raided and searched, actual proof of fornication must be discovered. The proprietors of these houses understand the kind and amount of evidence needed to obtain a conviction. It is hard to obtain this evidence. They know their legal rights. They regard lightly the sentences usually imposed. They will give up the business only when convinced by constant pressure that it has ceased to be profitable. Even if a conviction is obtained, different women appear as the ostensible proprietor, and the really nominal fine is charged to profit and loss.

The disposition of the persons arrested in Suffolk County from Jan. 1 to Sept. 1, 1913, for keeping houses of ill fame illustrates the results of law enforcement in these cases. It should be understood that the term " house of ill fame " is used for convenience; the wording of the statute is " a place resorted to for prostitution," and in Boston and some other cities such place is almost always an apartment, a hotel, lodging house, etc.

Number accused,	83
Defaulted,	5
For disposition,	78
Pleaded not guilty,	60
Of these, pleaded guilty later,	10
Admittedly guilty,	28
Found guilty by court,	37
Admittedly guilty or found to be guilty,	65

Disposition : —

Pending,	1
Defaulted,	2
On file,	3
On probation,	4
Acquitted,	13
Sentenced to imprisonment,	20
Sentenced to fine and imprisonment,	1
Fined,	34
	78

Imprisonment. — There were 21 sentences of imprisonment, out of 65 convictions.

8 to the House of Correction for three months.
6 to the House of Correction for four months.
6 to the House of Correction for six months.
1 to the House of Correction for one year.

Of these sentences, 10 were suspended while the person was tried on probation; 7 were appealed. Only 4 persons were actually committed to an institution by this court, if we except the cases of commitment for nonpayment of a fine. Of the 10 tried on probation under suspended sentence, 3 defaulted, 1 was discharged and 5 are still on probation. One was surrendered and committed.

On File. — Three cases were placed on file, 2 of them after guilt was admitted.

Probation. — Twelve were placed on probation. Of these, 3 defaulted; 2 were later discharged; 1 was surrendered and committed. The others are still pending.

Net Results. — Out of 65 guilty, the net result is 22 fines paid, 7 still on probation, 5 committed to an institution, 4 more for nonpayment of a fine, and the others escaped by default, etc. Of the 55 sentenced, 7 of those fined and 7 sentenced to imprisonment appealed to the Superior Court.

For the five years ending Nov. 30, 1912, 475 persons charged with keeping houses of ill fame have had their cases disposed of in the municipal courts in Suffolk County, as follows : —

Fined $100, ...	29
Fined $75, ...	6
Fined $50, ...	197
House of Correction 12 months, ...	11
House of Correction 11 months, ...	1
House of Correction 9 months, ...	3
House of Correction 8 months, ...	2
House of Correction 6 months, ...	27
House of Correction 4 months, ...	19
House of Correction 3 months, ...	19
House of Correction 2 months, ...	2
House of Correction 1 month, ...	1
House of Correction 9 months and $100 fine, ...	1
House of Correction 9 months and $50 fine, ...	1
House of Correction 6 months and $50 fine, ...	1
House of Correction 3 months and $100 fine, ...	1
House of Correction 3 months and $50 fine, ...	1
House of Correction 2 months and $75 fine, ...	1
Sherborn Reformatory, ...	2
Jail, ...	4
Placed on probation, ...	35
Placed on file, ...	31
Discharged, ...	68
Pending, defaulted or held for grand jury, ...	12
	475

In a recent special report of the police department of the city of Boston, Commissioner Stephen O'Meara, referring to the treatment by the courts of the offense of keeping a house of ill fame, says: —

With discharges no fault can be found, for doubtless the evidence was not strong enough to convince the courts. But that so many cases should be put on probation or on file, either of which dispositions implies guilt, is puzzling. No person goes into the business of keeping a house of ill fame by accident or impulse or through sudden temptation. All such persons are of mature years, and so hardened by vice as to be free from the danger of contamination by the inmates of any prison. The sentence of $50, which seems the most common, is not even the maximum money penalty provided by law. No money penalty can condone such an offense, and especially a small sum that can be charged to profit and loss account and not interfere with the business.

The maximum penalty under Revised Laws, chapter 101, section 7, the so-called " nuisance act," for keeping a house of ill fame, is $100 fine or one year's imprisonment, or both. In 407 convictions in Boston for keeping houses of ill fame since Dec. 1, 1907, the maximum combined penalty of $100 and one year's imprisonment under this law has not been imposed in a single instance.

For two years past in Boston no cases have been prosecuted under Revised Laws, chapter 212, section 19, the so-called " iron-clad act," which provides for imprisonment only for this offense.

Prosecutions for keeping a house of ill fame have been conducted in seven other counties of Massachusetts for the period from Jan. 1 to Sept. 1, 1913, as follows: —

Where found.

Springfield,	2
Lowell,	1
Gardner,	1
Plymouth,	1
Fall River,	4
New Bedford,	8
Attleborough,	6
Salem,	1
Haverhill,	3
Lynn,	10
Lawrence,	3
Amesbury,	1
Gloucester,	1
Totals,	42

Summary of Disposals.

Number of cases,	42
Acquitted,	9
Guilty,	33
Never arrested,	1
Defaulted,	1
Defaulted and on file,	1
Probation,	1
Continued for sentence,	1
Pending,	2

On file, ...	3
Sentenced, ...	10
House of Correction for 2 months, ... 2	
House of Correction for 3 months, ... 3	
House of Correction for 6 months, ... 2	
House of Correction for 9 months, ... 2	
House of Correction for 1 year, ... 1	
Fined, ...	13
$50, ... 8	
$75, ... 1	
$100, ... 3	
$150, ... 1	

Police Patrol in Front of Houses of Ill Fame.

In many cases where it has been found impossible to secure adequate evidence for court conviction, the police of Boston and other cities have stationed an officer in uniform in front of the house, who asks the names of those entering and warns them of the nature of the house. In this way the customers are driven away and the business ceases to be profitable. Some of the most notorious and long-established houses have been closed in this way.

Appeals to Superior Courts.

When a case is appealed from the sentence of the lower court, the complaining officer is called to the office of the district attorney and questioned as to the case. The defendant is not present, but is sometimes represented by counsel. The case goes from the district attorney's office to the Superior Court, and if a jury trial is not demanded and if the case is not nol prossed, the judge sentences in accordance with the recommendation of the district attorney.

Prosecution of Keepers of Houses of Ill Fame.

Results on Appeals to Superior Court in Suffolk County from Jan.
1 to Sept. 1, 1913.

Of the 7 who appealed from fines of $50 each : —

Fined $50 in upper court, ...	2
Defaulted, ...	1
Probation, ...	1
Nol prossed, ...	1
Pending (1 for three months and 1 for six months), . .	2

Results of appeal : —

Total fines in lower court, ...	$350
Total fines in upper court, ...	$100
Two cases still pending.	

Of the 7 who appealed from imprisonment sentences : —

Fined $50 in upper court, ...	3
Given same sentence, ...	1
Fined $100, ...	1
On file, ...	2

Results of appeal : —

Total imprisonment, lower court, ...	30 months.
Total imprisonment, upper court, ...	3 months.

Civil Proceedings against Houses of Ill Fame.

Within a few years the police commissioner of Boston has brought proceedings against two houses of ill fame by civil process, under Revised Laws, chapter 101, but the title to the property was immediately transferred, and as against the new owners the injunctions had no force.

Prosecutions under the Mann Act.

The Mann White Slave Act, so called, a federal statute which prohibits the transportation of female persons from one State to another for immoral purposes, has been in effect since July 23, 1910. The United States Court has since been open at Boston for the trial of all cases involving the transfer of such persons to or from Massachusetts, and federal officials especially charged with the discovery of violations of the act and the collection of evidence against the accused have been constantly on duty at Boston.

Up to Jan. 1, 1914, a period of three years and six months following the passage of the law, there have been 10 cases before the court at Boston, involving 12 defendants and 11 women or girls alleged to have been transported to or from other cities in violation of the Mann Act. A summary of the cases follows, the date given in each instance being that on which the transportation was alleged to have taken place, and the localities named being the places from which or to which the transportation took place: —

1. July 27, 1912; Boston to New York; not guilty.
2. Dec. 20, 1912; Lowell to Chicago; sentence, 6 months.
3. Nov. 27, 1912; New York to Springfield; sentence, 10 years.
4. Nov. 28, 1912; Springfield to New York; sentence, 10 years (same women as in No. 3).
5. Sept. 15, 1911; Providence, R. I., to Boston; on file.
6. Dec. 23, 1912; Hartford, Conn., to Springfield; two men; sentences, 1 year and 2 years.
7. March 1, 1911; March 3, June 3, June 8, 1913; one person, Woonsocket, R. I., to Manchester, N. H.; one person, Nashua, N. H., to Boston, Haverhill to Salem, N. H., Salem, N. H., to Tyngsborough; one person, Haverhill to Salem, N. H.; sentence, 12 years.
8. July 1, 1913; Lawrence to Nashua, N. H.; sentence, 2 years.
9. Aug. 9, 1913; Enfield, Conn., to Springfield; not guilty.
10. Dec. 5, 1913; Pawtucket, R. I., to Boston; pleaded not guilty and case pending.

Court Treatment of Arrested Prostitutes.

The records in the various courts show that women arrested for prostitution are arraigned as common nightwalkers, as idle and disorderly, or, when arrested in a house of ill fame, for fornication.

There is a variance in the disposition of cases in the different courts. In Boston, for a first offense as a common nightwalker, or idle and disorderly, they are put on probation or on file; for a second offense they are fined from $5 to $20; for a third or later offense they may be given a jail sentence. Those arrested for fornication are generally fined. Unfortunately, the imposition of a fine usually means that the woman must at once commit more prostitution in order to pay her fine.

In some courts probation is rarely used in the treatment of this class of offenders. Probationary supervision of such persons is necessarily a delicate task, and if the courts were disposed to place them on probation, the number of probation officers now in the field would be found entirely inadequate for the work.

In many courts cases are put on file or on probation with the proviso that the woman leave the city or the State. If such disposition is made in the effort to change an undesirable to a desirable environment, it would seem to be proper treatment; otherwise, it is of doubtful effect upon the woman and of doubtful effect upon the community to which she goes.

Prosecution for deriving Support from the Earnings of a Prostitute.

The difficulty of obtaining evidence sufficient to secure a conviction for this offense is illustrated by the fact that only 15 cases were brought before the courts under Revised Laws, chapter 212, section 2, as amended by the so-called Massachusetts White Slave Act, Acts of 1910, chapter 424, in the eight most populous counties of the State between Jan. 1 and Sept. 1, 1913.

The disposition of these 15 cases was as follows: —

1. Sentenced to House of Correction for 6 months. Committed.
2. Acquitted.
3. Acquitted.
4. Sentenced to House of Correction for 1 year. Committed.
5. Sentenced to jail for 1 year. Appealed; same sentence in upper court.
6. Never apprehended.
7. Acquitted.
8. Acquitted.
9. Acquitted.
10. House of Correction 1 year.
11. House of Correction 1 year. Appealed. Nol prossed.
12. Acquitted.
13. House of Correction 1 year. Pending since May 1. In jail.
14. Acquitted.
15. House of Correction 1 year. Committed.

Customers of Prostitutes.

The police court records show that relatively few male patrons of prostitutes are arrested for their share in the offense involved. Just here there seems to be a lack of even-handed justice. When men are found in a raided house they are not arrested unless taken in the act of fornication. The usual penalty for the offense for the man is a fine of $10. If unable to pay the fine he is usually placed on probation until he can pay it. Very rarely is even a short jail sentence imposed. Apparently no account is taken of the fact when a man has been arrested previously for this same offense.

As a rule these men give fictitious names and addresses. Apparently no attempt is made to verify names or addresses.

The disposition of the 223 men arrested for fornication, and considered by the Boston municipal court from Jan. 1, 1913, to Sept. 1, 1913, was as follows: —

Total number fined,	192
Fined $10 and paid,	108
Fined $20 and paid,	1
Fined $10 and committed for 15 days for nonpayment,	19
Fined $10 and on probation until payment,	62
Fined $20 and on probation until payment,	2
Total number given prison sentence,	5
House of Correction 20 days,	1
Common jail 20 days,	1
Common jail 2 months,	1
House of Correction 2 months.	1
House of Correction 3 months,	1
Acquitted,	2
On file,	11
On probation,	6
Default on probation,	1
Surrendered,	1
Pending,	4
Defaulted,	6
Pending,	1

223

The disposition of all the cases of male persons arrested for fornication in the eight most populous counties of the State from Jan. 1, 1913, to Sept. 1, 1913, was as follows: —

Total number fined, ... 79
　　　Fined $5 and paid, ... 4
　　　Fined $5 and committed for nonpayment, . . . 2
　　　Fined $10 and paid, ... 10
　　　Fined $15 and paid, ... 6
　　　Fined $15 and on probation until payment, . . 3
　　　Fined $15 and committed for nonpayment, . . 2
　　　Fined $20 and paid, ... 17
　　　Fined $20 and committed for nonpayment, . . 10
　　　Fined $25 and paid, ... 3
　　　Fined $25 and committed for·nonpayment, . . 1
　　　Fined $30 and paid, ... 16
　　　Fined $30 and committed for nonpayment, . . 5
Total number imprisoned, ... 13
　　　House of Correction 1 month, ... 4
　　　House of Correction 2 months, ... 4
　　　House of Correction 3 months, ... 3
　　　Common jail 2 months, ... 1
　　　Common jail 3 months, ... 1
Acquitted, ... 6
On file, ... 4
Defaulted, ... 2
Held for grand jury, ... 3
Probation, ... 2
Pending, ... 1
　　　　　　　　　　　　　　　　　　　　　　　———
　　　　　　　　　　　　　　　　　　　　　　　110

Solicitation by Men for Prostitutes.

Solicitation by men of business for prostitutes and the giving of information or directions to prospective customers of prostitutes, practices which the commission finds to play a conspicuous part in commercialized prostitution throughout the State, do not seem to be amenable to the present laws, as no prosecutions were recorded for the period studied, from Jan. 1 to Sept. 1, 1913. No prosecution for these offenses has been successfully conducted in Boston for seven years. The facts so apparent to our investigators do not receive official notice.

Disorderly Hotels.

The disorderly hotels used for purposes of prostitution are able to conduct this business with almost complete immunity.

In order to open and run a hotel the only requisite is the possession of an innholder's license. Revised Laws, chapter 102, provides for the granting of an innholder's license by the board of license commissioners in cities having such a board, by the mayor and aldermen in cities having no such boards, and by the selectmen of towns. The granting of these licenses is largely a matter of form. The hotel itself is not licensed. The law requires that the innholder must have upon his premises suitable rooms with beds and bedding, implements for cooking and serving of food, and " provision for hay and provender for horses and cattle, if required." It is provided that an innholder's or common victualler's license shall be immediately revoked if he ceases to be engaged in the business, or fails to maintain upon his premises the implements or facilities provided for by the law.

The law apparently does not recognize the possibility of the use of hotels for immoral purposes, and of course provides no special penalties for such use. On rare occasions the keeper of a disorderly hotel is convicted on the technical charge of keeping a house of ill fame. Sporadic and infrequent suspension of the liquor license, soon followed by nominal change of ownership and immediate renewal of the license, is the rare evidence of any effort to modify conditions. Some of the most notorious of these immoral hotels have been so conducted for years, and are known by reputation even beyond the State, and yet have never been molested by the authorities.

The fact that the average law-abiding citizen is not cognizant of the practices in the immoral hotels is one reason for the failure of public sentiment to demand better conditions. Here, also, the theory of " vested property interests " is used for the defense of a bald phase of commercialized prostitution.

An attempt to obtain the revocation of the license of the innkeeper responsible usually involves a formal hearing, with the inevitable publicity and annoyance so repugnant to a complainant.

The division of authority and responsibility between the
police and the licensing boards or officials is a vital factor in
the failure to suppress these immoral hotels. The information in the possession of the police, or to be easily obtained
by them or by any intelligent citizen, would justify the immediate closing of a majority of these immoral hotels by the
licensing authority.

The arrested and convicted prostitutes examined for the
commission of their own accord freely named the cafés, lodging houses and hotels where they secure their patrons and
where they take their customers. Certain resorts have been
so named by scores of women. There can be no difficulty in
securing evidence if evidence is desired.

No other form of criminal offense or violation of law so
flagrant and open and so harmful to the community would be
tolerated for a day in this State.

Immoral Cafés and Saloons.

The many cafés and saloons all over the State used by
known prostitutes for open solicitation of customers are prac-
ically undisturbed by the authorities. The licensing boards
and agencies have ample authority summarily to close these
immoral cafés and saloons so openly resorted to for immoral
purposes.

The commission has found few prosecutions, or cases in
which the license has been cancelled, for conducting a café or
saloon " used for purposes of prostitution." The warning and action of the authorities, if exerted at all, only serve
to keep the conduct of the place just within the letter of the
law. Here, again, the capital invested in plant and business
and the large profits constitute a " vested interest," which
seems to protect these places.

Apartment Houses.

The commission has found an almost complete lack of law
enforcement as to houses of prostitution in apartment houses,
or in telephone or call houses, or immoral lodging houses.
The business is carried on in these places with secrecy and
quietness, and few arrests are made or convictions obtained.

The present means of securing evidence available to the police are meagre. Although as a rule the police are aware of their existence, they seem at present almost immune to prosecution.

Enticing to Prostitution.

During the three years 1910, 1911 and 1912, in the entire State there were only 20 convictions for " enticing to prostitution " under the provisions of chapter 212, sections 1 and 2, Revised Laws, the so-called Massachusetts White Slave Act. Of these convictions, 1 was fined, 3 sentenced to terms of imprisonment up to six months, 6 to a term of six to ten months, 9 to a term of one to two years, and 1 to a term of three to five years. The limited number of persons arrested for this offense is due to the difficulty of corroborating the evidence of the girl who is enticed to prostitution.

Summary as to Law and Law Enforcement.

By comparison with the published reports of vice commissions in other States, it will be seen that Massachusetts has entered upon an advanced stage of the movement to suppress or eliminate commercialized prostitution. For practically a generation, in most of our cities public sentiment has demanded that the police actively enforce the existing laws against streetwalking and the old-time parlor house of prostitution. At the present time the money-making business of prostitution is largely carried on in cafés, saloons, call houses lodging houses, hotels and apartments. These new and comparatively subtile methods are not fully understood by the public and have not yet aroused public sentiment, and therefore have not been brought under control. In other words in this State prostitution can be prosecuted only under laws formulated long ago to meet comparatively simple conditions which have been supplanted by the present complicated system of commercialized prostitution. Under these laws, skillful and adroit lawyers, with long experience and a vast accumulation of ingenious expedients and precedents, are able so to advise their clients as to make them almost immune to arrest or prosecution, owing to the difficulty of securing evidence which will be accepted by the courts.

At the present time the greater part of the prosecutions and convictions for commercialized vice are of the individual prostitutes themselves, and do not reach the pimps and procurers, the male solicitors, the male customers, and the other purveyors of prostitutes, who as brokers buy and sell at retail the bodies of these wretched and degraded women.

In the investigation it has been noted that in the cities and towns where the prostitutes and their resorts have been consistently repressed for a long time there is now little evidence of prostitution and the moral conditions are by comparison good. In cities where it has been openly tolerated, prostitutes are numerous, their resorts well known, syphilis and gonorrhea prevalent, abortions easily procured, many young women who have not yet become professional prostitutes are openly immoral, and the young men of the city are familiar with all forms of sexual vice.

CONCLUSIONS AND RECOMMENDATIONS.

The resolve creating the commission directed that " it shall endeavor to devise plans for preventing such evils as it finds to exist."

The commission would fail in its duty to report its findings if it should omit reference to the widespread evidence of a strong public sentiment against the continuance of the conditions it has found to exist.

It has long been held that prostitution always has existed and always will exist, and that all remedies will be ineffective and of no avail, because it represents a variation of the most fundamental human instinct.

Modern methods of scientific study of first causes and the logical removal of those causes have prevented, alleviated or cured many physical and social ills of mankind which were considered necessary and inevitable.

Recent studies of prostitutes and prostitution in other cities, States and countries, and, in connection with this investigation, the study and analysis of the 300 prostitutes individually examined for the commission, the observation of prostitutes and prostitution, and of the immoral young girls who have not entered prostitution in cities and towns all over

the State, have convinced the commission that this evil is sus
ceptible of successful attack and treatment.

Such attack and treatment must be based upon long-con
tinued research and study of the prostitute herself, her ante
cedents and heredity, the conditions of her childhood, th
exposures and temptations of her adolescence, etc.; and upo>
information based on similar studies of the customer of th
prostitute, of his boyhood and youth, his associates, tempta
tions, etc.

The changes in habits and customs brought about by mod
ern industries and modern urban life must be recognized. I>
former times girls worked at home under their mothers
watchful eyes, and seldom went abroad unless accompanie
by women of mature years. Children were held in stric
discipline. The majority of families lived in small com
munities, and boys and girls helped on the farm, in the house
hold and in other home industries. Until late adolescence
when character and habits were formed, children selecte
their associates and found their interests and recreations i>
the home, the church and the neighborhood, under the watch
ful eyes of their parents. Religion was a controlling influ
ence over conduct.

Present conditions are vastly different. Modern inventio>
and business methods have transferred industry and it
products from the home to the factory, the big store and th
office. The great majority of our people live in large town
and cities. Young people work, and in many instances ar
obliged to live, away from home. The early economic inde
pendence of working girls brings temptations, and make
them intolerant of restraint. It has become the custom o>
young women to go about freely, unaccompanied. Our yout>
of both sexes are accorded great freedom in the pursuit o>
pleasures.

There have been several recent notable warnings by emi
nent citizens as to the significance of the changed condition
of living. The commissioner of police in our chief city i>
his annual report called attention to the lawlessness of yout>
of both sexes, and the absence of parental supervision an>
control.

The superintendent of schools in Boston has lamented the influence of vicious and exciting amusements, the weakening of home influence, and the fact that parents are expecting the schools to supply the moral training and develop the self-control which can be given only in the home.

A high dignitary of the church has emphasized the lack of home influences, the unrestrained liberty given to boys and girls, and the absence of religious training and influence.

The study of the individual prostitutes showed that the majority of these women began sex relations before they were eighteen, and entered on the life of prostitution for money before they were twenty-one. Nearly 75 per cent. of these prostitutes were of native birth.

The prostitutes of to-morrow are in our primary schools to-day. The future customers of these prostitutes are to-day innocent boys, with infinite possibilities of good as well as of evil. If our boys and girls are to be given sufficient moral fiber and the self-control to keep straight, certain old-fashioned agencies must assume their proper places. The fate of these boys and girls depends upon the home, the school, the church and the neighborhood, — and upon the administration of government by honest and high-minded public officials. Each of these agencies must do its part in the molding and forming of character. Until late adolescence boys and girls should be kept from evil associations, provided with wholesome and attractive recreation and amusement under the eyes of their parents, and not excited by unwholesome commercialized amusements which suggest and provoke sex impulse. If during this period they are taught the sacredness of the body, are warned of the dangers of bodily contact and the hazards of chance acquaintance, and self-control is inculcated by example and reinforced by knowledge of life imparted under conditions conducive to modesty and self-respect, they will be saved from the fate of these wretched women and their partners.

The best influence for girls is of course that of a loving home; but in the absence of such control in homes of their own, the community itself, in its own defence, should provide the best influence possible. Orphans and girls unprotected by those who should be their natural protectors should be the special care of religious, benevolent and friendly organizations.

The fact that one-half of the women examined were actually feeble-minded clears the way for successful treatment of this portion of this class. The mental status of the prostitutes under arrest should be determined, and such of them as are found to be feeble-minded or defective delinquents should be placed under custodial treatment. Thus would these women themselves be saved from an evil fate, pimps and procurers would lose their willing prey, and a non-self-supporting class who find in prostitution their only way of earning a living would be taken out of the community.

The recognition of feeble-minded girls at an early age in the public schools, and proper provision for their protection in the community or custodial care in an institution, would prevent much of the observed immorality among young girls and the resulting temptations to boys. Precocious sex interests and practices are well-known symptoms of feeble-mindedness.

The commission believes that well-qualified women with the proper authority as adjuncts to the police systems of the larger cities would be able to add to the effectiveness of the police in dealing with certain phases of the problem of prostitution, especially in the way of reaching and influencing reckless and unprotected young girls who have not become immoral or actually entered a life of prostitution.

The social and industrial system which fosters tenement life in congested areas has obligations towards the children and young people of these families which have not been adequately met. There are many modern evidences of the realization of these obligations in the way of movements for better living conditions, vocational school training, supervised playgrounds, and the utilization of schoolhouses and other municipal buildings for wholesome recreational purposes.

It has been stated that one of the obstacles to the prevention and prosecution of the various phases of prostitution, especially in the smaller cities and towns, is the unwillingness of citizens to testify in such cases, and the absence of opportunity for definite expression of public sentiment on these subjects. It is a commonplace that a law is not likely to be enforced which is not supported by expressed public opinion. The great majority of our citizens are opposed to immorality and prostitution. The conditions noted in the various cities and towns of the State would be favorably affected if there were influential local agencies for expressing the sentiment of law-abiding citizens, demanding the prevention and repression of prostitution and sex offenses in their localities. Such organizations would easily acquire knowledge of local vice problems, and, especially if they had the co-operation of some State agency, would compel action by the local authorities.

It would seem that existing organizations, such as boards of trade, medical, legal and educational organizations, labor unions, women's clubs and church societies, might well co-operate in efforts to repress the business of prostitution, — a business so costly to the State, so likely to affect the girls and boys of this and coming generations, and the cause of such distressing and deadly disease.

If especially selected and qualified officers of the State police were designated and required to prosecute those engaged in the business of prostitution, it would be possible to detect and convict offenders who are able to elude the vigilance of the local police. The utilization of unfamiliar police officers, untrammeled by local prejudicies or alliances, would be most effective in the repression of immoral resorts in the smaller cities and towns.

Syphilis and gonorrhea should be regarded as contagious diseases dangerous to the community rather than as evidences of evil-doing on the part of those who are suffering from them. Although prostitution plays a leading part in the spread of these diseases, they have leaped its barriers, and become a widespread source of danger to the innocent. The public should be taught that the protection of the innocent demands that steps be taken to check the scourge of these diseases. At present large classes of people who are afflicted with them, and who are unwilling to accept almshouse care, must continue at their work in order to support themselves, no matter how intimate their association with other people. Bakers, cooks, barbers, waiters, children's nurses, barkeepers and prostitutes are all alike thus forced to remain at their work, even when afflicted with these diseases. A very large proportion of these persons would accept hospital care during the dangerous period if it were available. Those who do not voluntarily seek such treatment when provided should be placed and forcibly detained under treatment during the period of danger to others. To one class of hospitals the unfortunate should be invited, in a second class the depraved should be confined. These two diseases should be included in the list of contagious diseases of which boards of health take cognizance. Hospital provision for their treatment is an imperative necessity.

The investigations and findings of the commission indicate that the most far-reaching " plans for preventing such evils as it finds to exist " are those which do not directly or immediately deal with law or law enforcement. It is nevertheless clearly evident that laws and their enforcement have a substantial and extremely important bearing upon the character and extent of the evil.

The commission therefore recommends certain new legislation and various changes and additions to existing laws, and urges more specific and thorough application of present laws and powers by the constituted authorities.

The recommendations relating to law and law enforcement are directed largely against the commercial aspects of prostitution, and look towards the diminution and suppression of the traffic in women rather than to punitive measures directed against the women themselves. It has been shown that in this State, to a large extent, the business of prostitution means the exploitation of the bodies of feeble-minded girls and women for the financial benefit of those who conduct the traffic.

Houses of Prostitution.

The laws for the suppression of " places resorted to for the purpose of prostitution " should provide for the penalizing of the property so used, and the commission recommends the following: —

AN ACT TO PUNISH AND PREVENT THE MAINTENANCE OF PLACES OF PROSTITUTION AND LEWDNESS.

Be it enacted, etc., as follows:

SECTION 1. Every building, part of a building, tenement or place used for prostitution, assignation or lewdness, and every place within which or upon which acts of prostitution, assignation or lewdness are held or occur shall be deemed a nuisance.

SECTION 2. Whoever keeps or maintains such nuisance shall be punished by a fine of not less than one hundred nor more than one thousand dollars, and by imprisonment for not less than three months nor more than three years.

SECTION 3. Whenever there is reason to believe that such nuisance is kept or maintained, or exists in any city or town, either the district attorney for the district in which the nuisance is believed to exist, or the attorney-general, in the name of the commonwealth, or one or more citizens, in his or their own names, may maintain a bill in equity to perpetually enjoin the person or persons conducting or maintaining the same, and the owner, lessee or agent of the building or place in or upon which such nuisance exists and their assignees from directly or indirectly maintaining or permitting such nuisance.

SECTION 4. The bill of complaint shall join the owner of record of the premises as a party respondent and shall be filed in the superior court for the county in which the nuisance is believed to exist, and shall be verified by oath of the complainant unless filed by the attorney-general or a district attorney. The bill shall forthwith after filing be presented to the court sitting in equity within the county, or to any judge of the court if the court is not sitting in equity within the county, or in vacation, and the proceeding shall have precedence over all other matters upon the docket except criminal proceedings, election contests and hearings upon petitions for other injunctions.

SECTION 5. If upon hearing, after two days' notice to the respondents of the time and place assigned for such hearing, the existence of such nuisance is shown to the satisfaction of the court or judge, either through verified complaint or through evidence in the form of affidavits, depositions, oral testimony, or otherwise as the complainant may elect, unless the court or judge by previous order shall have directed the form and manner in which such evidence shall be presented, a temporary injunction shall be ordered to issue forthwith restraining the maintenance of such nuisance and enjoining the occupants, owner and all other persons from removing fixtures, furniture, musical instruments and all movable property from the premises until further order of the court.

SECTION 6. If upon subsequent hearing in due course of equity procedure the existence of the nuisance shall be established, a decree permanently enjoining the maintaining of such nuisance shall be entered, and as a part of such decree shall be entered an order of abatement, which shall order the immediate removal from the building or place where the nuisance has been maintained of all furniture, musical instruments or movable property used in conducting and maintaining the nuisance, and shall direct the sale thereof in the manner provided for the sale of chattels under execution. If it shall appear that the bill of complaint was filed three or more days after notice to the record owner of the premises of the conditions alleged to exist and that the owner did not proceed forthwith to enforce his rights under the provisions of section ten of chapter one hundred and one of the Revised Laws, as amended by section twelve of this act, such order of abatement shall further direct the effectual closing of the building or place and the prohibition of its use for any purpose for a period of one year, unless sooner released as hereinafter provided. For the purpose of proving the existence of the nuisance the general reputation of the place shall be admissible as evidence.

SECTION 7. For removing and selling the movable property in accordance with the decree of the court the officer shall be entitled to charge and receive as fees the amounts which he would receive for levying upon and selling like property on execution, and for closing the premises and keeping them closed a reasonable sum shall be allowed by the court. The proceeds of the sale of the personal property by order of the court shall be applied: first, to the fees and costs of removal and sale; second, to the allowances and costs of so closing and keeping closed the building or place; third, to the payment of the complainant's costs, including a reasonable attorney's fee, in such proceeding; fourth, the balance, if any, to the owner of the property sold.

SECTION 8. If the owner of such building or place shall appear and pay all costs of the proceedings, and shall file a bond with sureties approved by the clerk in the full value of the property as ascertained by the court, or in vacation by the clerk, conditioned that such owner will immediately abate such nuisance and prevent the same from being established or kept therein within a period of one year thereafter, the court or judge may, if satisfied of such owner's good faith, order the premises so closed under the order of abatement to be delivered to such owner of the real estate, and the order of the abatement to be so modified as to dissolve the order that the building remain closed for one year: *provided, however,* that such release shall not be held to release such property from any judgment, lien, penalty or liability to which it may be subject by law.

SECTION 9. No bill of complaint filed under the provisions of this act shall be dismissed except upon a sworn statement made and filed by the complainant and by his attorney setting forth the reasons why such bill should be dismissed, and unless such dismissal is approved by the court in open court. If the court is of the opinion that the bill ought not to be dismissed he may direct the district attorney to prosecute the case to a final decree. If a bill of complaint brought by one or more citizens is continued more than one term of court any citizen of the county, or the district attorney of the district, or, if public interest so requires, the attorney-general, may be substituted for the original complainant and prosecute the case to a final decree. If the bill of complaint was brought by one or more citizens and the court finds that there was no reasonable ground therefor, the costs may be taxed to such complainants.

SECTION 10. Section six of chapter one hundred and one of the Revised Laws is hereby amended by striking out the words " prostitution, lewdness, or ", so as to read as follows: — *Section 6.* All buildings, places or tenements which are resorted to for illegal gaming, or which are used for the illegal keeping or sale of intoxicating liquor, shall be deemed common nuisances.

SECTION 11. Section eight of chapter one hundred and one of the Revised Laws is hereby amended by striking out the words " prostitution, lewdness or ", so as to read as follows: — *Section 8.* The supreme judicial court or the superior court shall have jurisdiction in equity, upon an information filed by the district attorney for the district or upon the petition of the board of police or police commissioners, or other authority having control of the police, or of not less than ten legal voters of a city or town, stating that a building, place or tenement therein is resorted to for illegal gaming, or is used for the illegal keeping or sale of intoxicating liquors, to restrain, enjoin or abate the same as a common nuisance.

SECTION 12. Section ten of chapter one hundred and one of the Revised Laws is hereby amended by·striking out the words " for any of the purposes enumerated in section six ", and by inserting in place thereof the words: — for the purposes of prostitution, assignation, lewdness, illegal gaming, or the illegal keeping or sale of intoxicating liquors, — so as to read as follows: — *Section 10.* If a tenant or occupant of a building or tenement, under a lawful title, uses such premises or any part thereof for the purposes of prostitution, assignation, lewdness, illegal gaming, or the illegal keeping or sale of intoxicating liquors, such use shall annul and make void the lease or other title under which he holds, and, without any act of the owner, shall cause the right of possession to revert and vest in him, and he may, without process of law, make immediate entry upon the premises, or may avail himself of the remedy provided in chapter one hundred and eighty-one.

SECTION 13. Section eleven of chapter one hundred and one of the Revised Laws is hereby amended by striking out the words " for any purpose enumerated in section six ", and by inserting in place thereof the words: — for the purposes of prostitution, assignation, lewdness, illegal gaming, or the illegal keeping or sale of intoxicating liquors, — so as to read as follows: — *Section 11*. Whoever knowingly lets a building or tenement owned by him, or under his control, for the purposes of prostitution, assignation, lewdness, illegal gaming, or the illegal keeping or sale of intoxicating liquors, or knowingly permits such building or tenement, or any part thereof, while under his control, to be used for such purpose, or after due notice of any such use omits to take all reasonable measures to eject therefrom the persons occupying the same as soon as it can lawfully be done, shall be deemed guilty of aiding in the maintenance of such nuisance and punished as provided in section seven.

SECTION 14. All persons found in or upon or proved to have been in or upon a building or place used for prostitution, assignation or lewdness shall be required to state under oath their true names and residences. Any person refusing to give his true name and residence shall be punished by a fine of not less than ten nor more than five hundred dollars, or by imprisonment for not more than two months, or by both such fine and imprisonment. Any person giving a name and residence other than his true name and residence shall be guilty of perjury and shall be subject to the penalties provided therefor.

SECTION 15. This act shall take effect upon its passage.

Hotels.

The many immoral hotels where commercialized prostitution is so freely and grossly practiced should be regulated and controlled. Innholders' licenses should be granted only after investigation and continued in force only so long as the conditions imposed are faithfully observed. Provision should be made for inspection of conditions. A permanent form of registration of every guest, subject to verification, should be required. A record of every assignment of every room should be made. This provision would prevent the letting of the same room, as at present, to sometimes a dozen couples in one night. This register should be open to the inspection of the police or other agents of the law at all times.

The use of closed private dining rooms in hotels by men

and women, now frequently resorted to for immoral purposes, and already prohibited by the licensing authorities of several cities, should be prohibited throughout the State. In general, there should be much closer co-operation between the police and the licensing authorities. The licensing authorities should have the right to such assistance as the police department can furnish.

The commission recommends the following: —

An Act to provide Supervision and Regulation of the Business of Innholders.

Be it enacted, etc., as follows:

Section 1. Innholders' licenses issued under chapter one hundred and two of the Revised Laws and its amendments shall be granted in cities and towns only after investigation by or under the direction of the licensing officer or board into the fitness of the applicant to receive such license, and shall be expressed to be subject to the provisions of this chapter, as well as the provisions of said chapter one hundred and two of the Revised Laws.

Section 2. Hotels and all premises maintained wholly or in part under innholders' licenses in all cities and towns shall be at all times subject to inspection, with reference to conditions existing upon the premises, by the police or other officials lawfully exercising the functions of police, and by inspectors and agents of the officer or board charged with the duty of licensing innholders, and by agents and inspectors authorized by any district attorney or by the attorney-general. Report of the unlawful conditions existing upon or about such premises shall forthwith be made to the licensing board or officer.

Section 3. All persons licensed as innholders shall keep, or cause to be kept by their employees, a register in permanent form for the recording of the true name and residence of every person occupying or sharing in occupying for any period of time whatever of the day or night a room upon the premises controlled by the licensee other than an open room exclusively devoted to and used for the convenience of all guests of either or both sexes, such as an office, reception, dining, reading or waiting room, together with a true and accurate record, made by the licensee or his employee for the time being in custody of such register, of the room or rooms assigned to such person or persons and of the time when each of such persons began and ceased to occupy the rooms. The register so kept shall at all times be open to the inspection of the police and to officers, inspectors and agents of the government.

Section 4. All persons occupying and sharing in occupying

rooms as described in the preceding section shall either sign their **true names and residences** in such register or shall cause their true names and residences to be entered upon the register for them, or shall state their true name and residence to the licensee or to his employee in custody of the register, who shall enter them upon the register.

Section 5. All persons refusing or neglecting or otherwise failing to comply with the provisions of the preceding sections of this act, including persons knowingly signing or entering or causing or permitting the entering of a false name or residence in a register required by the provisions of this act to be kept, shall be punished by a fine of not less than twenty-five nor more than five hundred dollars, or by imprisonment for not more than two months for each offence, or by both such fine and imprisonment.

Section 6. It shall be unlawful for any person holding an innholder's license or for any employee of such licensee to use, maintain for use or permit the use of closed private dining rooms in hotels and upon premises maintained wholly or in part under an innholder's license in any city or town by a number of persons more than one and less than five, unless the persons shall all be men or shall all be women: *provided, however,* that nothing herein contained shall be held to prevent the serving of meals to a family in its proper lodging room or suite of rooms. A space so enclosed that persons within it are shut off from public view, whether by walls, doors, curtains, portieres, screens or other device within which either food or drink is served or consumed, shall be deemed to be a private dining room within the meaning of this chapter.

Section 7. An innholder upon whose premises a room or space has been used in violation of this act shall be punished by a fine of not less than fifty nor more than five hundred dollars, or by imprisonment for a period not exceeding three months, or by both such fine and imprisonment.

Section 8. The clerk of a court in which any person is convicted of a violation of any of the provisions of this chapter shall forthwith send a copy of the record of such conviction to the officer or board charged with the duty of issuing innholders' licenses in the city or town where the offence occurred.

Section 9. Whoever being licensed as an innholder is convicted a second time under the provisions of chapter one hundred and two of the Revised Laws, or under the provisions of this chapter, shall in addition to suffering the penalties provided in the preceding sections of this chapter be adjudged to have forfeited his license as an innholder.

Section 10. This act shall take effect upon its passage.

Cafés and Saloons.

It is not easy to understand why the many immoral cafés and saloons, openly and impudently used nightly and almost solely for the bargaining places of prostitutes and their customers, are allowed to exist in every city of any size in the State. An officer of the law not known to the habitués in any one house could obtain evidence which would justify the permanent closing of any one of these places by the licensing authorities.

The separate booths, especially with drawn curtains, in cafés, restaurants and saloons, should be absolutely forbidden.

It is within the power of local licensing authorities to remedy this evil. There should be some definitely constituted State authority charged with the responsibility of securing action if the local authorities are inert.

The following is recommended : —

An Act to prevent Immorality in Cafés, Restaurants, Saloons, etc.

Be it enacted, etc., as follows:

SECTION 1. It shall be unlawful for any person owning or managing or controlling a café, restaurant, saloon or other place where food or drink is sold to the public to be consumed upon the premises in any city or town, and for any person employed by such person, to provide, maintain, use or permit the use of rooms, booths, stalls or enclosures of any description whatever which are so closed by walls, partitions, curtains, screens or other devices that the persons within cannot at any time be seen by all other persons in such café, restaurant, saloon or other place, or in any divisions thereof into which the premises may be divided under regulation of licensing authorities.

SECTION 2. Any person violating the provisions of the preceding section shall be punished by a fine of not less than fifty nor more than five hundred dollars, or by imprisonment for not more than two months, or by both such fine and imprisonment.

SECTION 3. Whoever shall resort to any café, restaurant, saloon or other place where food or drink is sold or served to be consumed upon the premises for the purpose of immoral solicitation, or immoral bargaining, or in any manner inducing another person to engage in immoral conduct, and whoever being in or about any such place shall engage in any such acts, shall be punished by a fine of not less than twenty-five nor more than five hundred dollars, or by imprisonment for not more than one year, or by both such fine and imprisonment.

SECTION 4. Whoever being licensed as an innholder or common victualler, and whoever being licensed to sell intoxicating liquors, shall himself or through his employees knowingly permit a café, restaurant, saloon or other such place maintained by him or under his direction or control to be used for any of the purposes described in section three of this act, shall be punished by a fine of not less than one hundred nor more than one thousand dollars, or by imprisonment for not more than two years, or by both such fine and imprisonment. A person shall be presumed knowingly to have permitted such use within the meaning of this section if by the exercise of reasonable diligence and watchfulness he could have learned of such use.

SECTION 5. In addition to the penalties provided in the preceding sections the license or licenses of a person convicted of a violation of the provisions of section four may upon the first conviction be suspended for such period as the licensing officer or board may determine, and upon the second conviction such license or licenses shall be adjudged to have been forfeited.

SECTION 6. The clerk of the court in which any person is convicted of a violation of any of the provisions of this chapter shall forthwith send a copy of the record of such conviction to the officers or boards having jurisdiction of such license or licenses in the city or town where the offence was committed.

SECTION 7. Innholders' licenses issued under chapter one hundred and two of the Revised Laws and its amendments shall be expressed to be subject to the provisions of this chapter.

SECTION 8. This act shall take effect upon its passage.

The Licensing of Lodging Houses.

The widespread and undisturbed use of lodging houses or rooming houses for purposes of prostitution in the State can be met by a long-needed legal regulation and control of these necessary adjuncts of present-day economic conditions. Such regulation could be made without injury to, or appreciable interference with, the legitimate business of letting rooms; indeed, it would be a protection and a financial benefit to properly conducted lodging houses. Every lodging house should be licensed and registered for a nominal fee or for no fee, and be subject to supervision. An approved permanent register should be kept, and every lodger should be required to record his correct name and address. The police authorities should be required to investigate and report upon the applicants for licenses and the conduct of such establishments.

The following is recommended: —

An Act to provide for the Licensing, Inspection and Regulation of Private Rooming and Lodging Houses.

Be it enacted, etc., as follows:

Section 1. No person owning, leasing, occupying or managing a building or part of a building used for private dwelling purposes in any city or town shall engage in the business of renting rooms for lodging except under a license therefor from the officer or board at the head of the police of a city and from the board of selectmen in a town. A person shall be deemed to be engaged in the business of renting rooms for lodging within the meaning of this act if the total number of occupants of all rooms rented by him is greater than five. Such license shall state the true name of the licensee and the location of the premises to which it relates, and shall not be assignable and shall not authorize the renting of rooms at any location other than that described. No fee shall be required to be paid for such license. A copy of every license issued and a record of the date when and the name and residence of the person to whom it was issued shall be kept by the licensing authority.

Section 2. No license shall be granted until the fitness of the applicant therefor has been established to the satisfaction of the licensing officer or board. The police shall, upon request of the licensing authority, investigate and report upon the fitness of applicants to receive such licenses.

Section 3. All persons managing or otherwise having or sharing the control of buildings or parts thereof in which rooms are rented for dwelling or lodging shall keep or cause to be kept in permanent form a register in which shall be entered the true name of every person and the city or town of permanent residence of every person renting and sharing in renting a room, and of every person occupying and sharing in occupying a room which has been rented upon the premises, together with a true and accurate statement of time when the renting and occupation by each and every person began and terminated. Such register shall at all times be open to the inspection of the police and of the licensing authorities and their authorized agents.

Section 4. The premises so occupied, used or controlled by the licensee shall at all times be subject to inspection by the licensing authorities and their authorized agents and by the police, who shall report the results of their inspection to the licensing authority.

SECTION 5. Every license shall be expressed to be granted subject to the conditions that the licensee shall not engage in, authorize or allow any disorderly conduct upon the premises, and that the provisions of this chapter shall be complied with.

SECTION 6. Persons failing to comply with the provisions of this act shall be punished for each offence by a fine of not less than five nor more than one hundred dollars, or by imprisonment for not more than one month, or by both such fine and imprisonment.

SECTION 7. A license issued under the provisions of this act shall be revoked if at any time the licensing authority, after investigation and after hearing, or after giving an opportunity to be heard, a notice of which shall be left at the premises of the licensee not less than twenty-four hours before the time set for the hearing, shall be satisfied that the licensee is unfit to hold such license.

Search Warrants for Houses of Ill Fame.

To obviate the necessity of using a search warrant for the illegal sale of liquor, as well as the danger of information of the issuing of the warrant being conveyed to the keepers of the places to be searched, it is suggested that the law be so amended as to provide for the granting of search warrants for the specific purpose of searching places suspected of being resorted to for purposes of prostitution, and that such service be lawful at any time within thirty days of the date of issue. Such a warrant would cover the purpose for which it is actually desired, and disclosure of its existence would be of less benefit to the keeper of a house of ill fame; for while such a person could afford to suspend business for the present limited time allowed for service, suspension would not be so practicable for the proposed period of thirty days.

The following is recommended: —

AN ACT TO PROVIDE FOR SEARCH WARRANTS FOR HOUSES OF ILL FAME.

Be it enacted, etc., as follows:

If a person makes oath before a police, district or municipal court or a trial justice that he suspects or has probable cause to suspect that a house, building, room or place is resorted to for purposes of prostitution, said court or trial justice shall, if satisfied that there is probable cause therefor, issue a warrant commanding the sheriff or any of his deputies, or any constable or police officer, to enter such house, building, room or place and search for evidence tending to show that such house, building, room or place is so resorted to, and to arrest any person found therein who the officer serving the said warrant may have reasonable cause to believe is violating any provision of chapter two hundred and twelve of the Revised Laws, or chapter four hundred and twenty-four of the acts of the year nineteen hundred and ten, and detain him for a reasonable time until he may be brought before said court or trial justice. Such warrant shall be served not later than thirty days after the date of its issue.

The Licensing and Supervising of Public Dance Halls.

Licenses should be required by the licensing authorities for all public dances. The expense of supervision, preferably by a matron chosen by the licensing authorities, should be included in the license fee.

The following is recommended: —

An Act to provide for the Licensing and Regulating and Supervision of Public Dances in Cities and Towns.

Be it enacted, etc., as follows:

SECTION 1. No public dance shall be held in any city or town unless a license therefor shall have been granted by the officer or board at the head of the police in cities and by the board of selectmen in towns to the person or persons promoting, managing or directing such dance. The license shall state the name and residence of the licensee and the location where such dance is to be held, and a copy of the license and record of its issue shall be kept by the licensing authority.

SECTION 2. A matron appointed by or approved by the licensing authority shall be required to be present throughout every such public dance, and shall be admitted without payment of admission fee. The duties of the matron shall be to require that the dance be conducted, and that all persons present at and about the dance conduct themselves, in an orderly, proper and decorous manner, and to afford protection and assistance to persons in need thereof. In the performance of her duties she may call upon the police and upon the persons in charge of the dance for such assistance as may be necessary, and may revoke the license for the dance for broken conditions, as hereinafter provided.

SECTION 3. A license fee which shall include the fee to be paid to the matron and shall be uniform in any one city or town shall be paid for every license to the licensing authority, to be paid into the treasury of the city or town, the amount of such uniform fee to be fixed by the mayor and aldermen or council or governing board in cities and by the boards of selectmen in towns.

SECTION 4. Such license shall be expressed to be granted subject to the following conditions, and to be subject to immediate revocation upon breach of any thereof: First, that the dance shall be conducted and that the persons in and about the dance hall or place where the dance is held shall be required to conduct themselves with propriety and decorum. Second, that the matron shall be permitted and required to occupy such position or positions as shall enable her clearly to see all parts of the premises where the dance is conducted, and shall be permitted to have free access to all parts of the premises used in connection with the dance or accessible to or used by those present and those who have been present at the dance. Third, that the person or persons to whom the license is issued will co-operate with and assist the matron in enforcing compliance with the conditions of the license.

SECTION 5. Upon breach of any of the conditions of the license the license may forthwith be revoked by the licensing authority, and a matron may at the time of her appointment or approval, or at any subsequent time, be vested with authority by the licensing power for and in its behalf forthwith to revoke a license upon breach of any of the conditions; and upon notice of such revocation to the manager or persons in charge of such dance, or any of them, or after a reasonable attempt to give such notice, the dance shall at once terminate and the hall or place of dancing shall be cleared and remain closed for the remainder of the time during which said dance might, under the terms of the license, have been continued.

SECTION 6. Any person managing, promoting or holding a public dance in violation of the provisions of this chapter, and any persons resisting or interfering with the matron in the performance of her duties, shall be punished by a fine of not less than ten nor more than two hundred dollars, or by imprisonment for not more than two months, or by both such fine and imprisonment.

SECTION 7. This act shall take effect upon its passage.

Pimps and Procurers.

The prosecution of this class of men would be simplified by adding the phrase " or shall share in such earnings, proceeds or moneys," after the phrase " or allowed," in section 5, chapter 424, Acts of 1910, so that said section as amended shall read as follows: —

SECTION 5. Whoever, knowing a female to be a prostitute. shall live or derive support or maintenance, in whole or in part, from the earnings or the proceeds of the prostitution. or from moneys loaned or advanced or charged against her by any keeper or manager or inmate of a house or other place where prostitution is practised or allowed, or shall share in such earnings, proceeds or moneys, shall be punished by imprisonment in the state prison for not more than three years or in the house of correction for not more than one year, or by a fine of not more than one thousand dollars, or by both such fine and imprisonment.

Providing for the Prosecution of Persons who accost Persons of the Opposite Sex in Public Places.

Successful prosecution of persons charged with being common nightwalkers, male or female, requires, under the statute and the usual court procedure, so much evidence of so positive a character that innumerable public actions tending to immorality or grievously offensive to respectable persons, especially women, are outside the present scope of lawful prevention or punishment. A woman may speak to men in the street, day or night, and even solicit them to commit immoral acts, without affording proof of violation of the present law. A man may, day or night, salute, accost or follow a respectable woman, to her annoyance or alarm, and unless he uses obscene or profane language, as he seldom does in such cases, he breaks no law. Even though he expose himself through profanity or obscenity, he still escapes unless a policeman is on the spot to arrest him, — and such men keep careful watch for the police, — and unless the respectable woman is willing to appear against him, and in open court repeat the profanity or obscenity which was addressed to her. The frequency with which such offenses are committed is well known, but the public, which looks to the police for a remedy, does not understand that in the present condition of the law neither prevention nor punishment can be secured.

It is recommended that the law be amended as follows: —

Section forty-six of chapter two hundred and twelve of the Revised Laws is hereby amended by inserting after the word " female ", in the fourth line thereof, the following: — persons who accost without legitimate reason or otherwise annoy in public places persons of the opposite sex, — so that said section as amended shall read: — *Section 46.* Rogues and vagabonds, persons who use any juggling or unlawful games or plays, common pipers and fiddlers, stubborn children, runaways, common drunkards, common nightwalkers both male and female, persons who accost without legitimate reason or otherwise annoy in public places persons of the opposite sex, pilferers, lewd, wanton and lascivious persons in speech or behavior, common railers and brawlers, persons who neglect their calling or employment, misspend their time by frequenting houses of ill fame, gaming houses or tippling shops, may be punished by imprisonment in the Massachusetts reformatory or at the state farm or for not more than six months in the house of correction or workhouse in the city or town in which the offender is convicted, or in the workhouse, if any, in the city or town in which the offender has a legal settlement, if such town is in the county. A female offender under the provisions of this section may in the discretion of the court be punished by imprisonment in the reformatory prison for women for not more than two years.

Arrests in the Daytime without a Warrant.

The restriction which limits to " the nighttime" arrests without a warrant for offenses enumerated in Revised Laws, chapter 212, section 46, is a relic of times long past, when practically all offenders were known personally to local peace officers. To be unable to arrest without a warrant in dealing with large numbers of persons who are strangers, who refuse to give their names and addresses or give those which are fictitious, is really to guarantee immunity for offenses committed by such persons. Offenses against chastity incident to the commercialized aspects of prostitution considered in detail in this report are especially likely to be committed under these conditions. An offense committed in the daytime should subject the offender to the same conditions of apprehension as if it were committed at night.

It is recommended that the law be amended as follows: —

Section forty-seven of chapter two hundred and twelve of the Revised Laws is hereby amended by striking out in the second line thereof the words " in the nighttime ". so that the section as amended shall read: — *Section 47.* Whoever is found in a street, highway or other public place committing any offence or disorder mentioned in the preceding section, may be apprehended by a sheriff. deputy sheriff, constable, police officer or watchman, or by any other person by the order of a magistrate or any of said officers, without a warrant, and be kept in custody for not more than twenty-four hours, Sunday or a legal holiday excepted. and at or before the expiration

of such time he shall be taken before a police, district or municipal
court or trial justice and proceeded against, as provided in the preceding section, or discharged, as such court or justice shall determine.

Wayward Children.

The following amendment to the law relative to the
treatment of wayward and delinquent children is recommended: —

Section one of chapter four hundred and thirteen of the acts of
the year nineteen hundred and six is hereby amended by adding at
the end of the fourth paragraph thereof the following: — or who
is found in the company of a person or persons who may reasonably be suspected of being vicious or immoral and under such
conditions as would lead to the belief that such child might be influenced thereby to lead an immoral, vicious or criminal life or to
commit an immoral, vicious or criminal act, — so that said paragraph as amended shall read as follows: — The words "wayward
child" shall be construed to mean a boy or girl between seven and
seventeen years of age who habitually associates with vicious or
immoral persons, or who is growing up in circumstances exposing
him or her to lead an immoral, vicious or criminal life, or who is
found in the company of a person or persons who may reasonably be
suspected of being vicious or immoral and under such conditions as
would lead to the belief that such child might be influenced thereby
to lead an immoral, vicious or criminal life or to commit an immoral, vicious or criminal act.

Disposition of Prosecutions of Offenses against Chastity.

It appears to the commission to be desirable that the nol
prossing and placing on file of prosecutions for offenses
against chastity should be subject to the same provisions of
law that have applied since 1885 to violations of the provisions of law relative to intoxicating liquors, and the following therefore is recommended: —

An Act regulating the Disposition of Prosecutions of Offences against Chastity.

Be it enacted, etc., as follows:

SECTION 1. A prosecution for the violation of any provision of
law relative to prostitution, assignation, lewdness, immoral solicitation, and any and all other offences against chastity, shall not, unless
the purposes of justice require such disposition, be placed on file

or disposed of except by trial and judgment, according to the regular course of criminal proceedings. It shall be otherwise disposed of only upon motion in writing stating specifically the reasons therefor and verified by affidavit if facts are relied on. If the court or magistrate certifies in writing that he is satisfied that the cause relied on exists, and that the interests of the public require the allowance thereof, such motion shall be allowed and said certificate shall be filed in the case.

SECTION 2. This act shall take effect upon its passage and shall apply to all prosecutions pending at the date of its passage.

Court Treatment of Prostitutes.

Those prostitutes who are found to be feeble-minded should be provided for as feeble-minded persons or as defective delinquents. The present laws provide for such commitment, but institution provision for the feeble-minded is inadequate, and for the defective delinquent entirely lacking.

For the arrested prostitute who is rated as of normal mentality, the present law provides for an adequate range of treatment, from probation to imprisonment.

The investigation has revealed clearly the interest of each community in the situation in neighboring and even distant communities. By reason of the recent development of methods of travel, the villages and smaller towns and cities of the State have a great deal at stake in the efficient or inefficient management of sex problems in the larger cities to which they are tributary.

Equally striking is the fact that under recent conditions the citizens of our metropolis, and also of our larger cities, have a similar interest in the policy pursued in these matters even in distant smaller towns and villages. Some of the worst resorts in the State are quite distant from centers of population, and yet are supported by patrons from such centers.

The highest interests of the individual communities are inextricably interwoven with those of the State as a whole.

SOCIAL PROBLEMS
AND
SOCIAL POLICY:
The American Experience

An Arno Press Collection

Bachman, George W. and Lewis Meriam. **The Issue of Compulsory Health Insurance.** 1948

Bishop, Ernest S. **The Narcotic Drug Problem.** 1920

Bosworth, Louise Marion. **The Living Wage of Women Workers.** 1911

[Brace, Emma, editor]. **The Life of Charles Loring Brace.** 1894

Brown, Esther Lucile. **Social Work as a Profession.** 4th Edition. 1942

Brown, Roy M. **Public Poor Relief in North Carolina.** 1928

Browning, Grace. **Rural Public Welfare.** 1941

Bruce, Isabel Campbell and Edith Eickhoff. **The Michigan Poor Law.** 1936

Burns, Eveline M. **Social Security and Public Policy.** 1956

Cahn, Frances and Valeska Bary. **Welfare Activities of Federal, State, and Local Governments in California, 1850-1934.** 1936

Campbell, Persia. **The Consumer Interest.** 1949

Davies, Stanley Powell. **Social Control of the Mentally Deficient.** 1930

Devine, Edward T. **The Spirit of Social Work.** 1911

Douglas, Paul H. and Aaron Director. **The Problem of Unemployment.** 1931

Eaton, Allen in Collaboration with Shelby M. Harrison. **A Bibliography of Social Surveys.** 1930

Epstein, Abraham. **The Challenge of the Aged.** 1928

Falk, I[sidore] S., Margaret C. Klem, and Nathan Sinai. **The Incidence of Illness and the Receipt and Costs of Medical Care Among Representative Families.** 1933

Fisher, Irving. **National Vitality, its Wastes and Conservation.** 1909

Freund, Ernst. **The Police Power:** Public Policy and Constitutional Rights. 1904

Gladden, Washington. **Applied Christianity:** Moral Aspects of Social Questions. 1886

Hartley, Isaac Smithson, editor. **Memorial of Robert Milham Hartley.** 1882

Hollander, Jacob H. **The Abolition of Poverty.** 1914

Kane, H[arry] H[ubbell]. **Opium-Smoking in America and China.** 1882

Klebaner, Benjamin Joseph. **Public Poor Relief in America, 1790-1860.** 1951

Knapp, Samuel L. **The Life of Thomas Eddy.** 1834

Lawrence, Charles. **History of the Philadelphia Almshouses and Hospitals from the Beginning of the Eighteenth to the Ending of the Nineteenth Centuries.** 1905

[Massachusetts Commission on the Cost of Living]. **Report of the Commission on the Cost of Living.** 1910

[Massachusetts Commission on Old Age Pensions, Annuities and Insurance]. **Report of the Commission on Old Age Pensions, Annuities and Insurance.** 1910

[New York State Commission to Investigate Provision for the Mentally Deficient]. **Report of the State Commission to Investigate Provision for the Mentally Deficient.** 1915

[Parker, Florence E., Estelle M. Stewart, and Mary Conymgton, compilers]. **Care of Aged Persons in the United States.** 1929

Pollock, Horatio M., editor. **Family Care of Mental Patients.** 1936

Pollock, Horatio M. **Mental Disease and Social Welfare.** 1941

Powell, Aaron M., editor. **The National Purity Congress;** Its Papers, Addresses, Portraits. 1896

The President's Commission on the Health Needs of the Nation. **Building America's Health.** [1952]. Five vols. in two

Prostitution in America: Three Investigations, 1902-1914. 1975

Rubinow, I[saac] M. **The Quest for Security.** 1934

Shaffer, Alice, Mary Wysor Keefer, and Sophonisba P. Breckinridge. **The Indiana Poor Law.** 1936

Shattuck, Lemuel. **Report to the Committee of the City Council Appointed to Obtain the Census of Boston for the Year 1845.** 1846

The State and Public Welfare in Nineteenth-Century America: Five Investigations, 1833-1877. 1975

Stewart, Estelle M. **The Cost of American Almshouses.** 1925

Taylor, Graham. **Pioneering on Social Frontiers.** 1930

[United States Senate Committee on Education and Labor]. **Report of the Committee of the Senate Upon the Relations Between Labor and Capital.** 1885. Four vols.

Walton, Robert P. **Marihuana, America's New Drug Problem.** 1938

Williams, Edward Huntington. **Opiate Addiction.** 1922

Williams, Pierce assisted by Isabel C. Chamberlain. **The Purchase of Medical Care Through Fixed Periodic Payment.** 1932

Willoughby, W[estal] W[oodbury]. **Opium as an International Problem.** 1925

Wisner, Elizabeth. **Public Welfare Administration in Louisiana.** 1930